Communications in Computer and Information Science 1149

Commenced Publication in 2007
Founding and Former Series Editors:
Phoebe Chen, Alfredo Cuzzocrea, Xiaoyong Du, Orhun Kara, Ting Liu,
Krishna M. Sivalingam, Dominik Ślęzak, Takashi Washio, Xiaokang Yang,
and Junsong Yuan

More information about this series at http://www.springer.com/series/7899

Weili Han · Liehuang Zhu · Fei Yan (Eds.)

Trusted Computing and Information Security

13th Chinese Conference, CTCIS 2019
Shanghai, China, October 24–27, 2019
Revised Selected Papers

 Springer

Editors
Weili Han
Fudan University
Shanghai, China

Liehuang Zhu (iD)
Beijing Institute of Technology
Beijing, China

Fei Yan
Wuhan University
Wuhan, China

ISSN 1865-0929   ISSN 1865-0937 (electronic)
Communications in Computer and Information Science
ISBN 978-981-15-3417-1   ISBN 978-981-15-3418-8 (eBook)
https://doi.org/10.1007/978-981-15-3418-8

This Springer imprint is published by the registered company Springer Nature Singapore Pte Ltd.
The registered company address is: 152 Beach Road, #21-01/04 Gateway East, Singapore 189721, Singapore

Preface

The 13th Chinese Conference on Trusted Computing and Information Security (CTCIS 2019) continued in a series of events dedicated to trusted computing and information security, focusing on new theories, mechanisms, infrastructures, services, tools, and benchmarks. CTCIS provides a forum for researchers and developers in academia, industry, and government to share their excellent ideas and experiences in the areas of trusted computing and information security in the broad context of cloud computing, big data, Internet of Things, etc.

This year, CTCIS received 247 submissions. After a thorough reviewing process, 38 English papers and 28 Chinese papers were selected for presentation as full papers, with an acceptance rate of 26.7%. This volume contains the 22 English full papers presented at CTCIS 2019.

The high-quality program would not have been possible without the authors who chose CTCIS 2019 as a venue for their publications. We are also very grateful to the Program Committee members and Organizing Committee members, who put a tremendous amount of effort into soliciting and selecting research papers with a balance of high quality and new ideas and new applications.

We hope that you enjoy reading and benefit from the proceedings of CTCIS 2019.

October 2019

Weili Han
Liehuang Zhu
Fei Yan

Organization

CTCIS 2019 was organized by the China Computer Federation, Fudan University.

Organizing Committee

Conference Chair

Changxiang Shen   Chinese Academy of Engineering, China

Conference Associate Chairs

Xiaoyang Wang   Fudan University, China
Huanguo Zhang   Wuhan University, China

Conference Chair Assistant

Bo Zhao   Wuhan University, China

Program Chair

Weili Han   Fudan University, China

Program Associate Chairs

Liehuang Zhu   Beijing Institute of Technology, China
Fei Yan   Wuhan University, China

Publicity Chair

Chao Shen   Xi'an Jiaotong University, China

Local Arrangement Chair

Chen Chen   Fudan University, China

Steering Committee

Changxiang Shen   Chinese Academy of Engineering, China
Huanguo Zhang   Wuhan University, China
Zhong Chen   Peking University, China
Kefei Chen   Hangzhou Normal University, China
Dengguo Feng   Beijing Science Technology Academy, China
Zhen Han   Beijing Jiaotong University, China
Yeping He   Chinese Academy of Sciences, China
Jiwu Huang   Shenzhen University, China

Jiwu Jing	Institute of Information Engineering, Chinese Academy of Sciences, China
Jianhua Li	Shanghai Jiao Tong University, China
Jianwei Liu	Beihang University, China
Zhoujun Li	Beihang University, China
Jianfeng Ma	Xidian University, China
Zhiguang Qin	University of Electronic Science and Technology of China, China
Jinshu Su	National University of Defense Technology, China
Wenchang Shi	Renmin University of China, China
Qingxian Wang	Information Engineering University, China
Xiaoyun Wang	Tsinghua University, China
Zhiying Wang	National University of Defense Technology, China
Xiaoyao Xie	Guizhou Normal University, China
Xiaoyuan Yang	Engineering University of CAPF, China
Yixian Yang	Beijing University of Posts and Telecommunications, China
Zhiqiang Zhu	Information Engineering University, China

Program Committee

Zuling Chang	Zhengzhou University, China
Fei Chen	Shenzhen University, China
Qingfeng Cheng	Information Engineering University, China
Zhongrui Du	Hebei University, China
Xiutao Feng	The System Science Institute of China Science Academy, China
ShaoJing Fu	National University of Defense Technology, China
Jianming Fu	Wuhan University, China
Huifang Guo	Huanghe Science and Technology College, China
Shanqing Guo	Shandong University, China
Yuanbo Guo	Information Engineering University, China
Debiao He	Wuhan University, China
Xinfeng He	Hebei University, China
Wei Hu	PLA Naval University of Engineering, China
Yupeng Hu	Hunan University, China
Qiang Huang	Naval Research Academy, China
Qiong Huang	South China Agricultural University, China
Zhen Li	Hebei University, China
Li Lin	Beijing University of Technology, China
Jinhui Liu	Shaanxi Normal University, China
Zheli Liu	Nankai University, China
Zhenxing Qian	Fudan University, China
Weizhong Qiang	Huazhong University of Science and Technology, China

Yu Qin	Institute of Software, Chinese Academy of Sciences, China
Longjiang Qu	National University of Defense Technology, China
Jun Shao	Zhejiang Gongshang University, China
Yulong Shen	Xidian University, China
Ming Tang	Wuhan University, China
Donghai Tian	Beijing Institute of Technology, China
Yan Tong	Huazhong Agricultural University, China
Ding Wang	Peking University, China
Chao Wang	Shanghai University, China
Houzhen Wang	Wuhan University, China
Juan Wang	Wuhan University, China
Wei Wang	Beijing Jiaotong University, China
Zhibo Wang	Wuhan University, China
Lifei Wei	Shanghai Ocean University, China
Qianhong Wu	Beihang University, China
Liang Xiao	Xiamen University, China
Peng Xu	Huazhong University of Science and Technology, China
Yang Xu	Guizhou Normal University, China
Li Xu	Fujian Normal University, China
Fajiang Yu	Wuhan University, China
Yong Yu	Shaanxi Normal University, China
Jianbiao Zhang	Beijing University of Technology, China
Liqiang Zhang	Wuhan University, China
Zijian Zhang	Beijing Institute of Technology, China
Lei Zhao	Wuhan University, China
Xueguang Zhou	Naval University of Engineering, China
Yajin Zhou	Zhejiang University, China

Contents

Generative Image Steganography Based on GANs

Yaojie Wang[1,2(✉)], Xiaoyuan Yang[1,2], and Hengkang Jin[1,3]

[1] Engineering University of PAP, Xi'an 710086, China
wangyaojie0313@163.com
[2] Key Laboratory of Network and Information Security of PAP,
Xi'an 710086, China
[3] Unified Communications and Next Generation Network Systems Laboratory,
Xi'an 710086, China

Abstract. According to the embedding method of secret information, steganography can be divided into: cover modification, selection and synthesis. In view of the problem that the cover modification will leave the modification trace, the cover selection is difficult and the load is too low, this paper proposes a generative image steganography scheme based on GANs, which combines with cover synthesis. Based on GAN, the scheme uses secret information as the driver and directly generates encrypted images for transmission, which can effectively resist the detection of steganalysis algorithms. The security of the scheme is based on the key of the encryption algorithm. Even if the attacker obtains the transmitted information, only the meaningless result will be obtained without the key. Experiments were carried out on the data set of CelebA, and the results verified the feasibility and security of the scheme.

Keywords: Information hiding · Cover synthesis · Generative adversarial networks · Security

1 Introduction

In Fridrich's groundbreaking work of modern steganography [1], steganographic channel is divided into three categories, cover selection, modification and synthesis. cover modification is the most common method of traditional information hiding, but it is inevitable to leave some traces of modification on the cover, which makes it difficult to resist the detection based on statistical analysis algorithm. Cover selection method does not modify the cover image, thereby avoiding the threat of the existing steganalysis technology. This method cannot be applied to practical applications because of its low payload [2]. Compared with the former two methods, the cover synthesis method is more suitable. However, this method is only a theoretical conception, rather than a practical steganography, because it is difficult to obtain multiple natural samples [3].

Fortunately, a data-based sampling technique, generative adversarial networks (GANs) [4] have become a new research hot spot in artificial intelligence. The biggest advantage and feature of GANs is the ability to sample real space and generate samples driven by noise, which provides the possibility for cover synthesis. Based on GANs,

W. Han et al. (Eds.): CTCIS 2019, CCIS 1149, pp. 1–15, 2020.
https://doi.org/10.1007/978-981-15-3418-8_1

this paper combines symmetric encryption and information hiding, and proposes a generative image steganography scheme. We do not make any modifications to the generated image, which can resist steganographic analysis detection. At the same time, a key-based coordinate encryption algorithm is proposed, which accords with the Kerckhoffs principle [5]. It enhances the ability to resist steganalysis and expands new ideas for the development of information hiding and cryptography.

The remainder of this letter is organized as follows: We detail the development and improvement of machine learning in steganography. Section. 3 shows how to build generative image steganography by GANs. Experiment results are demonstrated in Sect. 4. Section 5 concludes this research and details our future work.

2   Improvement of Generative Model in Steganography

In recent years, some researchers have tried to introduce the theory of confrontation into the field of information security. PassGAN [6] was introduced into the code-deciphering work, and the password generative method based on machine learning was used to replace the artificially formulated password rules, which made obvious progress. Biggo et al. [7] introduced the idea of confrontation into network attack and defense, and the concept of confrontation model was proposed, especially for the improvement of vulnerability repair. In terms of information hiding, some researchers have introduced the generation of confrontation networks into steganography, but the main method they use is still based on the framework of carrier modification. The representative schemes are as follows:

(1) SGAN & SSGAN

Volkhonskiy et al. [8] proposed the SGAN scheme, which first combined GAN with steganography, adding a message embedding module on the basis of original GAN. Different from the traditional method, the generated image is used as the carrier to embed the information. At the same time, an additional steganographic analysis discriminator is trained to ensure that the generated image of the generator cannot be distinguished from the encrypted image after embedded information, so that the steganographic security is further improved. The scheme structure is shown in Fig. 1 below:

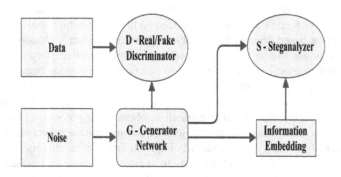

Fig. 1. The structure of SGAN

Similar to [8], Shi et al. [9] introduce WGAN [10] to increase convergence speed and achieve more stable image quality. At the same time, GNCNN was used as the steganographic analysis module to improve the safety of steganography. Wang et al. [11] improved the framework and reconstructed the discriminator of original GAN. The generated image is first embedded into the secret information, and then input into the discriminator for discriminating, forcing the generated image to be more suitable for embedding information while ensuring image quality.

The basic idea of the above solution is to introduce a simple LSB modification module to the GAN confrontation training to achieve steganography. On the one hand, the advantages of generating model in GAN are utilized to ensure that the generated carrier images meet the statistical characteristics of natural images. On the other hand, an additional steganographic discriminator and message embedding module are added to ensure that the generated vector image is effective against steganalysis. Therefore, these schemes can generate image carriers that meet specific steganographic security, but the general performance against steganographic analysis is poor and cannot effectively resist the detection of other steganalysis methods.

(2) ASDL-GAN

Tang et al. [12] proposed the automatic Steganographic Distortion Learning (ASDL) for the first time based on the additive distortion cost function. They use machine learning to obtain the probability matrix P of image pixel modification, then use the STC method to embed secret information. This scheme is called ASDL-GAN.

The scheme utilizes the adversarial network to improve the performance of the generator G, and the probabilistic matrix P is obtained by sampling the generator G to implement steganography. The discriminator D distinguishes both the encrypted carrier and the original carrier. The basic structure is shown in Fig. 2 below:

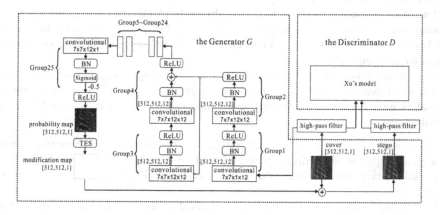

Fig. 2. The structure of ASDL-GAN

To learn the probability matrix P, they propose a miniature network TES as the activation function of the probability matrix. To further improve the security of ASDL-GAN, Yang et al. [13] proposed UT-SCA-GAN (U-net, Tanh-simulator function, Selection Channel Awareness). They use the Tanh-simulator function instead of the TES activation function to improve efficiency, using U-net as the basic structure of the generator. To resist SCA steganalysis, the scheme also introduces the absolute values of 30 high-pass filters in the rich model as auxiliary conditions. The basic framework is shown in Fig. 3:

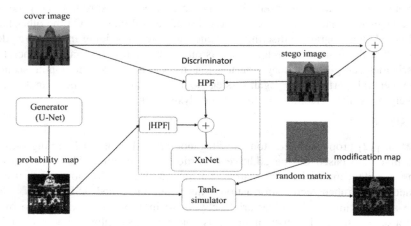

Fig. 3. The structure of UT-SCA-GAN

The main method of these representative schemes is still to embed secret information based on carrier modification. They do not fundamentally satisfy the statistical characteristics of the original image. That is to say, the transmitted encrypted carrier still has traces of modification, which makes it difficult to resist the detection of the steganographic algorithm.

For further study the application of adversarial training in steganography,we propose a novel method—generative image steganography based on GANs. Its feasibility and safety have been verified through experiments, and This paper has the following contributions:

1. According to the idea of carrier synthesis, the concept of generative image steganography is innovatively proposed, and no modification is made to the generated carrier information, which can fundamentally resist the detection of steganographic analysis.
2. Combining "two points, one line" mathematical principle, a coordinate encryption algorithm is proposed, which combines symmetric encryption and information hiding, and satisfies the Kerckhoffs' principle. Ideally, without shared keys, the extraction of secret information is equivalent to brute force cracking.

3   Generative Image Steganography

According to the characteristics of ACGAN [14] which can generate specific label messages, this paper proposes a GAN-based generative image steganography scheme, which directly generates secret cryptographic carriers driven by secret messages, and combines symmetric encryption with steganography to further improve security. The specific program framework is shown in Fig. 4.

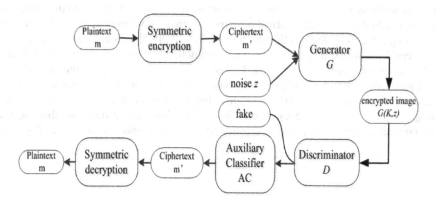

Fig. 4. The structure of the proposed scheme

The scheme consists of encryption algorithm and steganography algorithm. The encryption algorithm can be represented by coordinates, which can be encrypted and decrypted according to the "two points and one line" mathematical principle. Meanwhile, it can expand the dimension according to different security levels. This paper takes two-dimensional plane as an example to introduce the principle of the algorithm. The GAN-based steganographic algorithm replaces the category label with secret information as the driver, directly generates encrypted images for transmission, then the receiver extracts the embedded secret information through the discriminator, thereby realizing generative image steganography.

3.1   Symmetric Encryption Algorithm

First introduce the mathematical algorithm of the symmetric algorithm as shown below:

$$m' = E(m, K) \tag{1}$$

$$m = D(m', K) \tag{2}$$

Where m is the plain text, K is the shared key, and m′ is the encrypted ciphertext, that is, the encrypted information. $E(.)$ denotes an encryption algorithm and $D(.)$ denotes a decryption algorithm. In this scheme, both $E(.)$ and $D(.)$ are equivalent, both of which are represented by $L(.)$.

From a simple point of view, we take the two-dimensional plane as an example to introduce the structure of the algorithm. Suppose that a coordinate point (m,0) on the X-axis in the plane coordinate represents a secret information m. The Shared key $k(kx, ky)$ may be any point on the plane except for points on the X-axis, as shown in Fig. 5(a). Two points m and k define a unique straight line L(m, k) as shown in Fig. 5(b). In this case, L can be considered as the simplest ciphertext generator,which can generate different ciphertexts according to different samples. The sender selects a random number r, then sample a point $c(cx,cy)$ according to the line, which can be regarded as the corresponding ciphertext, as shown in Fig. 5(c). The receiver extracts the ciphertext c from the encrypted image. According to the mathematical principle of "two points and one line", it's easy for receiver to get the m by intersection of the L(c, k) and the X-axis as shown in Fig. 5(d).

We continue to expand this idea. The symmetric encryption of this paper is different from the classical cryptography. Under the same key condition, the ciphertext is not unique. This is also a groundbreaking work, which is worthy of further study. If the ciphertext follow a uniform distribution, this cipher (encryption algorithm) is a classical cryptography shown in Fig. 5(e). If the ciphertext follow a real data distribution, this cipher (steganography algorithm) is a generative steganography, as shown in Fig. 5(f).

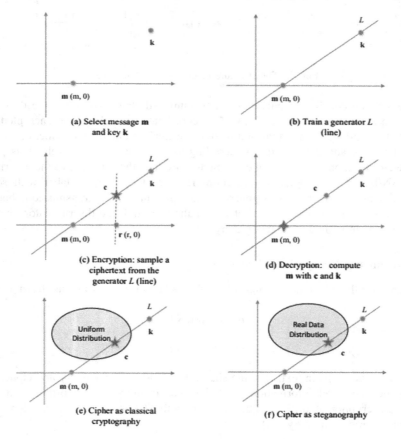

Fig. 5. Symmetric encryption algorithm

In this simple encryption scheme above, this scheme can only resist low-level Ciphtext-only attack. However, cryptographers can easily find the key by using statistical methods such as frequency analysis. Therefore, we can increase the dimension, increase the amount of calculation, and limit the frequency of use, such as changing the key periodically.

3.2   Image Steganography Algorithm

Before we apply the proposed scheme, we need to train ACGAN first. Since each generated sample in ACGAN has a corresponding category label, ACGAN's input consists of z and $C \sim P_C$, so generator G uses both z and C to generate the image $X_{fake} = G(C, z)$. Discriminator D outputs the probability distribution $P(S|X)$ of the real data and the category label's probability distribution $P(C|X) = D(X)$. The loss function has two parts: the likelihood log L_S of the real data and logarithmic L_C of correct category:

$$L_S = E[logP(S = real|X_{real})] + E[logP(S = fake|X_{fake})] \qquad (3)$$

$$L_C = E[logP(C = c|X_{real})] + E[logP(C = c|X_{fake})] \qquad (4)$$

Training discriminator D ultimately maximizes $L_S + L_C$, while training generator G targets $L_S - L_C$ to be minimal. ACGAN's characterization for z is independent of category label C. In training ACGAN, we use the same parameters so that the receiver and sender can get the same generator, and the above information is completely confidential.

Considering that the generator of ACGAN can be combined with noise z and category label C as drivers, which can directly generate specific image samples, and label $C(C_1, C_2, C_3, \cdots)$ can be composed of multiple sub-labels. Combined with the idea of carrier synthesis, the category label C is replaced with secret information m', and directly generate an encrypted image on the basis of ACGAN. This method realizes generative image steganography, which avoids the modification of the carrier. The detailed hiding and extraction process is as follows:

In the hiding process, we first encode the coordinate information m' that needs to be hidden into the corresponding sub-label, and combine the sub-label into label group G (m'). Then, we combine the label group $G(m')$ and random noise Z as the driver and input them into ACGAN, so that we can generate the encrypted image $G(m',z)$ of the specified category by the generator and realize the generated image steganography. The hidden process is shown in Fig. 6:

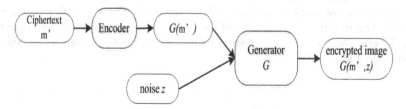

Fig. 6. The structure of the hidden algorithm

In the extraction process, after receiving the encrypted image, the receiver takes a reverse operation to extract information. First, we input the encrypted image into discriminator D in the ACGAN, but D can not directly output the secret information, the output is the likelihood logarithm of image category. Next, the probability of each category in the encrypted image is output by the softmax function [15]. Then, the probability of the image category is converted into a corresponding category label. Finally, we decode the obtained category labels, thereby obtaining embedded coordinate information to achieve information extraction. The extraction process is shown in Fig. 7.

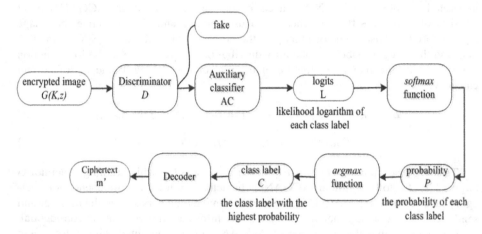

Fig. 7. The structure of extraction algorithm

4 Experiment and Analysis

The ACGAN network training for sender and receiver is as follows: the random noise z is uniformly distributed on $(-1,1)$, the real sample data set is CelebA celebrity face set, and the number of training steps is 10,000. The experimental environment is shown in Table 1. The secret information to be hidden is 10 articles randomly selected from the People's Daily official website.

The optimizer in ACGAN uses a momentum-based optimization method with a learning rate of 0.0002. At each training, the weight of the discriminator D is updated once, the weight of the generator G is updated twice, and the weight of the auxiliary classifier AC is updated once.

The generator consists of four deconvolutional layers. The 3×3 filters are used in each layer. The discriminator consists of four convolutional layers and four deconvolutional layers. The auxiliary classifier consists of four convolutional layers and one fully connected layer [16].

Table 1. Experimental environment

Software platform	Tensorflow v0.12	
Hardware environment	CPU	i7-8250U 3.2 GHz
	RAM	16 GB DDR3 1600 MHz
	GPU	NVIDIA 1080

4.1 Message Hiding and Extraction

In order to verify the feasibility of the proposed scheme, this paper only takes the two-dimensional plane space as an example. First, the code table dictionary can be built to cover 3755 Chinese characters in the national level font library. In addition, national secondary Chinese characters and some common phrases and special symbols should be covered as much as possible. Based on the mnist handwritten digit set with 0–9 total 10 category labels, this method selects 10000 category label combinations to construct a code table dictionary, that is, every 4 numbers are grouped (each number can be selected from 10 numbers)), a total of 10000 groups, each group corresponding to a Chinese character word or phrase, to construct a one-to-one mapping code table dictionary, while the mapping dictionary can be randomly established by the program to establish a corresponding relationship and add a plus or minus sign before the category label to ensure the randomness of the dictionary, As shown in Table 2. In order to increase the difficulty of deciphering, the mapping dictionary should be replaced periodically or the mapping relationship should be changed to reduce the frequency of use of the same mapping dictionary.

Table 2. Examples of the dictionary

Chinese character or phrase	Category label combination
福建 (Fujian)	−0021
火箭军 (Rocket army)	3024
运-20大型运输机 (Yun-20 large transport aircraft)	−0322
. . .	. . .

In the plane coordinates, the random selection message m is: 终南山 (Zhongnanshan). We can Find the category label combination in the code table dictionary is −1100, and the corresponding m coordinate is (−10.000, 0); assuming that the receiver and the sender share the key K coordinate (1.000, 11.000) in advance, the sampling generator L(m,k) is: y = x + 10, and the sampling is performed at random to obtain the sampling point m' coordinate (−3.124, 6.876), which is the delivery message to be hidden.

In this experiment, the input label setting vector length is 40, and the message m' (−3.124, 6.876) to be hidden is encoded (the first and 21st bits are positive and negative signs, and 1/0 is positive/negative signs respectively; 2nd Bits to the 20th place represent the x coordinate; the 22nd to 40th bits represent the y coordinate), and the obtained secret information $\phi(m')$ is as follows:

$$\phi(m') = \left\{ \begin{array}{l} \left. \begin{bmatrix} \boxed{1} & 0 & 0 & 0 & 0 \\ 0 & 1 & 1 & 0 & 0 \\ 0 & 1 & 0 & 0 & 1 \\ 0 & 0 & 1 & 0 & 0 \end{bmatrix} \right\} \text{X-axis cod-} \\ \left. \begin{bmatrix} \boxed{0} & 0 & 0 & 0 & 0 \\ 1 & 1 & 0 & 1 & 0 \\ 0 & 0 & 0 & 1 & 1 \\ 1 & 0 & 1 & 1 & 0 \end{bmatrix} \right\} \text{Y-axis} \end{array} \right.$$

According to the label mapping dictionary on the CelebA dataset, it corresponds to three labels: "pico opening", "smile", "dark".

As we have described, GS-GAN can generate multi-label samples by entering multiple tags in the generator, so you can use the trained generator to generate a dense image with labels. The experimental results are shown in Fig. 8. The "no-label" image is the process of input noise generation; the "+ pico-port" image is generated by the same noise and the "pico-port" label; Then add labels in order. In this manner, the last image is generated by the same noise z and 3 different labels.

Every time we train GS-GAN network 400 times in the experiment, we carry out a test that generates secret image by secret message K and extracts secret message from encrypted image.

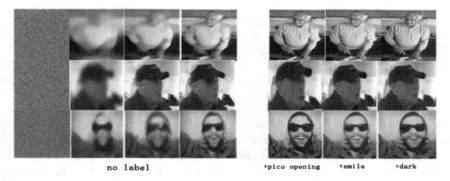

no label   +pico opening   +smile   +dark

Fig. 8. The generated encrypted pictures

The error rate of extracting information is shown in Fig. 9. After 6,000 trainings, the extracted information error rate is less than 0.07, and only the error correction code is added at the time of encoding to ensure the correctness of the decoding. It can therefore also be seen that the proposed solution allows for errors in the communication process without affecting the correct delivery of the communication information.

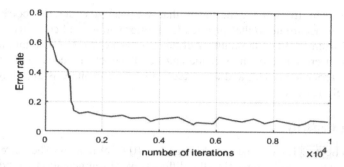

Fig. 9. The number of error class labels extracted

In order to further verify the scheme, we increase the amount of embedded information under the same conditions, that is, increase the number of labels in the dense image. As shown in Fig. 10(a), the number of labels is 3, 5, 7, and 9, respectively. As the number of labels increases, the error rate of extracting information increases with the same number of trainings. Figure 10(b) shows the average error rate of information extracted with different number of tags after 8000 training sessions. The error rate of the extracted information decreases as the number of labels decreases. When the number of labels is ≤ 7, after 8000 trainings, the error rate of the extracted information is less than 0.09. We can add error correction code to ensure the correctness of decoding.

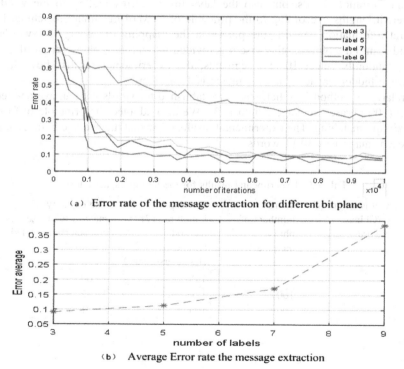

（a） Error rate of the message extraction for different bit plane

（b） Average Error rate the message extraction

Fig. 10. Error rate of the message extraction

It can be seen from the experiment that we can generate the corresponding encrypted image according to the specified label information, and correctly extract the selected label from it. When the number of labels does not exceed a certain threshold, the transmission error rate of the scheme can be effectively reduced, and no modification to the carrier is needed, and the detection of the steganalysis algorithm can be more effectively resisted.

4.2 Hiding Capacity

According to Sect. 3.1, each encrypted image has 10 label images. The corresponding hiding capacity is tested by changing the different word segmentation methods in the code dictionary. We conducted hidden capacity test experiments according to 3 different word segmentation methods. The experimental results are shown in Table 3.

1. We don't use the words segmentation in the dictionary but directly divide the text information into single Chinese character. In the hidden experiment, each word corresponds to a label image. That is,each encrypted image is composed of 10 label images, so the hidden capacity of each encrypted image is 10 words. Since no words segmentation dictionary is used, the number of phrases in the dictionary and the average word length are zero.
2. Select words with an average length of 2 to establish a dictionary (100 phrases, average length is 2). This dictionary not only includes label images corresponding to the common words, but also the label image corresponding to the words of different lengths. According to the principle of forward maximum matching, if the secret information contains the phrase in the mapping dictionary, the words are divided into the phrase, otherwise it is divided into a minor phrase or word, and so on. Randomly select 10 text segments, the experimental results show that the average hidden capacity of each image is 17.42 words.
3. Similarly to method 2, a dictionary is established for words with an average length of 3 (100 phrases, average length is 3). We also adopted the principle of forward maximum matching. The experimental results show that the average hiding capacity of each image was 30.11 words.

Table 3. Experimental results for the hiding capacity test

Average words length of dictionary (Chinese characters/words)	Words numbers of phrases dictionary	The capacity of literature [17] 's method (Chinese characters/image)	The capacity of our method (Chinese characters/encrypted-image)
0	0	1.00	10.00
2	100	1.57	17.42
3	100	1.86	30.11

The experimental results show that establishing a reasonable code dictionary and increasing the average length of the words in the dictionary can improve the information hiding capacity. Theoretically, the hidden capacity of a single label image is the number of Chinese characters in the dictionary. The average information hiding capacity of multiple images is the average length of secret information fragments after word segmentation:

$$\overline{C} = \frac{\sum_{i=1}^{n} C_i}{n} \tag{5}$$

Where: n is the number of secret information fragments, C_i is the length of the i-th secret information fragment.

It can be seen from Table 3 that the scheme of this paper has a large improvement in the hidden capacity. The reason is that each label image corresponds to one keyword, and the average length of the text information corresponding to the encrypted image containing multiple label images is greatly increased, making the capacity of hidden information. Each of the encrypted images in [17] corresponds to one high-frequency keyword, resulting in a relatively small amount of hidden information.

4.3   Security

The security of this paper is based on two aspects: First, a simple and easy encryption algorithm is proposed. According to the two-point and one-line mathematical principle, under the premise of no key, the single point cannot determine the straight line L(m, K), that is, brute force cracking is not feasible. That is to say, the security of the system depends on the confidentiality of the key used, not the confidentiality of the algorithm itself, in accordance with the Kerckhoffs criterion. At the same time, the spatial dimension can be expanded according to different confidential levels. When the security level is high, the spatial dimension is increased, so that the possibility of attacking the attacker is greatly increased, but the encryption and decryption operation still maintains a linear relationship, and the calculation amount is small and the encryption efficiency is high. Under the premise of regularly changing the key, the algorithm is easy to implement and difficult to decipher. Secondly, the secret image of hidden secret information is directly generated by ACGAN, and no modification is made to the carrier information, which greatly increases the anti-stealth analysis. Ability. Compared with the traditional methods of encryption and information hiding, the method proposed in this paper is more difficult to cause the suspicion of attackers, and it can cover secret communication more concealedly.

It is assumed that the attacker suspects that the transmitted image contains secret information, but since it does not have the same GS-GAN model as the communication parties, it is difficult to extract secret information from the dense image by the discriminator. Even if the hidden content is intercepted, only the meaningless result will be obtained without the key, thereby ensuring the security of the covert communication.

5 Conclusion and Future Work

This paper proposes a generative image steganography scheme (GS-GAN), which uses the latest technology of GAN to innovatively realize the new concept of "generative image steganography". At the same time, the combination of symmetric encryption and information hiding has opened up new ideas for the development of information security. On the one hand, the information that needs to be hidden is used as the driver to directly generate the dense image for transmission, and the embedded carrier is not modified, which conforms to the idea of carrier synthesis, and can effectively resist the detection of the steganographic analysis algorithm based on statistics; on the other hand, the security is based on Receiving the shared key of both parties, even if the hidden content is intercepted, only the meaningless result will be obtained without the key, thereby ensuring the security of the covert communication. We used the CelebA dataset to evaluate the performance of the GS-GAN scheme. Theoretical analysis and experimental results show the feasibility and safety of the proposed method.

How to improve the structure of the discriminant model D and improve the ACGAN extraction process is the key research direction of our next step.

Acknowledgment. This work was supported by National Key R&D Program of China (Grant No. 2017YFB0802000), National Natural Science Foundation of China (Grant Nos. 61379152, 61403417)

References

1. Fridrich, J., Kodovsky, J.: Rich models for steganalysis of digital images. IEEE Trans. Inf. Forensics Secur. **7**(3), 868–882 (2012)
2. Fridrich, J.: Steganography in Digital Media: Principles, Algorithms, and Applications. Cambridge University Press, Cambridge (2010)
3. Holub, V., Fridrich, J., Denemark, T.: Universal distortion function for steganography in an arbitrary domain. EURASIP J. Inf. Secur. **2014**(1), 1 (2014)
4. Goodfellow, I., Pouget- Abadie, J., Mirza, M.: Generative Adversarial Networks[DB/OL], 10 June 2014. http://arxiv.org/abs/1406.2661
5. Ke, Y., Zhang, M.Q., Liu, J., et al.: Generative steganography with Kerckhoffs' principle. Multimed. Tools Appl. **78**, 13805–13818 (2018)
6. Hitaj, B., Gasti, P., Ateniese, G., Perez-Cruz, F.: PassGAN: a deep learning approach for password guessing. In: Deng, R.H., Gauthier-Umaña, V., Ochoa, M., Yung, M. (eds.) ACNS 2019. LNCS, vol. 11464, pp. 217–237. Springer, Cham (2019). https://doi.org/10.1007/978-3-030-21568-2_11
7. Biggio, B., et al.: Evasion attacks against machine learning at test time. In: Blockeel, H., Kersting, K., Nijssen, S., Železný, F. (eds.) ECML PKDD 2013. LNCS (LNAI), vol. 8190, pp. 387–402. Springer, Heidelberg (2013). https://doi.org/10.1007/978-3-642-40994-3_25
8. Volkhonskiy, D., Nazarov, I., Borisenko, B., et al.: Steganographic generative adversarial networks (2017)
9. Shi, H., Dong, J., Wang, W., Qian, Y., Zhang, X.: SSGAN: secure steganography based on generative adversarial networks. In: Zeng, B., Huang, Q., El Saddik, A., Li, H., Jiang, S., Fan, X. (eds.) PCM 2017. LNCS, vol. 10735, pp. 534–544. Springer, Cham (2018). https://doi.org/10.1007/978-3-319-77380-3_51

10. Arjovsky, M., Chintala, S., Bottou, L.: Wasserstein GAN (2017)
11. Wang, Y., Yang, X., Liu, J.: Information hiding scheme based on generating confrontation network. J. Comput. Appl. **38**(10), 2923–2928 (2018)
12. Tang, W., Tan, S., Li, B., et al.: Automatic steganographic distortion learning using a generative adversarial network. IEEE Sig. Process. Lett. **24**, 1547–1551 (2017)
13. Yang, J., Liu, K., Kang, X., et al.: Spatial image steganography based on generative adversarial network. https://arxiv.org/abs/1804.07939
14. Odena, A., Olah, C., Shlens, J.: Conditional image synthesis with auxiliary classifier GANs (2016)
15. Lücke, J., Sahani, M.: Generalized softmax networks for non-linear component extraction. In: de Sá, J.M., Alexandre, L.A., Duch, W., Mandic, D. (eds.) ICANN 2007. LNCS, vol. 4668, pp. 657–667. Springer, Heidelberg (2007). https://doi.org/10.1007/978-3-540-74690-4_67
16. Krizhevsky, A., Sutskever, I., Hinton, G.E.: ImageNet classification with deep convolutional neural networks. In: International Conference on Neural Information Processing Systems (2012)
17. Zhou, Z.L., Cao, Y., Sun, X.M.: Coverless information hiding based on bag-of-words model of image. J. Appl. Sci. **34**(5), 527–536 (2016)

Partial Blind Proxy Re-signature
Scheme for Mobile Internet

Yanfang Lei[1], Zhijuan Jia[1(⊠)], Lipeng Wang[1], Bei Gong[2],
Yage Cheng[1], and Junjun Fu[1]

[1] Zhengzhou Normal University, Zhengzhou 450044, China
jzj523@163.com
[2] Beijing University of Technology, Beijing 100124, China

Abstract. Aiming at the problems of limited computing power and high security requirements of mobile Internet mobile terminal devices, we propose a server-assisted verification partial blind proxy re-signature scheme. Partial blind proxy re-signature algorithm protects both the trustee's privacy message and the agent's legal rights. In the server-assisted authentication protocol, the verifier transfers the complex bilinear pairing operation task to the server through the interaction, thereby reducing the amount of computation of the verifier. The numerical experiments show that the verification efficiency of the new scheme is improved by at least 71% and 74%, respectively, compared with the Yang's and Feng's schemes.

Keywords: Server-assisted authentication protocol · Partial blind proxy re-signature · Completeness · Unforgeability

1 Introduction

The development of mobile communication technology is changing with each passing day. Mobile terminals such as Ipad, smart phones, wireless sensors, and electronic keys have become an indispensable part of our lives and work. The rise of e-commerce and e-government has brought people from the real material world into a convenient electronic age. Through the network, you can conduct online shopping, stock operations, communication and access to network resources anytime and anywhere. However, due to the limitations of the mobile Internet terminal device itself, the computing power is generally weak, which makes it necessary for people to perform a large amount of time for verification in resource request and resource access. On the other hand, due to the intricate growth environment of the mobile Internet, this puts higher requirements and standards on the security of the mobile Internet. Therefore, it is necessary to design a solution that can solve terminal computing power, limited energy supply and high security to be applied in the mobile Internet environment.

A secure server-assisted verification signature scheme was given in [1]. However, this scheme does not satisfy the conditions of collusion against server and signer. Later, in [2], Niu proposed a server-assisted verification signature scheme and the scheme can resist the attack, but the scheme needs to consume large broadband expenditure. Combined with aggregation signature and server-assisted verification signatures, Yang

© Springer Nature Singapore Pte Ltd. 2020
W. Han et al. (Eds.): CTCIS 2019, CCIS 1149, pp. 16–30, 2020.
https://doi.org/10.1007/978-981-15-3418-8_2

et al. proposed a cryptosystem to save broadband expenditure in [3], which combines different signatures corresponding to multiple messages into one signature to reduce broadband expenditure, thus saving verification time and improving verification efficiency.

Agent re-signature is an important research direction of cryptography. Domestic and foreign scholars have done a lot of work in this direction. The security model of proxy re-signature was firstly proposed in [4], and two schemes with strict security under the random oracle model are given in this paper. A general combinable proxy re-signature scheme was proposed in [5]. However, some scholars have found that this scheme does not satisfy the conditions of unforgeability. In order to overcome this problem, a modification of the above scheme was proposed in the literature [6]. In recent years, the wide practicality of proxy re-signature has attracted the attention of scholars. Some proxy re-signature schemes with special properties have been proposed successively, such as proxy-based signature scheme based on polynomial isomorphism [7], lattice-based proxy re-signature [8], identity-based proxy re-signature [9], etc. However, these identity-based or certificate-based proxy re-signature schemes have issues such as certificate management and key escrow. In order to overcome these problems, a non-certificate proxy re-signature scheme with aggregation properties was designed in [10]. Effectively reduce the computational cost and communication cost in the verification process. In addition, Mi et al. proposed a blind proxy re-signature scheme in [11] in order to avoid the proxy getting the details of the converted message. However, the verifier in this scheme is pre-designated, which has limitations and low security in practical application. In addition, in order to avoid the agent obtaining the detailed content of the converted message, Mi et al. proposed a blind proxy re-signature scheme in [11]. However, the verifier in this scheme is pre-designated, which has limitations and low security in practical application. Aiming at this problem, in [12], the authors gave a partially blind proxy re-signature scheme with security. This scheme not only realizes the conversion of the signature between the trustee and the agent when the message content is not public. Moreover, the trustee's illegal use of the re-signature is effectively prevented. However, in the signature verification algorithm of this scheme, 4 bilinear pairing operations are needed, which is time-consuming and cannot be well applied to mobile Internet. Therefore, it is necessary to design a scheme that can reduce the verification overhead in partial blind proxy re-signature.

This paper combines the server-assisted authentication protocol and the partial blind proxy re-signature algorithm, and proposes a server-assisted verification part blind proxy re-signature scheme for low-end devices, and gives the security proof of the scheme. In the process of server-assisted verification protocol, the verifier and the server transfer the complex bilinear pairing operation task to the server through the interaction protocol between them, which makes the verifier verify the signature with a small computational cost and improves the verification efficiency of the signature. The verification algorithm reduces complex double-pair operations and has lower computational time overhead, so it can be better adapted to the mobile Internet environment.

2 Preliminaries

2.1 Bilinear Pairings

Let p be a large prime, G_1 and G_2 are two p-ordered cyclic groups, and g is a generator of group G_1. $e : G_1 \times G_2 \rightarrow G_2$ is a bilinear map and satisfies the following conditions:

(1) Bilinear: For arbitrary $x, y \in Z_q^*$, satisfied $e(g^x, g^y) = e(g, g)^{xy}$.
(2) Non-degenerate: There exist $g_1, g_2 \in G_1$, which satisfied $e(g_1, g_2) \neq 1$.
(3) Computability: There exists a valid algorithm $e(g_1, g_2)$, where $g_1, g_2 \in G_1$.

2.2 CDH Hypothesis

Definition 1 (CDH problem): For any unknown $x, y \in Z_q^*$, when $(g, g^x, g^y) \in G_1^3$ is known, we can calculate $g^{xy} \in G_1$.

Definition 2 (CDH Hypothesis): The CDH problem in the group G_1 can be solved with a large probability in polynomial time. The algorithm that satisfies the above conditions does not exist.

3 Scheme Model and Security Definitions

3.1 Server-Assisted Verification Partial Blind Proxy Re-signature Scheme

Combined with partial blind proxy re-signature algorithm and server-assisted authentication protocol, this paper proposes a partial blind proxy re-signature scheme for mobile internet. The participating entities involved in the scheme are the principal Bob, the trustee Alice, the verifier (SV), the semi-trusted proxy (P), and the server (SS). The details are as follows:

(1) The system parameter cp required by the signature algorithm is obtained through the initialization process, then disclosed the parameter cp.
(2) According to the disclosed system parameter cp, the user obtains the public and private key pairs (pk, sk) of the user by running a key generation algorithm.
(3) Generate a re-signature key $rk_{A \rightarrow B}$ for the agent by running the re-signature key algorithm by the given private keys sk_A , sk_B of principal and trustee.
(4) According to the public parameter cp, the trustee and the agent output a common message c by running an agreed message algorithm.
(5) The signature σ is obtained by running the signature algorithm by public message c, signature message m and private key sk.
(6) Given a blinding factor κ, Alice obtains the blinded message x corresponding to the message m and the blinded signature σ_A' corresponding to the message m, c by running the blinding algorithm, and sends (x, σ_A') to the agent.

(7) Firstly, we should judge σ'_A whether a legal signature corresponding to the trustee's public key pk_A, and if it is not a legal signature, output 0; if it is a legal signature, the agent obtains a partial blind proxy re-signature σ'_B by running a re-signature generation algorithm.

(8) The trustee uses the blinding factor κ to process the partial blind proxy re-signature to obtain the signature σ_B of the signed message m and the public message c.

(9) The verifier verifies whether the signature σ is a legal signature that corresponding to the public key pk for the signed message m and the public message c. If it is a legal signature, output 1; otherwise, it outputs 0.

(10) Generate server-assisted authentication parameters: from cp, generate a string vst for the verifier through this process.

(11) Server-assisted authentication protocol: for string vst, public key pk and message signature pairs (m, σ), if the server lets the verifier determine that σ is a valid signature, output 1; otherwise, output 0.

3.2 Security Definition

The security of the server-assisted verification part of the blind proxy re-signature should at least include the unforgeability of the proxy re-signature, the partial blindness and the completeness of the server-assisted authentication protocol. Unforgeability guarantees that an attacker cannot generate a legal signature for a new message. Partial blindness ensures that the agent generates a re-signature of the message without knowing the content of the converted message, and the agent cannot match the final re-signature of the message with a partial blind proxy re-signature. The completeness of the so-called server-assisted authentication protocol means that the server cannot enable the verifier to determine the legality of an illegal signature.

The unforgeability and partial blindness of proxy re-signature have been proved in [12]. In [13], the completeness of the server-assisted verification protocol under joint attack and adaptive selection message attack was defined by designing two games Game1 and Game2.

Definition 1: If the attacker's probability of winning in Game1 and Game2 in the literature [13] approaches, the server-assisted verification protocol in the scheme is said to be complete.

Definition 2: If the server-assisted verification part of the blind proxy re-signature scheme satisfies the following two conditions at the same time, it indicates that the scheme is secure under collusion attacks and selective message attacks.

(1) In the case of adaptive selection of message attacks, there is both unforgeability and partial blindness.

(2) The server-assisted verification protocol is complete.

4   Partial Blind Proxy Re-signature Scheme

In this part we construct a partial blind proxy re-signature scheme that is both secure and efficient and adapts to the mobile Internet environment. The bit length of the signature message is taken as $n_m bit$, and the bit length of the public message is $n_{m_1} bit$. Use the anti-collision hash function $H_1 : \{0,1\}^* \rightarrow \{0,1\}^{n_m}$ and $H_2 : \{0,1\}^* \rightarrow \{0,1\}^{n_{m_1}}$ to extend the fixed length of the message m and c to any length to enhance the flexibility of the solution.

(1) *Setup*: Given security parameter λ, disclose system parameter $(cp) = (e, p, G_1, G_2, g, g_1, u^*, u_1, \ldots, u_{n_m}, \mu^*, \mu_1, \ldots, \mu_{n_{m_1}})$, where $e : G_1 \times G_1 \rightarrow G_2$ is a bilinear map, G_1, G_2 are cyclic groups which prime number is p, g is a generator element of G_1, and g_1 is an element of the cyclic group G_1. $u^*, u_1, \ldots, u_{n_m}, \mu_1, \ldots, \mu_{n_{m_1}}$, which are randomly selected elements in the cyclic group G_1.

(2) *Keygen*: The user randomly selects $\alpha \in Z_p^*$ and obtains the corresponding public-private key pair $(pk, sk) = (g^\alpha, \alpha)$.

(3) *Rekey*: After inputting the private keys $sk_A = a$ and $sk_B = b$ of Alice and Bob, and outputting a re-signature key $rk_{A \rightarrow B} = \frac{b}{a}$ mod p of the agent, however, Alice and Bob's private key are not disclosed to the agent P in the process.

(4) *Agree*: Alice and Bob agree on a message $c = (c_1, c_2, \ldots, c_{m_1}) \in \{0,1\}^{n_{m_1}}$ with a bit length of n_{m_1} bit.

(5) *Sign*: Given the signed message m and the public message c, Alice then randomly selects $\varepsilon_1, \varepsilon_2 \in Z_p^*$ and then uses Alice's private key $sk_A = a$ to calculate

$$\sigma_{A1} = g_1^a \left(u^* \prod_{i=1}^{n_m} u_i^{m_i} \right)^{\varepsilon_1} \left(\mu^* \prod_{j=1}^{n_{m_1}} \mu_j^{m_{1j}} \right)^{\varepsilon_2}, \quad \sigma_{A2} = g^{\varepsilon_1} \text{ and } \sigma_{A3} = g^{\varepsilon_2}, \text{ finally, out-}$$

putting the original signature $\sigma_A = (\sigma_{A1}, \sigma_{A2}, \sigma_{A3})$ of the message m and c.

(6) *Blind*: For a signed message m and c are with bit lengths $n_m bit$, $n_{m_1} bit$ respectively. Alice randomly selects a blinding factor $\kappa \in Z_p^*$, calculates a blind message $x = \left(u^* \prod_{i=1}^{n_m} u_i^{m_i} \right)^\kappa$ of the signed message m, and then randomly selects

$\gamma_m, \gamma_{m_1} \in Z_p^*$, calculates $\sigma_{A1}' = g_1^a x^{\gamma_m} \left(\mu^* \prod_{j=1}^{n_{m_1}} \mu_j^{m_{1j}} \right)^{\gamma_{m1}}$, $\sigma_{A2}' = g^{\gamma_m}$ and $\sigma_{A3}' = g^{\gamma_{m_1}}$

finally, sends the blind message x, public message c, and blind signature $\sigma_A' = (\sigma_{A1}', \sigma_{A2}', \sigma_{A3}')$ to the agent P.

(7) *Resign*: After the agent P receives the blind message x, the public message c and the blind signature $\sigma_A' = (\sigma_{A1}', \sigma_{A2}', \sigma_{A3}')$ then verifies whether the equation

$$e(\sigma_{A1}', g) = e(g_1, pk_A) e(x, \sigma_{A2}') e\left(\mu^* \prod_{j=1}^{n_{m_1}} \mu_j^{m_{1j}}, \sigma_{A3}' \right) \tag{1}$$

is established, if not, output 0; if it is established, randomly selected $\gamma'_m, \gamma'_{m_1} \in Z_p^*$, then

use the re-signature key $rk_{A \to B}$ to calculate $\sigma'_{B1} = \left(\sigma'_{A1}\right)^{rk_{A \to B}} x^{\gamma'_m} \left(\mu^* \prod\limits_{j=1}^{n_{m_1}} \mu_j^{m_{1j}}\right)^{\gamma'_{m_1}}, \sigma'_{B2} =$

$\left(\sigma'_{A2}\right)^{rk_{A \to B}} g^{\gamma'_m}$ and $\sigma'_{B3} = \left(\sigma'_{A3}\right)^{rk_{A \to B}} g^{\gamma'_{m_1}}$ then send the partial blind proxy re-signature to Alice.

(8) *Unblind*: After receiving a partial blind proxy re-signature sent by the agent P, Alice uses Bob's public key pk_B to verify whether the equation

$$e\left(\sigma'_{B1}, g\right) = e(g_1, pk_B) e\left(x, \sigma'_{B2}\right) e\left(\mu^* \prod\limits_{j=1}^{n_{m_1}} \mu_j^{m_{1j}}, \sigma'_{B3}\right) \tag{2}$$

is established, if the equation is not established, it means that σ'_B is an invalid signature, and Alice refuses to accept it; if the equation is established, then randomly selects $\lambda \in Z_p^*$ which satisfied $\varepsilon_1 = \kappa\gamma_m + \lambda$ and $\varepsilon_2 = \gamma_{m_1} + \kappa\lambda$. The following is a blinding of partial blind proxy re-signatures. From calculating $\sigma_{B1} = \left(\sigma'_{B1}\right)$

$\left(\left(u^* \prod\limits_{i=1}^{n_m} u_i^{m_i}\right) \left(\mu^* \prod\limits_{j=1}^{n_{m_1}} \mu_j^{m_{1j}}\right)^\kappa\right)^\lambda$, $\sigma_{B2} = \left(\sigma'_{B2}\right)^\kappa g^\lambda$ and $\sigma_{B3} = \left(\sigma'_{B3}\right) g^{\kappa\lambda}$, we can obtain a

re-signature $\sigma_B = (\sigma_{B1}, \sigma_{B2}, \sigma_{B3})$ of the public message and the signed message.

(9) *Verify*: Enter the public key pk, signature message m, public message c and signature $\sigma = (\sigma_1, \sigma_2, \sigma_3)$, if the equation

$$e(\sigma_1, g) = e(g_1, pk) e\left(u^* \prod\limits_{i=1}^{n_m} u_i^{m_i}, \sigma_2\right) e\left(\mu^* \prod\limits_{j=1}^{n_{m_1}} \mu_j^{m_{1j}}, \sigma_3\right) \tag{3}$$

is established, outputs 1, otherwise outputs 0.

(10) *Server-setup*: The verifier randomly selects an element $y \in Z_p^*$ and further assumes a string $vst = y$, and requires the string to be undisclosed.

(11) *Server-verify*: The server helps the verifier to verify the validity of the signature through the following interactive protocol. Specific steps are as follows:

   (1) The verifier first enters the signature message m, the public message c, and computes $\sigma^* = \left(\sigma_1^*, \sigma_2^*, \sigma_3^*\right) = \left(\sigma_1^y, \sigma_2^y, \sigma_3^y\right)$ by using the string $vst = y$, and sends the information (m, c, σ^*) to the server.

   (2) After receiving the information (m, c, σ^*) sent by the verifier, the server

   calculates $\eta_1 = e\left(\sigma_1^*, g\right)$, $\eta_2 = e\left(u^* \prod\limits_{i=1}^{n_m} u_i^{m_i}, \sigma_2^*\right)$, $\eta_3 = e\left(\mu^* \prod\limits_{j=1}^{n_m} \mu_j^{m_{1j}}, \sigma_3^*\right)$

   and $\eta_4 = e(g_1, pk)$, and then sends $(\eta_1, \eta_2, \eta_3, \eta_4)$ to the verifier.

   (3) After obtaining $(\eta_1, \eta_2, \eta_3, \eta_4)$, the verifier verifies whether the equation

$$\eta_1 = (\eta_4)^y \eta_2 \eta_3 \tag{4}$$

is true, if it is true, output 1; otherwise output 0.

5 Safety Proof and Effectiveness Analysis

5.1 Correctness Analysis

Theorem 1: If the Eq. (1) holds, then the blind signature is correct.

Proof: From the natures of the bilinear pair and $\sigma'_{A1} = g_1^a x^{\gamma_m} \left(\mu^* \prod_{j=1}^{n_{m_1}} \mu_j^{m_{1j}} \right)^{\gamma_{m_1}}$, we

obtain

$$
\begin{aligned}
e\left(\sigma'_{A1}, g\right) &= e\left(g_1^a x^{\gamma_m} \left(\mu^* \prod_{j=1}^{n_{m_1}} \mu_j^{m_{1j}} \right)^{\gamma_{m_1}}, g \right) \\
&= e(g_1^a, g) e(x^{\gamma_m}, g) e\left(\left(\mu^* \prod_{j=1}^{n_{m_1}} \mu_j^{m_{1j}} \right)^{\gamma_{m_1}}, g \right) \\
&= e(g_1, pk_A) e(x, \sigma'_{A2}) e\left(\mu^* \prod_{j=1}^{n_{m_1}} \mu_j^{m_{1j}}, \sigma'_{A3} \right) .
\end{aligned}
$$

Theorem 2: If the Eq. (2) holds, then the partial blind proxy re-signature is correct.

Proof: From the natures of the bilinear pair and $rk_{A \to B} = \frac{b}{a} \bmod p$, $pk_B = g^b$, and

$$\sigma'_A = \left(\sigma'_{A1}, \sigma'_{A2}, \sigma'_{A3} \right) = \left(g_1^a x^{\gamma_m} \left(\mu^* \prod_{j=1}^{n_{m_1}} \mu_j^{m_{1j}} \right)^{\gamma_{m_1}}, g^{\gamma_m}, g^{\gamma_{m_1}} \right), \text{ we get}$$

$$
\begin{aligned}
\sigma'_{B1} &= \left(\sigma'_{A1} \right)^{rk_{A \to B}} x^{\gamma'_m} \left(\mu^* \prod_{j=1}^{n_{m_1}} \mu_j^{m_{1j}} \right)^{\gamma'_{m1}} \\
&= \left(g_1^a x^{\gamma_m} \left(\mu^* \prod_{j=1}^{n_{m_1}} \mu_j^{m_{1j}} \right)^{\gamma_{m_1}} \right)^{\frac{b}{a}} x^{\gamma'_m} \left(\mu^* \prod_{j=1}^{n_{m_1}} \mu_j^{m_{1j}} \right)^{\gamma'_{m_1}} \\
&= g_1^b x^{\frac{b}{a}\gamma_m + \gamma'_m} \left(\mu^* \prod_{j=1}^{n_{m_1}} \mu_j^{m_{1j}} \right)^{\frac{b}{a}\gamma_{m_1} + \gamma'_{m_1}} ,
\end{aligned}
$$

$$\sigma'_{B2} = \left(\sigma'_{A2} \right)^{rk_{A \to B}} g^{\gamma'_m} = (g^{\gamma_m})^{\frac{b}{a}} g^{\gamma'_m} = g^{\frac{b}{a}\gamma_m + \gamma'_m},$$

$$\sigma'_{B3} = \left(\sigma'_{A3}\right)^{rk_{A \to B}} g^{\gamma'_{m_1}} = \left(g^{\gamma_{m_1}}\right)^{\frac{b}{a}} g^{\gamma'_{m_1}} = g^{\frac{b}{a}\gamma_{m_1} + \gamma'_{m_1}}$$

then, using the properties of the bilinear pair again, we get

$$e\left(\sigma'_{B1}, g\right) = e\left(g_1^b x^{\frac{b}{a}\gamma_m + \gamma'_m}\left(\mu^* \prod_{j=1}^{n_{m_1}} \mu_j^{m_{1j}}\right)^{\frac{b}{a}\gamma_{m_1} + \gamma'_{m_1}}, g\right)$$

$$= e\left(g_1^b, g\right) e\left(x^{\frac{b}{a}\gamma_m + \gamma'_m}, g\right) e\left(\left(\mu^* \prod_{j=1}^{n_{m_1}} \mu_j^{m_{1j}}\right)^{\frac{b}{a}\gamma_{m_1} + \gamma'_{m_1}}, g\right)$$

$$= e\left(g_1, g^b\right) e\left(x, g^{\frac{b}{a}\gamma_m + \gamma'_m}\right) e\left(\mu^* \prod_{j=1}^{n_{m_1}} \mu_j^{m_{1j}}, g^{\frac{b}{a}\gamma_{m_1} + \gamma'_{m_1}}\right)$$

$$= e\left(g_1, pk_B\right) e\left(x, \sigma'_{B2}\right) e\left(\mu^* \prod_{j=1}^{n_{m_1}} \mu_j^{m_{1j}}, \sigma'_{B3}\right).$$

Theorem 3: If the Eq. (3) holds, then the proxy re-signature is correct.

Proof: For the sake of simplicity of writing, we write $\gamma_m^B = \frac{b}{a}\gamma_m + \gamma'_m$ and $\gamma_{m_1}^B = \frac{b}{a}\gamma_{m_1} + \gamma'_{m_1}$.

With Bob's public key and blind proxy re-signature, de-blinding the blind proxy re-signature in the following:

$$\left(\sigma'_{B1}\right)\left(\left(u^* \prod_{i=1}^{n_m} u_i^{m_i}\right)\left(\mu^* \prod_{j=1}^{n_{m_1}} \mu_j^{m_{1j}}\right)\right)^{\kappa\lambda}$$

$$= \left(g_1^b x^{\gamma_m^B}\left(\mu^* \prod_{j=1}^{n_{m_1}} \mu_j^{m_{1j}}\right)^{\gamma_{m_1}^B}\right)\left(\left(u^* \prod_{i=1}^{n_m} u_i^{m_i}\right)\left(\mu^* \prod_{j=1}^{n_{m_1}} \mu_j^{m_{1j}}\right)\right)^{\kappa\lambda}$$

$$= g_1^b\left(\mu^* \prod_{j=1}^{n_{m_1}} \mu_j^{m_{1j}}\right)^{\gamma_{m_1}^B + \kappa\lambda}\left(u^* \prod_{i=1}^{n_m} u_i^{m_i}\right)^{\kappa\gamma_m^B + \lambda}$$

$$= \sigma_{B1},$$

$$\left(\sigma'_{B2}\right)^{\kappa} g^{\lambda} = g^{\kappa\gamma_m^B} g^{\lambda} = g^{\kappa\gamma_m^B + \lambda} = \sigma_{B2},$$

$$\left(\sigma'_{B3}\right) g^{\kappa\lambda} = g^{\gamma_{m_1}^B} g^{\kappa\lambda} = g^{\gamma_{m_1}^B + \kappa\lambda} = \sigma_{B3},$$

then, from the properties of the bilinear pair, we get

$$e(\sigma_{B1}, g) = e\left(g_1^b\left(\mu^* \prod_{j=1}^{n_{m_1}} \mu_j^{m_{1j}}\right)^{\gamma_{m_1}^B + \kappa\lambda} \left(u^* \prod_{i=1}^{n_m} u_i^{m_i}\right)^{\kappa\gamma_m^3 + \lambda}, g\right)$$

$$= e\left(g_1^b, g\right) e\left(\left(u^* \prod_{i=1}^{n_m} u_i^{m_i}\right)^{\kappa\gamma_m^B + \lambda}, g\right) e\left(\left(\mu^* \prod_{j=1}^{n_{m_1}} \mu_j^{m_{1j}}\right)^{\gamma_{m_1}^B + \kappa\lambda}, g\right)$$

$$= e\left(g_1, g^b\right) e\left(u^* \prod_{i=1}^{n_m} u_i^{m_i}, g^{\kappa\gamma_m^B + \lambda}\right) e\left(\mu^* \prod_{j=1}^{n_{m_1}} \mu_j^{m_{1j}}, g^{\gamma_{m_1}^B + \kappa\lambda}\right)$$

$$= e\left(g_1, pk_B\right) e\left(u^* \prod_{i=1}^{n_m} u_i^{m_i}, \sigma_{B2}\right) e\left(\mu^* \prod_{j=1}^{n_{m_1}} \mu_j^{m_{1j}}, \sigma_{B3}\right).$$

Theorem 4: If the Eq. (4) holds, then the server-assisted verification algorithm is correct.

Proof: From the un-blind proxy re-signature $\sigma_B = (\sigma_{B1}, \sigma_{B2}, \sigma_{B3})$ and string $vst = y$ and using the properties of bilinear pairs, we obtain

$$\eta_1 = e(\sigma_{B1}^*, g)$$
$$= e((\sigma_{B1})^y, g)$$
$$= e\left(\left(g_1^b\left(u^* \prod_{i=1}^{n_m} u_i^{m_i}\right)^{\kappa\gamma_m^B + \lambda} \left(\mu^* \prod_{j=1}^{n_{m_1}} \mu_j^{m_{1j}}\right)^{\gamma_{m_1}^B + \kappa\lambda}\right)^y, g\right)$$
$$= e\left(g_1, g^b\right)^y e\left(u^* \prod_{i=1}^{n_m} u_i^{m_i}, \left(g^{\kappa\gamma_m^B + \lambda}\right)^y\right) e\left(\mu^* \prod_{j=1}^{n_{m_1}} \mu_j^{m_{1j}}, \left(g^{\gamma_{m_1}^B + \kappa\lambda}\right)^y\right)$$
$$= e\left(g_1, pk_B\right)^y e\left(u^* \prod_{i=1}^{n_m} u_i^{m_i}, \sigma_{B2}^y\right) e\left(\mu^* \prod_{j=1}^{n_{m_1}} \mu_j^{m_{1j}}, \sigma_{B3}^y\right)$$
$$= (\eta_4)^y \eta_2 \eta_3.$$

Through the derivation of the above four theorems, it is found that the obtained blind signature, partial blind proxy re-signature and proxy re-signature obtained after detachment processing are effective and the server-assisted verification protocol algorithm is correct. Because the original signature is indistinguishable from the proxy re-signature, this scheme satisfies transparency and versatility.

5.2 Security Analysis

The scheme of this paper is based on the scheme in [12]. In this scheme, the partial blindness and unforgeability have been proved under the standard model. Therefore, according to the definition of security of the scheme, in order to prove the security of the scheme, it is only necessary to prove that the server-assisted verification algorithm is complete.

Theorem 5: The server-assisted verification of the proposed scheme is complete.

The proof of this theorem needs to consider two aspects. Firstly, consider that the server and the trustee jointly generate an illegal signature, so that the verifier is convinced that the probability that an illegal signature is legal is negligible. Secondly, consider that the server and the agent jointly generate an illegal signature, and the probability that the signature convinced by the verifier that an illegal signature is legitimate is negligible. Next, the conclusion of Theorem 5 will be proved from the following two lemmas.

Lemma 1: If the server collides with Alice to become an attacker A_1, the attacker asks the challenger to determine that an illegal original signature is legal. The probability that the event is true is zero.

Proof: In this process, A_1 plays the role of the server and in the agreement, C plays the role of verifier. Given the illegal original signature of a message, the goal of A_1 is to let C make sure that the illegal signature is legitimate. The interaction between them is as follows:

Establishment: Challenger C performs the initialization algorithm to generate system parameter cp, randomly selects $y^*, \gamma \in Z_p^*$, lets $vst = y^*$ and calculates the public-private key pair $(pk_A, sk_A) = (e(g_1, g^\gamma), \gamma)$ of the trustee Alice and then sends $\{cp, pk_A, sk_A\}$ to the attacker A_1.

Query: The attacker A_1 can make a limited number of secondary verification queries to the server. In the process of each inquiry of (m_i, σ_i), both the challenger C and the attacker A_1 perform server-assisted verification to obtain the authentication protocol, and then respond to the output of the protocol and return it to the attacker A_1.

Output: Finally, the attacker A_1 outputs the forged messages m^*, c^* and the string $\sigma^{1*} = (\sigma_1^{1*}, \sigma_2^{1*}, \sigma_3^{1*})$, and let the set of all legal signatures that make the messages m^*, c^* corresponding to the public key pk_A is Γ_{m^*}, and satisfies $\sigma^{1^*} \notin \Gamma_{m^*}$. When the challenger C receives (m^*, c^*, σ^{1^*}), it computes $(\sigma^{1^*})^* = ((\sigma_1^{1*})^*, (\sigma_2^{1*})^*, (\sigma_3^{1*})^*) = ((\sigma_1^{1*})^{y^*}, (\sigma_2^{1*})^{y^*}, (\sigma_3^{1*})^{y^*})$ with the given string vst and sends it to the attacker A_1.

Then, A_1 obtains $\eta_1^* = e(\sigma_1^{1*}, g)$, $\eta_2^* = e\left(u' \prod_{i=1}^{n_m} u_i^{m_i}, \sigma_2^{1*}\right)$, $\eta_3^* = e\left(\mu^* \prod_{j=1}^{n_{ml}} \mu_j^{m_{1j}}, \sigma_3^{1*}\right)$ and $\eta_4 = e(g_1, pk_A)$ by operation and returns them to C. The following is a detailed derivation of the probability that the equation $\eta_1^* = (\eta_4)^{y^*} \eta_2^* \eta_3^*$ is established is $1/(p-1)$.

(1) Because of $(\sigma^{1*})^* = (\sigma^{1*})^{y^*}$ and $y^* \in Z_p^*$, the probability of attacker A_1 forging $(\sigma^{1*})^*$ from σ^{1*} is $1/(p-1)$.

(2) Assuming that the attacker A_1 returns $(\eta_1^*, \eta_2^*, \eta_3^*, \eta_4)$, which satisfies $\eta_1^* = (\eta_4)^{y^*} \eta_2^* \eta_3^*$, then we have

$$\log_{n_4} \eta_1^* = y^* + \log_{n_4} \eta_2^* + \log_{n_4} \eta_3^*,$$

Because y^* is an element selected arbitrarily from Z_p^*, the probability that the attacker tries to get y^* to make the above equation true is $1/(p-1)$.

From the above analysis, it can be seen that the probability that attacker A_1 makes C believe that message signature (m^*, σ^*) is legitimate is $1/(p-1)$. Since p is a large prime, the probability that attacker A_1 let C decide that an illegal original signature is legitimate is zero.

Lemma 2: If the server collides with the proxy to become an attacker A_2. The probability that A_2 lets C decide that an illegal re-signature is legal is negligible.

Proof: In this process, A_2 plays the role of the server and in the agreement, C plays the role of verifier. When an illegal signature of a message is given, the goal of A_2 is to let C make sure the illegal signature is legal. The interaction between the two is as follows:

Establishment: Challenger C obtains system parameter cp by running a system initialization algorithm, selects three elements y^*, α, β from Z_p^*, and computes $(pk_A, sk_A) = (e(g_1, g^\alpha), \alpha)$, $(pk_B, sk_B) = (e(g_1, g^\beta), \beta)$ and $rk_{A \to B} = \frac{b}{a} mod\, p$. Then Challenger C sends cp, pk_A, pk_B and $rk_{A \to B}$ to A_2.

Query: Same as the interrogation response process in Lemma 1.

Output: Finally, the attacker A_2 outputs the forged messages m^*, c^*, and the string $\sigma^{1*} = (\sigma_1^{1*}, \sigma_2^{1*}, \sigma_3^{1*})$, and let the set of all legal signatures that make the messages m^*, c^* corresponding to the public key pk_B is Γ_{m^*}, and satisfies $\sigma^{1^*} \notin \Gamma_{m^*}$. Similarly, in the analysis process in Lemma 1, attacker A_2 let C make sure that the probability that (m^*, c^*, σ^{1*}) is a legal signature is $1/(p-1)$. Therefore, the probability that attacker A_2 makes C convinced that (m^*, c^*, σ^{1*}) is a legitimate signature is negligible.

Based on the above analysis, we know that the partial blind proxy re-signature scheme proposed in this paper is safe in the case of adaptive selection of message attacks and collusion attacks.

Next, we present a performance analysis of the server-assisted verification partial blind proxy re-signature scheme.

5.3 Performance Analysis

5.3.1 Efficiency Analysis

The computational difficulty of the server-assisted verification partial blind proxy re-signature scheme proposed in this paper is equivalent to the CDH problem. In order to compare performance with the existing blind proxy re-signature algorithm, the following symbols are defined (Table 1).

Table 1. The symbolic representation of the solution.

Symbol	Description
$|G_1|$	The length of the element in G_1
$|G_2|$	The length of the element in G_2
C_p	Exponential calculation
C_q	Bilinear pairing calculation

It should be noted that since the calculation amount of addition, multiplication, HMAC algorithm and hash function are relatively small, we only consider the computational exponential operation and the bilinear pair operation with large computational complexity when considering the computational overhead.

The following analysis will be carried out from five aspects: the calculation amount of the signature algorithm, the calculation amount of the blind algorithm, the calculation amount of the re-signature algorithm, the calculation amount of the un-blind algorithm and the calculation amount of the verifier. The calculation amount of the algorithm in the scheme of this paper is shown in Table 2 below.

Table 2. Calculation amount of the scheme.

Procedure	Calculated amount
Sign algorithm	$5C_p$
Blind algorithm	$6C_p$
Re-signature algorithm	$7C_p + 4C_q$
Un-blind algorithm	$5C_p + 4C_q$
Verifier	$4C_p$

The literature [12, 14, 15] respectively gives three different blind proxy re-signature schemes. The signature algorithm proposed in this paper is compared with the existing three algorithms based on its computational cost and security attributes. The comparison results are shown in the following Table 3.

Table 3. Calculation overhead and security attributes of blind proxy re-signature algorithm.

Scheme	The length of signature	The length of Re-signature	Re-signature algorithm	Blind algorithm	Verifier	Versatility	Partial blindness
Alg. in [12]	$\|3G_1\|$	$\|3G_1\|$	$7C_p + 4C_q$	$6C_p$	$4C_p$	Yes	Yes
Alg. in [14]	$\|3G_1\|$	$\|3G_1\|$	$4C_q$	$2C_p$	$6C_q$	Yes	No
Alg. in [15]	$\|3G_1\|$	$\|2G_1\|$	$2C_p + 7C_q$	$5C_p$	$3C_q$	No	No
Ours	$\|3G_1\|$	$\|3G_1\|$	$7C_p + 4C_q$	$6C_p$	$4C_p$	Yes	Yes

It can be seen from Table 3 that on the one hand, from the perspective of storage overhead, the signature length and re-signature length of the scheme are similar to those of the literature [12, 14, 15], but the scheme in [14] does not have partial blindness. The scheme of [15] is neither versatile nor partially blind, so its practical applicability is small. On the other hand, from the calculation amount, the scheme in the literature [12] and the scheme proposed in this paper are slightly higher in the calculation of the re-signature algorithm and the blind algorithm than in the literature [12, 14, 15]. However, the scheme in this paper only needs four exponential operations in the verification process, and literature [12, 14, 15] needs six, three and four bilinear pairing operations with high computational complexity, respectively. In summary, the scheme has partial blindness and versatility security attribute features, which can effectively protect the trustee's privacy messages and the agent's legal rights can also be maintained. Moreover, the scheme has less computational complexity when verifying the validity of signatures, thus reducing the time required for verification and improving the efficiency of verification. Therefore, the scheme can be better applied to mobile communications.

5.3.2 Numerical Experiments

This part is a simulation experiment of the verifier's time overhead, verification efficiency and message signatures of different orders of magnitude in the schemes of this paper, the literature [12] and [14]. The environment of the simulation experiment is CPU for Intel Core i5-8300H processor, clocked at 2.3 GHz, memory 8 GB, software environment: 64-bit Window 10 operating system, MyEclipse2015.

It can be seen from Fig. 1 that for the signature messages of the same length, the verification time overhead of the scheme is lower than that in [12, 14] and is a bit higher than that in [15], however, the scheme in [15] is neither versatile nor partially blind. In addition, in the schemes of [12] and [14], the verifier needs to perform 4 and 6 bilinear pairing operations, respectively. As the length of the signature message increases, the time overhead of the verifier in the scheme increases greatly. However, in this scheme, the computationally complex bilinear pair operation is transferred to the server through the interaction protocol between the verifier and the server. The verifier only needs to perform 4 times exponential operation, so in this scheme as the length of the signature message increases, the time cost of the verifier changes little.

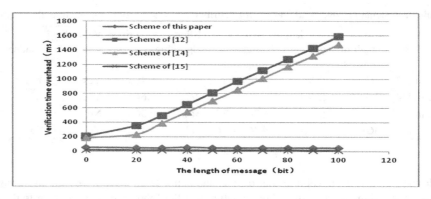

Fig. 1. Relationship between verification time overhead and message length.

It can be seen from Fig. 2 that the verification efficiency of the scheme is improved by at least 74% and 71%, respectively, compared with the schemes of [14] and [12], which greatly reduces the time cost of the verifier and saves the verification cost.

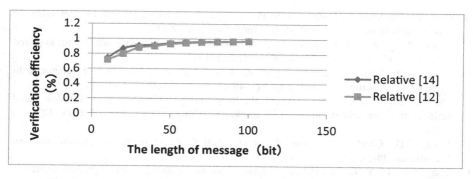

Fig. 2. Relationship between verification time overhead and message length.

6 Conclusion

This paper proposes a formal model of server-assisted verification of partial blind proxy re-signature, constructs a specific implementation scheme, and gives corresponding security proof. In this solution, on the one hand, in the process of the server-assisted authentication protocol, the verifier and the server transfer the complex bilinear pairing operation task to the server through the interaction protocol between them, so that the verifier compares the small computational cost verifies the signature and improves the verification efficiency of the signature. On the other hand, the use of partial blindness not only protects the privacy message of the trustee but also protects the legitimate rights and interests of the agent. Finally, simulation experiments show that the proposed scheme has higher verification efficiency than other existing blind proxy re-signature schemes, and satisfies the requirements of low-end computing equipment with weak computing power and limited energy supply. Therefore, it is suitable for use in the mobile Internet application environment.

References

1. Wei, W., Yi, M., Susilo, W., et al.: Provably secure server-aided verification signatures. Comput. Math. Appl. **61**(7), 1705–1723 (2011)
2. Niu, S.F., Wang, C.F., et al.: Server-assisted verification signature scheme against collusion attacks. Appl. Res. Comput. **33**(1), 229–231 (2016)
3. Yang, X.D., Li, Y.N., Zhou, Q.X., et al.: Security analysis and improvement of a server-sided authentication aggregation signature scheme. Comput. Eng. **43**(1), 183–187 (2017)
4. Ateniese, G., Hohenberger, S.: Proxy re-signatures: new definitions, algorithms, and applications. https://doi.org/10.1145/1102120.1102161
5. Hong, X., Chen, K.F., Wan, Z.M.: Simple universally combinable proxy re-signature scheme. J. Softw. **21**(8), 2079–2088 (2010)
6. Ai, H., Liu, X.J.: Research on universal combinable re-signature scheme based on bilinear pairs. Comput. Eng. Des. **34**(11), 3748–3751 (2013)
7. Li, H.X., Shao, L., Pang, L.J.: Proxy re-signature scheme based on polynomial isomorphism. J. Commun. **38**(2), 16–24 (2017)

8. Qiao, L.: Research on Lattice-Based Proxy Signature Scheme, pp. 40–46. University of Electronic Science and Technology of China, Chengdu (2016)
9. Huang, P., Yang, X.D., Li, Y., et al.: Identity-based proxy re-signature scheme for unpaired linear pairs. Comput. Appl. **35**(6), 1678–1682 (2015)
10. Yang, X.D., Yang, P., Gao, G.J., et al.: Uncertified proxy re-signature scheme with aggregation properties. Comput. Eng. Sci. **40**(6), 71–76 (2018)
11. Mi, J.L., Zhang, J.Z., Chen, S.T., et al.: Blind proxy signature scheme for designated verifiers that can tolerate information disclosure. Comput. Eng. Appl. **52**(22), 123–126 (2016)
12. Yang, X.D., Chen, C.L., Yang, P., et al.: Partially blind proxy re-signature scheme. J. Commun. **39**(2), 67–72 (2018)
13. Yang, X.D., Li, Y.N., Gao, G.J., et al.: Sever-aided verification proxy re-signature scheme in the standard model. J. Electron. Inf. Technol. **38**(5), 1151–1157 (2016)
14. Feng, T., Liang, Y.X.: Proven secure certificateless blind proxy re-signature. J. Commun. **33**(Z1), 58–78 (2012)
15. Hu, X.M., Yang, Y.C., Liu, Y.: Security analysis and improvement of a blind proxy re-signature scheme based on standard model. Small Microcomput. Syst. **2**(10), 2008–2011 (2011)

Information Flow-Based Security Construction for Compositional Interface Automata

Mingdi Xu[1], Zhaoyang Jin[1], Fan Zhang[2(✉)], and Feng Cui[1]

[1] Wuhan Digital and Engineering Institute, Wuhan 430205, Hubei, China
[2] School of Mathematics and Computer Science, Wuhan Polytechnic University,
Wuhan 430023, Hubei, China
whpuzf@whpu.edu.cn

Abstract. Information flow has been considered as a critical requirement to solve security related issues for complicated component-based system. However, security conditions are often fragile and general security properties may be not available to enforce the composition. Thus, this paper gives the computation model of interface automata (IA) and studies how the compositional interfaces behave to capture the information leakage with security process algebra (SPA) language. And we find that persistent bisimulation-based non deducibility property is preserved under composition, while it is not fully applicable to IA model. So several sufficient conditions for the property is developed to apply for composition of interface automata. Those conditions are given as theorems and proved efficiently to analyze security. Finally, we cite a classical instance to handle the composition and use an automatic verification software to test the correctness of our algorithms on compositional conditions.

Keywords: Information flow · Compositional security ·
Noninterference

1 Introduction

Compositional information flow security is an essential issue for the design of component-based software. It is complicated to enforce security properties on large compositional system. While some security issues can be pre-planned, the system may still face with confidential data leakage resulting from unanticipated changes in the environment. It could be the case that a system is completely secure, but it causes insecurity when interacting to another system. Because security conditions are often fragile under system behavior modifications. Adding, removing, or modifying some actions can break the whole security of a system [1,2]. Especially for the information flow security properties, the general theories on the composition are not available and some security properties are not preserved by composition [3]. So it is significant to unify security models for the construction and moreover to make the security property compositional.

© Springer Nature Singapore Pte Ltd. 2020
W. Han et al. (Eds.): CTCIS 2019, CCIS 1149, pp. 31–43, 2020.
https://doi.org/10.1007/978-981-15-3418-8_3

Information flow security which is known as noninterference (NI) has caused further research since the seminal work of Gogune [4]. NI is defined as an extensional property based on some observational semantics in the literature: the high part (confidential information) of a system is non-interfering with the low part (public informaiton) if whatever is done at the high level produces no visible effect on the low part of the system. And information are simply classified as confidential (H) and public (L). Currently compositional information flow security has already been studied by using different model-based approaches. Sufficient conditions for component-based systems that ensures and simplifies model-driven information flow security verification are proposed in [6]. And Rafnsson and Sabelfeld in paper [7] propose a general framework to model information flow of the interactive systems, and also give security conditions over general security lattices for the compositionality of the well-known noninterference properties. But practical enforcement for their compositional decision is still needed. Forcadi [5] introduces and develops stronger bisimulation based notion of NI, the so called persistent bisimulation-based non deducibility (PBNDC) properties, which is preserved under composition. While it is not fully applicable to interface automata (IA) And the models [8–11] are all for theory to cope with composition. The composition of IAs is a subset of all possible interleaved transition of two IAs, except for the actions that are shared [13]. Some states of the interleaved product where one component would have to wait are considered illegal, as illustrated in Figure 5 of [12]. Two agents may interact through interactive interfaces, but may also proceed independently by others that are not included in the compositional IAs. Thus for some system, the IA theory may be not suitable to formalize the concept of composition.

Due to the above analysis, key questions that have not been addressed by previous work are: (1) what is an appropriate general model to deal with security of component-based system, (2) how do we provide flexible ways to construct compositional secure property. Around the two questions, we are motivated to systematize the work in the area so far. Underlying weak bisimulaiton on enforcing secure information flow, PBNDC property is compositional and it allows to check security automatically. And IA is a lightweight interface model for describing the complex interfaces behavior of component based systems. Thus, we propose a new method to develop PBNDC property to support compositional information flow of component system combined with IA theory. We present several sufficient conditions and formally prove it to ensure compositional enforcement of IA model. And we also implement the refinement algorithm on CoPS tool to check its security.

This work is based on a line of work of bisimilation-based NI properties , and aims at satisfying compositional security for component-based system by constructing PBNDC property of multi-level security between interfaces. The rest of this paper is organized as follows. Section 2 gives the main concept of bisimilation-based NI properties. Section 3 presents a set of conditions of PBNDC property applied for compositonal IA security. And Sect. 4 implements and verifies the compositional system automatically by CoPS tool. Finally in Sect. 5, we draw conclusions and look forward to the next step of the research.

2   Noninterference Properties for Interface Automata

In this section we give the language that will be used to present and analyze NI security properties. First we present the computation model of the behavior of IA. Then we introduce a kind of general language to express IA transitions and cite several examples.

2.1   Computation Model

Our model of computation is an IA model [14,15]. An interface automata model is a tuple $S = (Q, q^0, A^I, A^O, A^H, \rightarrow)$, where Q is a finite set of states; q^0 is a distinct initial state with $q^0 \in Q$; A^I, A^O, A^H are the finite sets of input actions, output and hidden actions; $\rightarrow \subseteq Q \times A \times Q$ presents the state transition, where $A = A^I \cup A^O \cup A^H$ is the set of all actions. Let $\pounds = A^I \cup A^O$ to be the visible actions and thus $A = \pounds \cup A^H$.

Also, there are two security levels of visible actions to analyze NI properties. One carries public or low level confidential information (A^l) and the other carries private or high level confidential information (A^h). The information flow security analysis on IA are mainly based on the binary security lattice $A^l \sqsubseteq A^h$ [16]. It also can be defined as $\pounds = A^l \cup A^h$ and $A = A^l \cup A^h \cup A^H$.

The notation $(q, a, q') \in \rightarrow$ is equivalent to the transition $q \xrightarrow{a} q'$, which means that the model can move from the state q to the state q' by executing the action a. And we said an action $a \in A$ is enabled at state $q \in Q$, if $\exists q' \in Q$ then $q \xrightarrow{a} q'$. Conversely an action a is disable at q, if $\nexists q' \in Q$ then $q \xrightarrow{a} \!\!\!\!/$. If $\exists t = a_1 a_2 \dots a_n$ and $q_1 \xrightarrow{a_1} \xrightarrow{a_2} \dots \xrightarrow{a_n} q_n$, then we say q_n is reachable from q_1 and write $q_1 \xrightarrow{t} q_n$. If $\exists q_1 \xrightarrow{\tau} \xrightarrow{\tau} \dots \xrightarrow{\tau} q_n, \tau \in A^H$, then we write $q_1 \Rightarrow q_n$. If $\exists q_1 \Rightarrow \xrightarrow{a_1} \Rightarrow \dots \Rightarrow \xrightarrow{a_n} \Rightarrow q_n$, then we write $q_1 \Rightarrow q_n$. As a consequence, if $a \in \pounds, q_1 \Rightarrow q_n$ and if $a = \tau, q_1 \Rightarrow q_n$, then we write $q_1 \stackrel{\hat{a}}{\Rightarrow} q_n$.

The composition of two IAs is the subset of all possible interleaved transition, except when input actions of one of the IA coincide with some of the output actions of the other.

Definition 1. Considering two IAs, S and T, their set of shared actions is defined as: $Shared(S, T) = A_S \cap A_T$. If S and T are composable, then $Shared(S, T) = (A_S^I \cap A_T^O) \cup (A_S^O \cap A_T^I)$.

As usual, input actions are suffixed by ! and output actions by ?. And hiding or invisible actions are both replaced by τ. In a well-formed interfaces model, a binary composition operator is defined. IAs S and T are composable if one component is ready to issue an output action, the other should be ready to receive the action immediately. And a hidden action in the composition is created by shared actions. If $q_S \xrightarrow{a?} q_S'$ and $q_T \xrightarrow{a!} q_T'$, then $q_S | q_T \xrightarrow{\tau} q_S' | q_T'$.

A simple example of the rules with corresponding behaviors is as follows. If S represents the non-deterministic choice between the transitions $s_0 \xrightarrow{a_1?} s_1 \xrightarrow{a_2!} s_0$ and $s_0 \xrightarrow{b_1} s_3 \xrightarrow{b_2?} s_4$. T is an execution of $t_0 \xrightarrow{a_2?} t_1 \xrightarrow{a_3?} t_0$. The composition $S|T$ is able because of a shared action a_2 at state s_1 and t_0, and the composable part becomes $s_1|t_0 \xrightarrow{\tau} s_0|t_1$.

2.2 The Language

We present the security process algebra (SPA) language [5] that will simplify the IA transitions and be simple to analyze security properties. Besides the composition operator, there are also prefix, sum and restriction ones. The syntax of SPA is defined as: $S \models \underline{0} \mid a.S \mid S + S \mid S|S \mid S\backslash L$.

(1) $\underline{0}$ denotes the empty, which cannot do any action;
(2) Prefix operator $a.S$ can do an action a and transfers another state S. The rule is, $a.q_S \xrightarrow{a} q_S$;
(3) Sum operator $S + S$ represents the nondeterministic choice between two processes. If $q_S \xrightarrow{a} q'_S$, then $q_S + q_T \xrightarrow{a} q'_S + q_T$. And if $q_T \xrightarrow{a} q'_T$, then $q_S + q_T \xrightarrow{a} q_S + q'_T$;
(4) Operator $S|S$ is the parallel composition which is a little different from the composition of IA. If $q_S \xrightarrow{a} q'_S$, then $q_S|q_T \xrightarrow{a} q'_S|q_T$. If $q_T \xrightarrow{a} q'_T$, then $q_S|q_T \xrightarrow{a} q_S|q'_T$. And if $q_S \xrightarrow{a?} q'_S$ and $q_T \xrightarrow{a!} q'_T$, then $q_S|q_T \xrightarrow{\tau} q'_S|q'_T$;
(5) Finally, $S\backslash L$ can execute all actions that S can do, provided that they do not belong to L. That is, if $q_S \xrightarrow{a?} q'_S, a \notin \pounds$, then $q_S\backslash\pounds \xrightarrow{a} q'_S\backslash\pounds$.

Thus, the previous non-deterministic transitions $s_0 \xrightarrow{a_1?} s_1 \xrightarrow{a_2!} s_0$ and $s_0 \xrightarrow{b_1} s_3 \xrightarrow{b_2?} s_4$ can be depicted succinctly as $s_0 = a_1?.a_2!.s_0 + b_1.b_2?.s_4$. The initial state s_0 can alternative execute actions a_1a_2 or b_1b_2 to reach different states. Similarly, $t_0 \xrightarrow{a_2?} t_1 \xrightarrow{a_3?} t_0$ is equivalent to the process $t_0 = a_2?.a_3?.t_0$. SPA allows the specification of two-levels system, and can describe complex processes conveniently. All the compositional securities will be presented and applied to the analysis of systems based on such a language.

3   Compositional Information Flow Security

In this section, we present a bisimulation-based NI property PBNDC to support information flow security. This property guarantees that the composition of multiple interfaces will be secure. Also we propose sufficient conditions for the property to apply for interface automata.

3.1   Bisimilar NI Properties

For NI properties, it is expected that a low-level user can not distinguish whether high behavior occurrences. And system should behave the same if it does not execute any high actions or if it just hides them to the view of low users. In other words, it is the concept of observation equivalence between two processes, which have the same semantics if and only if they cannot be distinguished by an external observer [15]. We here define one of observational equivalences: weak bisimulation.

Definition 2. A binary relation $R \subseteq Q_S \times Q_T$ is a weak bisimulation between S and T, if $q_S^0 \, R \, q_T^0$ and for all $a \in A$,

if $q_S \xrightarrow{a} q_S'$, then $\exists q_T \xRightarrow{a} q_T'$ and $q_S' \, R \, q_T'$;

if $q_T \xrightarrow{a} q_T'$, then $\exists q_S \xRightarrow{a} q_S'$ and $q_S' \, R \, q_T'$.

Two processes S and T are weakly bisimilar, denoted by $S \approx T$, if there exists a weak bisimulation relation, $S \, R \, T$.

Relation $\approx$ is the largest weak bisimulation and is an equivalence relation. And it does not care about the invisible actions τ. So when S simulations an action of T, it also allows to do some τ actions before or after the action. For example, when there are two transitions $s_0 \xrightarrow{a} s_1 \xrightarrow{b} s_2 \xrightarrow{c} s_3$ and $t_0 \xrightarrow{a} t_1 \xrightarrow{\tau} t_2 \xrightarrow{\tau} t_3 \xrightarrow{b} t_4 \xrightarrow{c} t_5$, then we say $S \approx T$.

Lee argues that BSNNI is not suitable properties to formalize the concept of security interface in [12]. Indeed, the properties are both not enough strong for compositional systems. So, we present other NI properties BNDC and PBNDC to analyze the compositional security.

Definition 3. Let S be a process, $S \in BNDC$ if $\forall \, \Pi \in \xi^h$, $S \backslash A^h \approx (S|\Pi) \backslash A^h$

ξ^h is the set of all high actions. As a matter of fact, $S \backslash A^h$ prevent traces from high level actions; $(S|\Pi) \backslash A^h$ is the composition of S and Π except all high actions. If two terms are equivalent, S and $S|\Pi$ behave the same in lower level observation. High process Π cannot interfere with the low execution of S. In other words, a low level user cannot distinguish S from $S|\Pi$ and then believes the system is not modified by any high level process.

Definition 4. Let S be a process, $S \in PBNDC$ if $\forall S \Rightarrow S', S' \in BNDC$

Notice the difference between BNDC and PBNDC. It seems that PBNDC property requires a universal quantification over all the possible reachable states from initial process. While [17] defines an bisimulation equivalence notion to avoid this. If a system S is PBNDC, it never reaches insecure states. So PBNDC property is strong enough for system in dynamic execution process.

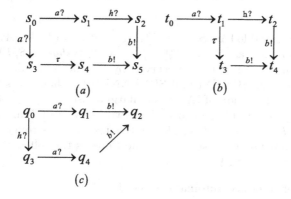

Fig. 1. The examples of bisimulation properties

Consider the IA S, T and Q in Fig. 1. s_0, t_0 and q_0 are the initial states of each IA. h is the confidential input action and a, b are the public input and output actions respectively. Thus, $h \in A^h$ and $a, b \in A^l$. And τ is the hidden actions, $\tau \in A^H$. Figure 1(a) presents a process $s_0 = a?. h?. b!. s_5 + a?. \tau. b!. s_5$. According to the Definition 3, S can be verified to be BNDC. Indeed, the transition between $h?$ and $b!$ in the first branch is hidden by the second branch τ and $b!$, which can simulate all the possible interactions with a high level compositional process. When s_0 executes $a?$ and reaches $h?.b!$, it is clear to know that the state s_0 is not secure. A direct causality between $h?$ and $b!$ is present. Thus, we say $S \in BNDC$ but $S \notin PBNDC$. For Fig. 1(b) and (c), we have $t_0 = a?. (h?. b!. t_4 + \tau. b!. t_4)$ and $q_0 = h?. a?. b!. q_2 + a?. b!. q_2$. In T the insecure state $h?$ is completely hidden by τ, lower Observer can not infer whether there is confidential information. And for $Q \backslash A^h$, only public actions $a?. b!$ exist and they behave the same in the two branches, which guarantees that $Q \backslash A^h$ can bisimulate any action of $(Q| \prod) \backslash A^h$. So the conclusion is $T \in PBNDC$ and $Q \in PBNDC$. That also motivates us to build PBNDC property for IA in simple ways.

3.2   Compositionality of Security Properties

The composition of two IA is the subset of all possible interleaved transition, except when input actions of one IA coincide with some output actions of the other IA. And a hidden action in the composition is created by shared actions.

Considering composable IA S and T, their leaved product $S \otimes T$ [13] may lead to some illegal states. The presence of illegal state is the evidence that one IA is violating the interfaces of the other. And if there is an illegal state reachable from $(q_S, q_T) \in Q_{S \otimes T}$ through an autonomous execution, q_S, q_T is considered as an incompatible state. Finally if the initial state $S \otimes T$ is compatible, then S and T are compatible.

Definition 5. Let S and T be compatible. The composition of S and T, denoted as $S|T$, is an IA with the same actions as $S \otimes T$ by removing all transition $q \xrightarrow{a}_{S \otimes T} q'$, if q is a compatible state in $S \otimes T$ and q' is an incompatible state in $S \otimes T$.

Given two composable IAs, $S = (S, A^h_S, A^l_S)$ and $T = (T, A^h_T, A^l_T)$, their composition $(S|T)$ is defined as $(S|T), (A^h_S \cup A^h_T \cup A^l_S \cup A^l_T) \backslash shared(S, T)$. Both BNNI and BSNNI properties cannot be preserved by interfaces parallel composition. The same happens for SIR_NNI and SIR_BNNI [10]. Then, we study PBNDC property for the composition of IAs. Bisimulation-based NI property PBNDC is naturally compositional. That means when two IAs S and T are PBNDC, the compositon of $S|T$ is PBNDC. Considering this useful and stronger property, we propose several unwinding construction conditions as the following theorem for the secure composition of IAs.

Theorem 1. For interface automata S and T,

(1) If all actions $a \in A^l_S$, then $S \in PBNDC$;

(2) If all actions $a \in A_S^h$, then $S \in PBNDC$;
(3) If $S \in PBNDC, a \in \mathcal{L}$, then $S \backslash a \in PBNDC$;
(4) If $S, T \in PBNDC$, then $S|T \in PBNDC$.

Proof. It is obvious for theorem (1) and (2), because IA S executes all actions in the same security level. Theorem (3) has been proved in [18,19]. Here is a brief description. Assume that state S' is reachable from S, that is $S \Rightarrow S'$. If $\exists S' \xrightarrow{h} S''$, $h \in A^h$, then $(S'/A^h) \backslash a \xrightarrow{\tau} (S''/A^h) \backslash a$ and $S'' \xrightarrow{h} S'''$, and $\exists (S'/A^h) \backslash a \xRightarrow{\tau} (S'''/A^h) \backslash a$. Thus we have $(S''/A^h) \backslash a \approx (S'''/A^h) \backslash a$. Similarly, if we analyze the process $(S'''/A^h \backslash a)$ in the same way, it exists $(S''''\backslash a)/A^h \approx (S''''\backslash a)/A^h$. So $(S'''/A^h) \backslash a$ and $(S''''\backslash a)/A^h$ is weak bisimilar. Every state of $S \backslash a$ is secure under PBNDC property, and we get the conclusion (3).

Then we prove (4) as following.

$S \in PBNDC \Rightarrow S \in BNDC \Rightarrow S \backslash A^h \approx (S|\Pi) \backslash A^h$, and $T \in PBNDC \Rightarrow T \in BNDC \Rightarrow T \backslash A^h \approx (T|\Pi) \backslash A^h$.

$(S|T) \backslash A^h \approx (S \backslash A^h)|(T \backslash A^h) \Rightarrow (S|\Pi)|(T|\Pi) \backslash A^h \approx ((S|\Pi) \backslash A^h)|((T|\Pi) \backslash A^h) \Rightarrow ((S|\Pi) \backslash A^h)|((T|\Pi) \backslash A^h) \approx (S \backslash A^h)|(\Pi \backslash A^h)|(T \backslash A^h)|(\Pi \backslash A^h) \approx (S \backslash A^h)|(T \backslash A^h) \approx (S|T) \backslash A^h$. And $(S|\Pi)|(T|\Pi) \backslash A^h \approx (S|\Pi|T|\Pi) \backslash A^h \approx (S|T|\Pi) \backslash A^h$. Thus, we have $(S|T) \backslash A^h \approx (S|T|\Pi) \backslash A^h \Rightarrow (S|T) \in BNDC$.

Also, $S, T \in PBNDC \Rightarrow S', T' \in BNDC \Rightarrow S' \backslash A^h \approx (S'|\Pi) \backslash A^h$ and $T' \backslash A^h \approx (T'|\Pi) \backslash A^h$, in the same way, we know $(S'|T') \in BNDC$. Finally, every reachable state in $S|T$ is BNDC property, $(S|T) \in PBNDC$. We mainly use those basic properties to build PBNDC property for complex compositional IAs.

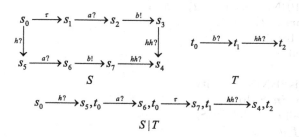

Fig. 2. The example of PBNDC compositional property

Theorem 2. For interface automata S and T,

(5) If $S|T \in PBNDC$, then $T|S \in PBNDC$;
(6) If $S, T \in PBNDC$, then $\sum (h_j.T_j + T_j) \in PBNDC$, where $h_j \in A^h$ and $\tau \in A^H$;
(7) If $S, T \in PBNDC$, then $\sum a_i.S_i + \sum (h_j.T_j + \tau.T_j) \in PBNDC$, where $a_i \in A^l, h_j \in A^h$ and $\tau \in A^H$.

Those properties almost cover all the transition for an IA. For example, let $s_0 = \tau.a?.b!.hh?.s_4 + h?.a?.b!.hh?.s_4$ and $t_0 = b?.hh!.t_2$ be two IAs. The transition is shown in Fig. 2. The verification of PBNDC property is as follows. Firstly, let the state $s_3 = hh?.s_4$, according to (2), $s_3 \in PBDNC$. And If $S \in PBNDC$, then $\sum a_i.S_i \in PBNDC$ in (5), we argue $s_1 = a?.b!.s_3 \in PBDNC$. Also, according to (6), it is $s_0 = \tau.s_1 + h?.s_1$ and $s_0 \in PBNDC$. The verification of T is similar to A. Finally, it is proved the composition $(S|T) \in PBNDC$ because of (4). The theorem is useful when we develop all the components of a complex system. As we can use this recursive algorithm to design each IA, it is possible to achieve full compatibility. The idea is simple, and only has to develop every IA to ensure the whole compositional security.

4   Implementation and Verification

We recall that any system can be proven NI property if the implementation of this system follows the constructive Theorems 1 and 2. And also it can be easily verified that all actions occurring in transitions within atomic component as well as interactions are sequential consistent.

For a complete check of a whole system, we focus on how to secure all transitions. The first step is to make each IA satisfies PBNDC property (cf. Algorithm 2) according to previous Theorems, and the second step is to check the composition of interfaces automata is also verified secure (cf. Algorithm 1).

Algorithm 1. isCompositionSecurity(IAs):
1:    **for** all $T_i \in$ IAs exists **do**
2:       **if** isPBNDCSecurity(T_i) **then**
3:          **print** T_i is true
4:       **else** break
5: **return** false

Algorithm 2. isPBNDCSecurity(S):
1: **for** all S_i *in* S **do**
2:     **for** all $a_j \in Act$ *in* S_i
3:        *if* $a_j \in A^l$
           then $S_i = a_j.S_i$, $a_j = a_{j+1}$
4:        *if* $a_j \in A^h$ *and* $\exists a_j.S_i + S_i$
           then $S_i = a_j.S_i + S_i$, $a_j = a_{j+1}$
5:        *if* $a_j \in A^h$ *and* $\exists a_j.S_i + \tau.S_i$
           then $S_i = a_j.S_i + \tau.S_i$, $a_j = a_{j+1}$
6: *if* $S_i = S$
7:     **return** true
8: **else**
9:     **return** false

We implement the Algorithms 1 and 2 of composition based on a CoPS software which is an automatic check of multilevel system security properties. The graphical interface of CoPS is implemented in Java to get a large portability and the kernel module is in standard C to obtain good performances. We use semantics graph generator to elaborate the syntax tree of the process and then verifier to transform the graph to perform the security check.

Now, we cite a classical example to illustrate the compositional IA framework and handle PBNDC security issues, web service reservation system. The case is the composition of three components as shown in Fig. 3. The framwork of this system has three interface automata parts denoted: S, T and Q, which respectively represent reservation, travel and pay process. $search$ action is supplied by a user through the S interfaces $dests$ and $dates$. Next, through the $search$ interaction, S can contact T to search for available flights and return explicit flights with corresponding prices by interfaces $list$. After that, S selects a ticket through $accept$ action and is approved to pay the ticket interacting with Q. Finally, if Q communicates T by action $complete$, T can confirm that the user does pay and will give $ticket$ to finish this transaction.

All the search actions $dests, dates, exit$ as well as the flights list $list$ are defined as low level information, since users are not identified while sending these requests and interface interactions can not disclose any confidential information about a customer's private trip. Other sensitive data like the personal information $identify$, the payment operator pay and the ticket data $ticket$ are set to high. Because the client destination can be deduced from the selection event through IA T in the view of observer. Specifically, we have actions $(accept, identify, ok, pay, complete, ticket, no, retry) \in A^h$, $(dest, dates, search, list) \in A^l$ and $exit \in A^H$.

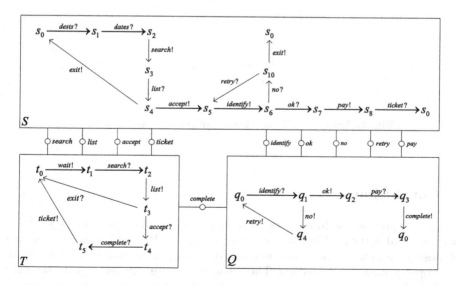

Fig. 3. Web service reservation system

The following is the process about the web reservation service system.

$$System = S \mid T \mid Q$$
$$S = dests?.\,dates?.\,search!.\,list?.\,(exit!.\,S + accept!.\,S_5)$$
$$S_5 = identify!.\,(no?.\,(exit!.\,S + retry?.\,S_5) + ok?.\,pay!.\,ticket?.\,S)$$
$$T = wait!.\,search?.\,list!.\,(exit?.\,T + accept?.\,complete?.\,ticket!.\,T)$$
$$Q = identify?.\,ok!.\,(no!.\,retry!.\,Q + pay?.\,complete!.\,Q)$$

It satisfies the syntactic security conditions from Theorems 1 and 2. Indeed, these conditions hold for the web service reservation system. Thus, we adopt the tactic of divide and rule to analyze subsystem through automatic checker of CoPS tool and translate the algorithm of system into CoPS syntax for SPA. The style used in specifying IA in CoPS is the same for SPA language. It uses bi to define the agent of system and $basi$ which binds a set of actions to an identifier. For example, $bi\ S\ a.'b.S\ +'\ h.0$ defines the process $S = a?.b!.S + h!.0$, and high actions define as $acth\ h!$. Finally, we automatically verify the composition security of the system shown in Fig. 4. So the compostion IA we improved is PBNDC security.

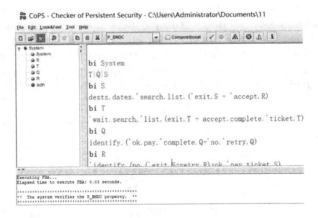

Fig. 4. Automatically verification of the compositonal IAs

5   Conclusion

This paper proposes a framework to manipulate automate interfaces for their compositional security. We have researched how the PBNDC property behaves composition and we formally provide a set of conditions to ensure preservation of the property under composition. These conditions are extensions with security typed SPA rules applied for component based system, and it also provides a new insight on the composition security for complex system. Finally, we give an example and use CoPS software which is an automatic check of multilevel security properties to verify security.

Our future work includes a more specific analysis of multiple security of compositional IAs. We plan to extend our composition to satisfy a stronger noninterference property. And it can be able to repair insecure components automatically and make the system perform the same from low level user's view.

6   Related Work

Information flow security can trace back to the original definition of noninterference [4]. Noninterference properties have been discussed on the multi-level security system using different model-based approaches [6,7,27,28]. Most of those work focus on binary security lattice $L \sqsubseteq H$ [8,29,30], and have rarely designed for the component-based system. Information flow security is a property on sets of traces and can also be defined as a safety property on two correlative traces of a system. And it can rely on a compositional algorithm to verify security properties with SPA specification [5,18] which is more expressive to describe the behaviors of interfaces automata composition [8,23–26].

Generally speaking, compositional information flow security property is different from the ordinary safety properties. The compositional IAs may interact through interactive interfaces, but proceed unexpected actions not included in the system. Thus for some system, the IA theory may be not suitable to formalize the concept of composition. Rafnsson [7] provides the compositional constraints and theorems for two probabilistic noninterference properties PINI and PSNI to achieve end-to-end security in a system built from parts. Lee presents some examples where the BSNNI/BNNI properties [17] are not suitable formalization of security, and introduces [12] SIR-SNNI and SIR-NNI properties to derive a secure interface and to ensure compositionality. Sun [10] presents a new extension of interface automaton and proposes two refinement-based security properties SIR-GNNI and RRNI. Compositional information flow security [20,21] divides the system into several components possibly along with sufficient conditions for composition. The compositionality of those work are mainly addressed on bisimulation-based noninterference, but those approaches cannot support infinite or unpredictable states in dynamic physical environment. As an alternative to those properties, PBNDC [18] is a strong enough security for the compositional IAs and can be proved automatically by CoPS tool. Further work is required to study a more stronger noninterference property for compositional security.

References

1. Hedin, D., Sabelfeld, A.: A perspective on information-flow control. Softw. Safe. Secur. **33**, 319–347 (2012)
2. Mclean, J.: A general theory of composition for trace sets closed under selective interleaving functions. In: IEEE Computer Society Symposium on Research in Security and Privacy. IEEE (1994)
3. Abadi, M., Lamport, L.: Conjoining specifications. ACM Trans. Prog. Lang. Syst. (TOPLAS) **17**(3), 507–535 (1995)
4. Goguen, J.A., Meseguer, J.: Security policies and security models. In: IEEE Computer Society Symposium on Research in Security and Privacy. IEEE Computer Society Press (1982)
5. Focardi, R., Gorrieri, R., Martinelli, F.: Classification of security properties. In: Focardi, R., Gorrieri, R. (eds.) FOSAD 2001. LNCS, vol. 2946, pp. 139–185. Springer, Heidelberg (2004). https://doi.org/10.1007/978-3-540-24631-2_4
6. Ben Said, N., Abdellatif, T., Bensalem, S., Bozga, M.: Model-driven information flow security for component-based systems. In: Bensalem, S., Lakhneck, Y., Legay, A. (eds.) ETAPS 2014. LNCS, vol. 8415, pp. 1–20. Springer, Heidelberg (2014). https://doi.org/10.1007/978-3-642-54848-2_1
7. Rafnsson, W., Sabelfeld, A.: Compositional information-flow security for interactive systems. In: Computer Security Foundations Symposium. IEEE (2014)
8. Lee, M., D'Argenio, P.R.: Describing secure interfaces with interface automata. Electron. Notes Theoret. Comput. Sci. **264**(1), 107–123 (2010)
9. Chi, Z., Chu, C.: Research on verifying of behavioral compatibility for software component composition. Computer Engineering and Applications (2016)
10. Cong, S., Ning, X., Ma, J.: Enforcing generalized refinement-based noninterference for secure interface Composition. In: IEEE Computer Software and Applications Conference (2017)
11. Sun, C., Xi, N., Li, J., et al.: Verifying secure interface composition for component-based system designs. In: Software Engineering Conference. IEEE (2015)
12. Lee, M., D'Argenio, P.R.: A refinement based notion of non-interference for interface automata: compositionality, decidability and synthesis. In: XXIX International Conference of the Chilean Computer Science Society (2010)
13. Esmaeilsabzali, S., Day, N.A., Mavaddat, F.: Interface automata with complex actions: limiting interleaving in interface automata. Fundam. Inform. **82**(4), 465–512 (2008)
14. de Alfaro, L., Henzinger, T.A.: Interface theories for component-based design. In: Henzinger, T.A., Kirsch, C.M. (eds.) EMSOFT 2001. LNCS, vol. 2211, pp. 148–165. Springer, Heidelberg (2001). https://doi.org/10.1007/3-540-45449-7_11
15. Bossi, A., Focardi, R., Piazza, C., Rossi, S.: A proof system for information flow security. In: Leuschel, M. (ed.) LOPSTR 2002. LNCS, vol. 2664, pp. 199–218. Springer, Heidelberg (2003). https://doi.org/10.1007/3-540-45013-0_16
16. Siirtola, A., Heljanko, K.: Parametrised modal interface automata. ACM Trans. Embed. Comput. Syst. **14**(4), 65:1–65:25 (2015)
17. Focardi, R., Rossi, S.: Information flow security in dynamic contexts. J. Comput. Secur. **14**(1), 307–319 (2002)
18. Focardi, R., Piazza, C., Rossi, S.: Proofs methods for bisimulation based information flow security. In: Cortesi, A. (ed.) VMCAI 2002. LNCS, vol. 2294, pp. 16–31. Springer, Heidelberg (2002). https://doi.org/10.1007/3-540-47813-2_2

19. Zhou, X., Li, Y., Li, W., Qiao, H., Shu, Z.: Bisimulation proof methods in a path-based specification language for polynomial coalgebras. In: Ueda, K. (ed.) APLAS 2010. LNCS, vol. 6461, pp. 239–254. Springer, Heidelberg (2010). https://doi.org/10.1007/978-3-642-17164-2_17

20. Mantel, H.: On the composition of secure systems. In: IEEE Symposium on Security and Privacy. IEEE Computer Society (2002)

21. Focardi, R., Gorrieri, R.: The compositional security checker: a tool for the verification of information flow security properties. IEEE Trans. Softw. Eng. **23**(9), 550–571 (1997)

22. Ben, H.N., Lafrance, S., Lin, F., et al.: On the verification of intransitive noninterference in mulitlevel security. IEEE Trans. Syst. Man Cybern. Part B Cybern. **35**(5), 948–958 (2005)

23. de Alfaro, L., Henzinger, T.A.: Interface-based design. In: Broy, M., Grünbauer, J., Harel, D., Hoare, T. (eds.) Engineering Theories of Software Intensive Systems. NSS, vol. 195, pp. 83–104. Springer, Dordrecht (2005). https://doi.org/10.1007/1-4020-3532-2_3

24. Emmi, M., Giannakopoulou, D., Pǎsǎreanu, C.S.: Assume-guarantee verification for interface automata. In: Cuellar, J., Maibaum, T., Sere, K. (eds.) FM 2008. LNCS, vol. 5014, pp. 116–131. Springer, Heidelberg (2008). https://doi.org/10.1007/978-3-540-68237-0_10

25. Li, J., Chen, S., Lin, J., et al.: A web services composition model and its verification algorithm based on interface automata (2011)

26. Changwei, M.A., Hongjiang, M.A.: Hybrid web service composition approach based on interface automata. J. Comput. Appl. **34**(6), 1774–1778 (2014)

27. Katkalov, K., Stenzel, K., Borek, M., et al.: Model-driven development of information flow-secure systems with IFlow. In: International Conference on Social Computing (2013)

28. Zeldovich, N., Boyd-Wickizer, S.: Securing distributed systems with information flow control. In: Usenix Symposium on Networked Systems Design and Implementation. USENIX Association (2006)

29. Sun, C., Xi, N., Gao, S., et al.: A generalized non-interference based on refinement of interfaces. J. Comput. Res. Dev. **52**, 1631–1641 (2015)

30. Abdellatif, T., Sfaxi, L., Lakhnech, Y., et al.: Automating information flow control in component-based. In: International ACM Sigsoft Symposium on Component Based Software Engineering. ACM (2011)

Provably Secure Server-Assisted Verification Threshold Proxy Re-signature Scheme

Guoning Lv[1], Yanfang Lei[1], Mingsheng Hu[1(✉)], Yage Cheng[1],
Bei Gong[2], and Junjun Fu[1]

[1] Zhengzhou Normal University, Zhengzhou 450044, China
13676951984@163.com
[2] Beijing University of Technology, Beijing 100124, China

Abstract. Aiming at the problems of limited computing power and high security requirements of terminal equipment, which affects people's good experience on some network resources, we proposes a provably secure server-assisted verification threshold proxy re-signature scheme. Threshold proxy re-signature can effectively disperse the power of the agent, and solve the security problem that the agent's rights are too concentrated. In the server-assisted authentication protocol, the verifier transfers the complex bilinear pairing operation to the server through the interaction, reducing the computational complexity of the verifier. Under the standard model, the scheme can effectively resist collusion attacks and adaptive selection of message attacks. Performance analysis results show that compared with Yang's scheme, the signature length of the new scheme is at least twice shorter and the verification efficiency is increased by at least 57%.

Keywords: Server-assisted authentication protocol · Threshold proxy re-signature · Secret sharing · Completeness · Unforgeability

1 Introduction

With the development of network technology and the continuous growth of technology in mobile communication, mobile devices become an important part of people's life. However, due to the limited computing power of terminal equipment and limited energy supply, it has affected people's good experience of some network resources. The emergence of server-assisted verification technology has effectively solved this problem. A secure server-assisted verification signature scheme was given in [1]. However, this solution does not effectively defend against server and signer collusion attacks. Later, in the [2], Niu et al. proposed a server-assisted verification signature scheme and the scheme can resist the attack, but the scheme needs to consume large broadband expenditure. Combined with aggregation signature and server-assisted verification signatures, Yang et al. proposed a cryptosystem that saves broadband expenditures in [3]. This scheme reduces broadband expenditure by converging different signatures corresponding to multiple messages into one signature. Saves verification time and improves verification efficiency.

© Springer Nature Singapore Pte Ltd. 2020
W. Han et al. (Eds.): CTCIS 2019, CCIS 1149, pp. 44–57, 2020.
https://doi.org/10.1007/978-981-15-3418-8_4

Agent re-signature is an important research direction of cryptography. Domestic and foreign scholars have done a lot of work in this direction. The security model of proxy re-signature was first proposed in the literature [4], and two schemes with strict security under the random oracle model are given in this paper. A general combinable proxy re-signature scheme was proposed in [5]. However, this scheme not unforgeable. In order to overcome this problem, a modification of the above scheme was proposed in the [6]. In recent years, the wide practicality of proxy re-signature has attracted the attention of scholars. Some proxy re-signature schemes with special properties have been proposed successively, such as proxy-based signature scheme based on polynomial isomorphism [7], lattice proxy re-signature [8], identity-based proxy re-signature [9], etc. However, these identity-based or certificate-based proxy re-signature schemes have problems such as certificate management and key escrow. In order to overcome these problems, a certificate-less proxy re-signature scheme with aggregation property was designed in [10]. This scheme effectively reduces the computational cost and communication cost in the verification process. In addition, in order to avoid the agent obtaining the detailed content of the converted message, Mi et al. proposed a blind proxy re-signature scheme in [11], however, the verifier in this scheme is pre-specified in practical application. Therefore, there are limitations in practical applications and lack of security. Aiming at this problem, a partial blind proxy re-signature scheme with security was given in [12]. This scheme not only realizes the conversion of the signature between the trustee and the agent when the message content is not public. Moreover, it also effectively prevents the trustee from illegally using the re-signature.

Although the proxy re-signature scheme has been widely used, it still has many drawbacks. For example, once the re-signature key is compromised, the security of the solution will be compromised. In addition, the agent's rights are too concentrated and need to be decentralized in order to make the solution more reliable. Then the concept of threshold proxy re-signature was proposed. Threshold proxy re-signature is a process of dealing with the threshold of proxy re-signature, so that the proxy's signature rights are dispersed. Threshold proxy re-signature schemes can be used to reduce public key management expenditures, space-saving specific path traversal certificates, and generate manageable weak group signatures [13, 14].

In [15], a server-assisted verification proxy re-signature scheme was proposed, which improves the efficiency of signature verification. However, in the proxy re-signature process of this scheme, there is only one agent, so the agent's rights are too concentrated. Once the agent is attacked, the re-signature key is leaked and the security of the scheme is destroyed. Aiming at this problem, we proposed a one-way variable threshold proxy re-signature scheme in [16]. In this paper, we introduce the secret sharing model and threshold technology, and propose a new provably secure server-assisted verification threshold proxy re-signature scheme. On the one hand, in the process of server-assisted authentication protocol, the verifier and the server transfer the complex bilinear pairing operation task to the server through the interaction protocol between them, so that the verifier has a smaller computational cost. The signature was verified to improve the verification efficiency of the signature. On the other hand, the dispersal of the agent's rights enhances the security of the scheme. Finally, simulation experiments show that the scheme is efficient.

2 Preliminaries

2.1 Bilinear Pairings

Let p be a large prime, G_1 and G_2 are two p - ordered cyclic groups, and g is a generator of group G_1. $e : G_1 \times G_1 \to G_2$ is a bilinear map and satisfies the following conditions:

(1) Bilinear: For arbitrary $x, y \in Z_q^*$, satisfied $e(g^x, g^y) = e(g, g)^{xy}$.
(2) Non-degenerate: There exist $g_1, g_2 \in G_1$, which satisfied $e(g_1, g_2) \neq 1$.
(3) Computability: There exists a valid algorithm $e(g_1, g_2)$, where $g_1, g_2 \in G_1$.

2.2 CDH Hypothesis

Definition 1 (CDH problem): For any unknown $x, y \in Z_q^*$, when $(g, g^x, g^y) \in G_1^3$ is known, we can calculate $g^{xy} \in G_1$.

Definition 2 (CDH Hypothesis): The CDH problem in the group G_1 can be solved with a large probability in polynomial time. The algorithm that satisfies the above conditions does not exist.

2.3 Secret Sharing Model

Distribution stage: Let q be a prime number and secret $s \in Z_q^*$ to be distributed. Suppose there is a threshold of (t, n), namely in a group with n members $P_i(i = 1, 2, \ldots, n)$, the secret s can be recovered when at least t members cooperate. The basic idea is: first randomly generate $a_1, a_2, \ldots, a_{t-1}$ and generate the function $F(x) = s + a_1 x + \ldots + a_{t-1} x^{t-1}$, then calculate $X_i = F(i) \in Z_q^*$ and issue (i, X_i) to each member P_i, note that we can get $X_0 = F(0) = s$, when $i = 0$.

Reconstruction stage: Let $\Phi \subseteq \{1, 2, \ldots, n\}$, $|\Phi| \geq t$, where $|.|$ represents the order of the set. Then, let the function, $F(x) = \sum_{j \in \Phi} \lambda_{x_j}^\Phi X_j$, $\lambda_{x_j}^\Phi \in Z_q^*$, where parameter $\lambda_{x_j}^\Phi = \prod_{k \in \Phi, k \neq j} \frac{x - k}{j - k}$. Finally, we can recover the $s = F(0) = \sum_{j \in \Phi} \lambda_{0j}^\Phi x_j$, where $\lambda_{0j}^\Phi = \prod_{k \in \Phi, k \neq j} \frac{0 - k}{j - k}$.

3 Scheme Model and Security Definitions

3.1 Two-Way Server-Assisted Verification Threshold Proxy Re-signature Scheme Model

The server-assisted verification threshold proxy re-signature scheme generally includes the following eight algorithms.

(1) *Setup*: Given a constant k, the system parameter cp are obtained by operation $(1^k) \to cp$ and disclosed.

(2) *Keygen*: Enter the system cp parameter obtained based on the (1) process, and by $(cp) \rightarrow (pk, sk)$, we obtain the public and private key pairs (pk, sk) of the user.

(3) *Rekey*: Firstly, enter the public and private key pairs (pk_B, SK_B), (pk_A, sk_A) of Bob and Alice, respectively. Secondly, the re-signature key $rk_{A \rightarrow B}$ is distributed n parts by the algorithm and randomly assigned them to the agents. Finally, a corresponding re-signature key $rk_{A \rightarrow B_i}$ and a re-signature public key $pk_{A \rightarrow B_i}$ are respectively generated for each agent, so that each agent can convert Alice's signature into Bob's partial re-signature through his own re-signed key. It should be noted that sk_A is not necessary in this algorithm.

(4) *Sign*: Randomly given the signature message m and Alice's private key sk_A can generate an original signature $\sigma_{A(m)}$ of the message m corresponding to the public key pk_A.

(5) *Resign*: Firstly, the compositor needs to collect a partial re-signature obtained by each agent through its own re-signature key. Secondly, when the compositor has at least t legal resigned parts, the compositor combines these legal parts into a signature to obtain a re-signature $\sigma_{B(m)}$ and outputs it.

(6) *Verify*: Given the public key pk, the signature message m, and the signature σ to be verified, if σ is a valid signature obtained by the public key pk for the message m, output 1; otherwise, output 0.

(7) *Server − setup*: Enter a parameter cp to generate a string Vst for the verifier.

(8) *Server − verify*: For the string Vst, public key pk and message signature pairs (m, σ), if the server lets the verifier determine that σ is a valid signature, output 1; otherwise, output 0.

3.2   Security Definition

The security of the scheme is ensured by the robustness and unforgeability of the threshold proxy and the completeness of the server-assisted authentication protocol. The so-called robustness and unforgeability means that even if the attacker can unite with $t - 1$ agents, the signature scheme can still be implemented correctly, but the attacker cannot re-sign. This ensures that a legal signature of a new message cannot be generated in the case of a joint attack. The so-called server-assisted authentication protocol completeness means that the server cannot enable the verifier to determine the legality of an illegal signature. In [15], the completeness of the server-assisted authentication protocol under joint attack and adaptive selective message attack is defined by designing two games, Game1 and Game2.

Definition 3: If the attacker approaches the probability that the game can be victorious in the Game1 and Game2 games in [15], the server-assisted verification protocol in the scheme is said to be complete.

Definition 4: If the threshold proxy re-signature scheme satisfies both of the following conditions, it indicates that the scheme is safe in the case of collusion attacks and selective message attacks.

(1) In the case of adaptive selection of message attacks, there is both unforgeability and robustness.
(2) The server-assisted verification protocol is complete.

4 A New Two-Way Server-Assisted Verification Threshold Proxy Re-signature Scheme

In this part we construct a provably secure server-assisted verification threshold proxy re-signature scheme. Participants in the program are: Trustee Alice (responsible for generating the original signature of the message), Delegator Bob, Verifier (by verifying the validity of the signature by interacting with a semi-trusted server), n semi-trusted agents and a server.

(1) *Setup*: Let q be a prime number of length k, and G_1, G_2 are respectively circular multiplicative groups of order q. Let g be a generator in group G_1, $e(G_1 \times G_1 \rightarrow G_2)$ is a bilinear map, arbitrarily select positive integers $q_0 < q_1 < q_2 < .. < q_{n-1}$, satisfying conditions $gcd(q_i, q_j) = 1$ and $gcd(q_i, q) = 1$, where $0 \leq i \leq j \leq n - 1$. Let $F = q_0 q_1 q_2 \ldots q_{n-1}$ and opening the parameter $(cp) = (e, q, G_1, G_2, g, H, F, q_0, q_1, q_2, \ldots, q_{n-1})$.

(2) *Keygen*: The user inputs the parameter and randomly selects $a \in Z_q$ and obtains the corresponding public-private key pair $(pk, sk) = (g^a, a)$.

(3) *Rekey*: After entering Alice and Bob's private keys $sk_A = a$ and $sk_B = b$, then proceed as follows:

 (1) In the interval $[1, q - 1]$, randomly select two numbers l, m and then calculate
 $$\alpha_i = l_i m_i \prod_{j=0}^{i-1} q_j (mod\, F), i = 1, 2, \ldots n - 1.$$ By applying the Chinese remainder theorem, we can calculate $\alpha_0 \in Z_F$, which satisfies $\alpha_0 = sk_B = b\, mod\, q_i$, $i = 0, 1, \ldots, n - 1$. Then, construct a $n - 1$ degree polynomial about the variable x. When a positive integer $t(1 \leq t \leq n)$ is given, there is a polynomial
 $$f_t(x) = f(x) mod_{q_{t-1}} = b + \sum_{i=1}^{t-1} \alpha_i x^i$$ corresponding to $t - 1$.

 (2) Let $X_j = g^{\alpha_j/a}$, $Y_j = g^{\alpha_j}$, $j = 0, 1, \ldots, n - 1$. Re-signature key $rk_{A \rightarrow B} \in Z_F$, $rk_{A \rightarrow B}^i = \frac{f_t(i)}{a} mod\, q_{t-1}$, $t = 1, 2, \ldots, n$ can be solved by Chinese remainder theorem. Then send the information $(i, rk_{A \rightarrow B}^i)$ to the agent $P_i, i = 1, 2, \ldots, n$, where $X_0 = g^{b/a}$, $Y_0 = pk_B = g^b$.

 (3) The agent $P_i(1 \leq i \leq n)$ first calculates $rk_{A \rightarrow B}^{n,i} = rk_{A \rightarrow B}^i mod\, q_{n-1}$ and then determines whether the obtained sub-key is valid by verifying the following Eqs. (1) and (2):

 $$g^{rk_{A \rightarrow B}^{n,i}} = \prod_{j=0}^{n-1} X_j^{i^j} \qquad (1)$$

$$e\left(\prod_{j=0}^{n-1} X_j, pk_A\right) = e\left(\prod_{j=0}^{n-1} Y_j, g\right) \tag{2}$$

If both of the above equations are true, then the generated sub-key $rk_{A\to B}^i$ is valid. Given any positive integer $t(1 \le t \le n)$, the agent P_i can compute $rk_{A\to B}^{t,i} = rk_{A\to B}^i mod q_{t-1}$ independently and publish its verification public key $vk_{t,i} = g^{f_t(i)} = \prod_{j=0}^{t-1} Y_j^{i^j}$ with the re-signature key $rk_{A\to B}^i$ originally obtained.

(4) *Sign*: We give the trustee's private key a and a message $m = (m_1, m_2, \ldots, m_{n_m}) \in \{0,1\}^{n_m}$ of length $n_m bit$, and then output an original signature $\sigma_A = H(m)^a = (\sigma_{A1}, \sigma_{A2}) = (g_1^a \varpi^\alpha, g^\alpha)$ of the message m corresponding to the public key pk_A,

where $g_1, g_2, u_1, \ldots, u_{nm} \in G_1, \alpha \in_R Z_q$ and $\varpi = g_2 \prod_{i=1}^{n_m} (u_i)^{m_i}$.

(5) Re*sign*:
   (1) Partial key generation: Assume that the threshold is $t(1 \le t \le n)$. Enter the threshold t, public key pk_A, message m, and signature σ_A. First check if $Verify(pk_A, m, \sigma) = 1$ is true. If the equation is true, enter the re-signature sub-key $rk_{A\to B}^{t,i}$ and output the partial re-signature $\sigma_{Bi} = (\sigma_A)^{rk_{A\to B}^{t,i}}$, where $i = 0, 1, \ldots, t$. If the equation is not true, namely it does not pass the verification, output 0.
   (2) Re-signature generation: After the re-signature combiner obtains some partial re-signatures, the following formula is verified:

$$e(\sigma_{B,i}, g) = e(vk_{t,i}, H(m)), \tag{3}$$

where $vk_{t,i}$ represents the verifiable public key of some agents. If the combiner obtains at least t legal partial re-signatures $(\sigma_{B,i_1}, \sigma_{B,i_2}, \ldots, \sigma_{B,i_k})$, its re-signature is $\sigma_B = (\sigma_{B,1}, \sigma_{B,2}) = (\prod_{i=1}^t (\sigma_{B,i_1})^{\gamma_{0,i}}, \prod_{i=1}^t (\sigma_{B,i_2})^{\gamma_{0,i}})$, where $\gamma_{0,i}$ is the coefficient of the Lagrange interpolation polynomial.

(6) *Verify*: When the public key pk_A, message m, and signature σ are entered,

$$\text{if the equation } e(\sigma, g) = e(H(m), pk_A) \tag{4}$$

is satisfied, output 1, otherwise output 0.

(7) *Server $-$ setup*: Given the system parameter cp, the verifier randomly selects an element $x \in Z_q^*$ and assumes a string $Vst = x$.

(8) *Server $-$ verify*: Given $Vst = x$, a public key pk and a signed message pair $(m, \sigma = (\sigma_1, \sigma_2))$, the server-assisted authentication interaction protocol between the verifier and the server is as follows:
   (1) The verifier calculates $\sigma' = (\sigma_1', \sigma_2') = ((\sigma_1)^x, (\sigma_2)^x)$ and sends (m, σ') to the server.

(2) The server calculates $\eta_1 = e(\sigma_1', g)$, $\eta_2 = e(\varpi, \sigma_2')$ and sends (η_1, η_2) to the verifier.

(3) The verifier needs to determine whether the verifier considers σ is the legal signature of the message m by calculating whether equation

$$\eta_1 = (pk)^x \eta_2 \tag{5}$$

is true. If it is true, it outputs 1; otherwise, it outputs 0.

5 A New Two-Way Server-Assisted Verification Threshold Proxy Re-signature Scheme

5.1   Correctness Analysis

Theorem 1: When the threshold is t, if the Eqs. (1) and (2) are true, the obtained re-signature sub-key is valid.

Proof: By $rk_{A \to B}^{n,i} = rk_{A \to B}^i mod q_{n-1}$, then $g^{rk_{A \to B}^{n,i}} = g^{rk_{A \to B}^i mod q_{n-1}} = \prod_{j=0}^{n-1} X_j^{i^j}$, and because of $X_j = g^{\alpha_j/a}$, $Y_j = g^{\alpha_j}$, then

$$e\left(\prod_{j=0}^{n-1} X_j, pk\right) = e\left(\prod_{j=0}^{n-1} g^{\frac{\alpha_j}{a}}, g^\alpha\right) = e\left(\prod_{j=0}^{n-1} g^{\alpha_j}, g\right) = e\left(\prod_{j=0}^{n-1} Y_j, g\right)$$

In addition, we have

$$rk_{A \to B}^{t,i} = rk_{A \to B}^i mod q_{t-1} = h^{\frac{f_t(i)}{a}},$$

$$vk_{t,i} = \prod_{j=0}^{t-1} Y_j^{i^j} = \prod_{j=0}^{t-1} g^{\alpha_j^{i^j}} = g^{\sum_{j=0}^{t-1} \alpha_j^{i^j}} = g^{f_t(i)}.$$

Theorem 2: When the threshold is t, if the Eq. (3) is established, the obtained partial re-signature is valid.

Proof: From the properties of the bilinear pair, we get

$$e(g, s_i) = e\left(g, H(m)^{f_t(i)}\right) = e\left(g^{f_t(i)}, H(m)\right) = e(vk_{t,i}, H(m)).$$

Theorem 3: When the threshold is t, if the Eq. (4) is established, the obtained threshold proxy re-signature is valid.

Proof: From the properties of the bilinear pair, we get

$$e(\sigma, g) = e(H(m)^{\alpha}, g) = e(H(m), g^{\alpha}) = e(pk, H(m)).$$

Theorem 4: If the Eq. (5) is true, the verifier is confident that σ is the legal signature of the message m.

Proof: From the re-signature $\sigma_B = (\sigma_{B1}, \sigma_{B2}) = \left(g_1^b \varpi^r, g^r\right)$ of Bob and string $Vst = x$, we obtain

$$
\begin{aligned}
\eta_1 &= e\left(\sigma'_{B1}, g\right) = e((\sigma_{B1})^x, g) = e\left(\left(g_1^b\varpi^r\right)^x, g\right) = e(g_1^b, g)^x e(\varpi^{rx}, g)\\
&= e(g_1, g^b)^x e(\varpi, g^{rx}) = (pk_B)^x e(\varpi, g^{rx}) = (pk_B)^x e(\varpi, (g^r)^x)\\
&= (pk_B)^x e(\varpi, (\sigma_{B2})^x) = (pk_B)^x e\left(\varpi, \sigma'_{B2}\right) = (pk_B)^x \eta_2.
\end{aligned}
$$

Through the above derivation process, it can be proved that when the threshold is t, the re-signature sub-key, partial re-signature and re-signature verification algorithm are effective, and the correctness of the server-assisted verification protocol is obtained. Since the length of the original signature and the length of the re-signature are the same, the scheme has the characteristics of transparency and versatility. We can get it through the operation $r_{A\to B} = b/a = 1/r_{B\to A}$, so the solution satisfies the two-way nature. In addition, because of $sk_A, sk_B, rk_{A\to B} \in Z_q^*$, this scheme has the characteristics of key optimality.

5.2 Security Analysis

The following analysis will analyze the scheme proposed in this paper with unforgeability and robustness, and the server verification protocol of the scheme satisfies the completeness. However, this scheme has unforgeability under the standard model. The proof has been given in [17], and its security problem can be attributed to the CDH hypothesis. Therefore, in order to prove the security of our proposed new solution, we only need to prove the robustness of the scheme and the completeness of the server-assisted verification protocol.

Theorem 5: Under the standard model, when $n \geq 2t - 1$, the scheme is robust to any attacker who can unite $t - 1$ agents.
Proof:

(1) Since the combiner has the ability to verify whether a partial re-signature is legal, it can be rejected when a malicious agent is found.
(2) Because there are at least t honest agents among the n agents, and these honest agents calculate their respective partial re-signatures through their own re-signature keys, and the combiner can also obtain the set $\Phi(|\Phi| \geq t)$ of the sequence number i of the honest agents, so the combiner can always have t legal partial re-signatures to synthesize and calculate the re-signature corresponding to the message m.
(3) When the combiner has t legal partial re-signatures to synthesize and calculate the re-signature corresponding to the message m, the number of joint attackers is up to

$2t - 1 - t = t - 1$. According to the (t, n) threshold condition, the attacker cannot succeed break through.

In summary, we can conclude that the scheme is robust when $n \geq 2t - 1$.

Theorem 6: In the case of adaptive selection of messages and collusion attacks, *Server − verify* is complete.

Before giving the proof of Theorem 6, we first introduce the following two lemmas.

Lemma 1: If the server collides with Alice to become an attacker A_1, the attacker asks the challenger C to determine that an illegal original signature is legal. The probability that the event is true is zero.

Proof: In this process, A_1 plays the role of the server and in the agreement, C plays the role of verifier. Given the illegal original signature of a message, the goal of A_1 is to let C make sure that the illegal signature is legitimate. The interaction between them is as follows:

Establishment: Challenger C performs the initialization algorithm to generate system parameter cp, randomly selects $x^*, \gamma \in Z_q^*$, lets $Vst = x$ and calculates the public-private key pair $(pk_A, sk_A) = (e(g_1, g^\gamma), \gamma)$ of the trustee Alice and then sends $\{cp, pk_A, sk_A\}$ to the attacker A_1.

Query: The attacker A_1 can make a limited number of secondary verification queries to the server. In the process of each inquiry of (m_i, σ_i), both the challenger C and the attacker A_1 perform server-assisted verification to obtain the authentication protocol, and then respond to the output of the protocol and return it to the attacker A_1.

Output: Finally, the attacker A_1 outputs the forged message m^* and the string $\sigma^* = (\sigma_1^*, \sigma_2^*)$, and let the set of all legal signatures that make the message m^* corresponding to the public key pk_A is Γ_{m^*}, and satisfies $\sigma^* \notin \Gamma_{m^*}$. When the challenger C receives (m^*, c^*, σ^{1*}), it computes $(\sigma^*)' = \left((\sigma_1^*)', (\sigma_2^*)' \right) = \left(\left((\sigma_1^*)^{x^*} \right), (\sigma_2^*)^{x^*} \right)$ with the given string Vst and sends it to the attacker A_1. Then, A_1 obtains $\eta_1^* = e\left((\sigma_1^*)', g \right)$ and $\eta_2^* = e\left(\varpi^*, (\sigma_1^*)' \right)$ by operation and returns them to C. The following is a detailed derivation of the probability that the equation $\eta_1^* = (pk_A)^{x^*} \eta_2^*$ is established is $1/(q-1)$.

(1) Because of $(\sigma^*)' = (\sigma^*)^{x^*}$ and $x^* \in_R Z_q^*$, the probability of attacker A_1 forging $(\sigma^*)'$ from σ^* is $1/(q-1)$.

(2) Assuming that the attacker A_1 returns (η_1^*, η_2^*), which satisfies $\eta_1^* = (pk_A)^{x^*} \eta_2^*$, then we have $log_{pk^*} \eta_1^* = x^* + log_{pk_A} \eta_2^*$, because x^* is an element selected arbitrarily from Z_q^*, the probability that the attacker tries to get x^* to make the above equation true is $1/(q-1)$.

From the above analysis, it can be seen that the probability that attacker A_1 makes C believe that message signature (m^*, σ^*) is legitimate is $1/(q-1)$. Since q is a large prime, the probability that attacker A_1 let C decide that an illegal original signature is legitimate is zero.

Lemma 2: If the server collides with the t proxy agents to become an attacker A_2. The probability that A_2 lets C decide that an illegal re-signature is legal is negligible.

Proof: In this process, A_2 plays the role of the server and in the agreement C plays the role of verifier. When an illegal signature of a message is given, the goal of A_2 is to let C make sure the illegal signature is legal. The interaction between the two is as follows:

Establishment: Challenger C obtains system parameter cp by running a system initialization algorithm, selects three elements x^*, α, β from Z_q^*, and computes $(pk_A, sk_A) = (e(g_1, g^\alpha), \alpha)$, $(pk_B, sk_B) = (e(g_1, g^\beta), \beta)$ and $rk_{A \to B} = b/a$. Then Challenger C sends cp, pk_A, pk_B and $rk_{A \to B}$ to A_2.

Query: Same as the interrogation response process in Lemma 1.

Output: Finally, the attacker A_2 outputs the forged message m^* and the string $\sigma^* = (\sigma_1^*, \sigma_2^*)$, and let the set of all legal signatures that make the message m^* corresponding to the public key pk_B is Γ_{m^*}, and satisfies $\sigma^* \notin \Gamma_{m^*}$. Similarly, in the analysis process in Lemma 1, attacker A_2 let C make sure that the probability that (m^*, σ^*) is a legal signature is $1/(q-1)$. Therefore, the probability that attacker A_2 makes C convinced that (m^*, σ^*) is a legitimate signature is negligible.

Based on the above analysis, we know that the two-way server-assisted verification threshold proxy re-signature scheme proposed in this paper is safe in the case of adaptive selection of message attacks and collusion attacks.

Next, we present a performance analysis of the server-assisted verification threshold proxy re-signature scheme.

5.3 Performance Analysis

5.3.1 Efficiency Analysis

In order to compare performance with the existing threshold proxy re-signature algorithm, the following symbols are defined in this paper (Table 1).

Table 1. The symbolic representation of the solution

Symbol	Description
$|G_1|$	The length of the element in G_1
$|G_2|$	The length of the element in G_2
E	Exponential calculation
P	Bilinear pairing calculation

It should be noted that since the calculation amount of addition, multiplication, HMAC algorithm and hash function are relatively small, we only consider the computational exponential operation and the bilinear pairing operation with large computational complexity when considering the computational overhead.

The following will be analyzed from secret segmentation, signature algorithm, re-signature algorithm, and signature verification, where the re-signature algorithm includes the partial re-signature algorithm and the synthetic re-signature algorithm. The calculation amount of the algorithm in the scheme of this paper is shown in Table 2 below.

Table 2. Calculation amount of the scheme

Procedure	Calculated amount
Secret partition	$2E + 2P$
Sign algorithm	E
Re-signature algorithm	$E + 2P$
Verifier	$3E$

Two different threshold proxy re-signature schemes are presented in [18] and [19]. The comparison between the proposed signature algorithm and the existing two algorithms based on their signature length and computational overhead is shown in Table 3 below.

Table 3. Calculation overhead and security attributes of blind proxy re-signature algorithm

Scheme	The length of re-signature	Re-signature algorithm	Verifier
Alg. in [18]	$\lvert 4G_1 \rvert$	$6E + 3P$	$8P$
Alg. in [19]	$\lvert 3G_1 \rvert$	$2E + 3P$	$5P$
Ours	$\lvert G_1 \rvert$	$E + 2P$	$3E$

From Table 3, it can be seen that the computational cost of the re-signature generation algorithm in this scheme only includes two bilinear pairing operations and one exponentiation operation compared with that in [18, 19], so the computational cost of this scheme is less than that in [18, 19]. In addition, the length of the signature in this scheme is shorter, and the computational cost in signature verification is also lower than that in [18, 19]. In this scheme, two bilinear pairings are needed in the process of signature verification, and only three exponentiation operations are needed in the server-assisted verification protocol. Therefore, the new algorithm proposed in this paper has more advantages than the previous ones.

In the new scheme of this paper, the bilinear pairing computation task with high computational complexity is transferred to the server by the interaction protocol between the server and the verifier, so the bilinear pairing operation with large computational complexity is not needed in signature verification, which solves the problem of limited computing power of mobile terminal devices in mobile Internet environment. In addition, under the standard model, the proposed scheme is unforgettable and complete in the case of adaptive selection of messages. Therefore, the server-assisted verification threshold proxy re-signature scheme proposed in this paper is secure under adaptive selection message attack and collusion attack, thus satisfying the high security requirements due to the complexity of mobile Internet environment. In conclusion, this paper proposes a server-assisted verification threshold proxy re-signature scheme, which can be better adapted to terminal devices in mobile Internet environment.

5.4   Numerical Experiments

In this part, we simulate the schemes of [18] and [19] for verifier's time overhead, verification efficiency and message signature of different orders of magnitude. The environment of the simulation experiment is CPU for Intel Core i5-8300H processor, clocked at 2.3 GHz, memory 8 GB, software environment: 64-bit Window 10 operating system, MyEclipse2015.

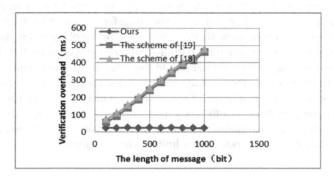

Fig. 1. Relationship between verification time overhead and message length.

It can be seen from Fig. 1 that for the signature messages of the same length, the verification time overhead of the scheme is lower than that of the literature [18] and [19]. In addition, in the schemes of [18] and [19], the verifier needs to perform 8 and 5 bilinear pairings, respectively. As the length of the signature message increases, the time overhead of the verifier in the scheme increases greatly. However, in this scheme, the computationally complex bilinear pair operation is transferred to the server through the interaction protocol between the verifier and the server. The verifier only needs to perform 3 times exponential operation, so in this scheme as the length of the signature message increases, the time cost of the verifier changes little.

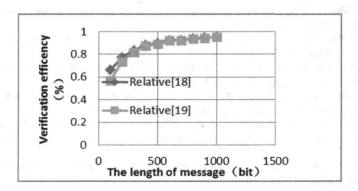

Fig. 2. Relationship between verification efficiency and message length.

It can be seen from Fig. 2 that the verification efficiency of the scheme is improved by at least 68% and 57%, respectively, compared with the schemes of [18] and [19], which greatly reduces the time cost of the verifier and saves the verification cost.

6 Conclusion

In this paper, we propose a provably secure server-assisted verification threshold proxy re-signature scheme. In this scheme, on the one hand, in the process of server-assisted verification protocol, the verifier and the server transfer the complex bilinear pairing operation task to the server through the interaction protocol between them, which makes the verifier verify the signature with a small computational cost and improves the verification efficiency of the signature. On the other hand, the decentralization of the rights of agents enhances the security of the scheme and meets the higher security requirements of the mobile internet. Finally, the simulation results show that the scheme has higher verification efficiency and shorter signature length than other existing threshold proxy re-signature schemes, which satisfies the low-end computing devices with weak computing power and limited energy supply.

References

1. Wei, W., Yi, M., Susilo, W., et al.: Provably secure server-aided verification signatures. Comput. Math Appl. **61**(7), 1705–1723 (2011)
2. Niu, S.F., Wang, C.F., et al.: Server-assisted verification signature scheme against collusion attacks. Appl. Res. Comput. **33**(1), 229–231 (2016)
3. Yang, X.D., Li, Y.N., Zhou, Q.X., et al.: Security analysis and improvement of a server-sided authentication aggregation signature scheme. Comput. Eng. **43**(1), 183–187 (2017)
4. Ateniese, G., Hohenberger, S.: Proxy re-signatures: new definitions, algorithms, and applications. https://doi.org/10.1145/1102120.1102161
5. Hong, X., Chen, K.F., Wan, Z.M.: Simple universally combinable proxy re-signature scheme. J. Softw. **21**(8), 2079–2088 (2010)
6. Ai, H., Liu, X.J.: Research on universal combinable re-signature scheme based on bilinear pairs. Comput. Eng. Des. **34**(11), 3748–3751 (2013)
7. Li, H.X., Shao, L., Pang, L.J.: Proxy re-signature scheme based on polynomial isomorphism. J. Commun. **38**(2), 16–24 (2017)
8. Qiao, L.: Research on Lattice-Based Proxy Signature Scheme, pp. 40–46. University of Electronic Science and Technology of China, Chengdu (2016)
9. Huang, P., Yang, X.D., Li, Y., et al.: Identity-based proxy re-signature scheme for unpaired linear pairs. Comput. Appl. **35**(6), 1678–1682 (2015)
10. Yang, X.D., Yang, P., Gao, G.J., et al.: Uncertified proxy re-signature scheme with aggregation properties. Comput. Eng. Sci. **40**(6), 71–76 (2018)
11. Mi, J.L., Zhang, J.Z., Chen, S.T., et al.: Blind proxy signature scheme for designated verifiers that can tolerate information disclosure. Comput. Eng. Appl. **52**(22), 123–126 (2016)
12. Yang, X.D., Chen, C.L., Yang, P., et al.: Partially blind proxy re-signature scheme. J. Commun. **39**(2), 67–72 (2018)

13. Hao, S.G., Zhang, L., Muhammad, G.: A union authentication protocol of cross-domain based on bilinear pairing. J. Softw. **8**(5), 1094–1100 (2013)
14. Sun, Y., Chen, X.Y., Du, Y.H., et al.: A proxy re-signature scheme for stream switching. J. Softw. **26**(1), 129–144 (2015)
15. Yang, X.D., Li, Y.N., Gao, G.J., et al.: Sever-aided verification proxy re-signature scheme in the standard model. J. Electron. Inf. Technol. **38**(5), 1151–1157 (2016)
16. Lei, Y., Hu, M., Gong, B., Wang, L., Cheng, Y.: A one-way variable threshold proxy re-signature scheme for mobile internet. In: Li, J., Liu, Z., Peng, H. (eds.) SPNCE 2019. LNICST, vol. 284, pp. 521–537. Springer, Cham (2019). https://doi.org/10.1007/978-3-030-21373-2_42
17. Jiang, M.M., Hu, Y.P., Wang, B., et al.: Proxy re-signature scheme over the lattice. J. Xidian Univ. **41**(2), 20–24 (2014)
18. Yang, D.X., Wang, F.C.: Flexible threshold proxy re-signature schemes. Chin. J. Electron. **20**(4), 691–696 (2011)
19. Li, H.Y., Yang, X.D.: One-way variable threshold proxy re-signature scheme under standard model. Comput. Appl. Softw. **12**, 307–310 (2014)

ReJection: A AST-Based Reentrancy Vulnerability Detection Method

Rui Ma[1], Zefeng Jian[1], Guangyuan Chen[1], Ke Ma[2(✉)], and Yujia Chen[1]

[1] School of Computer Science and Technology, Beijing Institute of Technology,
Beijing 100081, China
[2] Internet Center, Institute of Technology and Standards Research, China Academy
of Information and Communication Technology, Beijing 100191, China
make@caict.ac.cn

Abstract. Blockchain is deeply integrated into the vertical industry, and gradually forms an application ecosphere of blockchain in various industries. However, the security incidents of blockchain occur frequently, and especially smart contracts have become the badly-disastered area. So avoiding security incidents caused by smart contracts has become an essential topic for blockchain developing. Up to now, there is not generic method for the security auditing of smart contracts and most researchers have to use existing vulnerability detection technology. To reduce the high false rate of smart contract vulnerability detection, we use ReJection, a detection method based on abstract syntax tree (AST), to focus on the reentrancy vulnerability with obvious harm and features in smart contracts. ReJection consists of four steps. Firstly, ReJection obtains the AST corresponding to the contract by the smart contract compiler *solc*. Then, AST is preprocessed to eliminate redundant information. Thirdly, ReJection traverses the nodes of the AST and records the notations related to reentrancy vulnerabilities during the traversal, such as Danger-Transfer function, Checks-Effects-Interactions pattern and mutex mechanism. Finally, ReJection uses record information and predefined rules to determine whether the reentrancy vulnerability is occurred. ReJection is implemented based on Slither, which is an open-source smart contract vulnerability detection tool. Furthermore, we also use the open-source smart contract code as the test program to compare experimental results to verify the effects with the ReJection and Slither. The result highlights that the ReJection has higher detection accuracy for reentrancy vulnerability.

Keywords: Vulnerability detection · Smart contract · Abstract syntax tree · Reentrancy vulnerability

1 Introduction

Blockchain as an independent technology originates from Bitcoin designed by Satoshi Nakamoto [1]. In his paper ⟨Bitcoin: a peer-to-peer electronic cash

© Springer Nature Singapore Pte Ltd. 2020
W. Han et al. (Eds.): CTCIS 2019, CCIS 1149, pp. 58–71, 2020.
https://doi.org/10.1007/978-981-15-3418-8_5

system⟩ [2], Nakamoto describes an electronic digital currency system that does not rely on trusted third parties. The underlying technology that supports the system is called blockchain.

Blockchain 1.0 is a virtual digital currency represented by Bitcoin and Litecoin. Blockchain 2.0 refers to smart contracts represented by Ethereum [3]. Smart contracts have brought a qualitative leap to the blockchain, but security issues caused by smart contracts have also drawn increasing attention.

Smart contract represents a trusted blockchain platform where developers can't stop any smart contract or modify the content of smart contract after deploying a smart contract. While bringing a credible advantage to smart contracts, it also brings a considerable degree greatly of security risks. Essentially, each smart contract is a program that has the possibility for error. If there are vulnerabilities in the smart contract, the user's digital currency funds may be taken away by the attacker. And that even leads to serious consequences. Due to the inability to stop and modify the smart contracts, however, it will be difficult to repair it by upgrading when there is a potential vulnerability in the smart contracts. Therefore, the security audit of smart contracts is particularly necessary.

To address the issue, we propose the ReJection. It is a vulnerability detection method based on abstract syntax tree for smart contract reentrancy vulnerability. That vulnerability has obvious features and larger hazard. ReJection analyzes smart contracts source code by static analysis techniques. Generally, ReJection is able to detect the reentrancy vulnerability generated by the dangerous transfer function by analyzing the compile results of the smart contracts source code. At the same time, ReJection has better detection and analysis effects for the Checks-Effects-Interactions pattern and mutex mechanism, which is the key to reentrancy vulnerability prevention.

We make the following contributions:

- We study the causes of the smart contract reentrancy vulnerability, and analyze the existing security audit method of smart contract.
- A detection method, ReJection, is proposed for the smart contract reentrancy vulnerability. By compiling and parsing the source code of smart contracts, ReJection could determine whether there is reentrancy vulnerability. At the same time, ReJection also provides better detecting for Checks-Effects-Interactions pattern and mutex mechanism, which are the key of reentrancy vulnerability.
- We implemented ReJection based on the existing open source vulnerability detection tool Slither, and experimented with ReJection through open source smart contract source code as experimental dataset. By comparing ReJection with Slither, the results show that ReJection improves the accuracy of reentrancy vulnerability detection.

2 Related Works

2.1 Blockchain and Smart Contracts

In a narrow sense, the blockchain is a chained data structure that combines data blocks in a chronological order in a sequential manner, and it cryptographically guarantees non-tamperable and unforgeable distributed ledgers. At the same time, the blockchain is also an innovation application of traditional computer technologies such as distributed data storage, consensus algorithms, P2P transmission, and various encryption algorithms in the new Internet era. At present, blockchain technology has been budded off from Bitcoin and has developed in many fields including financial trade, logistics, smart contracts, and sharing economy.

Blockchain 1.0 is a virtual digital currency represented by Bitcoin and Litecoin including its functions of payment, circulation and other similar currencies. It represents a digital currency-based application for decentralized digital currency transactions.

Blockchain 2.0 refers to the smart contracts represented by Ethereum [4]. The combination of smart contracts and digital currency provides extensive application scenario for the financial field and forms "Programmable Finance". Smart contract is the core of Blockchain 2.0 and has Turing Completeness. It is an event-driven computer program that runs on a replicable shared blockchain distributed ledgers. It enables autonomous invoking data processing, accepting, storing and forwarding the value that corresponding to digital currency, as well as controlling and managing various types of intelligent digital assets on the blockchain. Smart contract is identified by a 160-bit identifier address whose code is compiled and deployed on the blockchain. All users can send a transaction to the address of the contract account through an external private account to sign a smart contract in the cryptocurrency. Therefore, smart contract makes the blockchain programmable and customizable, which gives the blockchain intelligence and indicates a development direction of the blockchain technology in the future.

2.2 Smart Contract Security Audit

Research on the smart contract security audits has just beginning.

Atzei analyzed the security vulnerabilities of Ethereum smart contracts [5], demonstrated a series of attacks that exploited these vulnerabilities, and provided a summary of the common programming pitfalls that could lead to vulnerabilities in Ethereum smart contracts.

Delmolino summarized the common mistakes made in coding smart contracts and the common pitfalls that are exposed when designing secure and reliable smart contracts, and proposed some suggestions for coding safety smart contracts [6].

Based on techniques such as symbolic execution, SMT solving and taint analysis, Bernhard Mueller proposed Mythril [7], a security analysis tool for

Ethereum smart contracts, to detect a variety of security vulnerabilities. He also analyzed the application of symbolic execution and constraint solving in smart contract security analysis.

Loi Luu analyzed several security vulnerabilities in smart contracts and found that about 44% of smart contracts have security risks. At the same time, a symbolic execution-based vulnerability detection tool Oyente [8] was proposed. It uses the decompiled code of the smart contract to construct a control flow graph based on basic blocks and further obtain the constraint path of the vulnerability by Z3 solver.

Bhargavan proposed a formal verification method for verifying smart contracts written by Solidity [9], and outlined a framework. The framework analyzes and verifies the safety of operational and accuracy of functional of Ethereum smart contracts by converting smart contracts to F*, which is a functional programming language for program verification.

To address the security problem of smart contracts, Petar Tsankov introduced Securify [10], a security analysis tool for Ethereum smart contracts. Securify extracts precise semantic information from the code by analyzing the function dependency graph of the contract, and then checks compliance and violation modes to capture sufficient conditions for verifying the vulnerability.

Grigory Repka developed the online smart contract static analysis tool SmartCheck to detect various security vulnerabilities in smart contracts [11], but he did not specify which detection techniques were used.

Hukai proposed a formal verification method for smart contracts [12], which can be used in the process of modeling, model checking and model validation.

Xin Wei analyzed the threat of smart contracts and the principle of the exiting vulnerabilities, summarized some common problems faced by smart contract vulnerability detection, and proposed an automatic vulnerability detection theory of smart contract [13].

Chengdu LianAn Technology [14] proposes an automatic formal verification platform VaaS for smart contract security issues.

2.3   Reentrancy Vulnerability

The occurrence of a smart contract reentrancy vulnerability means that the contract executes a callback operation. For smart contracts, function invocations can be made between the contract account and the external account to achieve more functionality of the smart contracts. Specifically, invoking to the fallback function is a kind of callback operation.

For each smart contract, there is at most one function without a function name. It does not need to be declared, and has no parameters and no return value. In addition, it needs to be visible to the outside. Such functions are called fallback functions. Once someone makes a transfer transaction to a contract account, the fallback function corresponding to the contract account is invoked.

Literally, reentrancy vulnerabilities are caused by repeated entry. In the Ethereum smart contracts, the attacker constructs malicious code in the fallback function of the contract address. Once the transfer function is executed to the vulnerable contract account, the contract account is forced to execute the fallback function of the attack contract due to its own vulnerability defect. That will trigger execution of the malicious code built by the attacker within the fallback function. The malicious code includes recalling the contract transfer function, which can result in the operation of reentering the contract to execute some operations like transfer Ether. Ultimately, it will lead to the theft of assets.

3　ReJection

3.1　Overview

After carefully analyzing the existing smart contract vulnerability detection methods and the reentrancy vulnerability characteristics, we propose the ReJection. ReJection is a detection method for smart contract reentrancy vulnerability based on abstract syntax tree (AST), which could improve the detection efficiency of the smart contract reentrancy vulnerability and the detection accuracy of the reentrancy vulnerability prevention condition.

ReJection detects vulnerability by traversing and parsing the source code of smart contract. It uses the open source smart contract compiler *solc* as the tool of syntax analysis to obtain the AST of the source code. By excluding the redundant information of the AST, ReJection could extract the key information about the vulnerability detection of the source code. That key information will be saved in the reserved nodes of AST. Then, the step-by-step nested traversal analysis is performed on the reserved nodes to detect the occurrence conditions of the reentrancy vulnerability. Specifically, that condition refers to whether the original contract account balance changes after executing the Danger-Transfer function. At the same time, the prevention conditions for reentrancy vulnerability are detected and analyzed. Generally, ReJection detects whether there is a change in the contract account balance and whether there exists the mutex mechanism after the execution of the Danger-Transfer function, respectively. Finally, the results of the analysis of the occurrence conditions and the prevention conditions are analyzed comprehensively to determine whether the contract is in danger of reentrancy vulnerability.

Figure 1 shows the detection scheme of ReJection, which can be divided into four parts.

(1) Obtaining AST. ReJection compiles the source code of smart contract by the *solc* compiler to generate an intuitive AST in *json* format and further outputs that to a local text file.
(2) Preprocessing the Redundant Node of AST. ReJection analyzes and preprocesses the AST to exclude redundant nodes and obtain the reserved nodes that reentrancy vulnerability may exist.
(3) Traversing the Reserved Nodes of AST. ReJection performs a step-by-step traversal analysis of the reserved nodes based on the attributes of the various nodes in the reserved nodes. For each contract, it detects whether there is

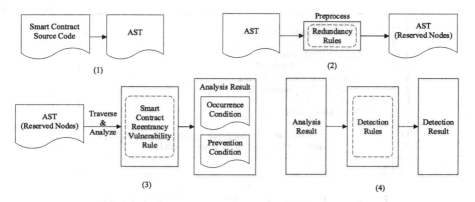

Fig. 1. Detection scheme of ReJection

a change in the contract account balance after the execution of the Danger-Transfer function, and whether there is a mutex mechanism in the contract. At the same time of traversing, ReJection also determines and assigns the parameters related to the reentrancy vulnerability so as to obtain the detection result of the Danger-Transfer function and the record list of the prevention conditions.

(4) Determining the Reentrancy Vulnerability. According to the analysis result of Step (3) and the reentrancy vulnerability determination rule summarized by the author, ReJection detects whether there is a reentrancy vulnerability generation condition. Finally, it could obtain the detection result of the reentrancy vulnerability.

3.2   Obtaining AST

AST is an abstract representation of the grammar structure of the source code. It intuitively expresses the structure in the programming language by the form of the tree. A node of AST represents one or more structures in the source code, while the AST contains a complete representation of the entire compilation unit. The AST in the Ethereum smart contract is obtained by the *solc* which is an open source compiler of the smart contract. In order to obtain intuitive representation of the AST, ReJection uses the *json* format to record the details of the AST.

Figure 2 shows a part of information of the AST of identifier node, where the *name* attribute represents the name of variable and the *typeDescriptions* attribute represents the details of return type. AST is represented with the form of the nested structure and each type of node has some special properties.

3.3   Preprocessing the Redundant Node of AST

In the AST obtained in the previous step, there is a considerable part of information that is not related to the reentrancy vulnerability detection, such as

```
1    {
2            "argumentTypes" : null,
3            "id" : 18,
4            "name" : "balances",
5            "nodeType" : "Identifier",
6            "overloadedDeclarations" : [],
7            "referencedDeclaration" : 15,
8            "src" : "292:8:0",
9            "typeDescriptions" :
10           {
11                   "typeIdentifier" : "t_mapping$_t_address_$_t_unit256_$",
12                   "typeString" : "mapping (address => unit256)"
13           }
14   }
```

Fig. 2. An Example of the AST of the identifier node

version information, compilation information. In order to improve the efficiency of the detection, it is necessary to preprocess the AST to exclude redundant information. The preprocessing divides all nodes into the reserved nodes and the redundant nodes. The information contained in the redundant nodes is independent of ReJection, while the information contained in the reserved nodes is closely related to the ReJection.

The preprocessing is described as follows:

(1) The root node, which is taken as a reserved node, represents all the information of the smart contract. ReJection further traverses the child nodes of the root node for analysis.
(2) ReJection traverses the child nodes of the root node to detect the node type *nodetype* of each child node. The values of the *nodetype* include *PragmaDirective*, *ContractDefinition*, and *ImportDirective*. The *PragmaDirective* represents the compiled version of the contract, the *ContractDefinition* indicates that the node is a library or contract, and the *ImportDirective* represents the other source files imported by the contract. The node of AST whose *nodetype* is *ContractDefinition* is identified as the reserved node and the other nodes are identified as the redundant nodes.
(3) ReJection further traverses the child nodes of the reserved node to detect its attribute *contractKind*. The node whose value of *contractKind* is *contract* is identified as the reserved node, and other child nodes are identified as the redundant nodes.

After the traversal, the remaining nodes in the AST are reserved nodes. The information of the nodes corresponds to the contract information.

3.4   Traversing the Reserved Nodes of AST

Traversing the reserved node is the most critical step in ReJection. The reserved nodes, which are obtained by the preprocessing of the redundant node, include all state variables and functions of the contract. The different types of the reserved nodes can be distinguished by the node type and return type. Aiming at different type of the reserved nodes, ReJection specifically analyzes it and assigns the value for the key parameters related to detecting reentrancy vulnerabilities. After the traversal of the reserved nodes has been fully completed, ReJection uses the above parameters to determine whether there is the reentrancy vulnerability in the contract according to the reentrancy vulnerability detection rule.

The key parameters associated with detecting reentrancy vulnerability are described in Table 1.

The method of traversing the reserved nodes is shown in Fig. 3. To conveniently explain the process of parsing AST, we give the following definition and abbreviations:

tCN: Current Node

$tULN$: Upper Level Node of Current Node

$tNLN$: Next Level Node of Current Node

Table 1. The definition of parameters

Variable name	Type	Initial value	The meaning of initial value
$reentrancyCode$	string	NULL	Save the Danger-Transfer function
$isReentrancy$	int	0	No Danger-Transfer function
$variableMutex$	array	NULL	Record a set of Mutex Mechanism variable
$isMutex$	int	0	No Mutex Mechanism
$isChange$	int	0	Exist the Checks-Effects-Interactions pattern
$ifList$	array	NULL	Used for Determination of Mutex Mechanism

Step 1. Traverse the reserved nodes and detect the node type based on the attribute $nodeType$ of the tCN. If the $nodeType$ is $VariableDeclaration$, the tCN represents a state variable and the return type $typeString$ of tCN should be detected; while the information of the node whose $typeString$ is bool or integer is recorded as state variable for further detection. If the $nodeType$ is $Function$-$Definition$, the tCN represents a function and the $tNLN$, which is the next level node of the tCN, should be traversed by Step 2.

Step 2. Detect the $nodeType$ of the node. If the $nodetype$ is $ExpressionStatement$, the tCN represents an expression statement and the $expression$ node of $tNLN$ should be analyzed by Step 3. If the $nodetype$ is $IfStatement$, $WhileStatement$, $DoWhileStatement$, or $ForStatement$, the tCN represents a statement of loop or judgment. Then, the $condition$ node of $tNLN$ should be processed as $expression$ node and $body$ node of $tNLN$ should be continued analyzing by Step 2. If the $nodetype$ is $Break$, $Continue$, or $Throw$, the tCN represents jumping out of the loop or judgement statement. So, it is necessary to return the node corresponding to the previous loop or judgement statement and continue performing Step 2.

Step 3. Detect $expression$ node. This step is mainly for analyzing different $nodeType$.

FunctionCall: If the *nodeType* of the *tCN* is *FunctionCall*, the *name* attribute of the *expression* node of the *tNLN* is detected. If there is no such *name* attribute or the value of the *name* attribute is NULL, that *expression* node should be continued processing according to Step 3. If the value of the *name* attribute is *require* or *assert*, the *arguments* node of the *tNLN* should be continued processing by Step 3. It is noted that if that *arguments* node has return value, that value should be recorded into the *ifList* to determine the mutex.

MemberAccess: If the *nodeType* of the *tCN* is *MemberAccess*, the return type *typeString* of the *tCN* is detected. If the *typeString* contains the *"payable"* field, the value of *memberName* attribute of the *tCN* should be recorded, and that value should be appended to the original value of parameter *reentrancyCode* to concatenate with the *reentrancyCode*. After that, the *expression* node of the *tNLN* is continued detecting by Step 3.

Identifier: If the *nodeType* of the *tCN* is *Identifier*, and if the value of the *name* attribute of the *tCN* belongs to the state variable recorded in Step 1, and the value of *isReentrancy* is 0 at this time, the value of *name* attribute of the *tCN* is returned. Otherwise, if the value of the *name* attribute of the *tCN* does not belong to the recorded state variable, or the value of *typeString* attribute of the *tCN* is *address*, the value of *name* attribute of the *tCN* is appended to the value of parameter *reentrancyCode*. While if the *reentrancyCode* is begins with *"valuecall"*, the value of parameter *isReentrancy* is assigned 1 and the value of *reentrancyCode* is assigned NULL. Otherwise, the *isReentrancy* and the *reentrancyCode* are unchanged.

Assignment: If the *nodeType* of the *tCN* is *Assignment*, it means that the node contains the assignment operator. If the value of *isReentrancy* is 1, the *leftHandSide* node of the *tNLN* should be continued detecting by Step 3; it is noted that if the *leftHandSide* node returns *true*, the value of parameter *isChange* should be assigned 0 at this time. If the value of *isReentrancy* is 0, the *leftHandSide* node of the *tNLN* should be continued detecting by Step 3. Meanwhile, if the return value of the *leftHandSide* node belongs to the state variable recorded in Step 1, the state variable should be assigned with the value of *value* attribute of the *rightHandSide* node of the *tNLN*.

Literal: If the *nodeType* of the *tCN* is *Literal*, it returns the value corresponding to the *value* attribute of the *tCN*.

BinaryOperation: If the *nodeType* of the *tCN* is *BinaryOperation*, the node represents a binary operation. If the value of *isReentrancy* is 0, both the *leftExpression* node and the *rightExpression* node of the *tNLN* should be continued detecting by Step 3. Meanwhile, if the return values of those two nodes belong to the state variable recorded in Step 1, the return values and the operator of the *tCN* are recorded in the *ifList* to further determine the mutex. And the result of current binary operation should also be returned.

Step 4. For each state variable recorded in Step 1, all the conditions recorded by the parameter *ifList* in Step 3 are used to judge one by one. If there is a state variable makes one of the conditions of *ifList* is unsatisfiable, the value of parameter *isMutex* is assigned 1.

3.5   Determining the Reentrancy Vulnerability

By analyzing, the execution of the Danger-Transfer function ⟨address⟩call. value()() may lead to the reentrancy vulnerability. Therefore, we summarize prevention ways including the following three types:

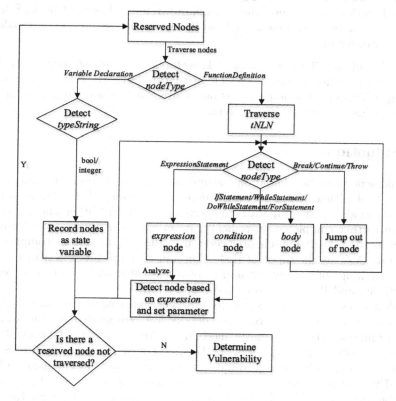

Fig. 3. Traversing the reserved nodes

(1) Use the secure transfer function, such as transfer(), instead of existing Danger-Transfer function;
(2) Use the Checks-Effects-Interactions pattern. Specifically, it completes all operations of the contract account before the transfer function is executed;
(3) Introduce mutex mechanism. Specifically, it avoids the occurrence of reentrancy vulnerability by using a flag of global variable.

According to the points (2) and (3) of that prevention ways, and combining with the analysis results obtained in Step 3 of Sect. 3.4, ReJection regulates 4 rules to determine reentrancy vulnerability.

Rule 1. If $isReentrancy = 0$, which indicates that the Danger-Transfer function does not appear, there is no reentrancy vulnerability.

Rule 2. If $isReentrancy = 1$ and $isMutex = 1$, which indicates that there appears the Danger-Transfer function, but mutex mechanism exists, there is no reentrancy vulnerability.

Rule 3. If $isReentrancy = 1$, $isMutex = 0$, and $isChange = 0$, there is no reentrancy vulnerability. This situation indicates that there appears the Danger-Transfer function and has not mutex mechanism, but it has the Checks-Effects-Interactions pattern which means it is no change in the contract account balance after the transfer function.

Rule 4. If and only if $isReentrancy = 1$, $isMutex = 0$, and $isChange = 1$, there must be a reentrancy vulnerability. This situation indicates that there appears the Danger-Transfer function and has not mutex mechanism, but it also has not the Checks-Effects-Interactions pattern.

4   Evaluation

We implement ReJection based on the open source smart contract vulnerability detection tool Slither. In order to verify detection accuracy of ReJection for reentrancy vulnerability, a comparative experiment between Slither and ReJection has been further completed. Specifically, it selects open source smart contract data set as the experimental source code; uses the smart contract compiler *solc* to generate AST as the input of ReJection and uses the smart contract source code as the input of the Slither; and records the vulnerability detection results of the Slither and ReJection to compare and analyze.

Table 2 shows the experimental results. The experiment compares 8 different contracts, in which the contract details are represented by the Danger-Transfer function (D-T), the mutex mechanism (Mutex) and the Checks-Effects-Interactions pattern (C-E-I). Here the Danger-Transfer function indicates that transfer function ⟨address⟩.call.value()(), and the mutex mechanism and the Checks-Effects-Interactions pattern is introduced in Sect. 3.5. For the value of corresponding cell, "Y" indicates that there exists Danger-Transfer function, the mutex mechanism or Danger-Transfer function in the contract, whereas "N" indicates that none of them exists. For the expected result, the detection result of the Slither and ReJection, "Y" indicates that the reentrancy vulnerability exists, and "N" indicates that there is no reentrancy vulnerability.

In Table 2, contracts *SimpleDAO*, *Reentrancy* and *BrokenToken* have the same contract details. They have Danger-Transfer functions and have no mutex mechanism and the Checks-Effects-Interactions pattern. According to the Rule 4 in Sect. 3.5, there must be existed a reentrancy vulnerability in the above contracts. The results of Slither and ReJection are consistent with the expected results, which shows the reentrancy vulnerability can be correctly detected by them.

Table 2. Comparison of experimental results

Contract	Contract details			Expected result	Detection result	
	D-T	Mutex	C-E-I		Slither	ReJection
SimpleDAO	Y	N	N	Y	Y	Y
Reentrancy	Y	N	N	Y	Y	Y
BrokenToken	Y	N	N	Y	Y	Y
ModifierEntrancy	N	N	N	N	N	N
SimpleDAOFixed	Y	N	Y	N	N	N
noCheck	Y	N	Y	N	Y	N
EtherStore	Y	Y	N	N	Y	N
EtherBankStore	Y	Y	Y	N	Y	N

Different from above contracts, contract *ModifierEntrancy* has no Danger-Transfer function. According to the Rule 1 in Sect. 3.5, there definitely has no reentrancy vulnerability in the contract. The results of Slither and ReJection are consistent with the expected results.

For contract *SimpleDAOFixed*, it has the Danger-Transfer function and the Checks-Effects-Interactions pattern, but there is no mutex mechanism. According to the Rule 3 in Sect. 3.5, there definitely has no reentrancy vulnerability in the contract. The results of Slither and ReJection are consistent with the expected results.

The contract details of contract *noCheck* is exactly the same as the contract *SimpleDAOFixed*, it should be no reentrancy vulnerability. However, in the real detection, ReJection got the correct result, whereas Slither had a false positive. Slither mistakenly believed that there was a reentrancy vulnerability in the contract.

Moreover, for contract *noCheck* and contract *EtherStore*, although they have different contract details, both of them have the Danger-Transfer function and have either a mutex mechanism or a Checks-Effects-Interactions pattern. According to the Rule 2 and Rule 3 in Sect. 3.5, there definitely has no reentrancy vulnerability in these two contracts. Unfortunately, in the real detection, Slither made a false result because it can not distinguish the difference between the two prevention ways. Instead, ReJection can detect these two kinds of prevention ways and report the correct detection result.

Similarity, for contract *EtherStore* and contract *EtherBankStore*, even although the contract details of them are not the same, both of them contain the Danger-Transfer function and a mutux mechanism. According to the Rule 2 of Sect. 3.5, there is no reentrancy vulnerability in them. While in the real detection, ReJection still got the correct result, and Slither had a false positive yet.

Although the examples of smart contracts involved in Table 2 are few, it is noted that they still cover all four types of determination rules proposed in

Sect. 3.5. For the above contracts, detection accuracy of Slither is 62.5%, while ReJection ones achieves 100%. ReJection is better than Slither in the detection effect. The main reason may be that ReJection fortifies with prevention conditions when detecting reentrancy vulnerability. Later, it is necessary to expand the number of testing contracts to further verify the detection capability of ReJection.

5 Conclusion

In this paper, we propose the ReJection, a method of smart contract reentrancy vulnerability detection based on abstract syntax tree (AST). By resolving the AST, ReJection uses the proposed redundancy rules to eliminate the nodes that are useless for vulnerability detection. That indirectly improves the efficiency of vulnerability detection. By traversing the reserved nodes in the AST, ReJection analyzes and records key information related to occurrence conditions and prevention conditions of the reentrancy vulnerability. Then, ReJection further detects whether there exists a reentrancy vulnerability generation condition depending on the reentrancy vulnerability determination rules summarized by the author. That improves the accuracy of the reentrancy vulnerability detection. Moreover, ReJection is implemented based on the Slither, which is an existing open source vulnerability detection tool of smart contract. The effectiveness of ReJection has been verified by comparing experimental results between ReJection and Slither.

References

1. Bitcoin Sourcecode. https://github.com/bitcoin/bitcoin/. Accessed 18 Jan 2016
2. Bitcoin: a peer-to-peer electronic cash system. https://bitcoin.org/bitcoin.pdf. Accessed 2018
3. Buterin, V.: Ethereum: A Next-Generation Smart Contract and Decentralized Application Platform. White paper, pp. 1–36 (2014)
4. Parizi, R.M., Dehghantanha, A.: Smart contract programming languages on blockchains: an empirical evaluation of usability and security. In: Chen, S.P., Wang, H., Zhang, L.J. (eds.) ICBC 2018. LNCS, vol. 10974, pp. 75–91. Springer, Cham (2018). https://doi.org/10.10007/978-3-319-94478-4_6
5. Atzei, N., Bartoletti, M., Cimoli, T.: A survey of attacks on Ethereum smart contracts (SoK). In: Maffei, M., Ryan, M. (eds.) POST 2017. LNCS, vol. 10204, pp. 164–186. Springer, Heidelberg (2017). https://doi.org/10.1007/978-3-662-54455-6_8
6. Delmolino, K., Arnett, M., Kosba, A., Miller, A., Shi, E.: Step by step towards creating a safe smart contract: lessons and insights from a cryptocurrency lab. In: Clark, J., Meiklejohn, S., Ryan, P.Y.A., Wallach, D., Brenner, M., Rohloff, K. (eds.) FC 2016. LNCS, vol. 9604, pp. 79–94. Springer, Heidelberg (2016). https://doi.org/10.1007/978-3-662-53357-4_6
7. Mueller, B.: Smashing Ethereum smart contracts for fun and real profit. In: The 9th Annual HITB Security Conference (2018)

8. Luu, L., Chu, D.H., Olickel, H., et al.: Making smart contracts smarter. In: Proceedings of the 2016 ACM SIGSAC Conference on Computer and Communications Security 2016, pp. 254–269. ACM, New York (2016). https://doi.org/10.1145/2976749.2978309

9. Bhargavan, K., Swamy, N., Zanella-Bguelin, S., et al.: Formal verification of smart contracts: short paper. In: Proceedings of the 2016 ACM Workshop on Programming Languages and Analysis for Security 2016, pp. 91–96. ACM, New York (2016). https://doi.org/10.1145/2993600.2993611

10. Tsankov, P., Dan, A., Drachsler-Cohen, D., et al.: Securify: practical security analysis of smart contracts. In: Proceedings of the 2018 ACM SIGSAC Conference on Computer and Communications Security 2018, pp. 67–82. ACM (2018). https://doi.org/10.1145/3243734.3243780

11. SmartCheck. https://tool.smartdec.net. Accessed 22 Oct 2017

12. Hu, K., Ai, X.M., Gao, L.C., et al.: Formal verification method of smart contract. J. Inf. Secur. Res. 2(12), 1080–1089 (2016)

13. Xin, W., Zhang, T., Zou, Q.C.: Research on vulnerability of blockchain based smart contract. In: The 10th Conference on Vulnerability Analysis and Risk Assessment 2017, pp. 421–437 (2017)

14. Chengdu LianAn Technology. http://www.lianantech.com. Accessed 10 June 2019

Identity Authentication Under Internet of Everything Based on Edge Computing

Zixiao Kong[1]([✉]), Jingfeng Xue[1], Yong Wang[1], Weijie Han[1,2], and Xinyu Liu[3]

[1] School of Computer Science and Technology, Beijing Institute of Technology, Beijing 100081, China
bit_kzx2017@126.com
[2] Space Engineering University, Beijing 101416, China
[3] The Experimental High School Attached to Beijing Normal University, Beijing 100081, China

Abstract. With the rapid development of the Internet, the application of the Internet of things and big data is more and more extensive. The era of Internet of everything (IoE) has come, and the traditional cloud computing model has been unable to efficiently process the massive data generated by a large number of edge devices. Therefore, edge-type big data processing which is oriented to massive data computing generated by network edge devices—edge computing comes into being. However, due to the complexity of edge computing, data security and privacy issues become more prominent. Aiming at the security authentication of edge equipment under the Internet of everything, this paper designs an identity authentication framework under the Internet of everything based on edge computing. In the framework, multi-factor identity authentication is applied to solve the weakness of edge equipment security authentication. Moreover, the software defined network technology (SDN) is adopted to realize the global management of the deployment and application of a large number of edge equipment, which can effectively realize the effective security protection of the Internet of everything. In the end, the formalized verification of the identity authentication process of the designed framework is carried out.

Keywords: Edge computing · Internet of everything · Identity authentication · SDN

1 Introduction

With the rapid development of Internet and Internet of things technology, online entity identity has been growing at an explosive pace. Nowadays society is changing from the industrial civilization to the information civilization, and to the intelligent development. A digital, networked, intelligent and cloud-based Internet of everything era is coming. As early as 2005, cloud computing has quietly changed our life, work and study. As for cloud computing platform of the rapid development of Internet of things, the number of sensors, smart phones, wearable devices, smart home appliances and other devices increases linearly. What follows is the massive amount of data generated by IOT terminals [1]. According to the cisco global cloud index [2], by 2019, 45% of the data

© Springer Nature Singapore Pte Ltd. 2020
W. Han et al. (Eds.): CTCIS 2019, CCIS 1149, pp. 72–85, 2020.
https://doi.org/10.1007/978-981-15-3418-8_6

generated by the Internet of things will be stored, processed and analyzed on the edge of the network. The total data traffic of the global data center is expected to reach 10.4 ZB. By 2020, the global data center traffic will reach 15.3 ZB [3]. At the same time, the number of IOT devices connected has also shown a linear growth trend in recent years. According to the Internet business solutions group, the number of wireless devices connected to the network will reach 50 billion by 2020 [4]. In this case, traditional cloud computing cannot meet the demand of Internet of everything (Fig. 1), and edge computing comes into being.

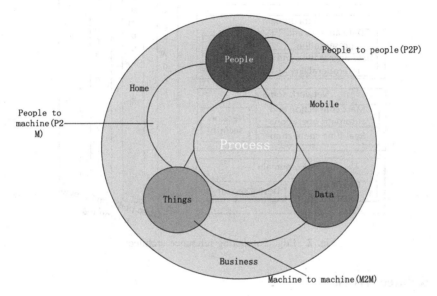

Fig. 1. Internet of Everything.

Edge contains applications, data calculation, network and equipment of four domains, which usually contain more than one function entity, such as data participants (the end user, infrastructure providers and service providers), service (virtual machine, data containers) and infrastructure (edge data centers, terminal infrastructure and core infrastructure) (Fig. 2) [5]. In this kind of multi-entity edge computing system, the demand of users' cross-domain networking increases rapidly. As a result, identity authentication faces huge challenges [6].

The main contributions of this paper include:

(1) presenting cloud computing, edge computing, SDN and other concepts to readers in different fields, and making a reasonable explanation of identity authentication based on edge computing instead of cloud computing under the IoE;

(2) combine SDN with edge computing model to give full play to the advantages of SDN;

(3) an identity authentication architecture based on edge computing under the IoE is proposed, which adopts multi-factor identity authentication with high security level.

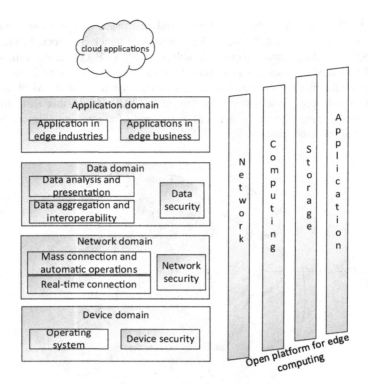

Fig. 2. Edge computing reference architecture.

2 Related Work

Identity authentication is an eternal war in the field of network security [7]. At present, identity authentication is mainly carried out on the basis of cloud computing platform. The information technology represented by cloud computing has profoundly changed people's way of production, work, study and life. This way of identity authentication is characterized by stable network, cost saving and high flexibility [8].

Bangui et al. proposed a transfer of services from a centralized cloud platform to a distributed platform. Edge computing is cited in the case. The integrated edge cloud computing brings many advantages, such as reducing network delay, dynamic flexibility, etc. However, there are still some network deficiencies in edge computing [9].

Liu et al. proposed an attribute based ciphertext access control optimization method for mobile cloud. The fusion of mobile Internet and cloud computing reduces the cost, has high reliability and is dynamic and extensible. Although the length of communication ciphertext increases in the process of data release, it is completely acceptable in the real environment [10].

Roy et al. proposed a mobile cloud computing security lightweight user authentication scheme based on encrypted graphics hash, bit XOR and fuzzy extraction function. ProVerif 1.93 simulation verifies that the authentication scheme has lower calculation cost and communication cost compared with relevant schemes, but it is more suitable for users of low-power computing devices [11].

Badr et al. proposed a technology to encrypt and share important medical data through cloud computing. Through this system, the decryption process is delegated to the cloud server to achieve scalability and low computational complexity on the data owner side, ensuring speed. Each cloud facilitates cost savings for users, and security challenges faced by cloud entities are addressed and addressed. In the cloud computing environment, data access has controlled access and access control permissions of multiple user roles, which realizes secure and confidential access to data [12].

Jin et al. designed a homomorphic encrypted communication protocol based on RLWE for user authentication and message management in the internet-of-things fusion environment based on cloud computing. By analyzing the performance of the existing Internet of things environment communication protocol and the proposed communication protocol, the security of the protocol is verified. Using the data in the cloud computing environment management server and the Internet of things in the environment of gateway between fully homomorphic encryption algorithm, designed the data validation techniques, is higher than traditional encryption algorithm efficiency and safety. In data leakage, infringement of user information and other vulnerabilities will continue to deepen [13].

Dhillon et al. proposed a multi-factor ECC authentication scheme for medical service security based on cloud Internet of things. This scheme uses the web-based AVISPA tool for formal analysis and verifies that the scheme is safe against both active and passive attacks, including replay attack and man-in-the-middle attack. Compared with the performance of the relevant scheme, the calculation cost of the scheme is lower. Nevertheless, there is still room for improvement in real-time heterogeneity and complexity [14].

Most of the solutions are cloud computing models under the Internet of things, and some of the solutions using edge computing models have shortcomings in the network surface. Considering the above reasons, this paper combines edge computing with SDN to make the network more flexible and dynamic and provide more efficient authentication.

3 Preliminaries

With the further development of IoE and the integration of IoE, many emerging industries will surely be derived [15]. The IoE will create new functions for enterprises, individuals and countries, and bring new experiences and development opportunities. At the same time, it also brings many challenges [16].

Computing is transitioning from single-user devices to the IoE. The IoE combines people, processes, data and things together. Cloud computing mostly adopts a centralized management method, which makes cloud services create high economic benefits. In the context of the Internet of Everything, application services require low latency, high reliability, and data security. The traditional cloud computing model (Fig. 3) can no longer efficiently process the massive data generated under the Internet of everything [17]. The main reasons are as follows [18]:

(1) Cloud computing is unable to handle the massive data with explosive growth. At present, big data processing has entered the era of edge computing centered on the IoE from the era of centralized processing centered on cloud computing. In the era of centralized big data processing, more is to centrally store and process big data. The approach taken is to build a cloud computing center and leverage the cloud computing center's superior computing power to centrally solve computing and storage problems. In contrast, in the era of edged big data processing, network edge devices generate massive amounts of real-time data. Moreover, these edge devices will deploy an edge computing platform that supports real-time data processing to provide users with a large number of services or functional interfaces, and users can call these interfaces to obtain the required edge computing services.

(2) Network transmission bandwidth load increases, leading to network delay. In the Internet of Everything environment, edge devices generate a large amount of real-time data, and cloud computing performance is gradually reaching a bottleneck. According to the Internet Data Center, by 2020, the total amount of global data will be greater than 40ZB. As the amount of data on edge devices increases, network bandwidth is becoming another bottleneck in cloud computing. Increasing network bandwidth alone does not meet the latency requirements of emerging Internet of Everything applications. For this purpose, performing some or all of the calculations on edge devices close to the data source is an emerging computing model that adapts to the needs of the Internet of Everything application.

(3) Marginal data involves personal privacy, which requires improved security protection. When users use e-shopping websites, search engines, social networks and so on, the users' private data will be uploaded to the cloud center. With the popularity of smart homes, many families install webcams in their homes. If video data is directly uploaded to the cloud data center, the transmission of video data not only occupies bandwidth resources, but also increases the risk of revealing user privacy data. To this end, for the data security problem of the existing cloud computing model, the edge computing model provides a better privacy protection mechanism for such sensitive data. On the one hand, before the user's source data is uploaded to the cloud data center, the data source is directly processed by the edge node of the near data end to implement protection and isolation of some sensitive data; on the other hand, the edge node establishes a functional interface with the cloud data, that is, the edge node only receives the request from the cloud computing center and feeds back the result of the processing to the cloud computing center, which can significantly reduce the risk of privacy leakage.

(4) Energy consumption of data transmission. As more and more user applications run in cloud computing centers, the demand for energy consumption in large-scale data centers will be difficult to meet in the future. To solve this energy consumption problem, the edge computing model proposes to decompose some computing tasks running on the original cloud data center, and then transfer the decomposed computing tasks to the edge nodes for processing. In this way, the computing load of the cloud computing data center is reduced, thereby achieving the purpose of reducing energy consumption.

Fig. 3. Traditional cloud computing models.

Currently, the linear growth of centralized cloud computing capabilities has been unable to match the explosive growth of massive edge data. A single computing resource based on cloud computing model can no longer meet the requirements of real-time, security and low energy consumption of big data processing. On the basis of the existing cloud computing model, the edge computing model emerges at the right moment. They complement each other and are applied to the processing of big data at the cloud center and edge to solve the problem of insufficient cloud computing services in the era of Internet of Everything. Edge computing refers to an open platform that integrates the core functions of network, computing, storage and application [19]. The edge computing model is shown in Fig. 4. Under the edge computing model, the main data processor is the edge device, and the cloud server is more used as the receiver of processing results. Therefore, the risk of privacy data exposure is effectively reduced [20].

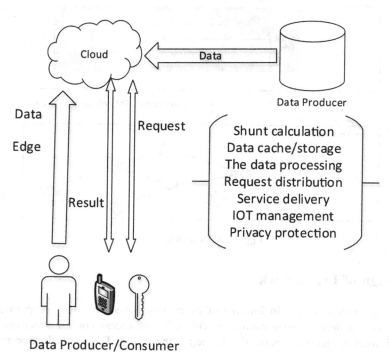

Fig. 4. Edge computing model.

With the rapid development of global network and communication, the traditional network has exposed many shortcomings: unclear division of service traffic, insufficient horizontal expansion ability, too large broadcasting domain, inability to quickly launch computing resources, and excessive network delay [21]. In 2008, clean slate research group of Stanford university proposed software defined network architecture (Fig. 5), which improved the shortcomings of traditional network [22]. SDN architecture has three layers: application layer, control layer and infrastructure layer. The SDN controller collects network topologies, calculates routes, creates and transfers flow tables, and manages and controls networks. Infrastructure devices only transmit traffic and execute policies. The normalized northern interface provides the required resources and services for the upper applications.

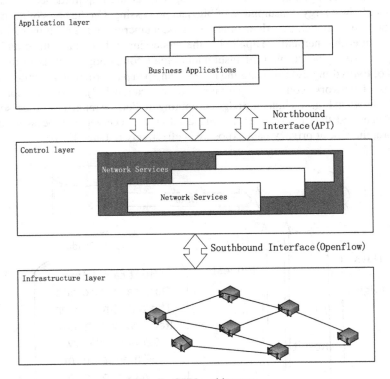

Fig. 5. SDN architecture.

4 Design of Framework

For identity authentication in Internet of everything based on edge computing, currently deployed technologies cannot provide efficient access control specification or authentication in traditional networks. In the framework of SDN, control plane and data plane are separated [23]. Administrators have the flexibility to control network traffic through centralized controllers without having to access physical devices. Centralized optimization of network resources, improve efficiency, simplify management, accelerate network innovation, shorten the start-up cycle of new functions [24].

This paper proposes a frame of reference to apply multi-factor identity authentication and SDN to edge computing [25]. Edge computing coordinator uses the nature of network management of SDN to conduct service discovery and choreography requirements of edge computing services. The centralized SDN controller has a global view of the network, and the edge computing coordinator can integrate with the SDN controller to collect information from the network [26]. The authentication module consists of a database server, an identity authentication server, a terminal and an application service provider. The database server stores the information of each network entity. Finally, multi-factor authentication method is used to complete the authentication, which includes password, fingerprint and digital certificate [27].

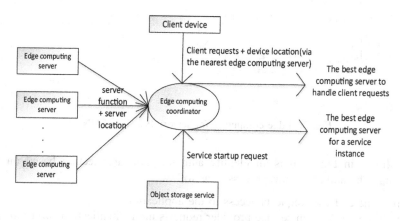

Fig. 6. Edge computing coordinator.

As shown in Fig. 6, edge computing coordinator is introduced to solve the limited computing capacity, critical latency, bandwidth and load balancing of edge computing servers. As a medium, edge computing coordinator connects applications to the right classes of edge computing servers [28].

As shown in Fig. 7, the edge computing coordinator is integrated with the SDN controller. Adding SDN can make the network more flexible and dynamic. Besides, the SDN controller can manage the edge computing coordinator northbound application, which can be programmed to handle a variety of situations. Therefore, edge computing coordinator can reuse SDN architecture. What is more, the northbound applications define the network behavior, SDN controller provides the northbound API for these applications to trigger commands. The controller also has a southbound interface (usually based on OpenFlow) that communicates with the managed device [29].

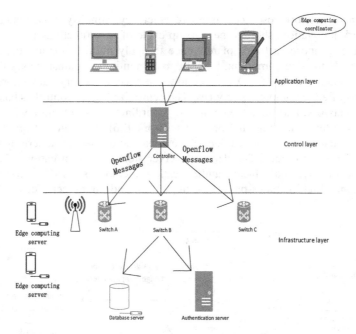

Fig. 7. Edge computing framework based on SDN.

As shown in Fig. 8, it is an identity authentication architecture based on edge computing. The authentication process is as follows:

Step 1: the end user requests access to the application;

Step 2: the application service provider requests the authentication server to verify the end user;

Step 3 and step 4: two-way authentication between the authentication server and the end user;

Step 5: the authentication server replies to the application service provider about the end user authentication results;

Step 6: the application service provider accepts or rejects the end user's request based on the authentication result of the authentication server.

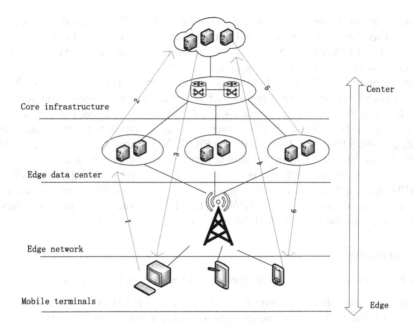

Fig. 8. Identity authentication architecture based on edge computing.

5 Formal Validation of Identity Authentication

The main authentication process is performed between the end user and the authentication server. For simplicity, only the authentication scheme between the user and the authentication server is described. Our scheme consists of the following three modules.

5.1 Registration

If an end user wants to become a valid user of secure applications on the Internet, they must register in advance. During the registration process, users should present their identity information to the authentication server for registration and apply for digital certificates from the authentication server. The main process is as follows:

(1) generate a pair of authentication server keys (SK_S, PK_S) based on the public key generation algorithm. SK_S is the private key of the verification server, and the corresponding public key is PK_S. After that, the verification server selects a robust security hash function $H(\cdot)$. Finally, the authentication server publishes its public key PK_S and hash function $H(\cdot)$ to all potential users.

(2) after obtaining the public key PK_S and hash function $H(\cdot)$, the user starts to register. Because fingerprint recognition is becoming more and more common, this paper adds fingerprint recognition to the authentication of users. First, after obtaining the user's fingerprint data b, the terminal calculates $Gen(b) \rightarrow (U,V)$. And let U become the user's private key SK_C, V is the public string produced

simultaneously, the corresponding public key is PK_C. Then the user sets ABC and PWD as the login username and corresponding password, and calculates M1 = E_{PKs} (ABC‖PWD‖PK_C‖H(SK_C)). In the end, the user sends M1 through the common channel to the authentication server.

(3) after obtaining M1, the authentication server decrypts D_{SKs}(M1) = (ABC‖PWD‖ PK_C‖H(SK_C)) with its private key SKS. Then the server verifies the legitimacy of ABC and PWD. If the authentication fails, the server will ask the user to send a new message, otherwise the server will give the digital certificate Cert = E_{PKc}(PWD‖ PK_C ‖PK_S‖Sig_{SKs}(PWD‖ PK_C ‖PK_S)). Finally, the server saves ABC, H(PWD), PK_C,H(SK_C) in the database and sends Cert to the user.

(4) after obtaining the Cert, the user decrypts D_{SKc}(Cert) = PWD‖PK_C‖PK_S‖Sig_{SKs} (PWD‖PK_C‖PK_S) through its private key SK_C. Then verifying the digital signature of the certificate—Sig_{SKs} (PWD‖ PK_C ‖PK_S), if successful, the user saves the certificate to the terminal and the registration process ends.

5.2 Verification

If a registered user wants to access the application, follow these steps:

(1) the user enters his user name ABC and password PWD in the login page.
(2) after obtaining the user name and password, the authentication server calculates H (PWD) and compares it with the information in the local database. If it is not equal, access is denied. Otherwise, go to step 3.
(3) the user enters his fingerprint on the client, using the fingerprint data b' and the help data V stored locally, and then the client calculates Rep(b', V) → U. The correctness of the fuzzy extractor method ensures that the string U is the user's private key SKC. The client calculates M2 = E_{PKs}(E_{SKc}(r1)), where r1 is a random number that sends the message M2 to the authentication server.
(4) after obtaining the message M2, the authentication server first encrypts it through its private key SK_S and the user's public key PK_C. Then the authentication server selects a different random number r2 and calculates M3 = E_{PKc}(H(SK_C)‖r1‖r2). Finally, the authentication server sends the message M3 to the client.
(5) after receiving the message M3, the client decrypts the message D_{SKc}(M3) = (H (SK_C))'‖r1' ‖r2. For receiving (H(SK_C))' and r1', the equation (H(SK_C))' = H (SK_C) and r1' = r1 need to be checked. The authentication server then computes the message M4 = E_{PKs} (r2) and sends it to the authentication server.
(6) after obtaining the message M4, the authentication server decrypts the message D_{SKc} (M4) = r2' and determines whether the equation r2' = r2 is true. If so, the authentication server accepts that the user is a legitimate user and allows him to access the application, otherwise access will be denied.

5.3 Cancellation

If a user does not want to use his digital certificate anymore, he can ask for the certificate to be canceled, as follows:

(1) the user calculates his digital certificate cancellation request Dele = E_{PKs} (ABC$\|$ PWD$\|$Sig$_{SKs}$ (ABC $\|$PWD)) and sends it to the authentication server.
(2) after obtaining Dele, the authentication server decrypts the message D_{SKc}(Dele) = ABC$\|$PWD $\|$Sig$_{SKc}$ (ABC$\|$PWD).

Signature ABC$\|$PWD and Sig$_{SKc}$(ABC$\|$PWD) will be verified later. If the signature cannot be verified, the cancellation request will fail. Otherwise, the authentication server changes the status of the user certificate to "cancel" by searching the records in the database of the keyword ABC. Finally, the authentication server sends the result of the cancellation request to the user.
(3) after obtaining the successful cancellation message, the client will delete the stored digital certificate, and the cancellation process is over.

Our proposed identity authentication scheme based on edge computing under the Internet of everything is multi-factor authentication. First, the account name ABC and password PWD are validated. Second, fingerprint data is validated to generate the correct private key for the end user. Finally, the end user's digital certificate is used in the interactive authentication process between the end user and the authentication server. Therefore, the proposed scheme has a high level of security and is difficult to break.

6   Conclusion

Under the Internet of everything, the traditional cloud computing model is no longer able to efficiently deal with the explosive growth of massive data, hence the emergence of the edge computing model. To solve the problem of identity authentication under the Internet of everything based on edge computing, this paper proposes a reference framework. It applies multi-factor identity authentication (including password, fingerprint and digital certificate) and software-defined network to edge computing, and formalizes the identity authentication process of the designed framework.

Acknowledgement. This work was supported by the National Key Research & Development Program of China (2016QY06X1205).

References

1. Shi, W., Sun, H., Cao, J., et al.: Edge computing: a new computing model in the Internet of everything era. Comput. Res. Dev. **54**(5), 907–924 (2017)
2. Cisco Global Cloud Index: Forecast and Methodology, 2016–2021 White Paper, 01 February 2018. https://www.cisco.com/c/en/us/solutions/collateral/service-provider/global-cloud-index-gci/white-paper-c11-738085.html
3. Cisco cloud index supplement. Cloud readiness regional details white paper (2017)
4. Evans, D.: The Internet of everything: how more relevant and valuable connections will change the world. Cisco IBSG **2012**, 1–9 (2012)
5. Zhang, J., Zhao, Y., Chen, B., Hu, F., Zhu, K.: Research review on edge computing data security and privacy protection. J. Commun. **39**(03), 1–21 (2008)

6. An, X., Cao, G., Miao, L., Ren, S., Lin, F.: Security review of intelligent edge computing. Telecommun. Sci. **34**(07), 135–147 (2018)

7. Han, W., Xue, J., Wang, Y., Liu, Z., Kong, Z.: MalInsight: a systematic profiling based malware detection framework. J. Netw. Comput. Appl. (125), 236–250 (2019). ISSN 1084-8045, https://doi.org/10.1016/j.jnca.2018.10.022

8. Han, W., Xue, J., Wang, Y., Huang, L., Kong, Z., Mao, L.: MalDAE: detecting and explaining malware based on correlation and fusion of static and dynamic characteristics. Comput. Secur. (83), 208–233 (2019). ISSN 0167-4048, https://doi.org/10.1016/j.cose.2019.02.007

9. Bangui, H., Rakrak, S., Raghay, S., et al.: Moving to the edge-cloud-of-things: recent advances and future research directions. Electronics **7**, 309 (2018)

10. Liu, J., Ming, M., Wang, H., et al.: Optimization method of attribute-based ciphertext access control for mobile cloud. J. Commun. **39**(373) (7), 43–53 (2018)

11. Roy, S., Chatterjee, S., Das, A.K., et al.: On the design of provably secure lightweight remote user authentication scheme for mobile cloud computing services. IEEE Access **5**, 25808–25825 (2017)

12. Badr, A.M., Zhang, Y., Gulfam, H., Umar, A.: Dual authentication-based encryption with a delegation system to protect medical data in cloud computing. Electronics **8**, 171 (2019). https://doi.org/10.3390/electronics8020171

13. Jin, B.W., Park, J.O., Mun, H.J.: A design of secure communication protocol using RLWE-based homomorphic encryption in IoT convergence cloud environment. Wirel. Pers. Commun. **105**, 599–618 (2018)

14. Dhillon, P.K., Kalra, S.: Multi-factor user authentication scheme for IoT-based healthcare services. J. Reliab. Intell. Environ. **4**(3), 141–160 (2018)

15. Zhang, X., Shao, Y., Sun, C.: Overall design of smart transportation for future cities. Urban Transp. (05), 1–7 (2018)

16. Mei, H.: Everything can be connected and everything can be programmed. Fangyuan (12), 58–59 (2018)

17. Liu, J., Xiao, Y., Chen, C.L.P.: Authentication and access control in the internet of things. In: International Conference on Distributed Computing Systems Workshops. IEEE Computer Society (2012)

18. He, W., Golla, M., Padhi, R., Ofek, J., Dürmuth, M., Fernandes, E., Ur, B.: Rethinking access control and authentication for the home internet of things (IoT). In: Proceedings of USENIX Security Symposium (2018)

19. Tu, Y., Dong, Z., Yang, H.: Key technologies and application of edge computing. ZTE Commun. **15**(02), 26–34 (2017)

20. Wang, F., Wen, H., Chen, S., Chen, L., Hou, W.: Protection method of mobile intelligent terminal privacy data under edge computing. Cyberspace Secur. **9**(02), 47–50 (2018)

21. Chen, Z., Guo, B., Zhang, Y.: MEC technology scheme and application analysis of 5G network edge computing. Mob. Commun. **42**(07), 34–38 (2018)

22. Qin, H., Liu, L.: Research on decentralized SDN access identity authentication. Appl. Comput. Syst. **27**(9), 243–248 (2018). http://www.c-s-a.org.cn/1003-3254/6509.html

23. Xu, F., Ye, H., Cui, S., Zhao, C., Yao, H.: Software defined industrial network architecture for edge computing offloading [J/OL]. J. China Univ. Posts Telecommun. 1–9 (2018). https://doi.org/10.19682/j.cnki.1005-8885.2018.0030

24. Tian, Y., Zhang, N., Lin, Y.-H., Wang, X., Ur, B., Guo, X., Tague, P.: SmartAuth: user-centered authorization for the internet of things. In: Proceedings of the USENIX Security Symposium (2017)

25. Wang, M.: A three-factor two-way identity authentication scheme in mobile internet. In: Proceedings of 2017 5th International Conference on Mechatronics, Materials, Chemistry and Computer Engineering (ICMMCCE 2017), Research Institute of Management Science and Industrial Engineering: Computer Science and Electronic Technology International Society, p. 5 (2017)
26. He, W., et al.: Rethinking access control and authentication for the home internet of things (IoT). In: Proceedings of the USENIX Security Symposium (2018)
27. Dong, H., Zhang, H., Li, Z., Liu, H.: Computational unloading of service workflow in mobile edge computing environment [J/OL]. Comput. Eng. Appl. 1–12 (2018). http://kns.cnki.net/kcms/detail/11.2127.TP.20181101.1416.033.html
28. Zhao, Y., Zhang, X.: New media identity authentication and traffic optimization in 5G network. In: 2017 IEEE 2nd Advanced Information Technology, Electronic and Automation Control Conference (IAEAC), pp. 1331–1334 (2017)
29. Fan, X., Lu, Z., Ju, L.: Security of SDN southbound channel. J. Beijing Univ. Electron. Sci. Technol. 24(04), 15–20 (2016)

STC: Improving the Performance of Virtual Machines Based on Task Classification

Jiancheng Zhao, Zhiqiang Zhu, Lei Sun, Songhui Guo,
and Jin Wu[✉]

Zhengzhou Information Science and Technology Institute,
Zhengzhou 450001, China
Wujin930716@foxmail.com

Abstract. Virtualization technology provides crucial support for cloud computing, and the virtual CPU (vCPU) scheduling in a virtualization system is one of the key factors to determine the system's performance. However, due to the semantic gap in the virtualization system, the mainstream current scheduling policy does not take the tasks' characteristics and spin lock into account, which leads to performance degradation in a virtual machine. This paper proposes a vCPU scheduling system STC (Virtual CPU Scheduling Based on Task Classification) in KVM to bridge the semantic gap. In STC, every virtual machine is configured with two types of vCPUs, among which the one with a shorter scheduling period is called the short vCPU (svCPU) and the ones with the default period are called the long vCPU (lvCPU). STC utilizes the Naïve Bayes classifier to classify the tasks, and the I/O-bound tasks are allocated to the svCPU, while the CPU-bound tasks are processed by lvCPUs. Correspondingly, in a host, two types of physical CPUs, the sCPU and lCPUs, are set to process the thread svCPU and lvCPUs. Moreover, lvCPUs adopt dispersive scheduling to alleviate Lock-Holder Preemption (LHP). STC improves the I/O response speed and saves the resources. Compared with the default algorithm, STC has achieved an 18% time delay decrease, a 17%–25% bandwidth improvement, and a 21% overhead decrease and ensured the fairness of the whole system.

Keywords: I/O virtualization · LHP · Virtual CPU scheduling · Task classification

1 Introduction

Cloud computing is a model for enabling ubiquitous, convenient, on-demand network access to a shared pool of configurable computing resources (e.g., networks, servers, storage, applications, and services) that can be rapidly provisioned and released with minimal management effort or service provider interaction [1]. With its development, Cloud computing emerges as one of the hottest topics in the field of information technology. Virtualization is crucial for cloud computing. For example, Amazon EC2 [2] and Microsoft Azure [3] are both typical cloud offerings that provide service in virtual instances. With virtualization technology, numbers of virtual instances, such as

© Springer Nature Singapore Pte Ltd. 2020
W. Han et al. (Eds.): CTCIS 2019, CCIS 1149, pp. 86–103, 2020.
https://doi.org/10.1007/978-981-15-3418-8_7

virtual machines (VM), can run on a physical server and effectively improve the utilization of resources.

However, in virtualization environments, there is a double scheduling phenomenon where the OS schedules processes on virtual CPUs (vCPU) and the hypervisor schedules vCPUs on physical CPUs (pCPU) [4]. Due to the semantic gap between the two schedulers, the hypervisor does not have information about the VM, and it introduces new problems that do not exist in no-virtualized environments, which include IRQ latency and Lock-Holder Preemption (LHP) [5]. The semantic gap keeps the hypervisor from having knowledge about the tasks in VMs and tracking which I/O event is destined for which blocked tasks and degrades the responsiveness [6]. The semantic gap also leads to LHP, since the hypervisor lacks perceptions of which vCPU is holding locks. The vCPU holding a lock may be preempted, which does not occur in a non-virtualized environment. Furthermore, the vCPUs waiting for the spinlocks have to spin for a longer time, significantly increasing the synchronization latency and the unnecessary resource waste.

Recently, there have been many studies on how to bridge the semantic gap, which will decrease the delay of I/O-bound tasks in the virtualization environment and relieve the LHP to improve the performance. One of the major solutions is the optimization of the vCPU scheduling algorithm. However, most of the researches just focus on one of the problems. Moreover, most of the researches are based on Xen rather than KVM, which will become the mainstream in the future.

In this paper, we propose a solution called STC (Virtual CPU Scheduler Based on Task Classification) in the KVM to bridge the semantic gap, which involves three ideas. First, we design an adaptive task classifier to classify the tasks in every VM through the extraction of the tasks' behavioral features based on statistical learning theory (SLT). Second, we designate a physical CPU (in this paper, we designate CPU0) called sCPU (short CPU) and a virtual CPU of VMs called svCPU (short virtual CPU), which have shorter scheduling periods and time slices and are dedicated for I/O-bound tasks processing in the guest OS. With the tasks classified and processed in their mapping CPU, the I/O latency is reduced, and the performance is greatly improved. Third, we modify the scheduling policy among lvCPUs, which will relieve the LHP and avoid unnecessary overhead.

The rest of the paper is structured as follows. We explain the I/O latency in the virtual environment in Sect. 2, which is followed by the work related to our research in Sect. 3. In Sect. 4, we present the design of the STC. In Sect. 5, we describe the implementation of the STC based on KVM. The evaluation of the STC is shown in Sects. 6 and in 7, we summarize the paper.

2 Related Work

The mainstream vCPU scheduling algorithm can be divided into two categories. One is the scheduling algorithm of the scheduler in the kernel, such as the CFS (Completely Fair Scheduler) used by the KVM. The other is exclusively designed for the hypervisor, such as the BVT, SEDF, and the Credit used in Xen. The Credit and CFS are more widely used at present.

Credit is the scheduling algorithm that Xen supplies, and it is based on Credit where VMs share CPUs according to their weighting. The vCPUs of VMs have four states, which are IDLE, OVER, UNDER, and BOOST, while the VCPUs of BOOST will be executed first.

As the CFS's name implies, it is aimed at fairness, which embodies that the processes of the system can all be executed in a scheduling period. Every process is distributed a time slice with a length proportional to its weight. However, to avoid context switches being too frequent, the time slice is required to be not less than a minimum slice, for example 3 ms in Linux 4.1. The processes allocated to the CPU are sorted from small to large according to their virtual runtimes (*vruntime* in the kernel code), the rate of growth of which is inversely proportional to the weighting of the progresses, and the one with the minimum *vruntime* will be scheduled first. The CFS algorithm is a part of the Linux kernel code, which is concise and has a simple mechanism. It can better achieve fairness, and has good interactivity with the application and server in Linux.

Many studies [7–12] have provided solutions to improve VMs' performance. Wiseman et al. [8] proposed paired gang scheduling. Since the I/O-bound tasks make light use of CPUs when I/O or blocking communications are performed, the processors remain idle. Hence, for improving the efficiency of CPUs, the paper proposed the idea of matching pairs of gangs in which one is compute-bound and the other is I/O-bound. They will hardly interfere in each other's work since they use different devices. However, the classification that the paper gives does not work in some cases, and in particular, poling and busy waiting may mask I/O activity and make it look like CPU activity [8]. Xu et al. [9] propose vSlicer to improve the performance of I/O-bound applications in VMs. vSlicer introduces a new class of VMs called latency-sensitive VMs (LSVM) in which I/O-bound applications are run, and contrary to LSVMs are non-latency-sensitive VMs (NLSVM) in which CPU-bound applications run. Under vSlicer, LSVM is given a shorter slice and higher scheduling frequency, while NLSVM retains the default slice and scheduling frequency. Therefore, both the LSVMs and NLSVMs sharing a physical core will still obtain the same amount of CPU time. This ensures fairness, and because of a smaller time slice, LSVMs achieve shorter CPU access latency, which will improve the performance. Unfortunately, vSlicer does not provide specific rules of VM classification and classifies the VM using a static method. Liu et al. [10] optimize vSlicer and propose FLMS. Based on the Credit in Xen, FLMS adds a file called IO_Boost to identify the I/O load of vCPUs and redesigns the load balancing strategy, which optimizes the migration of vCPUs. However, in a real cloud environment, the mixed workflow is more common in VMs, and there is difficulty in classifying the class of a specific VM. Moreover, the overhead of classification may offset the improvements that are achieved. vTurbo [11] is presented, which is based on the shortcoming of vSlicer. Different from vSlicer, vTurbo is styled with tasks as the objects of study and classification. According to vTurbo, besides regular vCPUs, each VM is configured with at least a new class of vCPU called a turbo vCPU, which relies on the new class of CPU cores named turbo cores with high-frequency scheduling. Turbo cores and turbo vCPU cores are used for the timely processing of the IRQs, which will accelerate I/O processing for VMs. vTurbo develops a simple but effective scheduling policy by giving regular CPU cores and turbo core magnitudes different time-slices, and the small slice provides I/O-bound tasks with lower latency and higher system performance. However, vTurbo does not take the LHP into account, and scheduling among the same types of vCPUs follows the default algorithm of the host system.

Chen et al. [13] improve the Credit scheduler by monitoring vCPUs and dynamically scale the context switching frequency by applying variable time slices, which make it more adaptive for concurrent applications in consideration of the LHP.

The existing approaches are mostly based on Xen. In the adolescent years of cloud computing, Xen had been provided more concerns and widespread applications because Xen is closely integrated with the system and occupies fewer resources. However, Xen runs on physical hardware as a microkernel, and its development and debugging are both more difficult than operating system virtualization [14]. In 2015, six security vulnerabilities of Xen were stated, which result in several cloud providers such as AWS and LINODE restarting some of their servers, thus causing a wide range of effects and huge losses. As a lightweight virtualization management module, KVM is built into Linux, which allows it to directly interact with the hardware and realizes virtualization without modifying the operating system. Compared with Xen, the KVM is more flexible. Mainstream cloud providers are increasingly turning the technology from Xen to the KVM. In 2017, AWS announced a new EC2 instance called C5 and explicitly indicated that C5 uses a new EC2 virtual machine management program based on the core KVM technology [15]. The mainstream vendors of Linux products, Ubuntu and Red Hat, both have made clear their choice on the KVM. In addition, the KVM is also recognized as the default open source software hypervisor for the Open Source Virtualization Alliance (OVA).

Therefore, this paper proposes STC, a virtual CPU scheduling algorithm based on task classification in the KVM, which schedules the vCPUs while taking tasks' characteristics and LHP into account. STC will bridge the semantic gap and achieve virtualization performance improvement.

3 Motivation

The performance of I/O-bound tasks in the virtual environment suffers from degradation, and one of the most important reasons is IRQ processing latency [9] caused by the semantic gap. To explain the problem, we illustrate it with a simple example in Fig. 1. This scenario uses 3 vCPUs (vCPU1, vCPU2, and vCPU3) which belong to 3 VMs (VM1, VM2, and VM3), respectively, and an I/O-bound task runs on vCPU1. Three vCPUs have equal priority, and their priorities are same as the VMs, which all inherit the priority of the parent process QEMU. According to the CFS, three vCPUs are allotted to time slices proportionally, and thus, the time slices that three vCPUs obtain are the same, which are equal to $\frac{1}{3}$(scheduling period). Taking Linux 4.1 as an example, the scheduling period is 24 ms, and thus, under this circumstance, the time slice is 24/3 = 8 ms.

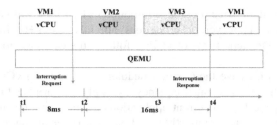

Fig. 1. I/O-bound task processing

We assume that the first slice (t1–t2) is allocated to vCPU1, and at t2, vCPU1 initiates an interruption request. Since the subsequent two slices (t2–t3 and t3–t4) are for vCPU2 and vCPU3, vCPU1 cannot receive the response until t4. For the I/O-bound task of VM1, the latency is approximately 16 ms (2 * *time slice*). To facilitate the analysis, we assume that there are only vCPUs in the CPU queue. Thus, latency is approximately equal to $((vCPU\ number - 1) * time\ slice)$. As mentioned earlier, the vCPUs of VMs have the same priority. Hence, according to CFS, the time slice is as follows:

$$time\ slice = \frac{sched\_period}{vCPU\_number} \qquad (vCPU\_number \le nr\_latency) \qquad (1)$$

$$time\ slice = \frac{sched\_period + \min\_granularity * (vCPU\_number - nr\_latency)}{vCPU\_number} \qquad (2)$$
$$(vCPU\_number > nr\_latency)$$

$nr\_latency$ is the maximum number of processes of the queue that are allowed to execute in a scheduling period, $sched\_period$ is a scheduling period and min_$granularity$ is the minimum slice allocated to the processes in the queue, which are both predefined in CFS. The relation between them is as follows:

$$nr\_latency = \frac{sched\_period}{\min\_granularity} \qquad (3)$$

If the number of processes is larger than $nr\_latency$, the *time slice* can be computed by following formula (2).

It suggests that we can lower the latency by decreasing the *time slice*, which is related to $sched\_period$ and min_$granularity$. Nonetheless, it will increase the costs if the *time slice* is too short since the more frequent context switches will hurt the performance of CPU-bound tasks, which is one of the reasons that $nr\_latency$ is predefined. Hence, a configuration with a shorter $sched\_period$ and min_$granularity$ cannot improve the overall performance.

We conduct a simple experiment to demonstrate the above analysis. In the experiment, 4 VMs with 3 vCPUs share a physical CPU. Each VM has two tests. The first is the Ping test with the same physical server in the same LAN, and the second is the AES encryption program, which is becoming a common CPU-bound task in the cloud. We conduct the experiment where the *sched_period* is 2.4 ms and 24 ms, and the corresponding min_*granularity* is 0.3 ms and 3 ms. The latter is the default value of *sched_period* and min_*granularity* in Linux 4.1. From Figs. 2 and 3, we can find that smaller *sched_period* and min_*granularity* achieve greater performance in Ping, while it is the opposite in the cryptography program. The experimental results agree well with the theoretical analysis and show that simply changing the *sched_period* and the min_*granularity* cannot improve the performance since mixed workloads are common in cloud environments.

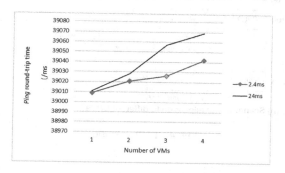

Fig. 2. Ping round trip time in different time period

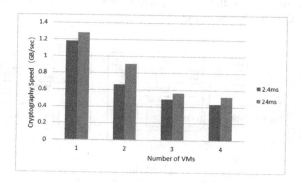

Fig. 3. Cryptography speed in different time period

As noted above, the semantic gap also causes LHP, which can be illustrated in Fig. 4. The scenario shown in Fig. 4 is that vCPU2 is the lock holder, and vCPU1 of the same VM is waiting for the lock. When the two vCPUs are allocated to the same CPU (CPU1), and vCPU2 is preempted by vCPU3, which is shown in Fig. 4(a). The waiting time of vCPU1 is equal to the sum of the executing times of vCPU2 and vCPU3. However, the waiting time is decreased when they are allocated to different

CPUs, as shown in Fig. 4(b). In this scenario, the waiting time of vCPU1 is equal to sum of the critical section and vCPU3's executing time, which is much less than that in Fig. 4(a).

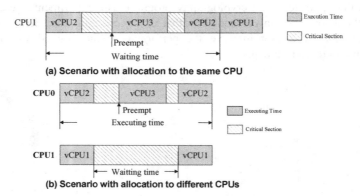

Fig. 4. LHP scenario

4 Design

We propose STC to improve the overall performance in the virtual environment. The framework of STC is as shown in Fig. 5.

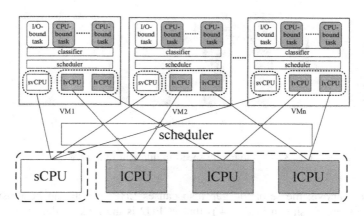

Fig. 5. Framework of STC

As the framework shows, we allocate two types of vCPUs, which are a short vCPU (svCPU) and long vCPUs (lvCPU). This step is performed during VM initialization. The svCPU is configured with short *sched_period* and min_*granularity* intended for

I/O-bound tasks processing, while the lvCPUs have the default configuration and process CPU-bound tasks. In the host, two corresponding types of CPUs are set, a short CPU (sCPU) and long CPUs (lCPU). In STC, the tasks of VMs are classified by the classifier and allotted to the corresponding vCPUs, which will be processed by the matched CPU in the host. Moreover, in order to alleviate LHP, we change the scheduling policy among lvCPUs by avoiding lvCPUs of the same VM from being allocated to the same lCPU.

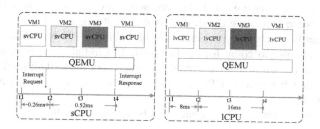

Fig. 6. I/O-bound task processing in STC

In STC, the I/O-bound task performances are improved without influencing the CPU-bound ones. As shown in Fig. 6, all I/O-bound tasks are allocated to the svCPU, which is configured with a shorter *sched_period* and min_*granularity* (e.g., 0.8 ms and 0.1 ms in Sect. 6). In the same scenario as that in the previous section, the latency of the I/O-bound task in VM1 is 0.52 ms, which is much lower than the previous 16 ms. Therefore, the I/O performance is greatly improved. The CPU-bound tasks are processed by lvCPUs with the default configuration, and hence, their performance does not degrade. Moreover, LHP can also be relieved since the dispersive allocation will reduce the waiting time of the lock waiter and improve the performance.

5   Implementation

A. *Task Classification*

In STC, different types of tasks are processed on different types of vCPUs, and we build a Naïve Bayes classifier to classify the tasks in VMs.

Naïve Bayes classification is a pattern recognition method based on the prior probability and conditional probability, with Bayes theorem as the basis. The Naïve Bayes classification has a small error rate, with the precondition that the properties are weakly correlated with each other [16, 17]. Moreover, it belongs to the generation model, and compared with the estimation model, its calculation is simpler, and it converges faster. Thus, it only requires a handful of data, a low memory footprint and few computing resources [18]. The two properties to be decided in the following pages are weakly correlated, which satisfies the application condition. Therefore, we classify the tasks of VMs utilizing the Naïve Bayes classifier. In STC, the tasks fall into two categories: I/O-bound and CPU-bound. The set of categories can be defined as follows:

$$C = \{I/O - bound, \quad CPU - bound\}$$

Characterizing the attributes of each category is also required in the classifier. In the KVM, when a I/O-bound task sends requests to the device, the function $qemu\_set\_irq$ $(qemu\_irq\ irq,\ int\ level)$ also needs to be accessed, which is the interface function used by the QEMU when emulating the device hardware. It suggests that if a task calls the function frequently when it is running, it is probably an I/O-bound task. We add a variable called $counter$ to count for the behavior. The initial value is 0, and when the function is called, the variable is updated by adding 1. For the CPU-bound tasks, one of the features is that it has high CPU utilization when running, which can also be an attribute of a task.

Given the above, the set of attributes can be defined as follows:

$$X = \{counter, CPU_{utilization}\}$$

For identification, we also add a flag $Cate$ in $task\_struct$ for the category mark, and tasks whose $Cate = 0$ are I/O-bound tasks, while ones with $Cate = 1$ are CPU-bound tasks.

When initializing the classifier, we input the training samples, which are collected from 20 common tasks. Early in the running time, all the tasks are treated as CPU-bound tasks by default and executed in lvCPU. To improve the adaptivity of the classifier and be more flexible in the cloud environment, the classifier is designed to periodically update the training samples. In particular, at the interval of T, 20 tasks in this period are randomly selected as the training samples to update the classifier, which is as shown in Algorithm 1 (Line 8–10). The CPU utilization uses a continuous value, which makes it difficult to directly obtain the probability. Therefore, in Algorithm 1, the four probabilities P(counter|I/O-bound), P(CPUU|I/O-bound),P(counter|CPU-bound), and P(CPUU|CPU-bound) are computed with the corresponding probability density functions, which are obtained by the training samples (Line 1–5). When classifying a task, its two attributes are plugged into these functions to get the probabilities, and then, with these probabilities, the probability of belonging to I/O-bound tasks and CPU-bound tasks (pro_task_IO and pro_task_CPU) can be obtained (Line 20–23). By comparing the two probabilities, the task's category can be determined.

Algorithm 1 Classification

Input: Sample={s1,s2,s3,...,s20}

task i={counter, CPUU} //Attribute features set of ith task

procate={procate_IO, procate_CPU} /*The probabilities of I/O-bound tasks and CPU-bound tasks*/

T /*A period updating the input sample*/

Output: task->Category

---

1 **Function** Sample_Probability(*Sample)

2   Normal_distribute_counter_IO(int counter,η_1,σ_1)

3   Normal_distribute_CPUU_IO (float CPUU,η_2,σ_2)

4   Normal_distribute_counter_CPU (int counter,η_3,σ_3)

5   Normal_distribute_CPUU_CPU (float CPUU,η_4,σ_4)

6 **end Function**

7 **Function** Classification NB(task i)

8   **if** timer==T

9   update Sample*

10   Sample_Probability(*Sample)

11   **end if**

12   p_counter_IO=Normal_distribute_counter_CPU(task i-> $counter,\eta_1,\sigma_1$)

13   /*Calculate p(counter|I/O-bound)*/

14   p_CPUU_IO=Normal_distribute_CPUU_IO (task i-> $CPUU,\eta_2,\sigma_2$)

15   /*Calculate p(CPUU|I/O-bound)*/

16   p_counter_CPU=Normal_disturibute_counter_CPU(task i-> $counter,\eta_3,\sigma_3$)

17   /*Calculate p(counter|CPU-bound)*/

18   p_CPUU_CPU=Normal_distribute_CPUU_CPU (task i-> $CPUU,\eta_4,\sigma_4$)

19   /*Calcluate p(CPUU|CPU-bound)*/

20   pro_task_IO=p_counter_IO * p_CPUU_IO * procate_IO

21   pro_task_CPU=p_counter_CPU * p_CPUU_CPU *

22   procate_CPU

23   **if** pro_task_IO > pro_task_CPU

24   task i->Category=0   /* task i is I/O-bound task*/

25   **else**

26   task i->Category=1   /* task I is CPU-bound task */

27   **end if**

28

B. *Task Scheduler*

We set the CPU0 and vCPU0 of every VM as sCPU and svCPU, respectively, whose *sched_period* and min_*granularity* are shorter than lCPU and lvCPU. In addition, the *sched_period* and min_*granularity* of lCPU and lvCPU are 24 ms and 3 ms, respectively, which are the default values in Linux 4.1. Different types of CPUs and vCPUs should be segregated, and it is not difficult to be achieved by changing the configuration file of the kernel in the host and the guests. Moreover, a category identification model is added into the scheduler of VMs. If the tasks are I/O-bound, they are allocated to vCPU0, while the CPU-bounds are allocated to other vCPUs except vCPU0. In the host, since the different types of CPUs have different scheduling periods, the scheduling algorithm should be modulated, as shown in Algorithm 2. The ratio of *sched_period* and min_*granularity* of sCPU to lCPU is α. If the CPU to be scheduled is sCPU, the *sched_period* and min_*granularity* are changed, and the realistic scheduling period can be obtained (Line 8–11). After determining the period, the slice of every task in the queue can be determined. Every time that a task runs out its time slice, it should update the *vruntime* of all tasks.

Algorithm 2 STC Scheduler

Require: *num sCPU* ≥ 1
Require: *num lCPU* ≥ 1
Require: *num vm* ≥ 1
Input : *ratio*
    sysctl_sched_latency   /*scheduling period of lCPU*/
    sysctl_sched_min_granularity   /*minimum slice of lCPU*/
    nr_latency= sysctl_sched_latency / sysctl_sched_min_granularity
/* maximum tasks in a scheduling period*/

1	**If** *CPU is sCPU*
2	*sysctl_sched_latency= sysctl_sched_latency/ratio* /* the
3	scheduling period of sCPU*/
4	*sysctl_sched_min_granularity=*
5	*sysctl_sched_min_granularity/ratio* /* the minimum slice of sCPU*/
6	*Calculate sum_period()*
7	**end if**
8	**If**(*sum of task* <=*nr_latency*)
9	*sum_period=sysctl_sched_latency*
10	**else**
11	*sum_period = sysctl_sched_min_granularity*sum of task*
12	**end if**
13	**Function** *Calculate time_slice()*
14	**Function** *Schedule()*
15	*triggered after another task is scheduled:*
16	*Update entity_se->vruntime*

C. *Dispersive Scheduling*

We change the scheduling policy in order to avoid lvCPUs of the same VM from being allocated to the same CPU. This will relieve LHP, which was proved in Sect. 3. It is not difficult to achieve by changing the CPU affinity in the host.

6 Evaluation

A series of experiments in this section evaluate the validity of the classifier and the performance and fair-share ability of STC. The hardware platform of our testbed has a quad-core processor configuration. The processor type is an Intel(R) Core(TM) i7-4790, 3.6 GHz. The total amount of physical memory is 8 GB with a 10-Gps network card. Our research work is based on qemu-kvm-1.5.3-126.el7 and Centos-7-x86_64–1511. Four VMs are established, all of which are configured with 1G memory and 3 vCPUs, 1 svCPU and 2 lvCPUs specifically, while in the host, there are 1 sCPU and 3 lCPUs. VMs all use the same operating system as the host. The updating period of the classifier is T = 10 s in the following experiments. As mentioned above, the *sched_period* and min_*granularity* of lCPUs are 24 ms and 3 ms by default.

To decide the *sched_period* and the min_*granularity* of the svCPU and sCPU, we evaluate the I/O performance by using Ping and IOzone [19]. IOzone is a benchmark to read/write a file from/to a disk and measure the throughput. The file size is 2G, and the record size is 2 MB. We record the throughput when the *sched_period* of CPU0 and vCPU0 is 24 ms, 8 ms, 2.4 ms, 0.8 ms and 0.24 ms, while the corresponding min_*granularity* is 3 ms, 1 ms, 0.3 ms, 0.1 ms and 0.03 ms. Meanwhile, we keep nr_*latency* unchanged. The experiment result is shown in Figs. 7 and 8, and the I/O performance is best when the *sched_period* and min_*granularity* are 0.8 ms and 0.1 ms, respectively, in which the network latency is the lowest and the file throughput is the highest. Based on the result, in this paper, the *sched_period* of the sCPU and svCPU is configured to be 0.8 ms, and the min_*granularity* is 0.1 ms.

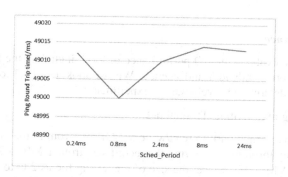

Fig. 7. Ping round trip time in different sched_periods

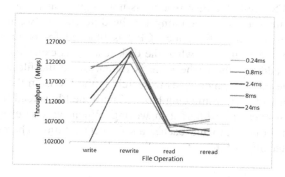

Fig. 8. File throughput in different sched_periods

A. *Classifying Veracity*

In the section, the tested VM is configured with three vCPUs (vCPU0, vCPU1, and vCPU2), and vCPU0 is a svCPU, while the other two are lvCPUs. In the experiment, different types of tasks run on the VM, including Super PI [20] and the AES encryption program, which are both typical CPU-bound tasks, and Ping and I/Ozone, which belong to I/O-bound tasks. Taking the time of feature extraction into account, we check that the vCPUs where each task is running on after tasks are running for 2 min and repeat the experiment 30 times. The results shown in Table 1 imply that the classifier is efficient and has high accuracy.

Table 1. Evaluation for classifying veracity

Task	vCPU0	vCPU1	vCPU2	Veracity
Super Pi	0	28	2	100%
I/Ozone	26	3	1	86.70%
Ping	28	1	1	96.70%
AESencrypt	0	5	25	100%

B. *I/O Performance*

In this section, we evaluate the I/O performance of STC, including the file reading and writing, the network bandwidth and latency. We use lookbusy [21] to keep the CPU utilization at the determined levels during experiments.

(1) File Reading and Writing Throughput

We use the I/Ozone benchmark to read/write a 2-GB file from/to the disk and measure the reading/writing throughput, varying the record size from 1 MB to 8 MB. Since the memory of each VM is 1G, we set the size of the testing file as 2 G to avoid the cache mechanism distorting the result. Figure 9 shows the reading and writing throughput in comparison with CFS. From Fig. 9, we can see that the disk write is improved by 15% compared with CFS, while the disk reading is non-significantly improved by approximately 5%. The main reason accounting for the difference between the writing and reading is that when reading files, the vCPU is blocked for periods of time while writing files are not. Specifically, when the disk reading is executed, read() is called. According to the address, the cache node is found. Since the file is larger than the memory, the cache misses, which leads to searching the file from the disk. The vCPU executes the reading to keep from being blocked until the file is read from the disk and read() returns. However, it is different in writing. When write is executed, write() is called, the file is written into the cache, and write() returns. Therefore, disk write throughput is better improved.

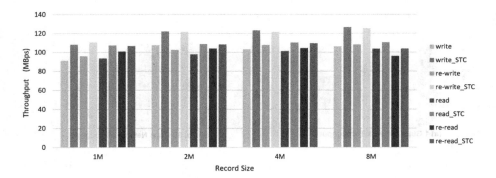

Fig. 9. File throughput evaluation

(2) Network Bandwidth and Latency

In the section, we use Iperf [22] and Ping to evaluate the network bandwidth and latency. Iperf is a benchmark for measuring the TCP/UDP throughput. We use Iperf to send a stream of UDP packets for 10 s to four VMs. The average throughputs (averaged over 10 runs) observed at the VMs are shown in Fig. 10. From both Fig. 10(a) and (b), we can see that the throughput of STC is higher than CFS by 17% to 25%, but it also suggests that the throughput starts to decrease when the number of VMs increases. The reason is that the packets first arrive at the host and are cached in the host. When the destination VM is scheduled, the host will forward the packets to its virtual port and write them to the VM's memory. However, the buffer in the host is limited, and hence, with the number of VMs increasing, the buffer fills up and packets will be dropped, thus causing the throughput to go down. To verify our analysis, we set the UDP kernel buffer (*net.core.rmem max* in kernel) to approximately 50 MB and repeat the experiment, and the results are shown in Fig. 10(c) and (d). The results show that the decrease eased as the VMs numbers changed.

A network latency test is also conducted, and its results are shown in Fig. 11. Compared with CFS, the latency of STC is lower by approximately 18%, thus proving that STC has better network performance.

C. *Computational Performance*

The section evaluates the computational performance utilizing the AES encryption program, and the result is shown in Fig. 12, which indicates that STC achieves the same level of performance as CFS. Therefore, STC can improve the I/O performance without impacting the computational performance.

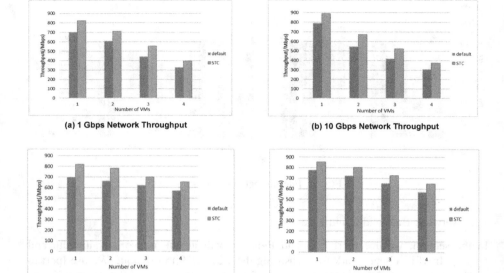

(a) 1 Gbps Network Throughput

(b) 10 Gbps Network Throughput

(c) 1 Gbps Network Throughput

(d) 10 Gbps Network Throughput

Fig. 10. Network throughput

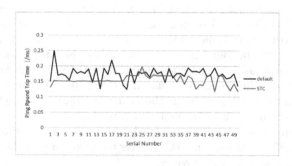

Fig. 11. Network latency

D. *Fairness Of Cpu Sharing*

We monitor the CPU utilization of each VM while running lookbusy in each VM, and we randomly select 5 moments to record them, which is shown in Fig. 13. The results show that STC maintains the same CPU sharing fairness as CFS. This is because STC only classifies tasks in VMs based on CFS, which do not change the resource allocation from a VM perspective. Therefore, STC inherits fairness from CFS.

E. *Parallel Performance*

In this section, we evaluate the parallel performance of STC by running a set of benchmarks from NASA Parallel Benchmark (NPB) [23], which consists of eight programs: EP (Embarrassingly Parallel), IS (Integer Sort), CG (Conjugate Gradient),

LU (Lower Upper Triangular), MG (Multi-Grid), FT (Fast Fourier Transformation), BT (Block Tridiagonal) and SP (Scalar Penta-diagonal). For these programs, the scale class of the problems can be specified by users, who are denoted as S, W, A, B, C, D, and E from the smallest to the largest (some classes are not available for some programs) [13]. The results are shown in Fig. 14, which shows the normalized standard deviation of the execution time of each program of NPB executed by CFS and STC. From the figure, we can see that for NPB programs, the standard deviation of STC is less than 21% of the CFS, thus implying the better performance of STC compared with CFS.

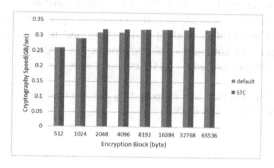

Fig. 12. Computational performance evaluation

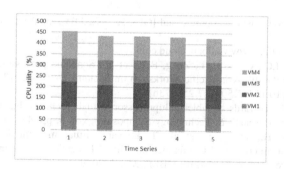

Fig. 13. Fairness evaluation of STC

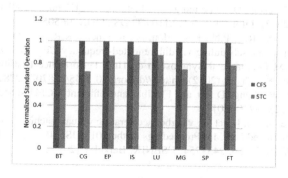

Fig. 14. Parallel performance

7 Conclusion

To bridge the semantic gap in virtualization, address I/O latency and allow LHP to improve the performance of VMs, we propose STC. More specifically, STC configures two types of vCPUs in every guest VM, which are a svCPU with a shorter *sched_period* and min_*granularity* and lvCPUs with a default *sched_period* and min_*granularity*. Meanwhile, the two types of vCPUs are processed by the corresponding types of CPUs in the host, which are the sCPU and lCPUs. A dispersive scheduling policy is adopted among lvCPUs to relieve LHP in STC. Our evaluation shows that STC can accurately classify the tasks. Compared with CFS, it achieves higher performance in I/O disk reading and writing and network performance, thus ensuring the high level of computational performance of VMs and fairness sharing. It also reduces the overhead caused by LHP and improves the performance.

Acknowledgment. This research was supported by the National Key Research Program of China under Grant No. 2012BAH94F03.

References

1. Mell, P., Grance, T.: The NIST definition of cloud computing. Commun. Acm **53**(6), 50–50 (2011)
2. Amazon. Amazon elastic compute cloud [OL]. Accessed 05 Aug 2010. http://aws.amazon.com/ecs2
3. AliCloud[OL]. https://www.alibabacloud.com
4. Song, X., Shi, J.C., Chen, H.B., Zang, B.Y., et al.: Schedule processes, not VCPUs. In: Proceedings of the 4th Asia-Pacific Workshop on Systems (APSys 2013), pp. 1–7 (2013). [https://doi.org/10.1145/2500727.2500736]
5. Uhlig, V., et al.: Towards scalable multiprocessor virtual machines. In: Proceedings of the Virtual Machine Research & Technology Symposium, vol. 3, pp. 43–56 (2004)
6. Kim, H., Lim, H., Jeong, J., et al.: Task-aware virtual machine scheduling for I/O performance. In: International Conference on Virtual Execution Environments, VEE 2009, Washington, Dc, Usa, pp. 101–110. DBLP, March 2009
7. Jin, H., Zhong, A., Wu, S., et al.: Research on virtual cpu scheduling in multi-core environment: problems and challenges. J. Comput. Res. Dev. **48**(7), 1216–1224 (2011)
8. Wiseman, Y., Feitelson, D.G.: Paired gang scheduling. IEEE Trans. Parallel Distrib. Syst. **14**(6), 581–592 (2003). https://doi.org/10.1109/TPDS.2003.1206505
9. Xu, C., Gamage, S., Rao, P.N., Kangarlou, A., Kompella, R.R., Xu, D.: vSlicer: Latency-Aware virtual machine scheduling via differentiated-frequency CPU slicing. In: Proceedings of the 21st ACM International Symposium on High Performance Distributed Computing, pp. 3–14. ACM, New York (2012). [https://doi.org/10.1145/2287076.2287080]
10. Liu, K., Tong, W., Feng, D., et al.: Flexible and efficient VCPU scheduling algorithm. J. Softw. **28**(2), 398–410 (2017)
11. Xu, C., Gamage, S., Lu, H., et al.: vTurbo: accelerating virtual machine I/O processing using designated turbo-sliced core. In: Proceedings of the 2013 USENIX Annual Technical Conf. (USENIX ATC 2013), pp. 243–254. USENIX, Berkeley (2013)

12. Jiang, W., Zhou, Y., Cui, Y., et al.: CFS optimizations to KVM threads on multi-core environment. In: Proceedings of the International Conference on Parallel and Distributed Systems, pp. 348–354. IEEE (2010). [https://doi.org/10.1109/icpads.2009.83]
13. Chen, H., Jin, H., Hu, K., et al.: Scheduling overcommitted VM: behavior monitoring and dynamic switching-frequency scaling. Fut. Gener. Comput. Syst. 29(1), 341–351 (2013). https://doi.org/10.1016/j.future.2011.08.006
14. Zhuang, J.: The designation and performance appraisement between virtualization solution of Xen and KVM. Beijing University of Technology, Beijing (2016)
15. https://amazonaws-china.com/cn/ec2/faqs/
16. Domingos, P., Pazzani, M.: Beyond independence: conditions for the optimality of the simple Bayesian classifier. In: Proceedings of the International Conference Machine Learning, pp. 105–112 (1996)
17. Dong, L., Wesseloo, J., Potvin, Y., et al.: Discrimination of mine seismic events and blasts using the fisher classifier, naive bayesian classifier and logistic regression. Rock Mech. Rock Eng. 49(1), 183–211 (2016). https://doi.org/10.1007/s00603-015-0733-y
18. Xuan, J., He, J., Ren, Z., et al.: Automatic bug triage using semi-supervised text classification. In: International Conference on Software Engineering & Knowledge Engineering, pp. 209–214. DBLP (2010)
19. IOzone Filesystem Benchmark. http://www.iozone.org/
20. Super Pi. http://www.superpi.net/
21. Lookbusy-a synthetic load generator. https://www.devin.com/lookbusy/
22. The Iperf Benchmark. http://www.noc.ucf.edu/Tools/Iperf/
23. NPB NASA. NAS parallel benchmarks. http://www.nas.nasa.gov/Software/NPB/

A Method for Realizing Covert Communication at Router Driving Layer

Jingsong Cui[1], Chi Guo[2(✉)], Manli Zhang[3], and Qi Guo[3]

[1] School of Computer Science, Wuhan University, Wuhan 430079, China
[2] GNSS Research Center, Wuhan University, Wuhan 430079, China
guochi@whu.edu.cn
[3] School of Cyber Science and Engineering, Wuhan University, Wuhan 430079, China

Abstract. The existing information hiding methods mainly focus on the analysis of the header field of the network protocol and the researches of VoIP. Well, the location of embedded covert data is easy to detect, its capacity is limited and the condition of covert communication is limited. In this paper, we propose a method which builds a covert channel between two routers for transmitting large-capacity information at the driver layer. The router is divided into sender and receiver, both of which mount our own driver and user application, intercept UDP packets generated during the user's voice or video call with instant message software. We analyze the UDP characteristics and construct UDP meta-model, and then split the secret information into the payload part of the meta-model with CRC check. The forged UDP is sent out with the common UDP traffic. The receiver router intercepts and identifies the forged UDP packets by CRC check and utilizes the obtained forged UDP to restore the original information. Moreover, we exploited WeChat and QQ voice call to conduct numerous simulations of covert communication, and successfully transmitted the secret information transparently from a network-restricted area to a more relaxed area of network supervision, verifying the concealment of the method.

Keywords: UDP packets · Covert channel · Instant message software · Router driver layer

1   Introduction

With the popularity of the Internet, there have been many security problems. How to ensure the security of data transmission over the Internet is an issue that needs to be urgently addressed. The existing methods for protecting data transmission are shown in Fig. 1, roughly including four fields: encrypt the network data, hide data in the static carrier, embed data in the redundant fields of network protocol, and embed data in the payload of voice packet. In detail, the mechanism of traditional information protection is to encrypt network communication. However, the encrypted data is disorganized and unusual, which is prone to cause the attacker's suspicions and will be attacked and destroyed. In addition, the static carrier such as image, text is not secure either, which can leave evidence for detection and is not real-time. Information hiding technology is

© Springer Nature Singapore Pte Ltd. 2020
W. Han et al. (Eds.): CTCIS 2019, CCIS 1149, pp. 104–118, 2020.
https://doi.org/10.1007/978-981-15-3418-8_8

an emerging technology. As one of information hiding, the covert channel was first proposed by Lampson [1]. He viewed covert communication as a process of communicating data, through a transferring channel that is neither designed nor intended. A covert channel is defined as a communication channel where information is transferred in a manner that violates the system security policy. As for covert channel, there are mainly two major areas. In the beginning, network protocols are popular used as carriers, where secret information can be embedded in fields such as redundant fields, fuzzy fields, extension bits, and padding bits for covert communication [2]. The fields that are often used to embed secret information include the ID of IP protocol, TTL, the ISN of TCP protocol, the time-stamp portion of the options field in the ICMP echo request, and so on. Because these fields are short in length (within 2 bytes), the secret information that can be embedded therein is limited. Moreover, the current covert channel detection can detect the hidden channel established by the network protocol, so the channel is not secure. Only a few researchers construct a covert channel through the payload of the audio packet (Lost Audio Packet [3]), but it has the risk of lost packets. And then more and more research tends to utilize the above methods to hide the secret information in VoIP streams, just as Fig. 1 shows. However, the effect of the covert channel based on VoIP voice stream depends on the specific speech coding format, and capacity is not very large.

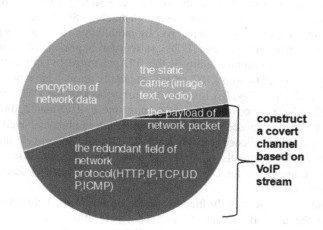

Fig. 1. Methods of protecting data transmission

The shortages in existing works motivate us to design a novel method. In this paper, we propose a method for realizing covert communication at router driving layer. The contributions of our work can be summarized as follows:

- We become the first one to realize a covert channel at router driving layer. At router driving layer, we utilize the Netfilter framework to intercept UDP packets, which is generated when the two parties use the instant message software to make a voice or video call. The system utilizes the UDP packets as carriers to mix the forged UDP.

- The covert channel has a large capacity. We take the intercepted voice UDP packet as a meta-model to construct a new UDP packet. The forged UDP is constructed by homomorphism using intercepted UDP as a meta-model. It keeps the header consistent and embeds secret information in the payload of forged UDP, which is much larger than information embedded in the specific field (about 2 bits) of the header of the network protocol.
- The covert channel has high concealment: the homomorphic construction allows forged UDP to be checked and modified by firewalls and NAT devices as well as instant message software dedicated servers. And there is no significant traffic change because covert Channel is only created when the usual UDP traffic is heavy.
- We have conducted numerous simulations of covert communication, and successfully transmitted the information transparently from a network-restricted area to a more relaxed area of network supervision, verifying the concealment of the method by installing soft routing as a security gateway on a multi-NIC computer.

2   Related Work

In recent years, relevant researchers have conducted a series of studies in the field of covert communications. Covert channels are characteristically categorized into covert timing channels (CTCs) [4] and covert storage channels (CSCs) [5].

CTC can transfer information to a receiver by modulating the timing behavior of an entity, such as the inter-packet delays (IPDs), or reordering packets of a packet stream. In this respect, the most common entity is the IPD generated by application [6]. Luo et al. [7] designed an IPD-based CTC which maintains normal burstiness patterns of TCP to ensure undetectability. To improve the robustness of the CTC, Wu et al. [8] proposed a CTC where the covert data was compressed by Huffman coding. Based on these, Zhang et al. [9] proposed a covert channel which modulates covert data by the postponing or extending silence periods in VoLTE traffic. Moreover, there are now ways to detect hidden channels in these locations. For example, Aiello et al. [10] proposed a profiling system for DNS tunnels which can be used to detect the covert channel based on DNS.

The researches on CSC mainly focused on the header of the network protocol and the payload of the network packet. Zander et al. [11] utilized TTL of IP header to construct a covert channel. They operate the TTL field of the continuous packet to embed the secret data. Dakhane et al. [12] used the IP ID reference model in the Linux kernel 3.0 to achieve covert communication. They took the Linux kernel and applications to generate new traffic into these packets (TCP), but this is a conceptual model without implementation.

What's more, there are many covert channels based on VoIP. Mazurczyk et al. [13] utilized the header field and data portion of VoIP packet to transmit authentication messages. They embedded the control commands into un-used header fields, and the data portion is embedded in the voice data. However, the embedded control commands are easily detected. Later, they provided a LACK method (Lost Audio Packets Steganography) [14], which provides a hybrid storage-timing covert channel by utilizing delayed audio packets. LACK uses the multicast of the RTP proto-col and sends the secret data to all the next nodes. LACK is suitable for LAN and has the risk of losing the secret information [15]. Hamdaqa et al. [16] applied a two-phase approach on the LACK steganography mechanism to improve reliability. Furthermore, Nair et al. [17] chose the payload length of the UDP packet as the carrier and realize a packet length channel in chatting applications. Liang et al. [18] proposed a covet channel scheme that communicates by rearranging the packet sending sequences. Their scheme focuses on building packet rearranging covert channel whose function is regardless of the variation on legitimate traffic. Schmidt et al. [19] exploited Voice Activity Detection, which suspends the transmission during the speech to reduce bandwidth requirements. Though they reduced and balanced the bandwidth during the speech, it is difficult to distinguish the noise and silence. These methods usually rely on speech coder and decoder and sometimes there are some errors in parsing and receiving secret data. Generally speaking, G.711 speech coding is more suitable to realize covert communication for VoIP.

In summary, none of them exploits the driving layer of the router and UDP packets generated by the instant message software's voice calling to implement covert communication.

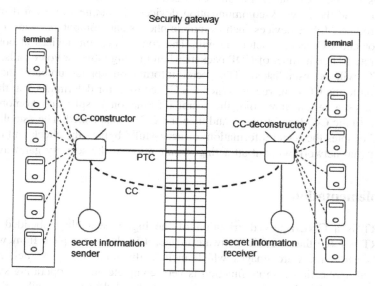

Fig. 2. Framework of covert communication

3 Covert Communication Modeling

The proposed system model for implementing covert communication at the router driver layer is shown in Fig. 2. The terms involved are explained as follows:

- PCC: public carrier channel, can transmit instant messaging voice data and can be used to hide secret information.
- CC: covert channel, is used to conceal information from one end to the other.
- CC-constructor: convert channel constructor, is the sending router that is used for homomorphism construction of covert information. Homomorphism construction refers to constructing a new UDP with the intercepted common UDP as a meta-model and embedding the secret data into the allowable position of the payload.
- CC-deconstructor: covert channel deconstructor, is the receiving router that is used to parse the received secret information.
- Security gateway: The security gateway sets a barrier between the internal network and the external network to prevent internal information leakage. It can protect the network by monitoring, limiting, and modifying the data traffic across the security gateway, shielding the internal information, structure, and operation of the network as much as possible. Specifically, the security gateway can analyze the packet, check the source and destination IP address, source and destination port, service type (such as HTTP or FTP), TTL value, domain name, etc., and monitor traffic changes and suspicious connections. Consequently, the security gateway protects data from being modified, inserted, deleted or replaced by unauthorized parties.

In this model. CC-constructor and CC-deconstructor mount our driver and user application, and the network communication devices can connect the wifi dispatched from the router. Mobile devices such as mobile phones and computers connect to CC-constructor and CC-deconstructor via wifi. The communication devices at both ends will generate a large number of UDP packets when making video or voice calls. At this time, PCC will be established. The secret information sender uploads the secret information to the CC-constructor. When the CC-constructor determines that the UDP traffic reaches a certain threshold, the secret information is split into homomorphic UDP, sent to the CC-deconstructor, and then the CC is established. The establishment of the CC enables the secret information to successfully bypass the check and transmit to the external network without attracting the attention of the security gateway.

4   Implementation

OpenWRT is a GNU/Linux distribution of the highly scalable embedded device. OpenWRT is more than a static firmware image, it is also a complete framework for building custom firmware images which include the boot loader, kernel, root file system, and applications. So its function is very complete and its operating system is easy to modify. Developers can customize an embedded system flexibly that only includes the features they need. In addition, OpenWRT system is more stable and more secure than others. Consequently, we take OpenWRT as the experimental platform. The method of implementing covert communication through OpenWRT mainly includes the following key points: UDP filtering, UDP construction and transmission, and packet information extraction, as shown in Fig. 3.

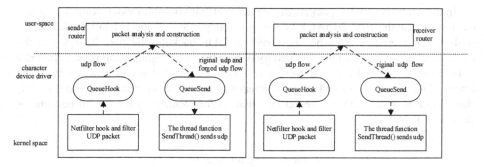

Fig. 3. Framework of covert Communication

In order to improve the stability of the system, an asynchrony should be achieved for drivers and applications. We used a time-stamp to prevent anomaly when the user application crashed unexpectedly. To prevent data interaction conflicts, we designed two circular queues to prevent the conflicts of hooked packets. If the queue is full, the last element will be discarded.

4.1 Protocol analysis

In this paper, we use the instant message software to make a secret information transfer when making a voice call. QQ and WeChat can use both TCP and UDP, but UDP is preferred. When the UDP protocol packet cannot be forwarded normally, they will select the TCP protocol.

After capturing the packets through the Wireshark soft-ware, it can be found that a large amount of UDP packets were generated during WeChat voice and video communications. Analysis of these UDP packets reveals that most of the information in the headers of both parties of the WeChat communication is identical to each other, which includes the source and destination physical addresses, the source and destination network addresses, and the source and destination port numbers, are the same. Therefore, we can use this identification information to construct a new packet that can be used to store secret information at the payload (payload refers to data part) field of the forged packet. The CRC check is performed on the secret information embedded in the payload, and the receiver can use the CRC check code to ensure the correctness of the data. Since the header information of forged packets is the same as that of the packets generated by WeChat communication, it helps the forged UDP pass the security gateway check and no connection anomalies emerge. And only when the UDP traffic passing through the sender router is very large, a small amount of constructed UDP traffic will be mixed in, so there will be no significant change in bandwidth. Moreover, forged UDP packets are not encrypted, so there is no clutter in the form. Even if the attackers intercept packets with secret information, they may also be regarded as ordinary WeChat communication packets. Consequently, the secret transmission is achieved.

In the analysis of UDP packets during the WeChat voice and video communication, we found that the first 20 bytes of the payload portion of these UDP packets have similar characteristics. So when constructing UDP packets, the first 20 bytes of the forged packet payload can be obtained by duplicating the original UDP packet. In order to facilitate the embedding and parsing of a large number of secret data, we fixed the length of the packet and filled the insufficient part with random numbers. And the CRC check code is added after the secret information for identifying the forged packets, as shown in Table 1.

Table 1. Forged packet forma

20 Bytes	The length of valid data	Valid data	Random number	CRC check code

4.2 UDP Filtering

Since WeChat voice and video communication mainly use the UDP protocol, it is necessary to filter out the UDP packets. To implement the filtering of UDP, we write a driver program. In the program, we call a hook function. Its main functions are as follows: the checkpoint packet is stored in Linux sk_buff structure; the head pointer of the data link layer is firstly obtained through the structure, judge whether the network layer protocol of the packet is IP protocol; if not, release the packet; if it is, move the pointer to point to the IP protocol header and judge whether the transport layer protocol of the packet is UDP protocol; if not, the package is released; if it is, the packet will be stored in a circular queue and wait for further processing.

Packets entering the router from outside all will go through the NF_IP_PRE_R-OUTING point; all packets sent from the router, including the packets forwarded by the router, will pass through the NF_IP_POST_ROUTING point before entering the network. Therefore, we can register the hook function for these two points that we can intercept all UDP packets generated during WeChat and QQ voice or video communication. In this paper, we register this hook function to the NF_IP_POST_ROUTING point. The reasons for selecting this point will be explained in the next chapter. By mounting the driver program on the OpenWRT router, we can achieve the operation of UDP filtering.

4.3 UDP Construction and Transmission

Because the router core has the low computing power and small storage capacity, the packet needs to be extracted from the kernel's address space to the user's address space for further analysis. In this paper, we adopt the device driver interface.

We extract the packets in the circular queue to user-space for further analysis. If it is found that there are multiple packets with the same physical address, network address, the port number of source and destination, or other the same key information, these packets can be considered to be generated by the voice or video communication of the instant message software. Using these key information, we can construct UDP packets that are very similar to that generated by the instant message software, and add secret information to constructed new UDP packets. These forged packets are mixed into common UDP data streams and sent back to the kernel. And finally, the kernel will reconstruct these UDP packets into the form of sk_buff structure and send them out to the destination.

Since NF_IP_POST_ROUTING point has a destination address translation function [20], we register a hook function here to filter all packets through this point. We analyze the intercepted packet and find that the source IP, destination IP, source port, and destination port have been changed while the physical addresses of the source and destination have not been changed. Therefore, we just need to do further processing of the physical addresses. Thus, the hook point NF_IP_POST_ROUTING is suitable for filtering UDP packets, which will result in less translation for us.

We write a new function for constructing packets in user-space. Taking the intercepted UDP packets as the meta-model, this function fills the corresponding ETH header, IP protocol header, and UDP protocol header into the same offset position of the forged packets and inserts the secret information in the payload. We check the secret information in the payload by CRC and then add the check code to the payload. For the ETH layer's physical addresses (source and destination), we modify them in kernel space according to the source and destination network addresses passed from user-space. The modification method is as follows:

- We search the ARP table according to the destination network address. If the destination is found, it is clear that the packet is sent to the local area network (LAN). The packet's destination physical address is changed to the physical address corresponding to the destination network address in the ARP table. The source physical address is changed to the same as that of LAN device. In the experimental environment, the network port of LAN network device is br-lan.
- If the destination network address of the packet is not found in ARP table, the packet will send to the wide area network (WAN). Then we look for the gateways IP in routing table; then we use the IP to search in the ARP table, and finally get the physical address of the gateway. We modify the destination physical address as the physical address of the gateway, and modify the source physical address as the physical address of the network interface of the WAN network device. In the experiment, the network port of the WAN network device is eth0.2.

In addition, the checksum also needs to be recalculated. In the driver, the skb_checksum, ip_fast_csum, and csum_tcpudp_magic functions are called to calculate the checksum. After the packet is constructed, it is sent by the dev_queue_xmit function. For intercepted UDP packets, the source and destination physical address of the ETH layer is also replaced as described above and then released.

4.4 Packet Information Extraction

As same as packet filtering, we need to filter out UDP packets through the router. We used the same driver program and mount it on the receiver's router. After the UDP packet is intercepted, it is extracted from the kernel space to user-space for analyzing.

In user-space, we perform CRC check on the data in the payload and then extract the packet with the successful verification, and merge and restore the packets to complete the secret information extraction. Packets that failed the verification are sent back to the kernel, which achieves the purpose of not affecting the normal UDP traffic transmission. As described in Sect. 4.3 the header of the constructed packet and the specific header of the payload field are consistent with the normal UDP traffic, so they are not detected and recognized by the security gateway. Forged packets are not encrypted and in a normal form, so they won't attract the attention of an attacker. Even if an attacker modifies or deletes our packet, the receiving router will release the modified UDP when there is an error verification of the CRC check.

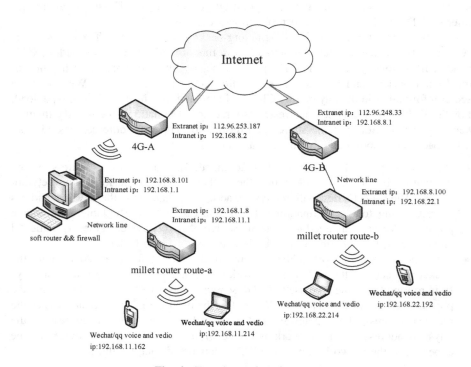

Fig. 4. Experimental environment

5 Experiment Result

In order to verify the feasibility and the concealment of the covert communication proposed in this paper, we conducted the following experiments. The experiments used CC-constructor and CC-deconstructor that were installed OpenWRT system. In the experiment, we applied the character device driver to exchange information between the kernel and user-space. We took WeChat and QQ as the instant message software to make a voice call for generating a large amount of UDP packets. We simulated the real work environment by using the method shown in Fig. 4: 4G-A and 4G-B are ordinary 4G routers that can connect to the Internet. Route-a and route-b are routers with

OpenWRT system which installed driver and user app that we have written. Two mobile phones are used to make video or voice calls in the wifi environment of CC-constructor and CC-deconstructor to simulate real communication. The construction of the security gateway: in the experiment, we performed the following settings to simulate the security gateway. The 64bit Windows 7, which installed with the grass soft router, was used for the security gateway. The grass soft router can perform an online audit, flow control, and some communication behavior control. We set the grass soft router to prevent the interception of outgoing UDP data from port 8000 to port 9000 with IP addresses of 192.168.1.100-192.168.1.200. When the PCC was not established, the TCP/UDP debugging tool failed to send any data whose IP address and port number were within the range above. However, when the PCC was established, the data was successfully sent to the external network.

5.1   Packet Construction and Transmission

In user application, we split the complete secret information into pieces of data that can be sent. Replace the header of the forged packet (ETH header, IP header, UDP header, the first 20 bytes of payload) with the intercepted common UDP header. And then fill the secret data piece and CRC check code in the payload. The forged and com-mon packets are sent back to the kernel and will be reconstructed and sent to the destination. At the other end of the router, we also mounted the driver and intercepted the packet and forwarded it to the TCP & UDP test tool. We took the message "Uh-oh, I am a secret message-_-" for the example to show that how the secret message mixed into the usual message "Hello, this is an ordinary message as the carrier.". The usual messages were sent by the TCP & UDP test tool and the secret messages were generated by the user application. As shown in Fig. 5, all messages intercepted by the receiving router were transmitted to the TCP & UDP test tool.

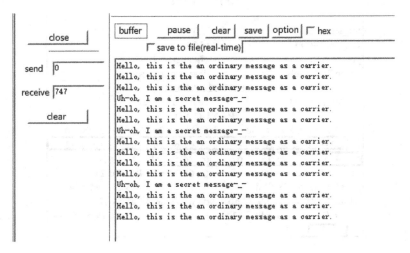

Fig. 5. Forged packets with specific flags

5.2   Packet Information Extraction

In user-space, we embedded information with the content "Uh-oh, I am a secret message-_-" to simulate the secret information. At the other party of the router, we also intercepted all UDP packets passing through the router, and uploaded the packet to user-space. In the user-space, we analyzed the payload field of the packet sent from the kernel and forwarded the valid data of the packet with the successful verification of CRC check to the TCP & UDP test tool. The result is shown in Fig. 6.

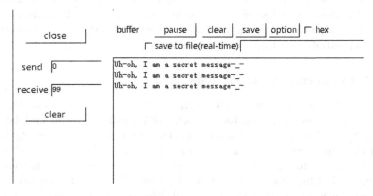

Fig. 6. Intercept forged packets

ETH HEADER	
DEST_MAC:	64:09:80:06:9e:06
SOURCE_MAC:	f4:83:cd:a7:73:30
IP HEADER	
version&hil:45	tos:0
tot_len:00a8	id:0
frag_off:4000	ttl:34
protocol:11	checksum:9905
src ip:7060fdbb	dest ip:c0a816c0
UDP HEADER	
source port:1f40	dest port:c872
PAYLOAD	
5b 00 8c 00 00 00 00 00 00	61 bb c4 28 00 00 00 00 00 00
00 55 68 2d 6f 68 2c 20 49	20 61 6d 20 61 20 73 65 63 72
65 74 20 6d 65 73 73 61 67	65 2d 5f 2d 00 25 64 2e 25 64
2e 25 64 2e 25 64 00 6c 6f	63 6b 20 65 e4 aa 8d 21 80 4c
94 35 b7 f9 d3 78 f7 d0 8c	d3 f0 c7 48 38 53 24 5e bb bc
ad 0a 1e d5 dc 1e b9 87 ab	da 07 f8 6e 3c af 68 10 27 5f e0
b3 33 d1 7a 7b 09 cd 9f 67	88 5c 14 93 7a e9 6f 99 a3 f6 44
7d a4 e8 fd 2d	

Fig. 7. Forged packets with specific flags

What's more, we showed the complete packet format including ETH header, IP header, UDP header and the pay-load on the router screen which was put in Fig. 7. The first rectangular box circled the valid data part (from 0x55 to 0x2d), and the second rectangular box circled the CRC check code (0xa4 0xe8 0xfd 0x2d).

5.3 Covert Communication Verification

In order to verify the concealment of the CC, we have con-figured a dual-NIC computer with a Windows7 system as the operating system and installed the grass soft router on it. The grass soft router is a firewall with routing function. Through the configuration, the computer can have the function of the router and firewall.

We first closed all apps on the mobile phone that connected to the router at the side of the grass soft router. At this time, check the number of connections and the connection information on the grass soft router. Then we turned on the WeChat or QQ on the mobile phone to make a voice call. The connection information and UDP traffic are shown in Fig. 8(a) to (d). In the connection interface of the grass soft router, there were some connections and UDP traffic when voice is generated. Then we mounted the driver and application on the OpenWRT routers at both ends. If we dial the WeChat or QQ voice again, we could find that the connection number and connection information are the same as the situation that we did not install the driver and the application. Moreover, UDP traffic change of these connections is not obvious. In Fig. 8(b), the connection between 192.168.1.8 and 157.255.132.53 showed that only 5 Kbps increased than that with no driver. As for the traffic of 233 Kbps, 5 Kbps is negligible. In Fig. 8(d), though the total traffic is smaller that WeChat, the traffic change can also be negligible. That is to say, the firewall does not detect new connections or significant traffic change when sending forged packets. This verifies that the communication is of high concealment.

seq	type	connection type	source IP	source port	dest IP	dest port	total traffic
1	other data	UDP	192.168.1.8	40753	157.255.132.53	16285	233Kbps(145Kbps/87Kbps)
2	QQ	UDP	192.168.1.8	4027	220.249.244.174	8000	200bps(0bps/200bps)
3	DNS	UDP	192.168.1.8	61158	180.76.76.76	53	0bps(0bps/0bps)
4	DNS	UDP	192.168.1.8	54824	180.76.76.76	53	0bps(0bps/0bps)
5	DNS	UDP	192.168.1.8	34911	180.76.76.76	53	0bps(0bps/0bps)
6	not determined	UDP	192.168.1.8	43896	193.228.143.23	123	0bps(0bps/0bps)

(a) dial WeChat voice

seq	type	connection type	source IP	source port	dest IP	dest port	total traffic
1	other data	UDP	192.168.1.8	40753	157.255.132.53	16285	238Kbps(148Kbps/82Kbps)
2	DNS	UDP	192.168.1.8	34911	180.76.76.76	53	0bps(0bps/0bps)
3	DNS	UDP	192.168.1.8	61158	180.76.76.76	53	0bps(0bps/0bps)
4	not determined	UDP	192.168.1.8	43896	193.228.143.23	123	0bps(0bps/0bps)
5	QQ	UDP	192.168.1.8	4027	220.249.244.174	8000	200bps(0bps/200bps)
6	DNS	UDP	192.168.1.8	54824	180.76.76.76	53	0bps(0bps/0bps)

(b) dial WeChat voice and send forgd UDP

seq	type	connection type	source IP	source port	dest IP	dest port	total traffic
1	QQ	UDP	192.168.1.8	53692	163.177.93.149	8000	122Kbps(50Kbps/71Kbps)
2	other data	UDP	192.168.1.8	48653	59.175.19.185	56191	2Kbps(944bps/1Kbps)
3	QQ	UDP	192.168.1.8	4027	220.249.244.174	8000	600bps(0bps/600bps)
4	DNS	UDP	192.168.1.8	27139	192.168.8.2	53	0bps(0bps/0bps)
5	DNS	UDP	192.168.1.8	34556	192.168.8.2	53	0bps(0bps/0bps)
6	DNS	UDP	192.168.1.8	14041	192.168.8.2	53	0bps(0bps/0bps)
7	DNS	UDP	192.168.1.8	57522	111.206.63.16	53	0bps(0bps/0bps)
8	DNS	UDP	192.168.1.8	55398	192.168.8.2	53	0bps(0bps/0bps)
9	DNS	UDP	192.168.1.8	58578	111.206.63.16	53	0bps(0bps/0bps)
10	DNS	UDP	192.168.1.8	55941	111.206.63.16	53	0bps(0bps/0bps)
11	DNS	UDP	192.168.1.8	55942	111.206.63.16	53	0bps(0bps/0bps)
12	DNS	UDP	192.168.1.8	56362	192.168.8.2	53	0bps(0bps/0bps)
13	DNS	UDP	192.168.1.8	14834	192.168.8.2	53	0bps(0bps/0bps)
14	DNS	UDP	192.168.1.8	64598	111.206.63.16	53	0bps(0bps/0bps)
15	DNS	UDP	192.168.1.8	65137	111.206.63.16	53	0bps(0bps/0bps)

(c) dial QQ voice

seq	type	connection type	source IP	source port	dest IP	dest port	total traffic
1	QQ	UDP	192.168.1.8	53692	163.177.93.149	8000	126Kbps(51Kbps/74Kbps)
2	other data	UDP	192.168.1.8	48653	59.175.19.185	56191	1Kbps(200bps/834Kbps)
3	QQ	UDP	192.168.1.8	4027	220.249.244.174	8000	534bps(0bps/534bps)
4	DNS	UDP	192.168.1.8	55941	111.206.63.16	53	0bps(0bps/0bps)
5	DNS	UDP	192.168.1.8	34556	192.168.8.2	53	0bps(0bps/0bps)
6	DNS	UDP	192.168.1.8	14041	192.168.8.2	53	0bps(0bps/0bps)
7	DNS	UDP	192.168.1.8	57522	111.206.63.16	53	0bps(0bps/0bps)
8	DNS	UDP	192.168.1.8	55398	192.168.8.2	53	0bps(0bps/0bps)
9	DNS	UDP	192.168.1.8	64598	111.206.63.16	53	0bps(0bps/0bps)
10	DNS	UDP	192.168.1.8	58578	111.206.63.16	53	0bps(0bps/0bps)
11	DNS	UDP	192.168.1.8	55942	111.206.63.16	53	0bps(0bps/0bps)
12	DNS	UDP	192.168.1.8	65137	111.206.63.16	53	0bps(0bps/0bps)
13	DNS	UDP	192.168.1.8	14834	192.168.8.2	53	0bps(0bps/0bps)
14	DNS	UDP	192.168.1.8	56362	192.168.8.2	53	0bps(0bps/0bps)
15	DNS	UDP	192.168.1.8	27139	192.168.8.2	53	0bps(0bps/0bps)

(d) dial QQ voice and send forged UDP

Fig. 8. Detected network connection

5.4 Performance

In the experiment, we used 1.09 MB information as test data to test the transmission efficiency. The constructed UDP contains 100Bytes of private data.

As shown in Fig. 9, it can be seen that with the sending speed becomes larger within 20 UDP/s to 50 UDP/s, the time for sending complete hidden information is gradually shortened. However, when the speed exceeds the 50UDP/s, the time required increases with the increase of the packet trans-mission speed. The anomaly is due to the fact that with the increase of the sending speed, the UDP loss is aggravated, and the time of resending UDP increase. The dotted curve in the figure indicates the number of packets received by the receiver per second. Therefore, the speed of receiving UDP decreases. In the entire system, the system efficiency is the highest when the UDP transmission speed is 50 UDP/s (5 KB/s). The number of UDP sent per second exceeding 50 will cause the communication to become blocked, and the UDP loss rate will increase, making CC-constructor and CC-deconstructor worse.

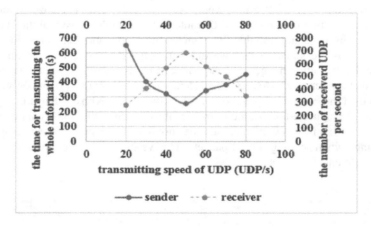

Fig. 9. The comparison of different information hiding

We also investigated other information hiding methods and compared them with ours. The results are shown in Table 2. It shows that information hiding in the field of network protocol' header is of high real-time but with a small capacity. The methods of JPEG and BMP are of low real-time and the capacity is not large too. By contrast, our method based on the router driver is of large-capacity and higher real-time.

Table 2. The performance of the existing covert communications

Information hiding methods	Carrier	Capacity	Real-time
The hiding in JPEG image	JPEG image	One byte per 2.5 bytes	Low
The hiding in audio	Audio	16 bps (phase coding)	High
The hiding based on LSB algorithm	24-bit BMP image	One byte per 8 usual bytes	Low
The hiding in IP header	The fields such as checksum, identification, TTL, TOS, etc.	About 2 bytes per TCP packet	High
The hiding in TCP header	The fields such as ISN, ACK, RST, etc.	One byte per TCP packet	High
The hiding in ICMP header	The field of time-stamp and ID	One byte per ICMP packet	High
Our method	The payload of a new constructed UDP	100 bytes per UDP packet (40 Kbps)	High

6 Conclusion

Based on the CC' large-capacity, we have first embedded the secret information in the UDP data stream generated by the voice or video call of the instant message software at CC-constructor. Furthermore, we add CRC check code in the payload of forged UDP at CC-constructor, and check the CRC code at CC-deconstructor for the extraction. The feasibility and concealment of the method have been perfectly proved through experiments. Furthermore, we have built firewall between CC-constructor and CC-deconstructor. No new connections or obvious data flow changes are detected, which can prove our method of high concealment. The downside of our system is that we have only studied two kinds of instant message tools WeChat and QQ to verify our system so the universality of our system still needs to be improved.

In a further study, we will analyze UDP data on more instant message software such as Skype, MSN, UC, and others to develop a self-adaptive covert communication system. In addition, our method is likely to be applicable to other Linux-based platforms. Therefore, we plan to investigate the possibility of applying our method to other router platforms to find its universalities, such as SuperWRT or RouterOS.

References

1. Lampson, B.W.: A note on the confinement problem. Commun. ACM **16**(10), 613–615 (1973)
2. Chuanchuan, G.: Research and implementation on the system of storage network covert channels detection, Ph.D. dissertation, University of Electronic Science and Technology (2016)

3. Mazurczyk, W., Szczypiorski, K.: Steganography of VoIP streams. In: Meersman, R., Tari, Z. (eds.) OTM 2008. LNCS, vol. 5332, pp. 1001–1018. Springer, Heidelberg (2008). https://doi. org/10.1007/978-3-540-88873-4_6

4. Luo, X., Chan, E.W.W., Chang, R.K.C.: TCP covert timing channels: design and detection. In: 2008 IEEE International Conference on Dependable Systems and Networks with FTCS and DCC (DSN), pp. 420–429. IEEE (2008)

5. Chow, J., Li, X., Mountrouidou, X.: Raising flags: detecting covert storage channels using relative entropy. In: 2017 IEEE International Conference on Intelligence and Security Informatics (ISI), pp. 25–30. IEEE (2017)

6. Zhang, X., Tan, Y.A., Liang, C., et al.: A covert channel over volte via adjusting silence periods. IEEE Access **6**, 9292–9302 (2018)

7. Peng, T., Liu, Q., Meng, D., et al.: Collaborative trajectory privacy preserving scheme in location-based services. Inf. Sci. **387**, 165–179 (2017)

8. Xiao, Y., Chen, H.H., Du, X., et al.: Stream-based cipher feedback mode in wireless error channel. IEEE Trans. Wirel. Commun. **8**(2), 622–626 (2009)

9. Zhang, X., Tan, Y., Xue, Y., et al.: Cryptographic key protection against FROST for mobile devices. Cluster Comput. **20**(3), 2393–2402 (2017)

10. Aiello, M., Mongelli, M., Cambiaso, E., et al.: Profiling DNS tunneling attacks with PCA and mutual information. Log. J. IGPL **24**(6), 957–970 (2016)

11. Zander, S., Armitage, G., Branch, P.: Covert channels in the IP time to live field (2006)

12. Zander, S., Armitage, G., Branch, P.: Dynamics of the IP time to live field in Internet traffic flows (2007)

13. Alsaffar, H., Johnson, D.: Covert channel using the IP timestamp option of an IPv4 packet. In: Proceedings of the International Conference on Electrical and Bio-medical Engineering, pp. 48–51 (2015)

14. Guan, X.X., Wang, C.D., Li, Z.G., et al.: Reliable and double-blind IP covert timing channel. J. Comput. Appl. **6**, 40 (2012)

15. Mazurczyk, W., Kotulski, Z.: New security and control protocol for VoIP based on steganography and digital watermarking. arXiv preprint cs/0602042 (2006)

16. Mazurczyk, W.: Lost audio packets steganography: the first practical evaluation. Secur. Commun. Netw. **5**(12), 1394–1403 (2012)

17. Nair, A.S., Kumar, A., Sur, A., et al.: Length based network steganography using UDP protocol. In: 2011 IEEE 3rd International Conference on Communication Software and Networks, pp. 726–730. IEEE (2011)

18. Liang, C., Wang, X., Zhang, X., et al.: A payload-dependent packet rearranging covert channel for mobile VoIP traffic. Inf. Sci. **465**, 162–173 (2018)

19. Schmidt, S.S., Mazurczyk, W., Keller, J., et al.: A new data-hiding approach for IP telephony applications with silence suppression. In: Proceedings of the 12th International Conference on Availability, Reliability and Security, p. 83. ACM (2017)

20. Yun, L.: Packet filtering algorithm based on netfilter under linux. Comput. Eng. **35**(11), 143–145 (2009)

A Secure Multi-party Signature Scheme Based on Trust Mechanism

Yage Cheng[1], Mingsheng Hu[1(✉)], Lipeng Wang[1], Yanfang Lei[1],
Junjun Fu[1], Bei Gong[2], and Wei Ma[1]

[1] Zhengzhou Normal University, Zhengzhou 450044, China
15652698433@163.com
[2] Beijing University of Technology, Beijing 100124, China

Abstract. Aiming at the problem of trust, we propose a secure multi-party signature scheme based on trust mechanism. In this scheme, we introduce a trust vector with time-stamped and form a trust matrix composed of multi-dimensional vectors to record the behavior of the participants periodically. Finally, a trusted evaluation mechanism is established for the participants. Under the premise of participant trustworthiness, a secure multi-party dynamic threshold signature scheme is constructed by secret sharing technology. The security analysis shows that the scheme can effectively suppress the vandalism of malicious participants. it is forward security and can resist mobile attacks. Performance analysis shows that the scheme has lower computational complexity and higher execution efficiency.

Keywords: Secure multi-party computation · Trusted mechanism · Trust matrix · Secret sharing · Threshold signature

1 Introduction

Secure multi-party computing (SMC) protocol is an academic field that is very active in cryptography. It has strong theoretical and practical significance. Broadly speaking, all cryptographic protocols are a special case of secure multiparty computing. It plays an important role in data mining, statistical analysis, privacy protection and confidential electronic voting etc. It was first proposed by Yao in the 1980s, which was an extension of the millionaire problem [1]. After extensive research by Goldreich et al. [2], secure multi-party computing has become a research hotspot in the international cryptography.

In [3], a secure routing decision scheme based on trust mechanism is proposed. This scheme introduces a trust vector to realize the collection of the evidence chain. The literature [4] sets behavioral trust and energy trust of the nodes to the same weight, and comprehensively considers historical behavior and existing behavioral to record the trusted behavior of the node. In [5], a rational secure multi-party computing protocol based on reputation mechanism is proposed. The scheme is based on Lagrange difference polynomial, which requires many polynomial calculations and is less efficient. The literature [6] proposes a weight-based way to calculate the trust value of the nodes.

W. Han et al. (Eds.): CTCIS 2019, CCIS 1149, pp. 119–132, 2020.
https://doi.org/10.1007/978-981-15-3418-8_9

There are many signature schemes based on secret sharing, such as the literature [7–9]. They can verify the credibility of the participant in the secret share generation stage but cannot verify the credibility of the participant behavior in the signature phase. The literature [10] is based on the Lagrange interpolation polynomial, which has a large amount of computation. The literature [11] is based on the bilinear pairing algorithm. The scheme requires bilinear pairing calculation in the signature and verification process, which makes the signature efficiency low. The literature [12] is based on a secure multi-party fair secret sharing scheme. In recovery phase, the scheme implements the privacy protection function through secure multi-party computing.

In the signature scheme based on trust mechanism, Literature [13] first proposed a conceptual model of "Virtual identity authentication based on trust delivery". The model proposes the establishment, authorization, storage and maintenance rules of trust to ensure the security of the virtual identity authentication process. Literature [14] designed a dynamic credibility evaluation model in a distributed environment. In this scheme the Shapley entropy is introduced into the process of credibility evaluation, so that the credibility evaluation result of the new scheme can more accurately reflect the dynamic behavior of the node. Literature [15] based on the basic automatic trust negotiation model combine with the idea of secure multi-party computing theory, proposes an automatic trust negotiation protocol based on secure multi-party computing to achieve privacy protection.

Based on the above research, this paper designs a secure multi-party signature scheme, introduces a trust matrix to record the participant's trusted behavior, and dynamically binds it to the signature process as evidence. Its overall structure is shown in Fig. 1:

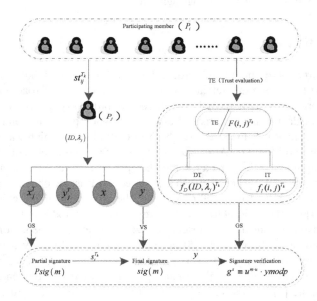

Fig. 1. Secure multi-party signature scheme based on trust mechanism

2   Prerequisite

2.1   Secure Multi-party Computation

Secure Multi-party Computation [16] is used to solve the problem of privacy protection between a group of untrusted participants. It must ensure the independence of the input, the correctness of the calculation, and the confidentiality of the participants' privacy. It is an effective way to solve the privacy calculation problem between two or more participants. It can ensure that the participants complete the computing task without revealing the privacy data. The model is as follows:

Suppose that in a distributed network, there are a group of n participants $P = \{P_1, P_2, \cdots, P_n\}$ who do not trust each other. Each member has the secret data $x = \{x_1, x_2, \cdots, x_n\}$. The participants secretly input the secrets x_i, and cooperate with each other to execute functions $f : (x_1, x_2, \cdots, x_n) \rightarrow (y_1, y_2, \cdots, y_n)$. Finally, each participant gets their own output y_i. In this process, each participant cannot obtain any information from other participants except for their own output information.

In a secure multiparty computing protocol, the person who attempts to destroy the agreement is called an attacker. An attacker can corrupt a subset of participants, and depending on the type of attacker's corrupted participants, the attacker can be divided into two categories [17]:

Passive Attacker: If the corrupted are half-honest participants, that is, the attacker can only get the input, output and intermediate results of the corrupted participant, but it cannot change the input and intermediate results, nor can it stop the operation of the agreement, then the attacker called a passive attacker.

Active Attacker: The corrupted person has malicious participants, that is, the attacker can not only get the input, output and intermediate results of the corrupted participant, but also can cause the corrupted participant to change the input, the intermediate result information, and even can stop the operation of the agreement, then call this attacker an active attacker.

2.2   Asmuth-Bloom Secret Sharing Scheme

In 1983, Asmuth and Bloom [18] proposed the Asmuth-Bloom secret sharing scheme. It mainly includes three steps:

Initialize. Suppose DC is a secret distributor, $P = \{P_1, P_2, \cdots, P_n\}$ is a collection of n members, the threshold is t and the secret is S. DC selects a large prime $q(q > S)$, A is an integer, $d = \{d_1, d_2, \cdots, d_n\}$ is a strictly increasing sequence of positive integers, and d satisfies the following conditions: (1) $0 \leq A \leq D/q - 1$;   (2) $d_1 < d_2 < \cdots < d_n$;   (3) $\gcd(d_i, d_j) = 1, (i \neq j)$;   (4) $\gcd(d_i, q) = 1, (i = 1, 2, \cdots, n)$;   (5) $D = \prod_{i=1}^{t} d_i > q \prod_{i=1}^{t-1} d_{n-t+1}$.

Secret Distribution. DC calculation $z = S + Aq$, here, $z_i = z \bmod d_i$, DC send (z_i, d_i) to P_i as a secret share of P_i.

Secret Recovery. Any t members can recover secrets. After exchanging secrets between members, any member can establish the following congruence equations: $z = z_i \bmod d_i$. According to the Chinese remainder theorem, the congruence equation has a unique solution: $z = \sum_{i=1}^{t} \frac{D}{d_i} e_i z_i \bmod D$. Here, $\frac{D}{d_i} e_i \equiv 1 \bmod d_i$ So, we can find $S = z \bmod q$.

3 Proposed Scheme

This paper evaluates the credibility of participants by introducing a time-stamped trust matrix, and dynamically binds them to the signature process as the evidence to record the participants' behavior. Based on the trustworthiness of participants, a secure multi-party trusted threshold signature scheme was designed by using secret sharing technology and threshold signature scheme.

3.1 A Secure Multi-party Signature Scheme Based on Trust Mechanism

Key Generation

1. System initialization: $P = \{P_1, P_2, \cdots, P_n\}$ denotes a set of n members. p, q are large primes satisfy $\frac{q}{p-1}$. There is a strictly monotonically increasing positive integer sequence $d = \{d_1, d_2, \cdots, d_n\}$ satisfies the Asmuth-Bloom secret sharing scheme, and $D = \prod_{i=1}^{t} d_i$ is the product of the t smallest d_i. The threshold is t, and $g \in GF(p)$ is the generated element. m is the message to be signed. Published p, q, g, t, d, D.

2. Select the secret tag information: $P_i (i = 1, 2, \cdots, n)$ secretly selects the secret tag $st_{ij}^0 = (c_{i1}^0, c_{i2}^0, \cdots, c_{in}^0)$ and sends them to P_j , $(j = 1, 2, \cdots, n, j \neq i)$. At the same time, P_i keeps c_{ii}^0. Then calculate $st_i^0 = c_{i1}^0 + c_{i2}^0 + \cdots + c_{in}^0 = \sum_{j=1}^{n} c_{ij}^0$ and broadcasts $g^{c_{ii}^0}$ and $g^{st_i^0}$

3. Generate identity tag information: The participant selects the random number r_i and calculates $r = \sum_{i=1}^{n} r_i$, then broadcasts g^{r_i} and g^r. Let $ID_i = \lambda_i (\bmod d_i)$, and its solution is $ID = \sum_{i=1}^{n} \frac{D}{d_i} e_i \lambda_i \bmod D$, then the identity tag information of the participant P_i is (ID, λ_i). Here $\lambda_i = r + st_i^0$, and e_i satisfies $\frac{D}{d_i} e_i \equiv 1 \bmod d_i$.

4. Calculate verification information: Let $\mu_i^0 = st_i^0 + c_{ii}^0$, $\alpha_i^0 = \lambda_i + c_{ii}^0$, $\beta_i^0 = st_i^0 q + r$. According to the broadcast information $g^{c_{ii}^0}$, $g^{st_i^0}$ and g^r, if

$$\left(g^{\left(\alpha_i^0 - \mu_i^0 \right)} \bmod p \right) \cdot \left(\left(g^{st_i^0} \right)^q \bmod p \right) \bmod p = \left(g^{\left(\beta_i^0 \right)} \right) \bmod p,$$

then P_j receives the information $c_{ij}^0 (i \neq j)$ sent by $P_i (i \neq j)$.

5. Generate secret share: Then $P_j(j = 1, 2, \cdots, n)$ calculates its own secret share $ss_j^0 = c_{1j}^0 + c_{2j}^0 + \ldots\ldots + c_{nj}^0 = \sum\limits_{i=1}^{n} c_{ij}^0.$

6. Generate keys: $P_i(i = 1, 2, \cdots, n)$ calculate $x_i^0 = (ss_i^0 q + r_i) \bmod d_i$ together to generate the personal private key x_i^0. Then the public key of the participant is $y_i^0 = g^{x_i^0} \bmod p$. The system private key is $x = \sum\limits_{i=1}^{n} r_i \bmod p$, and the system public key is $y = g^x \bmod p$.

Trust Evaluation (TE)

A time-stamped trust vector is generated by dynamically updating interaction information between participants. Then, as the basis for the trustworthiness of the participants a trust matrix (TM) is constituted by the trust vectors. The specific process is as follows:

The trusted evaluation function is:

$$F(i,j)^{T_k} = \frac{1}{2} \left[f_D(i,j)^{T_k} + f_I(i,j)^{T_k} \right]$$

As shown above, $F(i,j)^{T_k}$ represents a trusted evaluation of participant i by $j(i = 1, 2, \cdots, n)$ during the k update cycle, which consists of direct trust and indirect trust. Direct trust (DT) $f_D(i,j)^{T_k}$ is the identity tag metric trust evaluation value of P_i, here $f_D(ID, \lambda_j)^{T_k} \subseteq \{0, 1\}$. The indirect trust (IT) $f_I(i,j)^{T_k}$ is the trust metric evaluation of P_j on P_i, here $f_I(i,j)^{T_k} \subseteq \{0, 1\}$. Let $f(x) = [x]$ be the rounding function, so $F(i,j)^{T_k} = \{0, \frac{1}{2}, 1\}$. Here T denotes the update cycle.

The direct trust calculation is based on the function $g^{\lambda_i} = g^r \cdot g^{st_i^0}$. If the equation $g^{\lambda_i} = g^r \cdot g^{st_i^0}$ is true, the participant identity information is credible, that is P_i is trusted then $f_D(i,j)^{T_k} = 1$, otherwise 0.

The indirect trusted calculation is determined by the verification equation

$$\left(g^{\left(\alpha_i^{T_k} - \mu_i^{T_k} \right)} \bmod p \right) \cdot \left(\left(g^{st_i^{T_k}} \right)^q \bmod p \right) \bmod p = \left(g^{\left(\beta_i^{T_k} \right)} \right) \bmod p$$

if the equation is true, then $f_I(i,j)^{T_k} = 1$,otherwise equal to 0.

The participant $P_j(j = 1, 2, \ldots\ldots, n)$ generates the trust vector TV by the trust value of P_i in cycle k.

$$TV_i^{T_k} = \begin{bmatrix} F_{i1}^{T_k} & F_{i2}^{T_k} & \cdots & F_{in}^{T_k} \end{bmatrix}$$

here $F_{ii}^{T_k} = 1$, and the trust vector of $P_i(i = 1, 2, \cdots\cdots, n)$ is formed into the trust matrix (TM) is a reliable judgment basis for the participant behavior.

$$TM_{ij}^{T_k} = \begin{bmatrix} F_{11}^{T_k} & F_{12}^{T_k} & \cdots & F_{1n}^{T_k} \\ F_{21}^{T_k} & F_{21}^{T_k} & \cdots & F_{2n}^{T_k} \\ \vdots & \vdots & \vdots & \vdots \\ F_{n1}^{T_k} & F_{n2}^{T_k} & \cdots & F_{nn}^{T_k} \end{bmatrix}$$

So, every participant P_i retains the credible estimates of the first k cycles of all participants.

$$TM_i^{T_k} = \begin{bmatrix} F_{i1}^1 & F_{i2}^1 & \cdots & F_{in}^1 \\ F_{i1}^2 & F_{i2}^2 & \cdots & F_{in}^2 \\ \vdots & \vdots & \vdots & \vdots \\ F_{i1}^{T_k} & F_{i2}^{T_k} & \cdots & F_{in}^{T_k} \end{bmatrix}$$

In cycle $k+1$, P_i update TM_i^k and save it.

$$TM_i^{T_k} = \begin{bmatrix} F_{i1}^1 & F_{i2}^1 & \cdots & F_{in}^1 \\ F_{i1}^2 & F_{i2}^2 & \cdots & F_{in}^3 \\ \vdots & \vdots & \vdots & \vdots \\ F_{i1}^{T_k} & F_{i2}^{T_k} & \cdots & F_{in}^{T_k} \end{bmatrix} \rightleftharpoons \begin{bmatrix} F_{i1}^{T_{k+1}} & F_{i2}^{T_{k+1}} & \cdots & F_{in}^{T_{k+1}} \end{bmatrix} = TV_{ij}^{T_{k+1}}$$

$$\downarrow$$

$$TM_i^{T_{k+1}} = \begin{bmatrix} F_{i1}^1 & F_{i2}^1 & \cdots & F_{in}^1 \\ F_{i1}^2 & F_{i2}^2 & \cdots & F_{in}^2 \\ \vdots & \vdots & \vdots & \vdots \\ F_{i1}^{T_{k+1}} & F_{i2}^{T_{k+1}} & \cdots & F_{in}^{T_{k+1}} \end{bmatrix}$$

When the participant is not trusted, it will be excluded.

Generating a Signature (GS)

1. $P_i(i = 1, 2, \cdots, t)$ select random numbers $P_i(i = 1, 2, \cdots, t)$, and calculate $u_i = g^{l_i \cdot \frac{\sum_{j=1}^t F(i,j)^{T_k}}{n}} \bmod p$. Then $P_i(i = 1, 2, \cdots, t)$ send it to P_j and broadcast it.

2. After P_j receive u_i, the intermediate variable $u = g^{\frac{1}{t}\sum_{i=1}^t \left(l_i \cdot \sum_{j=1}^t F(i,j)^{T_k} \right)} \bmod p = \prod_{i=1}^t g^{l_i \cdot \frac{\sum_{j=1}^t F(i,j)^{T_k}}{t}} \bmod p = \prod_{i=1}^t u_i \bmod p$ is calculated together by $P_j(j = 1, 2, \cdots, t)$.

3. $P_i(i = 1, 2, \cdots, t)$ calculate the partial signature $s_i^0 = m \cdot u \cdot l_i + w_i^0 \bmod D$ together, so the partial signature of each participant is (m, u, s_i), where $w_i^0 = \sum_{i=1}^t \frac{D}{d_i} e_i x_i^0 \bmod D$.

4. P_i co-calculates $s = \left(\sum_{i=1}^{t} s_i^0 \bmod D \right) \bmod q$ to generate the final signature $sig(m)$, then the signature of message m is $sig(m) = (m, u, s)$.

Verification Signature (VS)

P_i Verifies the equation $g^s \equiv u^{m \cdot u} \cdot y \bmod p$ by the system public key y. If the equation is true, the signature of the message m is valid.

Dynamic Update

Due to the existence of mobile attacks, an attacker may obtain somebody's private key of the participant through a long-term stable attack. However dynamically updating the keys of the participants' can effectively prevent mobile attacks and increase the security. The solution keeps the system public key unchanged during the whole update process, retains the function of using the system public key to access historical signature information. Set the update period to be T.

Every T cycle, the participants update secret tag $C^{T_k} = \left(st_{ij}^{T_k} \right)^{t \times t}$, and co-calculate the private key generation function $x_i^{T_k} = (ss_i^{T_k} q + r_i) \bmod d_i$, and then update the private keys $x_i^{T_k}$.

After the update is complete, the participants can also generate the signature according to the signature process 1–4.

3.2   A Secure Multi-party Signature Protocol Based on Trust Mechanism

Protocol: Trust-based secure multi-party signing protocol

Input: $P_1, P_2, \cdots, P_n$ enter the secret tag information $st_{ij}^{T_k}{}'$ and the random positive integers r_i and l_i.

Output: signature of message m.

1. Initialize to select system parameters. The participants select secret tag information $st_{ij}^{T_k}$ and random positive integers r_i and l_i.
2. $P_i(i = 1, 2, \cdots, n)$ co-calculates private keys $x_i^0 = (ss_i^0 q + r_i) \bmod d_i$, then the public key of P_i is $y_i^0 = g^{x_i^0} \bmod p$. The system private key is $x = \sum_{i=1}^{n} r_i \bmod p$, and the system public key is $y = g^x \bmod p$. Public y_i^0 and y.
3. The credibility of the participants are evaluated according to the trusted evaluation function $F(i, j)^{T_k}$, and the untrusted are eliminated.
4. P_i calculates $u_i = g^{l_i \frac{\sum_{j=1}^{t} F(i,j)^{T_k}}{t}} \bmod p$ and broadcasts it. Then P_i calculates the intermediate variable $u = g^{\frac{1}{t} \sum_{i=1}^{t} \left(l_i \cdot \sum_{j=1}^{t} F(i,j)^{T_k} \right)} \bmod p = \prod_{i=1}^{t} g^{l_i \frac{\sum_{j=1}^{t} F(i,j)^{T_k}}{t}} \bmod p = \prod_{i=1}^{t} u_i \bmod p$.

5. P_i calculates the partial signature $s_i^0 = m \cdot u \cdot l_i \cdot \dfrac{\sum\limits_{j=1}^{t} F(i,j)^0}{t} + w_i^0 \bmod D$, so the partial

   signature is (m, u, s_i), where $w_i^0 = \sum\limits_{i=1}^{n} \frac{D}{d_i} e_i x_i^0 \bmod D$.

6. P_i co-calculates $s = \left(\sum\limits_{i=1}^{n} s_i^0 \bmod D \right) \bmod q$ and generates the final signature $sig(m)$.

   Then, the signature of the message m is $sig(m) = (m, u, s)$.

7. P_i Verify the equation $g^s \equiv u^{m \cdot u} \cdot y \bmod p$. If it is true, the signature of the message m is valid.

8. Every T cycle, the participants jointly calculate $x_i^0 = (ss_i^0 q + r_i) \bmod d_i$ and get their own new private keys, and with the new private keys they execute the signature process from 1 to 7.

4   Correctness and Safety Analysis

4.1   Correctness Analysis

Theorem 1: The signatures generated by the participants jointly calculated are valid. According to the construction of the protocol, the private key of P_i is

$$x_i^{T_k} = (ss_i^{T_k} q + r_i) \bmod d_i.$$

Let
$$\alpha = ss_i^{T_k} q + r_i \tag{1}$$

so
$$x_i^{T_k} = \alpha \bmod d_j.$$

According to the Chinese remainder theorem, we can solve the congruence equations:

$$\begin{cases} x_1^{T_k} \equiv \alpha \bmod d_1 \\ x_2^{T_k} \equiv \alpha \bmod d_2 \\ \quad \vdots \\ x_t^{T_k} \equiv \alpha \bmod d_t \end{cases}$$

get a unique solution: $\alpha = \sum\limits_{i=1}^{t} \frac{D}{d_i} e_i x_i^{T_k} \bmod D$

Let $w_i^{T_k} = \sum\limits_{i=1}^{t} \frac{D}{d_i} e_i x_i^{T_k} \bmod D$

Then $\alpha = \sum\limits_{i=1}^{t} w_i^{T_k} \bmod D$

When $t > 2$, according to [19], $m \cdot u \cdot \frac{1}{t} \sum\limits_{i=1}^{t} \left(l_i \cdot \sum\limits_{j=1}^{t} F(i,j)^{T_k} \right) + \alpha < D$, so there is

$$s = \left(\sum_{i=1}^{t} s_i^{T_k} \bmod D \right) \bmod q$$

$$= \left[\sum_{i=1}^{t} \left(m \cdot u \cdot l_i \cdot \frac{\sum\limits_{j=1}^{t} F(i,j)^{T_k}}{t} + w_i^{T_k} \right) \bmod D \right] \bmod q$$

$$= \left(m \cdot u \cdot \frac{1}{t} \sum_{i=1}^{t} \left(l_i \cdot \sum_{j=1}^{t} F(i,j)^{T_k} \right) + \alpha \right) \bmod q$$

From (1) $\alpha = ss_{ij}^{T_k} q + r_i$, we can get

$$s = \left[m \cdot u \cdot \frac{1}{t} \sum_{i=1}^{t} \left(l_i \cdot \sum_{j=1}^{t} F(i,j)^{T_k} \right) + \sum_{j=1}^{t} ss_{ij}^{T_k} q + r_i \right] \bmod q$$

$$= \left(m \cdot u \cdot \frac{1}{t} \sum_{i=1}^{n} \left(l_i \cdot \sum_{j=1}^{t} F(i,j)^{T_k} \right) + \sum_{i=1}^{t} r_i \right) \bmod q$$

So

$$g^s \equiv g^{m \cdot u \cdot \frac{1}{t} \sum\limits_{i=1}^{t} \left(l_i \cdot \sum\limits_{j=1}^{t} F(i,j)^{T_k} \right) + \sum\limits_{i=1}^{t} r_i} \bmod p$$

$$\equiv g^{m \cdot u \cdot \frac{1}{t} \sum\limits_{i=1}^{t} \left(l_i \cdot \sum\limits_{j=1}^{t} F(i,j)^{T_k} \right)} \cdot g^{\sum\limits_{i=1}^{t} r_i} \bmod p$$

$$\equiv u^{m \cdot u} \cdot y \bmod p$$

If the equation is established by verification, we can say that the signature is valid. So, the correctness of the agreement is proved.

4.2   Security Analysis

Theorem 2: It has the forward security.

The private keys of the participants were updated regularly to ensure the forward security.

Suppose that if an attacker who wants to get the private key $x_i^{T_k} = (ss_i^{T_k} q + r_i) \bmod d_i$ of participant P_i in cycle k, the attacker needs to obtain both the secret tag information $ss_i^{T_k}$ and the personal privacy r_i. He needs to calculate $ss_i^{T_k} q + r_i$, but $ss_i^{T_k} = c_{i1}^{T_k} + c_{i2}^{T_k} + , \cdots,$ $+ c_{in}^{T_k}$, which is obtained from the other participants $P_i(i = 1, 2, \cdots, n-1)$. It is difficult for an attacker to attack all participants simultaneously in a finite time to get $ss_i^{T_k}$.

The attacker may want to calculate $ss_i^{T_k}$ by $g^{ss_i^{T_k}}$, however the problem is based on the discrete logarithm problem that he cannot obtain it by calculation. Similarly, r_i is secretly selected by the participant, and the attacker cannot directly obtain it. The attacker may want to calculate $ss_i^{T_k}$ through the broadcast information $g^{ss_i^{T_k}}$, which also belongs to the discrete logarithm calculation problem, so it is difficult for the attacker to obtain it.

Therefore, it is difficult for an attacker to obtain the participants' private keys by calculating the discrete logarithm problem. It has the forward security.

Theorem 3: It is resistant to mobile attacks.

The mobile attack means that when an attacker successfully invades and controls a participant, he can transfer the attack target to other participants of the system. A mobile attacker may not be able to completely invade and control all participants in a short period of time, but if there is enough time, he can obtain almost all secret shares to damage the system security. So, it is necessary to update the private keys regularly to prevent the mobile attacks.

This paper is based on the (t, n) threshold secret sharing scheme, which requires at least t thresholds for solving congruence equations. Less than t cannot be solved. So, only the attacker successfully invades t or more participants in the same period, which may affect the security of the system.

Suppose an attacker invades in k cycle, and the private key of P_i is $x_i^{T_k} = (ss_i^{T_k}q + r_i) \bmod d_i$. If the attacker wants to obtain the private key, it is necessary to obtain the secret tag $ss_i^{T_k}$ and the random number r_i of t members simultaneously within the finite time. The attacker may intercept the broadcast information $g^{ss_i^{T_k}}$ and g^{r_i}, and try to calculate $ss_i^{T_k}$ and r_i to obtain the private keys. But through calculate $g^{ss_i^{T_k}}$ and g^{r_i} to get $ss_i^{T_k}$ and r_i are discrete logarithm problems, it is impossible for the attacker to calculate it within the effective time. So, it can effectively resist mobile attacks.

Theorem 4: Trusted evaluation mechanism can effectively identify malicious participants.

The trusted evaluation mechanism dynamically monitors the behavior of participants in times to ensure the participants are dynamically trusted.

The trusted evaluation function is

$$F(i,j)^{T_k} = \frac{1}{2}\left[f_D(i,j)^{T_k} + f_I(i,j)^{T_k}\right]$$

here $f_D(ID, \lambda_j)^{T_k}$ is the direct trust metric function, and $ID_i = \lambda_i(\bmod d_i)$ is the participant's identity tag. It has a unique solution $ID = \sum_{i=1}^{n}\frac{D}{d_i}e_i\lambda_i \bmod D$. If an attacker pretends to be a trusted participant to forge a pseudo-private key $x_i^{T_l} = (ss_i^{T_l}q + r_i) \bmod d_i$, according to the participant identity information, there must be $ss_i^{T_l} \neq ss_i^{T_k}$, $\lambda_i^{T_l} \neq \lambda_i^{T_k}$, so $ID' \neq ID$. Then, it can be judged that the participant behave is abnormally and it is not trusted. In addition, based on the Chinese remainder theorem to solve the congruence equations is a large modulus decomposition problem. So it is impossible for an attacker to solve e_i by D and d_i, then it is also impossible to obtain the private keys through the identity information ID of the participant.

In addition, $f_I(i,j)^{T_k}$ is the indirect trusted metric function, which is generated by interaction verification:

$$\left(g^{\left(\alpha_i^0 - \mu_i^{T_k}\right)} \bmod p\right) \cdot \left(\left(g^{st_i^0}\right)^q \bmod p\right) \bmod p = \left(g^{\left(\beta_i^0\right)}\right) \bmod p$$

due to,

$$\mu_i^0 = st_i^0 + c_{ii}^0, \ \alpha_i^0 = \lambda_i + c_{ii}^0,$$
$$\beta_i^0 = st_i^0 q + r, \ \lambda_i = st_i^0 + r_i,$$

So,

$$= \left(g^{\left(st_i^0 + r_i + c_{ii}^0 - st_i^0 - c_{ii}^0\right)} \bmod p\right) \cdot \left(\left(g^{st_i^0}\right)^q \bmod p\right) \bmod p$$
$$= \left(g^{r_i} \bmod p\right) \cdot \left(\left(g^{st_i^0}\right)^q \bmod p\right) \bmod p$$
$$= \left(g^{r_i} \cdot g^{st_i^0 \cdot q}\right) \bmod p$$
$$= \left(g^{r_i + st_i^0 \cdot q}\right) \bmod p$$
$$= g^\beta \bmod p$$

If it passes the verification, P_i is trusted. Then $f_D(i,j)^{T_k} = 1$ and $f_I(i,j)^{T_k} = 1$. So

$$F(i,j)^{T_k} = \frac{1}{2}\left[f_D(i,j)^{T_k} + f_I(i,j)^{T_k}\right] = 1,$$

otherwise it is 0.

5 Performance Analysis

5.1 Efficiency Analysis

The scheme is based on the Asmuth-Bloom secret sharing scheme, which mainly involves calculations such as modular multiplication, modular addition, and modular subtraction, and it requires only one inverse calculation. So, it reduces the computational complexity, decreases time consumption, and improves computational efficiency. Compared with the Shamir secret sharing scheme based on the Lagrange difference polynomial and the bilinear pairing operation, the scheme has obvious advantages.

For convenience of description, this paper defines the symbolic representation method of Table 1 below.

Table 1. Symbol description

Description	Symbol	Complexity representation
Logarithm operation	e	$o(e(x))$
Modular power operation	m	$o((lbn)^k)$
Modular inverse	u	$o((lbn)^{-1})$
Hash function calculation	h	$o(h(x))$

Table 2 is the comparison of the computational complexity of this paper and the literature [10] and [11]. The literature [10] is based on the Lagrange difference polynomial. It has higher polynomial order and complicated calculation, which leads to lower execution efficiency. In [11], a forward-and-secure signature algorithm is constructed by using bilinear pairwise properties. The scheme introduces bilinear pairwise operations and hash calculations when generating the signature. In the verification process, two bilinear operations are required to verify. It greatly increases the system calculation complexity and the execution efficiency.

From Table 2, we can find that the calculation efficiency of this paper is significantly higher than the others.

Table 2. Computational complexity comparison

Scheme	Signature generation	Signature verification
Ours	$t\left[o((lbn)^k) + 3o(\cdot lbn)\right]$	$o((lbn)^k) + o(\cdot lbn)$
Lit. [10]	$(4t+1)o(lbn)^k + 3o(h(x))$	$3to(lbn)^k + 2to\left((lbn)^{-1}\right) + o(h(x))$
Lit. [11]	$2to(h(x)) + 2to((lbn)^k) + to(e(x)) + to((lbn)^{-1})$	$t\left[2o(e(x)) + o(h(x)) + o((lbn)^k)\right]$

5.2 Simulation

The environment of the simulation experiment is: 64-bit, Window 10 operating system, MyEclipse2015 system, CPU is Intel Core i5-8300H processor, clocked at 2.3 GHz, memory 8 GB. The simulation experiment was carried out on the time overhead of the scheme and the literature [10] in the signature and verification phase. The result is shown below:

It can be seen from Fig. 2 that ours' scheme and the literature [10] both have an increasing trend with the increase of the number of members, this is because the signature process is positively related to the number of the members. From the experimental data, the literature [10] takes more time than ours' scheme. This is because the literature [10] requires bilinear pairing in the signature generation and verification stages, and the computational complexity is relatively high.

It can be seen from Fig. 3 that the efficiency of this paper is improved by about 90% compared with the literature [10], which greatly reduces the time overhead and improves the execution efficiency.

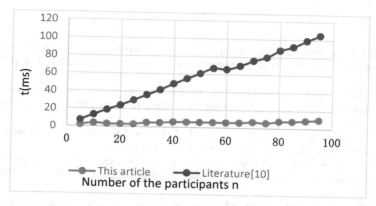

Fig. 2. Relationship between the number of members n and time overhead

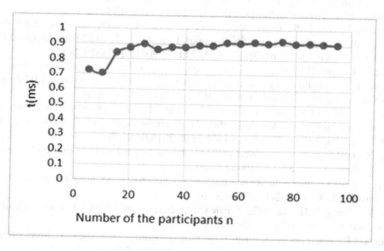

Fig. 3. Relationship between efficiency and number of members

6 Summary

Based on secure multi-party computing, this paper establishes a trust evaluation mechanism to detect the credibility of the participants. A time-stamped trust matrix is introduced to record the behavior of the participants, which is traceable. It has no trusted center and the secret shares are generated by the interaction among the participants, which has verifiable function. Regularly update the private keys to make it forward-secure and resistant to mobile attacks. And it is based on the Chinese remainder theorem, which reduces the computational complexity, has a small amount of computation, and improves the efficiency of execution.

References

1. Yao, A.C.: Protocols for secure computations. In: Proceedings of the 23rd Annual IEEE Symposium on Foundations of Computer Science, Piscataway, NJ, pp. 160–164. IEEE Press (1982)
2. Goldreich, O., Micali, S., Wigderson, A.: How to play any mental game. In: Proceedings of the 19th Annual ACM Conference on Theory of Computing, pp. 218–229. ACM Press, New York (1987)
3. Li, F., Si, Y.L., Chen, Z., Lu, N., Shen, L.M.: Trust-based security routing decision method for opportunity network. J. Softw. **29**(09), 2829–2843 (2018)
4. Qin, D.Y., Jia, S., Yang, S.X., Ma, J.Y., Zhang, Y., Ding, Q.: Research on secure routing mechanism of wireless sensor networks based on trust perception. J. Commun. **38**(10), 60–70 (2017)
5. Zheng, W.: Research on rational and secure multi-party computing protocol based on secret sharing under multiple mechanisms. Beijing University of Technology, Beijing (2018)
6. Jiang, J., Han, G., Wang, F., et al.: An efficient distributed trust model for wireless sensor networks. IEEE Trans. Parallel Distrib. Syst. **26**(5), 1228–1237 (2015)
7. Cheng, Y.G., Hu, M.S., Gong, B., Wang, L.P., Xu, E.F.: Dynamic threshold signature scheme with strong forward security. Comput. Eng. Appl., 1–13 (2019). Accessed 04 June 2019. http://kns.cnki.net/kcms/detail/11.2127.tp.20190417.1134.006.html
8. Cheng, Y.G., Jia, Z.J., Hu, M.S., Gong, B., Wang, L.P.: A threshold signature scheme applying for blockchain electronic voting scene, pp. 1–9 (2019). Accessed 04 June 2019. http://kns.cnki.net/kcms/detail/51.1307.TP.20190507.1540.002.html
9. Wang, L.P., Hu, M.S., Jia, Z.J., Gong, B, Zhang J.L.: Blockchain voting scene signature scheme based on Chinese remainder theorem. Comput. Appl. Res., 1–8. Accessed 16 June 2019. https://doi.org/10.19734/j.issn.1001-3695.2018.08.0566
10. Yang, X.D.: Research on improved verifiable strong forward security ring signature scheme. Comput. Appl. Softw. **30**(4), 319–322 (2013)
11. Xu, P.: Proactive threshold RSA signature scheme based on polynomial secret sharing. J. Electron. Inf. **38**(09), 2280–2286 (2016)
12. Fu, Z.Y., Zhang, Y.H., Xu, J.G.: A Fair secret sharing scheme based on secure multi-party. Math. Model. Appl. **7**(02), 30–35 (2018)
13. Wang, L.: Research on Mobile Business Virtual Identity Authentication Mechanism based on Trust Transfer. Beijing Jiaotong University, Beijing (2015)
14. Zhu, Y.W.: Research on Privacy Protection Technology and its Application in Distributed Environment. University of Science and Technology of China, Hefei (2012)
15. Wang, W.: Research on Automatic Trust Negotiation Protocol based on Secure Multi-party Computing. Hunan University, Changsha (2012)
16. Dou, J.W., Li, S.D.: Study on secure multi-party computing scheme for data equality problem. Acta Electronica Sinica **46**(05), 1107–1112 (2018)
17. Li, Q.: Research and Application of Secure Multi-party Computing Protocol. Shanghai Jiaotong University, Minhang (2003)
18. Asmuth, C., Bloom, J.: A modular approach to key safeguarding. IEEE Trans. Inf. Theor. **29** (2), 208–210 (1983)
19. Hou, Z.F., Tan, M.N.A.: CRT-basted (t, n) threshold signature scheme without a deeler. J. Electron. Inf. Technol. **11**(3), 975–986 (2015)

Virtual FPGA Placement with an Efficient Ant Colony Optimization

Yingxin Xu$^{(\boxtimes)}$, Lei Sun, Songhui Guo, and Haidong Liu

Zhengzhou Information Science and Technology Institute,
Zhengzhou 450001, Henan, China
xxyyxx151@163.com

Abstract. Virtualization allows integrating Field Programmable Gate Arrays (FPGAs) into a resource pool at the infra-structure layer. So as to improve the FPGA resource utilization while ensuring the quality of service, a virtual FPGA (vFPGA) Scheduling algorithm has been presented in our early work. At the meantime, we noticed that the initial deployment of vFPGAs has obvious effect on resource utilization ratio. Finding an optimal deployment of vFPGAs onto FPGAs which can be summed up in virtual FPGA placement (VFP) problem is a NP-hard problem. With a widespread of reconfigurable cryptographic resource pool, regarded it as a combinatorial optimization problem have offered higher efficiency than linear programming (LP) problem. In this paper, an optimized ant colony optimization (ACO) algorithm, where given ants the ability to perceive resource status, is presented to achieve the VFP goal. Finally, CloudSim toolkit is extended to evaluate our solution through simulations on synthetic workloads. The obtained results show that our algorithm can reduce the number of active FPGAs by improving the resource utilization.

Keywords: Cloud computing · FPGA virtualization · Virtual FPGA placement · ACO algorithm

1 Introduction

In the era of cloud computing and big data, the demand for centralized security services is highlighted. The major cloud security service vendors have proposed their cloud security solutions. AWS used hardware security module (HSM) to be responsible for user's private key and storage and management 1; Ali Cloud and Tass based on hardware cipher machines that have been recognized by the State Encryption Administration to provide tenants with a trusted data encryption service 2. Among these solutions, FPGAs and Application Specific Integrated Circuits (ASICs) are used to work as coprocessors of crypto-operations. On the other hand, FPGA virtualization technology allows division of a single FPGA device that supports partial reconfiguration into multiple vFPGAs. When tenants modify their demands, only one or more portions of the FPGA logic needs modifying while the remaining portions are not altered 3. In our early work, a reconfigurable cryptographic resource pool scheme has been put forward to provide tenants with crypto-operation service on-demand 4.

© Springer Nature Singapore Pte Ltd. 2020
W. Han et al. (Eds.): CTCIS 2019, CCIS 1149, pp. 133–143, 2020.
https://doi.org/10.1007/978-981-15-3418-8_10

In our scheme, vFPGAs are allocated according to the capacity of required crypto-operations such as AES, RSA, and MD5, specified by the customers and then run on a virtual cipher machine to work as coprocessors of crypto-operations. Through our Scheduling algorithm, vFPGAs is enabled to be consolidated automatically, and the FPGA utilization is at the ratio between 50% and 90%. However, during the experiment and evaluation stage, we found that the initial vFPGA placement strategy may have significant impact on the number of active FPGAs. So as to allocate the maximum number of vFPGAs in the minimum number of FPGAs, a substantially extension of research on VFP problem is needed.

For the resource utilization objective, The VFP problem is an NP-hard problem. It was solved as a linear programming (LP) problem at the first. With a rapid growth in the quantity of tenants, using heuristic methods such as genetic algorithm (GA) or ACO may offered higher efficiency. Particularly, the adoption of global shared pheromone in ACO allows the experience information to be spread rapidly among the colony and thus help the cooperation among multiple ants. This can enhance the global exploration capacity to receive better performance.

The contributions of this paper include the following aspects.

- In this paper, we first extensively study the ACO based algorithm for VFP optimization.
- We propose an ACO-based algorithm to reduce the number of active FPGAs while ensuring the quality of service (QoS).
- Synthetic workloads are created to evaluate our solution by simulations on the extended CloudSim [5]. The obtained results show that our algorithm can offer more efficiently use of FPGA resources without affecting the service level agreement.

This paper organized as follows. Section 1 describes the works of virtual resource allocation. Section 2 designs an ACO based algorithm for solving the VFP on the basis of system abstraction and modeling. Section 3 verifies the superiority of the proposed scheme by experimental analysis. Finally, we summarize the full text in Sect. 4.

2 Related Work

Several efforts have been made to solve the resource allocation problem for cloud computing. Linear programming was first used to the similar problems. For example, Speitkamp and Bichler [6] presented a mathematical programming approach that using various decision models to optimally the server placement. Teyeb et al. [7] presented two integer linear programming formulations for reducing energy consumption. Whereas the perceived lag of requirement changes often leads to imbalances allocation while using these static strategies. In [8], a virtual resource allocation problem is also formulated as an LP problem, solved with two greedy approximation algorithms to reduce energy consumption.

In comparison, heuristic methods such as genetic algorithm (GA) have offered higher efficiency in solving the VFP problem. Based on the multi-objective GA, an efficient framework is operationalized on a real cloud platform to minimize resource wastage [9]. In [9], a GA is applied to deal with FPGA placement problem to ensure the minimization of the critical path. A modified GA with the k-means clustering was developed for providing a good trade-of between effectively reduce energy consumption of Data-centers and sustained quality of service [11].

ACO is another heuristic approach that has been recently applied to these problems with good results. Yang et al. [12] designed an improved ACO by adding a performance perceptive strategy and changing the single ant pheromone update rule to avoid hardware resources competition and reduce the misleading. In [13], the ant colony system, a variant of ACO, coupled with a novel strategy for pheromone deposition is used to minimize the number of active physical servers from a global optimization perspective. The ACO-based algorithms proposed for energy efficient scheduling or tasking mapping still can be used for reference [14, 15].

On dynamically reconfigurable systems, several challenges have to be addressed, such as, reconfiguration overhead, communication bandwidth and resource utilization. To address these challenges approaches that are put forward from a general point of view, should be further optimization. Taking characteristics of FPGA into consideration is necessary when applied to the FPGA resource pool.

3   ACO Algorithm for Solving the VFP

In this section, we first define the VFP problem and establish the mathematical model; Then, a vFPGA deployment strategy based on ant colony algorithm is proposed.

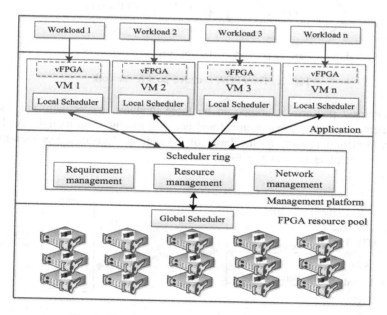

Fig. 1. Framwork of cryptographic resource pool.

3.1 System Abstraction and Modeling

In reconfigurable cryptographic resource pool, according to the infrastructure as a service delivery model, computing resources are provided to the tenant in the form of virtual machine (VM) instance. Each VM carries a vFPGA which is working as coprocessors of crypto-operations. The system can be divided into three parts: FPGA resource pool, management platform and application layer. The specific framework is shown in Fig. 1.

As it's shown in Fig. 2, the FPGA resource pool is a cluster of servers, where each server is supporting reconfigurable FPGAs as computing entities. By FPGA virtualization technology, each FPGA can be divided into multiple vFPGAs.

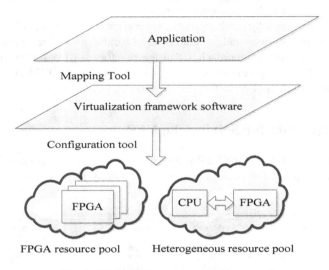

Fig. 2. The FPGA resource pool framework

Management platform is composed by three modules, respectively are resource management, requirement management and network management module. And monitoring information is used as the basis of scheduling decisions. Decision-making process of scheduling is shown in Fig. 3.

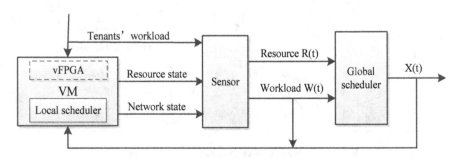

Fig. 3. Decision-making process of scheduling.

Firstly, management platform obtains system information, such as tenants' workflow, resource status, and network status, and forecast the workflow in the future;

Secondly, the global scheduler will solve the VFP problem by optimizing ant colony algorithm, and get vFPGA deployment matrix. The global scheduler is shown in Algorithm 1.

algorithm 1. Global scheduler

Algorithm 1: Global_Scheduler()
INPUT: R(t), W(t)
OUTPUT: X(t)
1 if $\mathbf{R}(t)$ & $\mathbf{W}(t)$ do
2   ACO($\mathbf{R}, \mathbf{W}, \mathbf{X}$)
3   partitions regions for f_j
4   allocate vf_{ij} to VM_j
5 done

Finally, the local scheduler, which is working within the VM, o dynamic reconfigures vFPGAs according to the tenant demand. Local scheduler is shown in Algorithm 2.

Algorithm 2. Local scheduler

Algorithm 2: Local_Scheduler ( )
INPUT: W(t), vFPGA
1 for $\forall vf_{ij}$ in f_j do
2   if $S^{t+1}_{vf_{ij}} \neq S^{t}_{vf_{ij}}$ then
3   partitions regions for vf_{ij}
4   end if
5   if $r^{t+1}_c \neq r^{t}_c$ then
6   reconfigure vf_{ij}
7   end if
8 done

In application layer, the workflow is produced by the tenants, and dynamic change with tenants' requirements. VFPGAs are provided to VMs to work as crypto-operation coprocessor.

Based on previous work, we establish a mathematical model by the entity abstraction. Parameters and their corresponding meanings are shown in Table 1.

The VFP problem for minimizing the number of active FPGAs is formulated as:

$$\min \text{Num}(K) = \sum_{i=1}^{N} \text{state}_i \tag{1}$$

Table 1. Parameter and meanings

Parameters	Meanings
$f = \langle f_i, \text{vf}, S_f, r_c \rangle$	FPGA
$vf = \langle \text{vf}_{ij}, S_{\text{vf}}, r_c \rangle$	vFPGA
$f_i \in \{f_1, f_2, \ldots, f_N\}, i \in \{1, 2, \ldots, N\}$	A set of FPGAs
$\text{vf}_j \in \{\text{vf}_1, \text{vf}_2, \ldots, \text{vf}_M\}, j \in \{1, 2, \ldots, M\}$	A set of vFPGAs
S_f	Number of logical units of the FPGA
S_{vf}	Logical units of the vFPGA
S_S	Logical units of the static area
S_D	Logical units of the dynamic area
K	vFPGA placement solution
$\mathbf{X} = [x_{ij}], i \in \{1, 2, \ldots, N\}, j \in \{1, 2, \ldots, M\}$	vFPGA placement matrix
state_i	FPGA status

subject to:

$$x_{ij} = \begin{cases} 1, & \text{if } \text{vFPGSA} \, j \text{ is assigned to FPGA } i \\ 0, & \text{otherwise} \end{cases} \tag{2}$$

$$\text{state}_i = \begin{cases} 1, & \text{if } \sum_{j=1}^{M} x_{ij} \geq 1 \\ 0, & \text{otherwise} \end{cases} \tag{3}$$

$$\sum_{i=1}^{N} x_{ij} = 1, \forall j \in M \tag{4}$$

$$S_{D_i} = S_{f_i} - S_{S_i}, \forall i \in N \tag{5}$$

$$\sum_{j=1}^{M} x_{ij} S_{\text{vf}_j} \leq S_{D_i} * 90\%, \forall i \in N \tag{6}$$

Communications across the FPGAs often leads to great overhead on bandwidth. Hence, we use constraint (4) to ensure that a vFPGA is assigned to one and only one of the FPGAs. In Constraints (5) and (6) 10% of the logic area is reserved to avoid aggressive migration that caused by prediction errors.

3.2   ACO Algorithm for Solving the VFP

The ACS was proposed initially for solving the traveling salesman problem (TSP). While the VFP problem in reconfigurable cryptographic resource pool is not a standard

TSP problem. For the requirements are changing dynamically, idle resources should be reserved to guarantee resource flexibility and avoid frequent migration. Therefore, a load-balancing method is added to our algorithm. We dramatically reduce pheromones to make overload nodes hard to be found, and moderately improve pheromones to encourage ants to assign vFPGA to underload nodes.

The overall flowchart of the optimized ACO algorithm is shown in Fig. 4, and is described in the following seven steps.

Step 1: Initializing pheromone matrix $\tau = \begin{bmatrix} \tau_{00} & \cdots & \tau_{0M} \\ \vdots & \ddots & \vdots \\ \tau_{N0} & \cdots & \tau_{NM} \end{bmatrix}$.

Step 2: Initializing the placement matrix. Set the feasible solution K_0 as placing the M vFPGAs on N FPGAs with $\lceil M/N \rceil$ vFPGAs mapping to one FPGA. Therefore, min Num$(K_0) = N$. Then generate and initialize an ant.

Step 3: Pairing vFPGAs and FPGAs. Probability of ant z placing vf$_j$ on f_i at time t can be calculated by formula (7). Among them, T_{vf} represents a table that contains the vFPGAs waiting to be placed, and T_f represents the FPGAs that haven't overload.

$$P_{ij}^z(t) = \begin{cases} \dfrac{[\tau_{ij}(t)]^\alpha [\eta_{ij}(t)]^\beta}{\sum\limits_{l \in T_f, T_{vf} \in vf} [\tau_{lh}(t)]^\alpha [\eta_{lh}(t)]^\beta}, & \text{if } j \in T_{vf} \\ 0, & \text{otherwise} \end{cases} \tag{7}$$

Step 4: Update T_f and T_{vf}. Assume that vf$_j$ is placed on f_i in step 3, remove it from T_{vf}. As for f_i, it will be removed from T_f when overload. If T_{vf} is not empty, return to step 3, otherwise jump to step 5.

Step 5: Each ant constructs a solution, and find out the current iteration best solution.

Step 6: Update pheromone matrix τ by formula (8), ρ is volatile factor.

$$\tau_{ij}(t+1) = \begin{cases} (1-\rho)\tau_{ij}(t+1) + \Delta\tau, & \text{if } i \in T_f \\ 0, & \text{otherwise} \end{cases} \tag{8}$$

Step 7: Get the global optimal solution by repeat from steps 2 to step 6, until the number of iterations reaches the maximum. Finally, execute on the extended CloudSim simulator, and statistical the results.

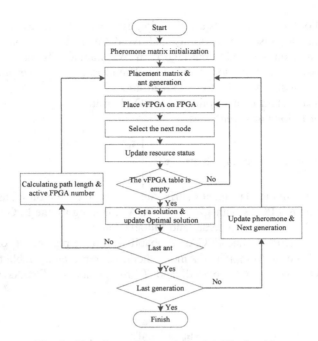

Fig. 4. Flowchart of the optimized ACO algorithm.

4 Experiment and Evaluation

We extend CloudSim by adding FPGA class and vFPGA class that deployed on Host class and VM class respectively. There are different types of function modules on the vFPGA for processing crypto-operations. During the experiment, random workflows that satisfy the normal distribution are regarded as input. The time span of the workflows is 48 h, sampling in a 10 min interval. The first 24 h are used as the training set, while the last 24 h are used as the test set. A vFPGA scheduling algorithm, which has been proposed in our other work, is embedded in the data center agent. Finally, the performance of the algorithm is evaluated by counting the number of vFPGA migrations, the SLA conflict rate, and the average number of active FPGA enabled under different experimental settings.

4.1 System Configuration

When CloudSim is initialized, create a Datacenter with 600 Hosts. Each Host is configured with 3.5G Mips, 16 GB RAM and an FPGA. FPGAs are setup with reference to the XC7VX690T FPGA the Xilinx VC709 FPGA development board. Their on-board memory is 8 GB, and the total number of logical units is 693,120, of which 7% is a static logic area and the rest are dynamic reconfigurable areas [16]. The Quartus II 13.0 and ModelSim are used for integrated wiring and simulate the number of logical units required to implement the AES, RC4, RSA, and MD5 algorithm IP cores and their processing speeds. The specific data is shown in Table 2. Reconfiguration delay of each algorithm IP core is 16 ms. The SLA conflict rate is defined as shown in Eq. (9), where the number of SLA collisions is expressed, and the value is incremented by one when the vFPGA resources owned by the tenant cannot satisfy their computational requirements.

$$p = \frac{1}{143} \sum_{t=2}^{144} \frac{CTS}{2000} \tag{9}$$

Table 2. IP core parameters of different algorithm.

Algorithm	Logical unit	Frequency	Speed
AES	4797	100 MHz	560 Mbps
RC4	1271	100 MHz	140 Mbps
RSA	10892	100 MHz	4800 times/sec
MD5	4624	100 MHz	800 Mbps

4.2   Analysis of Results

Experimental tests are carried out in this subsection to verify the performance of our vFPGA placement algorithm ($\alpha = 1$, $\beta = 1$, $\rho = 0.1$). The algorithm performance is evaluated by comparing with the corresponding results obtained by four schemes, namely: without scheduler (WS), with vFPGA scheduling (VFS) algorithm, and both vFPGA placement (VFP) and vFPGA scheduling (VPVS) algorithm. Particularly, in the VPVS algorithm, vFPGA placement algorithm is used for vFPGA deployment in the system initialization phase, and the scheduling algorithm is working in the service supply phase. In the without scheduler algorithm, the number of vFPGAs deployed on each FPGA is 4, 8, and 12. Moreover, ARIMA model with a three-step prediction is designed to sense the requirements of tenants in advance. The number of tenants is 500, 1000, 1500 and 2000 respectively. Each tenant needs a vFPGA to provide cryptographic computing services.

The results are given in Fig. 5. As shown in the figure, when 12 vFPGAs are deployed on a single FPGA without scheduler, where SLA conflict is more serious than the other case. This is caused by the competition for logical areas between different tenants, when there are too much vFPGAs deployed on a single FPGA. The VFP algorithm can use the minimum number of active FPGAs while guaranteeing SLA, but it requires aggressive migration, especially in large scale problems. This is because that the dynamic changes in requirements of tenants often lead to changes in the optimal deployment location of the vFPGA. It demonstrates that the VFP algorithm is more suitable for scenarios where resources are scarce. Moreover, it can be observed that VPVS can make better trade-off between migration times and resource usage.

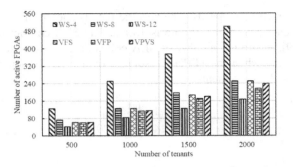

(a). Number of active FPGAs under different algorithms.

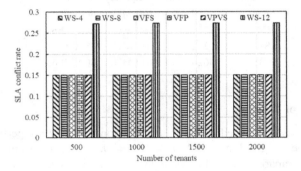

(b). SLA conflict under different algorithms.

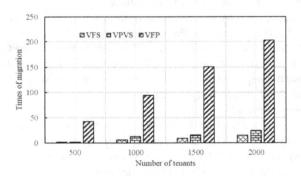

(c). Number of migrations under different algorithms.

Fig. 5. The effect of different algorithms on system performance.

5 Conclusion

In this paper, we design an ACO based vFPGA placement algorithm, which can dynamically schedule vFPGA as CPU and memory-like hardware resources according to changes in tenant requirements. We also examine the performance of the algorithm in synthetic workloads, and compare it to other alternatives presented in our early work. Results demonstrate that our VFP algorithm has achieved the objectives of minimizing the number of active FPGAs and guaranteeing the quality of service.

References

1. Amazon Web Services. AWS CloudHSM User Guide. https://docs.aws.amazon.com/cloudhsm/latest/userguide/cloudhsm-user-guide.pdf. Accessed 23 Apr 2019
2. QI, K.: The first Cloud Data Encryption Service released by Alibaba Cloud and JN TASS. Inf. Secur. Commun. Priv. (1), 87 (2016)
3. Vipin, K., Fahmy, S.A.: FPGA dynamic and partial reconfiguration: a survey of architectures, methods, and applications. ACM Comput. Surv. (CSUR) 51(4), 72 (2018)
4. Xu, Y., Sun, L., Guo, S., et al.: Research and design of reconfigurable security resource pool framework. In: Proceedings of the 2018 2nd International Conference on Computer Science and Artificial Intelligence, pp. 620–626. ACM, Shenzhen (2018)
5. Calheiros, R.N., Ranjan, R., Beloglazov, A., et al.: CloudSim: a toolkit for modeling and simulation of cloud computing environments and evaluation of resource provisioning algorithms. Softw.: Pract. Exp. 41(1), 23–50 (2011)
6. Speitkamp, B., Bichler, M.: A mathematical programming approach for server consolidation problems in virtualized data centers. IEEE Trans. Serv. Comput. 3(4), 266–278 (2010)
7. Teyeb, H., Balma, A., Hadj-Alouane, N.B., Tata, S.: Optimal virtual machine placement in a multi-tenant cloud. In: Toumani, F., et al. (eds.) ICSOC 2014. LNCS, vol. 8954. Springer, Cham (2015). https://doi.org/10.1007/978-3-319-22885-3_27
8. Dai, X., Wang, M., Bensaou, B.: Energy-efficient virtual machines scheduling in multi-tenant data centers. IEEE Trans. Cloud Comput. 4(2), 210–221 (2016)
9. Riahi, M., Krichen, S.: A multi-objective decision support framework for virtual machine placement in cloud data centers: a real case study. J. Supercomput. 74, 2984–3015 (2018)
10. Veredas, F.J., Carmona, E.J.: FPGA placement improvement using a genetic algorithm and the routing algorithm as a cost function. In: 2018 21st Euromicro Conference on Digital System Design (DSD). IEEE (2018)
11. Haghighi, A.M., Mehrdad, M., et al.: An energy-efficient dynamic resource management approach based on clustering and meta-heuristic algorithms in cloud computing IaaS platforms. Wirel. Pers. Commun. 104(4), 1367–1391 (2019)
12. Yang, X., Ma, Z., Sun, L.: Research on batch deployment of virtual machines based on improved ant colony algorithm in cloud environment. Comput. Sci. 39(9), 33–37 (2012)
13. Liu, X.F., et al.: An energy efficient ant colony system for virtual machine placement in cloud computing. IEEE Trans. Evol. Comput. 22(1), 113–128 (2018)
14. Jing, C., Zhu, Y., Li, M.: Energy-efficient scheduling on multi-FPGA reconfigurable systems. Microprocess. Microsyst. 37(6–7), 590–600 (2013)
15. Jing, C.: Ant-colony optimization based algorithm for energy-efficient scheduling on dynamically reconfigurable systems. In: Ninth International Conference on Frontier of Computer Science & Technology. IEEE Computer Society (2015)
16. Fahmy, S.A., Vipin, K., Shreejith, S.: Virtualized FPGA accelerators for efficient cloud computing. In: IEEE, International Conference on Cloud Computing Technology and Science, pp. 430–435. IEEE Computer Society, Dubai, UAE (2015)

Identity-Based Threshold Group Signature Scheme of Blockchain Verification

Lipeng Wang[1,2(✉)], Mingsheng Hu[1], Zhijuan Jia[1], Yage Cheng[1], Junjun Fu[1], Yubo Wang[1], and Bei Gong[1]

[1] Zhengzhou Normal University, Zhengzhou 450044, China
wlpscu@126.com
[2] Peking University, Beijing 100871, China

Abstract. In the e-commerce scenario, the signature schemes generally have to meet four requirements: public verification, integrity, traceable and efficiency. To achieve the above goals, the paper proposes a identity-based threshold group signature scheme which can not only simplify the process of key management, but also allow to trace the user identities. To protect the user privacy, the scheme blinds the user identities and stores them on the blockchain to prevent the malicious members from tampering with the content. Security analysis shows that the proposed signature, whose difficulty is equivalent to solve the discrete logarithm problem, achieves a high level of anonymity and can resist impersonation attacks. Computational complexity analysis shows that the new method with low computation overhead and high communication efficiency can be effectively adapted to the electronic commerce scene.

Keywords: Blockchain · Confidential computation · Threshold group signature · Traceability · E-commerce

1 Introduction

Electronic commerce is a business activity, which focuses on commodity exchange technology. However the security situation of e-commerce has been getting worse. Billions of accounts have been stolen or controlled by the hackers, and millions of the user identities are leaked, even publicly traded. Therefore, it is necessary to study the signature schemes applicable to the e-commerce scenarios, which can protect the user privacy and information behaviors, prevent message forgery and repudiation, and guarantee integrity of the trading contents.

The identity-based signature scheme can verify the message content to ensure that the message is not tampered with during transmission. In the e-commerce scenario, the available signature schemes generally have to meet four requirements: public verification, integrity, traceable and efficiency. Previously, the user identities were the pseudonym information used by the user to participate in the signing process and the temporary identify labels were usually generated through the public key encryption algorithm with anonymity. For the identity-based signature scheme, the user can select his ID number, E-mail, mobile phone number as his identity for tracing after the event, which simplifies the key management process.

© Springer Nature Singapore Pte Ltd. 2020
W. Han et al. (Eds.): CTCIS 2019, CCIS 1149, pp. 144–158, 2020.
https://doi.org/10.1007/978-981-15-3418-8_11

Blockchain is a distributed database technology which can record the transactions. The characteristics of blockchain are decentralization, anonymization and non-tampering. It handles distrust among nodes and has been widely applied in the fields of e-money, financial investment and IoT. As described above, the signatures and the blinded user identities can be stored in the blockchain, which guarantees the public verification of the signatures, and prevents the third party from maliciously tampering with the public information.

2   Related Work

In 1994, Marsh firstly proposed the concept of trusted computing and elaborated on the canonical representation of trust metrics. Based on the typical mathematical problems, existing threshold group signature schemes can be divided into three categories: 1. Based on prime factorization of large numbers. 2. Based on the discrete logarithm problem. 3. Based on the elliptic curve discrete logarithm problem. According to the way of key distribution, the threshold group signature schemes are mainly divided into two categories: 1. The ones with the trusted center. 2. The ones without the trusted center.

In 2004, Chen [1] proposed a signature scheme based on the elliptic curve encryption algorithm, and the length of the private key was short. However, it lacked the revoking operation and could not trace the user identities. In 2018, Wang [2] proposed a threshold group signature scheme which was introduced through collaboration between the blockchain and the trusted center. Dong [3] proposed an ECC threshold signature scheme with the elliptic curve discrete logarithm difficulty, which could trace the user identities with the help of the trusted center and effectively resist the malicious participants forging the final signature. The above threshold group signature schemes are based on the Shamir secret sharing method. Some other secret sharing methods will be discussed in the following part.

Yage [4] proposed a threshold signature scheme with strong forward security based on the Chinese Remainder theorem. The scheme updated the private key regularly to improve the security level and excluded the trusted center to increase the availability. Wang [5] proposed a scheme based on Asmuth-Bloom scheme applying on the blockchain voting scene. The method without the participation of the trust center was able to synthesize the final signature with the signature shares, during which the group private key was not exposed and the sensitive data would be validated to protect the user privacy during data transmitting in the blockchain unsafe transmission channel.

The paper [6] proposed an identity-based threshold group signature scheme based on the bilinear mapping. The master key of the scheme was distributed into the whole group and the user's signature key was stored in a threshold way. In [7], the threshold group signature scheme with the elliptic curve discrete logarithm difficulty was proposed. The method allowed signature verification and thresholds modification. The paper [8] proposed a threshold group signature scheme based on Elliptic Curve Cryptosystem with characteristics of easy verification, unforgeability and undeniability. The scheme had a shorter key length, lower computation and bandwidth requirement. [9] and [10] proposed two ECDSA threshold signature schemes. Both schemes allowed participants to reconstruct keys. Gennaro et al. [11] proposed a threshold signature scheme which realized the multi-party control on the Bitcoin scene.

The concept of secret sharing was first proposed by Shamir [12] and Blackey [13]. The idea is to split the target secret S into N copies and each share will be sent to its corresponding participant. When need to reconstruct the secret, we should involve a certain number of participants, the number of whom should be greater than or equal to a specified threshold t. In the e-commerce scenario, the signature schemes generally have to meet four requirements: public verification, integrity, traceable and efficiency. To achieve the above goals, the paper proposes an identity-based threshold group signature scheme, which can not only simplify the process of key management, but also allow us to trace the user identities. To protect the user privacy, the scheme blinds the user identities and stores them on the blockchain to prevent the malicious members from tampering with the content.

3 Proposed Scheme

3.1 Architecture

The participants in the proposed scheme include user (U), trust center (TC), signature compositor (SC) and signature verifier (V). The proposed threshold group signature scheme includes seven parts: setup, registration, signature shares generation, combining signature shares, signature verification, signature opening and revocation.

The following section describes the details of the proposed threshold group signature scheme. For convenience, the symbols are defined as Table 1.

Table 1. Symbols defined for the proposed scheme

Symbol	Description	Symbol	Description
TC	Trusted center	ID_i	The identity of i th node
U_i	i th user	d_i	Private key for i th user
g_s	Private group key	D_i	Public key for i th user
g_p	Public group key	P	Set which comprises t members
T_s	Private key of trusted center	ID	Set which comprises t member identities
T_p	Public key of trusted center	ID_{i1}	Blinded member identity
SC	Signature compositor	ID_{i2}	Secondary blinded member identity
V	Signature verifier	UL	User information list

1. *System initialization*

   TC initializes the system parameters, and then mainly accomplishes two tasks: the first is to set the parameters for the proposed threshold group signature scheme and build the system template parameters; the second is to generate the key information and hash function for TC. The process is as follows:

1.1 Determine the participant number N and its corresponding threshold t for the proposed method, where $t \leq N$. F_p denotes the finite field, wherein p is a large prime number and the generator is g.

1.2 TC generates its private key and other related information depending on the template parameters generated in the previous step. First, TC selects its private key $T_s = s$, $s \in Z_p^*$, and its corresponding public key is $T_p = g^s \bmod p$. Then TC selects a

$$(t-1) \text{ degree polynomial } f(x) = \sum_{i=1}^{t-1} a_i x^i + a_0 \bmod p, a_j \in [1, p-1], j = 0, 1, \ldots,$$

$t - 1$, where $a_0 \in Z_p^*$ is the secret to be shared. The variable $a_0 = g_s = f(0)$ represents the group private key, and its group public key is $g_p = g^{g_s} \bmod p$.

1.3 Select a one-way hash function $h : \{0, 1\}^* \rightarrow F_p$.

1.4 $(s, g_s, f(x))$ is the private information of TC, and (T_p, g_p, h, g, p) is the public information.

2. *User Registration*

When the user U_i wants to join the group, the registration process is performed. First, U_i sends its identity to TC, and TC will verify it. After the verification is passed, the identity will be blinded and sent to U_i. The blinded identity is verified and blinded for the second time. The secondary blinded identity along with the partial key which is generated by U_i is sent to TC. After TC receives the above information, it performs the verification operation, and stores the result on the blockchain. After that, TC generates another part of the private key for the user and sends it to U_i. After U_i verifies the information, the user synthesizes the key generated by himself and the partial key generated by TC to generate his own private key and the public key. The details are as follows:

2.1. The user U_i sends his identity ID_i to TC.

2.2. After TC receives ID_i, it checks whether the user has already registered or not. If the user does, TC rejects his request. Otherwise, TC generates $u \in Z_p^*$ randomly and calculates: $U = g^u \bmod p$, $ID_{i1} = s \times h(ID_i) + u$. After that, TC sends (U, ID_{i1}) to the user U_i.

2.3. After the user U_i receives (U, ID_{i1}), the data pair will be verified with $g^{ID_{i1}} \bmod p = \left(T_p^{h(ID_i)} \times U \right) \bmod p$. If the verification fails, it means that the data is tampered with during the transmission process, and the user U_i requests TC to resend the data. If the verification succeeds, the user U_i selects his partial private key $x_i \in Z_p^*$ and calculates $X_i = g^{x_i} \bmod p$. The user U_i needs to perform the secondary blindness operation on his identity to increase the security of the solution. First, the user U_i randomly selects $v_i \in Z_p^*$ and calculates $V_i = g^{v_i} \bmod p$. Then he performs the secondary blinding operation on his identity with $ID_{i2} = x_i \times h(ID_{i1}) + v_i$. After that, U_i sends $(X_i, V_i, ID_{i1}, ID_{i2})$ to TC.

2.4. After TC receives $(X_i, V_i, ID_{i1}, ID_{i2})$, it first checks the data pair with $g^{ID_{i2}} \bmod p = (X_i^{h(ID_{i1})} \times V_i) \bmod p$. If the verification succeeds, it denotes that the user has successfully generated his blinded identity, and TC will store

(X_i, ID_i, ID_{i2}) in the user information list UL, which will be used to trace the user identity afterwards. Then TC assigns another private key y_i to the user where

$$y_i = f(ID_{i2}) = \sum_{j=1}^{t-1} a_j(ID_{i2})^j + a_0 \bmod p.$$ In order to prevent the malicious third

party from intercepting y_i, y_i needs to be encrypted to $E_{PK_{U_i}}(y_i)$ with the public key of U_i.

5. 2.5 After the user receives $E_{PK_{U_i}}(y_i)$, the user decrypts it with his private key to obtain the plaintext y_i. The user U_i can then generate his own private key with $d_i = x_i + y_i$. The corresponding public key for U_i is $D_i = g^{d_i} \bmod p$. At this point, the user registration process ends.

3. *Generating Signature Shares*
   For the proposed threshold group signature scheme, the set of participants is denoted as $U' = \{U_1, U_2, \ldots, U_N\}$, and the final legal signature can be generated with at least t $(t \leq N)$ signature shares. For convenience, we will only consider t signature shares to combine the final signature, and the user set is denoted as $U = \{U_1, U_2, \ldots, U_t\}$. After registration, the user in the set firstly generates his signature share corresponding to the message, and then delivers it to SC for synthesizing. In the end, V checks the final signature and stores it in the blockchain. For the user U_i, when to generate his signature share, he first generates a random number $k_i \in Z_p^*$, and then obtains $r_i = g^{k_i} \bmod p$. We can obtain the corresponding hash value $z = h(m)$ from the message m, and then calculates the

   signature share with $s_i = k_i - z d_i I_i$, where $I_i = \prod_{j=1, i \neq j}^{t} \frac{ID_{j2}}{ID_{j2} - ID_{i2}} \bmod p$, $1 \leq i \leq t$.

   Since I_i is public, it can be pre-computed and published to reduce the computational complexity. Finally, the user U_i sends the signature share (r_i, s_i), the message m and its corresponding identity ID_{i2} to SC.

4. *Combine signature shares*
   After SC receives greater than or equal to t signature shares, the final signature can be synthesized. Before that, we need to verify the received signature shares. In order to trace the user identify afterwards and prevent the third party from tampering with the content, the final signature needs to be stored into the blockchain. When SC verifies (r_i, s_i) and ID_{i2}, he first calculates the corresponding hash value $z = h(m)$ from the message m, and then performs the verification with $g^{s_i} D_i^{zI_i} = r_i \bmod p$. If the above equation holds, we can perform the subsequent signature synthesis operation, otherwise the signature compositor will reject the signature share. When performing

   signature synthesis, we first calculate $R = \prod_{i=1}^{t} r_i$, $S = \sum_{i=1}^{t} s_i$, and (R, S) is the final

   synthesized signature. In order to verify the synthesized signature, we should cal-

   culate $W = \prod_{i=1}^{t} X_i^{I_i} \bmod p$. SC sends (R, S, W) and the message m to V for verification.

5. *Signature verification*

After V receives the above information, it needs to verify the signature. First, V performs a hash function $z = h(m)$ on the received message m, and then verifies the final signature with $R = g^s \times (g_p W)^z$. When the verification holds, V stores (ID_{i2}, r_i, s_i) and the synthesized signature (R, S, W) in the blockchain for traceability.

6. *Signature Opening*

When dispute occurs, we need to access the blockchain and TC to trace the target identities from the given signature. During the process, the participation of SC and V is not required, and the feature of the blockchain guarantees the data against tampering, which not only increases the security level of the system, but also reduces the number of interactions to increase the efficiency. For the synthesized signature (R, S), we need to access the blockchain when to trace its corresponding identity. When accessing the blockchain, we need to search for (ID_{i2}, r_i, s_i) corresponding to (R, S). Among them, ID_{i2} is the secondary blinding identity, and the third party cannot infer the user identity. Then we need to access TC and obtain (X_i, ID_i, ID_{i2}) through ID_{i2}, among which ID_i is the user identity.

7. *Members Revoking*

When a member withdraws from the group, only TC needs to perform most of the calculation tasks. The revocation message along with attached information needs to be broadcast to other users. Other users only need to perform a small number of operations to revoke the target member. First, TC needs to reselect a $t - 1$ order polynomial, then recalculate the new partial key $y_i = f(ID_{i2})$ for each member ID_{i2}, and send the revocation message together with the encrypted message $PK_{U_i}(y_i)$ to other users. Other users only need to update their private keys with $d_i = x_i + y_i$, and their corresponding public keys with $D_i = g^{d_i} \bmod p$. After that, TC can delete the specified member ID_{i2} from the group.

4   Security Analysis

4.1   Correctness Analysis

Theorem 1. Two verification equations $g^{ID_{i1}} \bmod p = (T_p^{h(ID_i)} \times U) \bmod p$ and $g^{ID_{i2}} \bmod p = (X_i^{h(ID_{i1})} \times V_i) \bmod p$ are established when any user registers.

Proof: When the user U_i begins to register, the user U_i and TC are required to perform the two-way authentication. The corresponding verification formula is $g^{ID_{i1}} \bmod p = (T_p^{h(ID_i)} \times U) \bmod p$, $g^{ID_{i2}} \bmod p = (X_i^{h(ID_{i1})} \times V_i) \bmod p$. Because of $ID_{i1} = s \times h(ID_i) + u$, we can obtain $g^{ID_{i1}} \bmod p = g^{(s \times h(ID_i) + u)} \bmod p = (g^s)^{h(ID_i)} g^u \bmod p$. From

$U = g^u \bmod p$ and $T_p = g^s \bmod p$, we can get $g^{ID_{i1}} \bmod p = (g^s)^{h(ID_i)} g^u \bmod p = (T_p^{h(ID_i)} \times U) \bmod p$. Because of $ID_{i2} = x_i \times h(ID_{i1}) + v_i$, we can obtain $g^{ID_{i2}} \bmod p = g^{(x_i \times h(ID_{i1}) + v_i)} \bmod p = (g^{x_i})^{h(ID_{i1})} g^{v_i} \bmod p$. From $X_i = g^{x_i} \bmod p$ and $V_i = g^{v_i} \bmod p$, we can calculate $g^{ID_{i2}} \bmod p = (g^{x_i})^{h(ID_{i1})} g^{v_i} \bmod p = (X_i^{h(ID_{i1})} \times V_i) \bmod p$.

Theorem 2. When to generate the synthesized signature, the verification equation $r_i = g^{s_i} D_i^{zl_i} \bmod p$ of SC holds.

Proof: The user U_i begins to sign the message m and generate the signature share which will be sent to SC for signature synthesis. After receiving the information, SC should verify the message to ensure that the message is not maliciously tampered by a third party with $r_i = g^{s_i} D_i^{zl_i} \bmod p$. Because of $s_i = k_i - zd_i l_i$, we can obtain $g^{s_i} = g^{k_i - zd_i l_i} = g^{k_i} (g^{d_i})^{-zl_i} \bmod p$. From $r_i = g^{k_i} \bmod p$ and $D_i = g^{d_i} \bmod p$, we can get $g^{s_i} = r_i (D_i)^{-zl_i} \bmod p$, and then we can obtain $g^{s_i} D_i^{zl_i} = r_i \bmod p$.

Theorem 3. After generating the final signature, the verification equation $R = g^S \times (g_p W)^z$ of the signature verifier holds.

Proof: After the signature compositor synthesizes the signature shares, the final signature is sent to the signature verifier for verification with $R = g^S \times (g_p W)^z$. Because of $s_i = k_i - zd_i l_i$, $S = \sum_{i=1}^{t} s_i$, we can obtain $g^S = g^{\sum_{i=1}^{t} s_i} = g^{\sum_{i=1}^{t} (k_i - zd_i l_i)} = g^{\sum_{i=1}^{t} k_i} g^{-\sum_{i=1}^{t} (zd_i l_i)} = \prod_{i=1}^{t} g^{k_i} \prod_{i=1}^{t} g^{-zd_i l_i}$. From $d_i = x_i + y_i$, $r_i = g^{k_i} \bmod p$ and $R = \prod_{i=1}^{t} r_i$, we can get $g^S = \prod_{i=1}^{t} g^{k_i} \prod_{i=1}^{t} g^{-zd_i l_i} = \prod_{i=1}^{t} r_i \prod_{i=1}^{t} g^{-z(x_i + y_i) l_i} = R \prod_{i=1}^{t} g^{-z(x_i + y_i) l_i}$. Then we can calculate $g^S \prod_{i=1}^{t} g^{z(x_i + y_i) l_i} = R = g^S \prod_{i=1}^{t} (g^{zx_i l_i} g^{zy_i l_i}) = g^S g^{z\sum_{i=1}^{t} f(ID_{i2}) l_i} \prod_{i=1}^{t} g^{zx_i l_i}$. According to Lagrange interpolation formula, we can obtain $z \sum_{i=1}^{t} f(ID_{i2}) l_i = za_0 = zg_s$. Then we can get $R = g^S g^{zg_s} \prod_{i=1}^{t} g^{zx_i l_i}$. Because of $g_p = g^{g_s} \bmod p$ and $X_i = g^{x_i} \bmod p$, we can obtain $R = g^S g^{zg_s} \prod_{i=1}^{t} g^{zx_i l_i} = g^S g_p^z \prod_{i=1}^{t} g^{zx_i l_i} = g^S (g_p \prod_{i=1}^{t} X_i^{l_i})^z$. Because of $W = \prod_{i=1}^{t} X_i^{l_i} \bmod p$, we can obtain $R = g^S \times (g_p W)^z$.

4.2 Threshold Safety Analysis

The threshold feature of the proposed scheme means that for a (t, n) threshold signature scheme, the secret will be dispersed into a group comprising of n members, and the subset of no less than t members can use their respective possessions to produce the final signature. On the other hand any subset of less than t members cannot recover the secret or obtain the correct result.

The process to obtain the threshold group signature includes generation of signature shares and synthesis of signature shares. For n participants, when to generate the signature shares, each user utilizes its own private key $k_i \in Z_p^*$ to sign the message and generates the signature share with the formula $s_i = k_i - zd_il_i$. After the trusted center receives the signature shares $\{(r_i, s_i)|t \leq i \leq n\}$ from participants, the trusted centers will perform the synthesis operations with $R = \prod_{i=1}^{t} r_i$ and $S = \sum_{i=1}^{t} s_i$. (R, S) is the final synthesized signature which needs to be verified with the formula $R = g^S \times (g_p W)^z$.

At least t nodes are required to synthesize the signature shares. When to combine less than t signature shares, the synthesis will fail. When obtain the final signature, the content must be verified with $R = g^S \times (g_p W)^z$. According to Lagrange interpolation formula, we can obtain $z \sum_{i=1}^{t} f(ID_{i2})I_i = za_0 = zg_s$. If a malicious third party wants to obtain the private group key g_s, he needs at least t participants cooperating to succeed.

If the attacker has obtained the public key g_p and g, he wants to calculate the private group key g_s through $g_p = g^{g_s} \bmod p$, and the difficulty of the operation is reduced to the discrete logarithm problem which is computationally infeasible. In the end, the above analysis shows that the proposed scheme is safe.

4.3 Anonymity Analysis

The anonymity of the proposed threshold signature scheme means that for a given group signature, no one else can know the true identities of the participants except for TC or themselves.

When a user U_i wants to join the group, he first sends his identity ID_i to TC. TC will check its repeatability, and then blinds the user identity with $ID_{i1} = s \times h(ID_i) + u$, which takes $u \in Z_p^*$ and his private key s as input. ID_{i1} will be sent to the user who will check its integrity. After that, the user U_i will use his partial private key $x_i \in Z_p^*$ and a random value $v_i \in Z_p^*$ to perform the secondary blinding operation on his identity with $ID_{i2} = x_i \times h(ID_{i1}) + v_i$.

The two items ID_{i1} and ID_{i2} which are respectively generated by the user and TC are public, while the user id ID_i is secret. Other unauthorized nodes are not able to obtain the user true identity without the knowledge of the values of s, u, x_i and v_i. Even the attacker obtains those values, it is still difficult for him to retrieve the identities through the one-way hash function $h(x)$. The two items ID_{i1} and ID_{i2} are stored into the blockchain which cannot be tampered with. Based on the above analysis, the user identity can achieve a high level of anonymity which could prevent the malicious third party from tampering with the user sensitive information.

4.4 Unforgeability Analysis

Unforgeability means that any participant cannot impersonate another one to generate the legal signature. In real life, TC and the user may impersonate each other to sign the

given message with another identity. The attack scenes can be divided into two cases:
Case 1: TC masquerades as member U_i, and signs the message m with the identity of
U_i. Case 2: The user U_j masquerades as member U_i, and signs the message m with the
identity of U_i.

For the first case, TC spoofs the identity of U_i. The blinded identity set
$\{ID_{i1}, ID_{i2}, , ID_{it}\}$ is public, and TC can know the $(t-1)$ degree polynomial
$f(x) = \sum_{i=1}^{t-1} a_i x^i + a_0 \bmod p$. The trusted center randomly selects $u'_i \in Z_p^*$ to generate
(U', ID'_{i1}) and selects $x'_i \in Z_p^*$ as the user U_i partial private key to calculate
$X'_i = g^{x'_i} \bmod p$. TC performs secondary blindness on the identity of the user U_i by
randomly selecting $v'_i \in Z_p^*$ to calculate $V'_i = g^{v'_i} \bmod p$. Then he performs the secondary blinding operation with $ID'_{i2} = x'_i \times h\left(ID'_{i1}\right) + v'_i$. After that, TC stores
$\left(X'_i, ID'_i, ID'_{i2}\right)$ in the information list, and then generates the final signature. In the end,
TC stores $\left(ID'_{i2}, r'_i, s'_i\right)$ and the synthesized signature (R', S') in the blockchain. However, the user U_i can obtain the data pair $\left(ID'_{i2}, r'_i, s'_i, R', S'\right)$ from blockchain and
$\left(X'_i, ID'_i, ID'_{i2}\right)$ from TC with his own X_i. If TC wants to pass the verification, he must
generate the value X'_i guaranteeing $X'_i = X_i$, which means that TC has to obtain $x_i \in Z_p^*$
from $X_i = X'_i = g^{x_i} \bmod p$. The question is reduced to discrete logarithm problem, and
the operation is computationally infeasible.

For the second scenario, the user U_j poses as the node U_i to sign the message m. At
this time, the user U_j only knows ID_{i2} of the user U_i. The user U_j randomly selects
$u'_i \in Z_p^*$, and selects $x'_i \in Z_p^*$ as the user U_i partial private key to calculate
$X'_i = g^{x'_i} \bmod p$. Then the user U_j will perform the secondary identity blind operation to
generate $\left(X'_i, ID'_i, ID'_{i2}\right)$. In the end, TC will combine the signature shares to generate
the final signature (R', S'), which will be sent to SC for verification with
$R' = g^{S'} \times (g_p W)^z$. If the user U_j wants to pass the verification, he must guarantee the
following equation holds $z \sum_{i=1}^{t} f(ID_{i2}) I_i = za_0 = zg_s = z \sum_{i=1}^{t} f'(ID_{i2}) I_i$. I_i is public, and
the user U_j can obtain $z = h(m)$ from the message m, so the user U_j should obtain the
function $f'(ID_{i2})$ which meets $f(ID_{i2}) = f'(ID_{i2})$. Because of $f(x) = \sum_{i=1}^{t-1} a_i x^i +$
$a_0 \bmod p$, the user U_j needs to guess the values of $a_i, 0 \le i \le t-1$, which probability is
$Pr = \frac{1}{(p-1)^t}$. Because p is a large prime number, the adversary can only succeed with a
negligible probability.

5 Performance Analysis

5.1 Functionality Comparison

In this part, we give the functionality comparison of the proposed scheme with other related ones as shown in the following Table 2. We mainly focus on the five properties: public verifiability, sensitive information hiding, members revocable, traceability and anti-collusion.

Table 2. Functionality comparison

Schemes	Public verifiability	Sensitive information hiding	Members revocable	Traceability	Anti collusion
Dahshan et al. [14]	Yes	Yes	No	Yes	Yes
Yage et al. [4]	Yes	Yes	Yes	No	No
Lipeng et al. [15]	Yes	Yes	Yes	No	No
Shacham et al. [16]	Yes	No	Yes	No	No
Wang et al. [17]	Yes	No	Yes	No	No
Yannan et al. [18]	Yes	No	Yes	No	No
Wang et al. [19]	No	No	Yes	No	Yes
Shen et al. [20]	Yes	No	Yes	No	Yes
Shen et al. [21]	Yes	Yes	No	Yes	Yes
Ours	Yes	Yes	Yes	Yes	Yes

Public verifiability means that the final signature can be verified by the others apart from SV. Sensitive information hiding denotes that anyone else can not fetch the user identity from the public information advertised in the method. This property allows participants to opt out of the group, which is especially important in mobile Internet scenarios. Traceability represents that the supervisor can perform post hoc analysis to trace the identity information of the signer from the synthesized signature, mainly used in the auditing scenario. Anti-collusion means that any participant cannot impersonate another one to generate the legal signature. Note that the proposed scheme supports all the five properties compared with other related algorithms.

5.2 Performance Comparison

We define several notations to denote the operations in the proposed scheme as Table 3.

Table 3. Defined symbols for computational complexity

Symbols	Descriptions
T_{mul}	Modular multiplication operation
T_{exp}	Modular exponentiation operation
T_{inv}	Modular inverse operation
T_h	Hashing operation
T_{add}	Modular addition operation
T_{sub}	Modular subtraction operation

We mainly consider the three steps in the scheme, which are signature shares generation, signature shares combing and the final signature verification. We do not consider the step of user registration. This is because registration only needs to be performed only once when a user attempts to join the group. The time-consuming operations of the system are mainly signature synthesis and verification. The computation overhead comparison is described as the Table 4.

Table 4. Comparison of computation overhead

Schemes	Shares generation	Shares combining	Signature verification
Yage et al. [4]	$tT_{exp} + (6t-1)T_{mul} + tT_{add} + tT_{inv}$	$(t-1)T_{add}$	$2T_{exp} + T_{mul}$
Shen et al. [21]	$32tT_{mul} + tT_h + tT_{sub}$	$34tT_{mul} + (3t-2)T_{add}$	$30T_{mul} + T_h + 2T_{add}$
Lipeng et al. [15]	$(2t-1)T_{add} + (6t-1)T_{mul} + tT_{inv}$	$(t-1)T_{add}$	$2T_{exp} + 2T_{mul}$
Ours	$tT_{exp} + tT_h + tT_{sub} + 2tT_{mul}$	$tT_h + (4t-2)T_{mul} + 3tT_{exp} + (t-1)T_{add}$	$2T_{exp} + 2T_{mul} + T_h$

Generally speaking, $T_{\exp}$ is the most time consuming operation, followed by T_{inv}. The operation execution time rankings are usually as follows:

$$T_{\exp} > T_{inv} > T_{mul} > T_{add} > T_{sub}.$$

Although in the two stages of signature combining and signature verification, Yage et al. [4] takes less time. For the signature shares generation, the proposed scheme consumes less time than Yage et al. [4], which includes the inversion operation. Shen et al. [21] mainly contains the modular multiplication and modular addition operations without modular exponentiation operation, which seems more efficient than the proposed one. But during the process of user registration and the following steps, the method involves bilinear pairing operations which will take more time. That is because a bilinear pair operation is slightly equal to 50 exponentiation operations in general. The performance of the proposed scheme is inferior to Lipeng et al. [15] in the signature shares combining and the final signature verification, but the proposed one can take the user identities as input during registration, which simplifies the key management process for users.

In real-world scenarios, the effectiveness of the proposed scheme depends on the expression execution time and the communication overhead. According to the description of the proposed algorithm, we can know that the communication overhead mainly comes from user registration, signature shares generating, signature shares combing and signature verification. For simplicity, the two steps of signature shares generating and signature shares combing are combined in one step which is denoted as signatures generating. Assuming $|\varsigma|$ is the size of an element in $\mathbf{Z}_p^*$, $|\Gamma|$ is the size of the message m, $|\eta|$ is the size of user identification and the length of $E_{PK_{U_i}}(y_i)$ is $|\varsigma|$ during the process of user registration, communication overhead of the proposed scheme is shown as Table 5.

Table 5. Communication overhead of the proposed scheme

Signature length	Registration	Signatures generating	Signature verification
$3|\varsigma|$	$|\eta| + 7|\varsigma|$	$t(3|\varsigma| + |\Gamma|)$	$8|\varsigma| + |\Gamma|$

5.3 Experimental Results

In this subsection, we will evaluate the performance of the proposed scheme with several experiments. The details of the running environment are as following:

Hardware

CPU: Intel(R) Core(TM) i5-7500 CPU @ 3.40 GHz 3.40 GHz; *RAM: 8.00 GB.*

Software

OS: Windows 7 64; MyEclipse: 2015 CI; JAVA: 1.7.

Specifically, we will run the test 10 times and calculate the average value to eliminate errors. The running time of each step varies with N and t which will be recorded. The details are shown in Table 6, and the time measurement unit is milliseconds (ms).

Table 6. Execution time between different phases varying from N and t.

N	t	Setup	Register	Generate Shares	Combine Shares	Verify
5	2	1.84	17.96	0.78	2.38	0.8
10	5	0.77	31.21	1.87	5.66	0.76
15	7	0.78	46.02	2.61	7.76	0.75
20	10	0.74	61.43	3.67	11.1	0.76
25	12	0.73	75.09	4.39	13.16	0.85
30	15	0.74	90.4	5.56	16.42	0.74
35	17	0.74	105.4	6.33	18.64	0.74
40	20	0.73	121.8	7.34	21.71	0.73

(continued)

Table 6. (*continued*)

N	t	Setup	Register	Generate Shares	Combine Shares	Verify
45	22	0.75	137.61	8.14	24.22	0.75
50	25	0.74	154.19	9.26	27.47	0.71
55	27	0.73	170.23	9.82	29.43	0.74
60	30	0.74	188.98	11.1	33.25	0.74
65	32	0.77	207.47	11.78	35.37	0.75
70	35	0.74	220.4	12.87	38.37	0.73
75	37	0.75	238	13.5	40.52	0.74
80	40	0.74	255.53	14.57	43.6	0.74
85	42	0.77	273.31	15.41	45.65	0.74
90	45	0.74	290.62	16.46	49.19	0.73
95	47	0.75	308.36	17.36	51.44	0.73
100	50	0.75	328.68	18.3	54.79	0.79

From the data in the table, as N and t increase, the running time of the setup phase and the signature verification phase remains almost unchanged. The experimental results show that these two steps have no direct correlation with N and t, which is consistent with the implementation. We can also know the registration phase consumes most of the time, followed by the signature shares combing phase. That is because the two steps consist a lot of modular exponentiation operations and modular inverse operations which is demonstrated in Table 4.

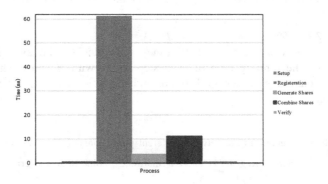

Fig. 1. Execution time of different steps

Figure 1 shows the execution time of the five steps when N is 20 and t is 10. We can know that the registration phase takes most of the overall running time of the system, almost 90%. It also shows that the step is the bottleneck of the overall performance, which denotes that we should focus on this step if we want to optimize the performance of the proposed algorithm.

6 Conclusion

The paper proposes an identity-based threshold group signature scheme, which can not only simplify the process of key management, but also allow tracing the user identities. To protect the user privacy, the scheme blinds the user identities and stores them on the blockchain to prevent the malicious members from tampering with the content. Security analysis shows that the proposed signature, whose difficulty is equivalent to solve the discrete logarithm problem, achieves a high level of anonymity and can resist impersonation attacks. Computational complexity analysis shows that the new method with low computation overhead and high communication efficiency can be effectively adapted to the e-commerce scenario.

Acknowledgments. This work was supported by Henan Province Higher Education Key Research Project (20B520040).

References

1. Chen, T.S., Hsiao, T.C., Chen, T.L.: An efficient threshold group signature scheme. In: TENCON 2004, pp. 13–16 (2004)
2. Wang, L., et al.: A voting scheme in blockchain based on threshold group signature. In: Zhang, H., Zhao, B., Yan, F. (eds.) CTCIS 2018. CCIS, vol. 960, pp. 184–202. Springer, Singapore (2019). https://doi.org/10.1007/978-981-13-5913-2_12
3. Dong, X., Jiajia, L., Zhonghua, S.: A new threshold signature scheme based on elliptic curve cryptosystem. J. Hangzhou Normal Univ. (Nat. Sci. Ed.) 12(1), 57–60 (2013)
4. Yage, C., Mingsheng, H., Bei, G., Lipeng, W., Erfeng, X.: Dynamic threshold signature scheme with strong forward security. Comput. Eng. Appl. 1(23), 1–12 (2019)
5. Wang, L., Hu, M., Jia, Z., Gong, B., Lei, Y.: A signature scheme applying on blockchain voting scene based on asmuth-bloom algorithm. In: IEEE 4th International Conference on Computer and Communications (2018)
6. Hongwei, L., Weixin, X., Jianping, Y., Peng, Z.: Efficiency identity-based threshold group signature scheme. J. Commun. 30(5), 122–127 (2009)
7. Jie, Y., Xuri, Y., Wujun, Z.: Research on group signature with threshold value based on elliptic curve. J. Southeast Univ. (Nat. Sci. Ed.) 38(1), 43–46 (2008)
8. Yufang, C., Tzerlong, C., Tzer-Shyong, C., Chihsheng, C.: A study on efficient group-oriented signature schemes for realistic application environment. Int. J. Innov. Comput. Inf. Control 8(4), 2713–2727 (2012)
9. Gennaro, R., Goldfeder, S.: Fast multiparty threshold ECDSA with fast trustless setup. In: Proceedings of the 2018 ACM SIGSAC Conference on Computer and Communications Security, pp. 1179–1194 (2018)
10. Yehuda, L., Nof, A.: Fast secure multiparty ECDSA with practical distributed key generation and applications to cryptocurrency custody. In: Proceedings of the 2018 ACM SIGSAC Conference on Computer and Communications Security, pp. 1837–1854 (2018)
11. Gennaro, R., Goldfeder, S., Narayanan, A.: Threshold-optimal DSA/ECDSA signatures and an application to Bitcoin wallet security. In: Manulis, M., Sadeghi, A.R., Schneider, S. (eds.) ACNS 2016. LNCS, vol. 9696, pp. 156–174. Springer, Cham (2016). https://doi.org/10.1007/978-3-319-39555-5_9

12. Shamir, A.: How to share a secret. Commun. ACM **22**(11), 612–613 (1979)
13. Blakley, G.R.: Safeguarding cryptographic keys. In: AFIPS Conference Proceedings, pp. 313–317 (1979)
14. Dahshan, H., Kamal, A., Rohiem, A.: A threshold blind digital signature scheme using elliptic curve dlog-based cryptosystem. In: IEEE Vehicular Technology Conference, pp. 1–5 (2015)
15. Lipeng, W., Mingsheng, H., Zhijuan, J., Bei, G., Jialei, Z.: A signature scheme applying on blockchain voting scene based on chinese remainder theorem. Appl. Res. Comput. **29**(1), 1–8 (2018)
16. Shacham, H., Waters, B.: Compact proofs of retrievability. J. Cryptol. **26**(3), 442–483 (2013)
17. Wang, B., Li, B., Li, H.: Panda: public auditing for shared data with efficient user revocation in the cloud. IEEE Trans. Serv. Comput. **8**(1), 92–106 (2015)
18. Yannan, L., Yong, Y., Geyong, M., et al.: Fuzzy identity-based data integrity auditing for reliable cloud storage systems. IEEE Trans. Dependable Secure Comput. **14**(8), 72–83 (2017)
19. Wang, H.: Proxy provable data possession in public clouds. IEEE Trans. Serv. Comput. **6**(4), 551–559 (2013)
20. Shen, J., Shen, J., Chen, X., Huang, X., Susilo, W.: An efficient public auditing protocol with novel dynamic structure for cloud data. IEEE Trans. Inf. Forensics Secur. **12**(10), 2402–2415 (2017)
21. Wenting, S., Jing, Q., Jia, Y., et al.: Enabling identity-based integrity auditing and data sharing with sensitive information hiding for secure cloud storage. IEEE Trans. Inf. Forensics Secur. **14**(2), 331–346 (2019)

ByteDroid: Android Malware Detection Using Deep Learning on Bytecode Sequences

Kewen Zou[1], Xi Luo[2], Pengfei Liu[1], Weiping Wang[1(✉)], and Haodong Wang[3]

[1] School of Computer Science and Engineering, Central South University,
Changsha 410083, China
wpwang@csu.edu.cn
[2] Department of Information Technology, Hunan Police Academy,
Changsha 410138, China
[3] Department of Electrical Engineering and Computer Science,
Cleveland State University, Cleveland, OH 44115, USA

Abstract. The explosive growth of the Android malware poses a great threat to users' privacy and sensitive personal information. It is urgent to develop an effective and efficient Android malware detection system. Existing studies usually require the manual feature engineering for the feature extraction. In fact, the detection performance is heavily relied on the quality of the feature extraction. Additionally, the feature extraction becomes extremely difficult in the malware detection due to the fact that malware developers often deploy the obfuscation techniques. To address this issue, we focus on the Android malware detection using the deep neural networks without the human factors. In this paper, we propose ByteDroid, an Android malware detection scheme that processes the raw Dalvik bytecode using the deep learning. ByteDroid resizes the raw bytecode and constructs a learnable vector representation as the input to the neural network. Then, ByteDroid adopts a Convolutional Neural Networks (CNNs) to automatically extract the malware features and perform the classification. Our experiment results demonstrate that ByteDroid not only can effectively detect Android malware, but also has a great generalization performance given untrained malware. Moreover, ByteDroid maintains resilience to obfuscation techniques.

Keywords: Android malware detection · Dalvik bytecode · Convolutional Neural Networks

1 Introduction

The growth of Android malware has become a crucial security problem for users' privacy and sensitive information. It is impractical to analyze every single application manually given millions of Android applications in the application stores. Many Android malware detection systems heavily rely on human factors, using

W. Han et al. (Eds.): CTCIS 2019, CCIS 1149, pp. 159–176, 2020.
https://doi.org/10.1007/978-981-15-3418-8_12

handcrafted rules to detect the malware from unknown applications and determine the malware type. These rules, however, may not work when the malware equipped with obfuscation techniques. Meanwhile, it is still difficult for malware detector to keep up with the process of malware evolution. To address this issue, we develop a deep learning based malware detection scheme that does not require the domain knowledge and the human factors. In particular, the proposed detection system works in the rapidly variant malware ecosystem.

In recent years, the deep neural networks have achieved great success in the fields of computer vision and natural language processing. The deep neural networks can learn feature representation and classification simultaneously to achieve the best results. Motivated by this, we seek to use the raw bytecode sequences of the Android application as the input to train the deep neural networks. There are three reasons for choosing the Android bytecode sequences instead of the source code. First, studies [1–3] show that malicious applications often contain the similar bytecode sequence due to the fact that malware development usually shares the same libraries or modules. Second, the deep neural networks can learn directly from raw data such as pixels, words and signals. The bytecode sequence is a great form of raw data. Third, malware often use some obfuscation techniques to evade detection by renaming identifiers and inserting junk code. Yet, the bytecode is resilient to these obfuscation techniques and the model we proposed does not rely on the semantics like strings.

Recent work [4–7] strives to extract semantics as the features for the malware detection. Based on the features used to classify the malware, these approaches can be categorized into static analysis and dynamic analysis. The approaches based on static analysis usually obtain the Android application source code through the reverse engineering tools like ApkTool. The features are extracted from the API calls, the permissions, the control flows and the data flows, and then are used for classification tasks. This type of approaches is resource and time efficient because the application does not need execution. The dynamic analysis based detection approaches extract the behavioral characteristics while the application is running and therefore are more effective in detecting the malicious activities even if the evasion techniques, such as native code and dynamic code loading, are used. Nevertheless, these approaches require complicated feature extraction and are not resilient to typical obfuscation techniques.

In this paper, we propose ByteDroid, a deep learning based Android malware detection approach that does not require domain knowledge and manual feature extraction. Different from the studies that extract semantic features, ByteDroid directly processes the raw bytecode for malware detection. The raw bytecode is extracted from the Android application packages (APKs), which is subsequently represented by a series of vectors. The generated vectors are then fed to a Convolutional Neural network (CNN) to learn the bytecode sequential features for the classification.

To evaluate the performance of our model, we implement the Android malware detection model based on the opcode sequences [8]. The results show that bytecode-based method outperforms opcode-based method. In addition, we

evaluate the robustness of ByteDroid. Experimental results indicate that Byte-
Droid can effectively detect unknown malware. Meanwhile, ByteDroid is resilient
to obfuscated Android malware. Our contributions can be summarized as follow:

- We propose ByteDroid that directly processes the raw Dalvik bytecode and
  automates the Android application bytecode feature extraction through the
  deep neural networks to detect the Android malware. ByteDroid does not
  require any domain knowledge and manual feature extraction.
- We implement ByteDroid and the malware detector [8] relying on the Android
  opcode. The experimental results demonstrate that ByteDroid outperforms
  the opcode based detector.
- We conduct the extensive experiments on several datasets to evaluate ByteDroid's capability in detecting the malware from the untrained application
  pool. The results show that ByteDroid has the ability to detect the unknown
  malware. Moreover, for 10479 malware that applied seven typical obfuscation
  techniques, ByteDroid successfully detects 92.17% of them.

2   Related Work

Methods Based on Traditional Machine Learning. Machine learning and
data mining based methods have been proposed for Android malware detection
[9–15]. In particular, most of studies mainly focus on handcrafted features such
as the sensitive APIs, the permissions, the data flow and the control flow. After
encoding these features as vectors, the machine learning algorithm is applied for
classification.

DroidMat [9] extracts the sensitive API calls, the permission and the intent
message through static analysis. Then it uses k-means algorithm for clustering
and applies k-NN for classification. DroidMiner [10] also performs static analysis to extract activities, services, broadcast receivers and sensitive API calls to
construct a behavioral graph. The malicious patterns can be mined from the
behavioral graph and then encoded as vectors to train a classifier. DREBIN
[11] is another static-analysis based method that extracts features including the
hardware, the permissions, the system API calls and the URLs from the manifest files and the source code. These features is then applied for building a linear
SVM. Since DREBIN applies the linear SVM for classification, it can determine
the contribution of every features and provide explanation. Crowdroid [12] uses
dynamic analysis to extract the system calls. The system calls are clustered
by using k-means algorithm to distinguish malware from benign applications.
DroidDolphin [13] also utilizes dynamic analysis to extract 13 features of run-
time activities, including API calls, network access, file I/O and services. Then
a SVM is trained on these features to detect malware. Marvin [14] performs
the combination of the static analysis and dynamic analysis to fully capture
the behaviors of malware, which uses a linear SVM for binary classification
and assesses the risk of unknown apps with a malice score. HinDroid [15] represents the Android applications and the corresponding APIs as a structured

heterogeneous information network, and it uses a meta-path based approach to characterize the semantic information of the application and its corresponding APIs. Ultimately, HinDroid applies the multi-kernel learning to build a malware prediction model.

Methods Based on Deep Learning. Since the deep neural networks perform much better than the traditional machine learning in many application tasks, many studies begin to use the deep neural networks instead of the traditional machine learning algorithms.

Droiddetector [16] associates static analysis and dynamic analysis to extract 192 features and applies Deep Belief Networks (DBNs) whose performance outperform machine learning algorithms such as Random Forest and SVM. Li et al. [17] also build a DBN based model that uses the combinations of sensitive API calls and permissions as the input features. S. Hou et al. [18] propose an approach to categorize the API calls inside a single method and represent the Android application by blocks of API calls. The classification is then performed on API call blocks using Stacked AutoEncoders. Nix et al. [19] design a pseudo-dynamic program analyzer to track a possible execution path and generate a series of the API calls along the path. They build a CNN taking the API call sequences as input to either detect malware or classify the benign applications. Xu et al. [20] propose a malware detection system DeepRefiner consisting of two layers. In the first layer, DeepRefiner classifies the applications into benign, malware and uncertain type based on the features extracted from the manifest files. For the applications that labeled as uncertain, DeepRefiner builds a Long Short Time Memory (LSTM) model to perform refined inspection on the simplified Smali code in the second layer. Mclaughlin et al. [8] take the opcode as the input of a CNN model, which is similar to us. The opcode is extracted from the Smali code dissembled by reverse engineering tools. The author discards the operands in the execution statement, which has a certain impact on the performance of the model. In our experiments, we take this approach as a comparison.

As far as we know, there are little published studies directly process the raw Dalvik bytecode for Android malware detection. Of all the studies described above, though they use the deep neural networks, the manual feature extraction is still required. Consequently, the effectiveness of deep neural networks is limited. Instead, we leverage the potential of the deep neural networks, which use as little human labors as possible to detect Android malware.

3   ByteDroid

In this section, we describe the details of how to process the bytecode and the overall architecture of ByteDroid.

3.1   System Architecture

The system architecture of ByteDroid is shown in Fig. 1. ByteDroid consists of two stages: training and testing. In the training stage, ByteDroid first extracts

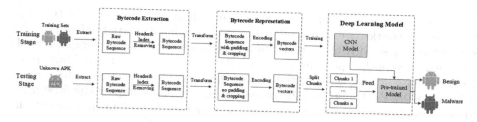

Fig. 1. System architecture of ByteDroid.

the bytecode from the training set containing both malicious and benign applications. Then, the extracted bytecode is resized to a fixed length and encoded to the corresponding vectors to fit the input of CNN. Finally, we train the CNN model using the bytecode vectors. In the testing stage, ByteDroid performs the same operation as in the training stage to deal with the unknown applications. After the bytecode sequence is encoded, ByteDroid splits the bytecode sequence into several chunks to accelerate the malware detection process because the bytecode with larger size will generate larger intermediate results and introduce the extra time consumption. Finally, the chunks are fed to the trained model to complete the classification. Both in training stage and testing stage, there are three components: Bytecode Extraction, Bytecode Representation and the Deep Learning Model. In the rest of this section, we discuss each component in detail.

3.2 Bytecode Extraction

The Android application bytecode is contained in file "classes.dex" and is interpreted by the Dalvik Virtual Machine (DVM) during the execution. Since each APK file is a zipped file, we can easily get the classes.dex file by extraction. After extraction, we use HexDump to obtain hexadecimal bytecode.

The dex file is mainly composed of three parts: the header section, the index section, and the data section. The header contains the basic information such as magic, check sum and file size. The index section stores the offset attribute of string, type, proto, field and method. The data section contains the actual executable code and data where we are most concerned about. The bytes of the header section and the index section are constants that vary in different applications. These bytes normally cannot contribute to malware detection. Therefore, ByteDroid removes the header section and the index section, only preserving the data section of an application.

3.3 Bytecode Representation

Size Padding and Cropping. The Android application bytecode has a highly variable size. Since CNN requires a fixed-size input, we need to pad the bytecode of a smaller APK to a pre-determined size and crop the bytecode of a larger APK to the same size so that all bytecode sequences have the same size for training the neural networks. We do not select the pre-determined size to be the bytecode size of the largest APK because that would significantly incur the computational complexity. Note that padding the bytecode will not cause additional false positives because adding zeros at the end of the bytecode is equivalent to adding a bunch of NOPs. Unfortunately, bytecode cropping does impact the false negatives because the bytecode containing the malicious operations may be cut off and therefore cannot be "learned" during the training stage.

In this work, we carefully select the pre-determined size in the training stage to keep the false negative low. Let α be the maximum size of the sequence. The value of α in our system is determined to 1,500 KB by our experiments (as will be discussed in Sect. 4.5). In the testing stage, considering the unknown application may have large size of bytecode, we split the input sequence into multiple chunks and then feed to our CNN model respectively. At last, we take the summation of all chunks' output as the results. The size of each chunk can be arbitrary and is limited by the physical memory size.

Bytecode Encoding. Since the operation instruction of Android bytecode is strictly limited to one byte, the bytecode can be considered as a sequence of single bytes. Assuming that the pre-determined bytecode size is α, then a given bytecode sequence B can be represented as $B = \{b_1, b_2, b_3, ..., b_\alpha\}, b_i \in [0, 255]$, where b_i refers to a single of the bytecode.

We encode each byte using a one-hot vector. A one-hot vector for byte is a vector of length 256 with a single element equals one and other elements being zero. Therefore, the respective dimension of each bytecode value is set to one and others are zeros. Using the one-hot vector representation, an Android application's bytecode sequence is constructed as the input, a sparse matrix B' of size $\alpha \times 256$ to our CNN.

3.4   Deep Learning Model

ByteDroid builds a CNN model consisting of embedding layer followed by a convolutional layer, a global max pooling layer, a fully connected layer and an output layer. The proposed CNN architecture is shown in Fig. 2.

Bytecode Vectors. Given a bytecode sequence $B' = \{b'_1, ..., b'_i, ..., b'_\alpha\}$ representing an APK file and b'_i refers to a one-hot form bytecode, our task is to construct a classifier to label the APK to be either benign or malicious.

Embedding Layer. The bytecode in the one-hot form would result in very large vector space. For reducing the dimensions of the vector space, ByteDroid chooses embedding layer to transform the vectors of one-hot form into the dense vectors with P dimensions. The dense vectors not only reduce the dimensions and therefore lower the computational cost, but also capture the bytecode sequence information surrounding each vector. In particular, if a sub-sequence consisting of two or more vectors appears frequently in the bytecode sequence, the similarity score between these vectors is higher than any other vector pairs. For example,

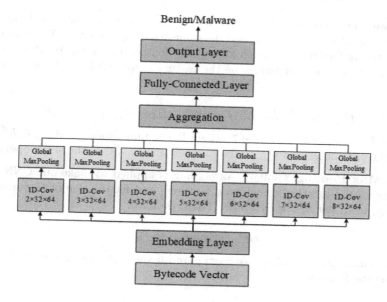

Fig. 2. The architecture of CNN.

if the vector of "invoke-virtual" frequently follows the vector of "iget-object", the similarity score between "iget-object" vector and "invoke-virtual" vector is higher than the similarity score between "iget-object" and any other vectors. Note that the size (P) of dense vector is a hyperparameter that requires to be tuned. A larger P can capture longer sub-sequence patterns, but does introduce much higher computational cost. Actually, our experiment results (as will be discussed in Sect. 4.5) show that the system only achieves a marginal performance improvement when P is set to 64 and 128. Therefore, we set the value of P to 32 for the practical reason. We project each of bytecode in $B^{'}$ into a P-dimensional space by multiplying a weight matrix $W_E \in R^{256 \times P}$:

$$b_i^E = b_i^{'} W_E, i \in [1, \alpha]. \tag{1}$$

Thus, a bytecode sequence is mapped into a matrix $B_E \in R^{P \times \alpha}$. The initial value of W_E is pre-trained by using Word2Vec [21] and can be fine-tuned during training.

Convolutional Layer. ByteDroid then applies one-dimensional convolutional layer whose input is matrix B_E. As each row in B_E represents a bytecode, the width of convolutional kernels should be same as the embedding size P. In the convolutional layer, we select the multiple-sizes of kernels, ranging from 2 to 8, and apply them in parallel to improve the receptive field of the CNN model. Formally, let W_{cov} be the convolutional kernels which are size of $K \times P$. K is the height of convolutional kernel, which is the number of bytecode bytes participating in each convolution operation. For different size of the convolutional kernels, we arrange to use 64 different filters. Each convolutional kernel produces a feature map of size $\alpha \times 1$ as we use the same-padding in convolution operation. Since there are 64 filters for each kernel, the feature maps can be stacked to a matrix of size $\alpha \times 64$. Let out_{cov}^j be the feature maps produced by a kernels of size j:

$$out_{cov}^j = CC_{i=1}^{64}(ReLU(Cov(W_{cov}^i, B_E) + b_{cov}^i)), j \in [2, 8], \qquad (2)$$

where $ReLU = max\{0, x\}$ is the rectified linear unit function. $W_{cov}^j \in R^{P \times j}$ is the weight parameter and b_{cov}^j is the bias parameter. CC is the stack operation.

Global Max Pooling. Global max pooling is applied to make our CNN work regardless of the location of detected features, and fix the size of feature maps given any arbitrary size of bytecode. Then, we have:

$$out_{mp}^j = max(out_{cov}^j). \qquad (3)$$

After global max pooling, we aggregate all the features in a matrix of size 7×64 as the following:

$$out_{aggr} = \{out_{mp}^2, out_{mp}^3, ..., out_{mp}^8\}, \qquad (4)$$

where out_{aggr} refers to the results of the aggregation operation.

Fully Connected Layer and Output Layer. Finally, out_{aggr} is flattened and fed to the fully connected layer and the Output layer to obtain the label of the bytecode sequence. In the fully connected layer, 512 neurons are used. We also use dropout between the fully connected layer and the output layer to reduce over-fitting. Therefore, we have the fully connected layer as following:

$$out_{fc} = ReLU(W_{fc}out_{aggr} + b_{fc}), \qquad (5)$$

where W_{fc} and b_{fc} respectively represent the weight and bias of the fully connected layer.

The output layer uses the output of the fully connected layer to calculate the probabilities of a bytecode sequence being benign and being malicious. Thus, there are two neurons in this layer. The Softmax function is then applied for normalizing the probabilities. The description of output layer is as following:

$$P(out_{fc}) = Softmax(W_{out}out_{fc} + b_{out}), \qquad (6)$$

where W_{out} and b_{out} respectively represent the weight and the bias of the output layer. The classification result of the bytecode sequence is expressed in Eq. 7 and the result with the probability greater than 0.5 is used as the prediction.

$$Predict(B_E) = argmax(P(out_{fc})), \qquad (7)$$

We denote the label of the bytecode sequence by L_i which is a two-dimensional vector (i.e., [0, 1] representing a malware, [1, 0] representing a benign application). Given M training samples, we use the categorical cross entropy as the loss function:

$$Loss = -\frac{1}{M} \sum_{i=1}^{M} L_i \log Predict(B_i) + \frac{\lambda}{2M} \sum_{W} W^2, \tag{8}$$

where $\frac{\lambda}{2M} \sum_W W^2$ is the L2 regularization and λ is the attenuation coefficient. The loss function is minimized by using Adam [22] optimizer. In our system, we set the value of λ to 0.01. The learning rate is set to 0.01 and the dropout rate is 0.5.

4 Experiments

In this section, we show the experimental result of our proposed method. In the first set of experiments, we evaluate the detection performance of ByteDroid. In the second set of experiments, we evaluate the Generalization performance of ByteDroid using real-world datasets. In the third set of experiments, we evaluate the robustness of ByteDroid against typical obfuscation techniques. In the last set of experiments, we evaluate the hyper-parameters of our CNN.

4.1 Datasets

We use four datasets in our experiments, as depicted in Table 1.

Table 1. Description of the datasets.

Datasets	# Benign	# Malware	Source from
Dataset A	6420	4554	Kang et al. [23]
Dataset B	6982	6575	FalDroid [24]
Dataset C	-	9389	VirusShare [25]
Dataset D	-	979	VirusShare [25]
Dataset E	-	10479	Android PRAGuard [28]

Dataset A. This dataset is obtained from Kang et al. [23], with 10,874 samples in total. Among them, there are 6,420 benign samples and 4,554 malware samples. All of the benign samples are scanned by VirusTotal [26]. We only keep the applications that are not reported as malware by any anti-virus scanners.

Dataset B. This dataset is provided by FalDroid [24]. It contains 6,982 benign samples and 6,575 malware samples. Benign samples are obtained from Google Play Stores and are scanned by VirusTotal. All malware samples are labeled into 30 malware families as described in FalDroid.

Dataset C and D. There two datasets are obtained from VirusShare [25]. There are 9,389 samples from 2014 and 979 samples from 2017 to 2018.

Dataset E. is obtained from Android PRAGuard [28] that contains 10479 malware obfuscated by seven different obfuscation techniques. Particularly, each obfuscation category contains 1497 samples, which are from the Mal-Genome [2] and the Contagio Minidump [27] datasets.

We use Dataset A and Dataset B as the training sets, and Dataset C and Dataset D are used to evaluate the Generalization performance of ByteDroid. Then, we evaluate the performance of ByteDroid against obfuscation techniques using the Dataset E. The proposed CNN model is implemented by using the Python package of Tensorflow [30]. We train the CNN model with 4 Nvidia Titan X. As depicted in Table 2, we evaluate the performance of ByteDroid using accuracy, precision, recall and f1 score.

Table 2. Evaluation metrics

Metrics	Abbr.	Description
True Positive	TP	# of malware correctly detected
True Negative	TN	# of benign samples correctly classified
False Positive	FP	# of benign samples predicted as malware
False Negative	FN	# of malware predicted as benign sample
Accuracy	Acc.	(TP+TN)/(TP+TN+FP+FN)
Precision	Pre.	TP/(TP+TN)
Recall	Rec.	TP/(TP+FN)
F1-score	F1	2*Precision*Recall/(Precision + Recall)

4.2   Detection Performance

In this experiment, we measure the detection performance of ByteDorid using ten-fold cross validation based on the Dataset A and the Dataset B. To prevent over-fitting, cross validation is performed in ten rounds. In each round, we split the dataset into the training sets, validation sets and testing sets. The split ratio is 8:1:1.

Single Dataset Cross Validation. We firstly evaluate the performance of ByteDroid in single dataset. At the same time, we implement the method of N. Mclaughlin et al. [8] as a comparison and we refer this method as DAMD in the following experiments. Table 3 shows the detection results of ByteDroid and DAMD based on Dataset A and Dataset B. In addition, the result threshold is set to 0.5.

We can see that ByteDroid outperforms DAMD with the accuracy improvement as much as 6%. The reason can be explained as the following. First, ByteDroid utilizes both the opcode and the operands of the applications, while

Table 3. Single dataset cross validation of ByteDroid and DAMD.

Method	Data type	Datasets	Acc.	Pre.	Rec.	F1
Ours	Bytecode	A	0.984	0.972	0.991	0.981
DAMD	Opcode	A	0.968	**0.996**	0.927	0.960
Ours	Bytecode	B	**0.995**	0.992	**0.998**	**0.995**
DAMD	Opcode	B	0.936	0.957	0.887	0.920

DAMD only relies on the opcode. We believe the operands do carry the partial malware features and that is the reason why DAMD is less accurate than ByteDroid. Second, ByteDroid uses the multiple sizes of the convolutional kernels to improve the performance of the model architecture, while DAMD only has a single sized convolutional kernel.

Cross-Dataset Testing. It is commonly believed that the deep learning based malware detection cross the datasets is more challenging because the malware from different datasets may not share the features as the malware from the same dataset does. In this experiment, we test ByteDroid's detection accuracy on different datasets. In particular, we conduct the cross-dataset testing. We first train ByteDroid with Dataset A, and then use Dataset B as the testing set to evaluate ByteDroid's performance. We repeat the same experiment by swapping the training set and the testing set. Similarly, we also perform the same test for DAMD for the comparison purpose.

Table 4. Cross-dataset testing of ByteDroid and DAMD.

Method	TrainSet	TestSet	Acc.	Pre.	Rec.	F1
Ours	A	B	0.854	0.857	0.837	0.847
DAMD	A	B	0.682	**0.997**	0.551	0.710
Ours	B	A	**0.969**	0.974	**0.952**	**0.963**
DAMD	B	A	0.885	0.971	0.828	0.894

Table 4 shows the results of cross-dataset tests. Obviously, ByteDroid achieves the significant improvement in all metrics. It indicates that ByteDroid has much better cross-dataset testing performance than DAMD. In addition, it is interesting to find that both methods have much better detection accuracy when dataset B is used as the training set and the dataset A is used as the testing set. By examining the both datasets, we find the dataset B contains approximately 500 more benign applications and 2,000 more malicious applications than dataset A. It demonstrates that the size of the training set does affect the malware detection performance of both methods. When the training set is larger, the deep learning model has better chances to capture more malware features and therefore achieves higher accuracy in the detection stage. Nevertheless, the testing results show ByteDroid is much more effective in the malware detection than DAMD.

Manual Analysis. When we use dataset B as the training set, ByteDroid correctly classifiers 96.9% of 10,874 applications (Dataset A), with 69 benign samples being misclassified as malware and 236 malware samples being misclassified as benign applications. To investigate the actual reasons that cause the above false positive and false negative, we perform the following manual analysis.

We use VirusTotal to rescan 69 benign samples that are reported incorrectly as malware. The results show that all of them are clean. After manual analysis, we find that 52 benign samples have the behaviors that are commonly performed in the malware, such as reading contact, reading SMS, collecting device ID, obtaining geographical location and device IMEI. We believe the behaviors' corresponding bytecode sequences are detected during the test and thus cause the false positive.

There are also 236 malware samples misclassified as benign applications. We find 194 malware out of 236 have their APK sizes less than 500 KB. These APKs have the short bytecode sequences, and thus lack the sufficient sequence patterns that match the malicious ones. The rest of the misclassified malware either hide the malicious code in its resources or disguise itself as an image such as install.png. The detection of these behaviors is out of the scope of our malware detection.

4.3   Generalization Performance

In this experiment, we evaluate the generalization performance of our proposed method in realistic scenarios. Based on the model trained using Dataset B, we use the Dataset C and the Dataset D to measure the Generalization performance of ByteDroid. Again, we take DAMD as a comparison. Table 5 shows the detection rates of ByteDroid and DAMD using the Dataset C and the Dataset D.

Table 5. Detection rates of ByteDroid and DAMD using Dataset C and D.

Method	Datasets	Years	# of malware	# of detected	Detected rate
Ours	C	2014	9389	7923	**84.38%**
DAMD	C	2014	9389	7253	77.24%
Ours	D	2017–2018	979	822	**83.96%**
DAMD	D	2017–2018	979	611	62.41%

We can clearly see that the malware detection rate of ByteDroid is at least 7% higher than DAMD. One may notice that the overall detection rate of ByteDroid is less than 85%. The reason is that the dataset (B) used for training is relatively old, and the datasets (C&D) under the test are relatively newer. We believe many newer malicious patterns of the malware in dataset C and D are not learned in the training stage. To further investigate the reason of the false negative, we perform the following manual analysis.

Manual Analysis. In Dataset C, ByteDroid fails to detect 1,466 malware samples. We discover that 191 samples only detected by 1 out of 62 anti-scanners in VirusTotal. There are 146 samples used native code or dynamic code loading to evade the detection. The malicious behaviors of these malware samples are not obviously under the static analysis.

In Dataset D, ByteDroid misses 157 malware samples. One-half of the 157 samples contain the dynamically load code from a library. It is obvious that the obfuscation techniques become more popular in the newer malware. In addition, 10 malware samples use MultiDex technique to generate multiple DEX files in their APKs.

Nevertheless, experiment results demonstrate that ByteDroid is capable of catching the various malicious patterns once the malicious behaviors are present during the training.

4.4   Against the Obfuscation

In this experiment, we evaluate the robustness of ByteDroid in catching the Android malware with the obfuscation techniques. Currently, obfuscation techniques on Android platform have been very mature, and there are many automated obfuscation frameworks [28, 29] available, which allow attackers to reduce the labor cost or even achieve the obfuscation capability without understanding the detailed obfuscation techniques.

We use the datasets (E) from the Android PRAGuard [28] for the evaluation. The Dataset E contains seven obfuscation techniques including trivial obfuscation, class encryption, string encryption, reflection and their combinations. We also train the CNN model using the Dataset B. Table 6 shows the detection results.

Table 6. Detection rate of ByteDroid against obfuscated malware.

ID	Obfuscation method	Detected rate	Miss rate
1	Trivial obfuscation	94.07%	5.93%
2	String encrption	88.02%	11.98%
3	Class encryption	89.90%	10.10%
4	Reflection	93.52%	6.48%
5	Combined 1, 2	90.48%	9.52%
6	Combined 1, 2, 4	90.40%	9.60%
7	Combined 1, 2, 3, 4	98.81%	1.19%
Average	-	92.17%	7.83%

The results shown in Table 6 indicate that ByteDroid effectively detect Android malware despite the use of different types of obfuscation techniques.

ByteDroid is more effective for detecting the malware applied with trivial obfuscation. As described in Android PRAGuard [28], the trivial obfuscation only affects the string and does not change the instructions in the bytecode. Yet, ByteDroid learns the malicious behaviors by the bytecode sequences rather than by the semantics of the strings.

ByteDroid has a poorer performance in defending other obfuscation techniques such as string encryption, class encryption and reflection because these techniques affect both the strings and the bytecode sequence. They introduce some noises may break the key bytecode sequence of a malware, which makes ByteDroid difficult to classify them correctly.

4.5   Hyperparameter

In this experiment, we evaluate the effectiveness of hyperparameters in ByteDroid, including embedding vector size, the maximum size of the bytecode sequence, the convolutional kernel sizes and the number of epochs. In the validation process, we explore these hyperparameters with ten-fold validation using the Dataset B.

Embedding Size P. In Fig. 3(a), the embedding size of the outermost ROC curve is 128. The ROC curves corresponding to the embedding size exceeding 32 are close to each other. Since the larger embedding vector size requires the longer training time and the higher computational cost, we choose to set the embedding size to 32 to make a balance between performance and efficiency.

Convolutional Kernel Sizes. In our CNN, the convolutional kernel with sizes are ranging from 2 to 8, and the stride is set to 1. Compared with the kernel sizes of 3, 5 and 7, which are commonly used in other CNN-based schemes, we find that the sizes with the powers of 2 (i.e., 2, 4, and 8) achieve better performance. Figure 3(b) shows the ROC curves with different convolution kernel sizes.

Maximum Length of the Bytecode Sequence α. Figure 3(c) shows the distribution of the bytecode size of the dataset. Nearly 90% of the bytecode samples are less than 2,500 KB. Consider that 2,500 KB is still a large number that incurs much computational cost, we search for a shorter size that fits the best for our system. To do that, we test the malware detection true positive rate with the bytecode sizes starting from 500 KB and gradually increasing at an interval of 500 KB. It can be seen from Fig. 3(d) that the receiver operating characteristic (ROC) curve does not improve much when the bytecode size is 1,500 KB or more. Based on the above result, we set 1,500 KB as the size of the bytecode sequence in the training stage.

Number of Epochs. We train the model for 20 Epochs and record the accuracy, the precision, the recall and the f1 score of every single epoch. The results are plotted in Fig. 4. It can be observed that all of the metrics keep a small range fluctuation after 9 epochs. Consequently, the CNN model can be trained to achieve good performance quickly after several epochs.

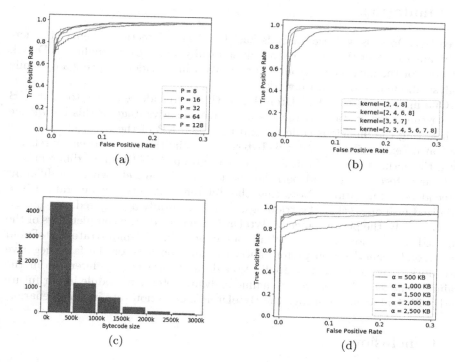

Fig. 3. Effectiveness of different hyperparameters. Figure 3(a) shows the ROC curves with different embedding vector sizes. Figure 3(b) shows the ROC curves for different convolutional kernel sizes. Figure 3(c) shows the size distribution of the bytecode. Figure 3(d) shows the ROC curves for different α.

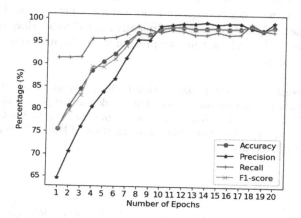

Fig. 4. The metrics versus the number of epochs.

5   Limitations

Since ByteDroid is a static analysis based malware detection scheme, it inherently fails to detect the malware that dynamically launches the malicious Dalvik bytecode or the native code from a library. We will consider adopting a dynamic analysis module in our future work.

One may notice that ByteDroid limits that bytecode sequence to 1,500 KB during the training stage. Attackers may take the advantage of this knowledge by inserting the malicious code beyond the 1,500 KB of the bytecode to evade the feature extraction. In fact, this bytecode size limitation can be easily relaxed given the actual dataset. In practice, we can group the APKs into different sets by their bytecode sizes and perform the training separately with the different bytecode size limitations. Note that the different datasets can be trained in a serialized fashion so that the training result is naturally aggregated.

Obviously, the performance of ByteDroid depends on the completeness of the Android application datasets. While our experiments demonstrate ByteDroid has a good generalization performance, the false positive or the false negative rate does increase when the application datasets are very different from the training datasets. We believe a dynamic malware detection module in our future work will significantly improve the ByteDroid's detection rate in this scenario.

6   Conclusion

In this paper, we propose ByteDroid, an automatic Android malware detection system using Convolutional Neural Network. ByteDroid eliminates the need of manual feature extraction. It applies multiple convolutional kernels to learn the sequential patterns of the bytecode. The effectiveness and generalization performance of ByteDorid are evaluated in our experiments. In addition, ByteDroid is robust against several typical obfuscation techniques.

In future work, we plan to explore more complex network architecture and consider dynamic analysis to detect dynamically loaded code. Moreover, to better understand malware behaviors, the interpretability of the neural networks is also what we concerned about.

Acknowledgements. We would like to thank the anonymous reviewers for their insightful comments to improve our paper. This work was supported by the National Natural Science Foundation of China under Grant No. 61672543, by the Open Research Fund of Key Laboratory of Network Crime Investigation of Hunan Provincial Colleges Grant No. 2017WLFZZC002.

References

1. Comparetti, P.M., Salvaneschi, G., Kirda, E., Kolbitsch, C., Kruegel, C., Zanero, S.: Identifying dormant functionality in malware programs. In: 2010 IEEE Symposium on Security and Privacy, pp. 61–76. IEEE (2010)

2. Zhou, Y., Jiang, X.: Dissecting android malware: characterization and evolution. In: 2012 IEEE Symposium on Security and Privacy, pp. 95–109. IEEE (2012)
3. Zhou, W., Zhou, Y., Jiang, X., Ning, P.: Detecting repackaged smartphone applications in third-party Android marketplaces. In: Proceedings of the Second ACM Conference on Data and Application Security and Privacy, pp. 317–326. ACM (2012)
4. Chen, S., Xue, M., Tang, Z., Xu, L., Zhu, H.: Stormdroid: a streaminglized machine learning-based system for detecting Android malware. In: Proceedings of the 11th ACM on Asia Conference on Computer and Communications Security, pp. 377–388. ACM (2016)
5. Narudin, F.A., Feizollah, A., Anuar, N.B., Gani, A.: Evaluation of machine learning classifiers for mobile malware detection. Soft Comput. **20**(1), 343–357 (2016)
6. Milosevic, N., Dehghantanha, A., Choo, K.K.R.: Machine learning aided Android malware classification. Comput. Electr. Eng. **61**, 266–274 (2017)
7. Li, J., Sun, L., Yan, Q., Li, Z., Srisa-an, W., Ye, H.: Significant permission identification for machine-learning-based Android malware detection. IEEE Trans. Industr. Inform. **14**(7), 3216–3225 (2018)
8. McLaughlin, N., et al.: Deep Android malware detection. In: Proceedings of the Seventh ACM on Conference on Data and Application Security and Privacy, pp. 301–308. ACM (2017)
9. Wu, D.J., Mao, C.H., Wei, T.E., Lee, H.M., Wu, K.P.: Droidmat: Android malware detection through manifest and API calls tracing. In: 2012 Seventh Asia Joint Conference on Information Security, pp. 62–69. IEEE (2012)
10. Yang, C., Xu, Z., Gu, G., Yegneswaran, V., Porras, P.: DroidMiner: automated mining and characterization of fine-grained malicious behaviors in Android applications. In: Kutyłowski, M., Vaidya, J. (eds.) ESORICS 2014. LNCS, vol. 8712, pp. 163–182. Springer, Cham (2014). https://doi.org/10.1007/978-3-319-11203-9_10
11. Arp, D., Spreitzenbarth, M., Hubner, M., Gascon, H., Rieck, K., Siemens, C.: Drebin: effective and explainable detection of Android malware in your pocket. In: NDSS, vol. 14, pp. 23–26 (2014)
12. Burguera, I., Zurutuza, U., Nadjm-Tehrani, S.: Crowdroid: behavior-based malware detection system for Android. In: Proceedings of the 1st ACM Workshop on Security and Privacy in Smartphones and Mobile Devices, pp. 15–26. ACM (2011)
13. Wu, W.C., Hung, S.H.: Droiddolphin: a dynamic android malware detection framework using big data and machine learning. In: Proceedings of the 2014 Conference on Research in Adaptive and Convergent Systems, pp. 247–252. ACM (2014)
14. Lindorfer, M., Neugschwandtner, M., Platzer, C.: Marvin: efficient and comprehensive mobile app classification through static and dynamic analysis. In: 2015 IEEE 39th Annual Computer Software and Applications Conference (COMPSAC), vol. 2, pp. 422–433. IEEE (2015)
15. Hou, S., Ye, Y., Song, Y., Abdulhayoglu, M.: Hindroid: an intelligent Android malware detection system based on structured heterogeneous information network. In: Proceedings of the 23rd ACM SIGKDD International Conference on Knowledge Discovery and Data Mining, pp. 1507–1515. ACM (2017)
16. Yuan, Z., Lu, Y., Xue, Y.: Droiddetector: Android malware characterization and detection using deep learning. Tsinghua Sci. Technol. **21**(1), 114–123 (2016)
17. Li, W., Wang, Z., Cai, J., Cheng, S.: An Android malware detection approach using weight-adjusted deep learning. In: 2018 International Conference on Computing, Networking and Communications (ICNC), pp. 437–441. IEEE (2018)

18. Hou, S., Saas, A., Chen, L., Ye, Y., Bourlai, T.: Deep neural networks for automatic android malware detection. In: Proceedings of the 2017 IEEE/ACM International Conference on Advances in Social Networks Analysis and Mining, pp. 803–810. ACM (2017)
19. Nix, R., Zhang, J.: Classification of Android apps and malware using deep neural networks. In: 2017 International Joint Conference on Neural Networks (IJCNN), pp. 1871–1878. IEEE (2017)
20. Xu, K., Li, Y., Deng, R.H., Chen, K.: Deeprefiner: multi-layer Android malware detection system applying deep neural networks. In: 2018 IEEE European Symposium on Security and Privacy (EuroS&P), pp. 473–487. IEEE (2018)
21. Le, Q., Mikolov, T.: Distributed representations of sentences and documents. In: International Conference on Machine Learning, pp. 1188–1196 (2014)
22. Kingma, D.P., Ba, J.: Adam: a method for stochastic optimization. arXiv preprint arXiv:1412.6980 (2014)
23. Kang, H., Jang, J.W., Mohaisen, A., Kim, H.K.: Detecting and classifying Android malware using static analysis along with creator information. Int. J. Distrib. Sens. Netw. **11**(6), 479174 (2015)
24. Fan, M., et al.: Frequent subgraph based familial classification of Android malware. In: 2016 IEEE 27th International Symposium on Software Reliability Engineering (ISSRE), pp. 24–35. IEEE (2016)
25. Roberts, J.M.: Virus share (2011). https://virusshare.com
26. Total, V.: Virustotal-free online virus, malware and URL scanner (2012). https://www.virustotal.com
27. Mobile, C.: Mobile malware mini dump (2013). http://contagiominidump.blogspot.com
28. Maiorca, D., Ariu, D., Corona, I., Aresu, M., Giacinto, G.: Stealth attacks: an extended insight into the obfuscation effects on Android malware. Comput. Secur. **51**, 16–31 (2015)
29. Rastogi, V., Chen, Y., Jiang, X.: Droidchameleon: evaluating Android anti-malware against transformation attacks. In: Proceedings of the 8th ACM SIGSAC Symposium on Information, Computer and Communications Security, pp. 329–334. ACM (2013)
30. Abadi, M., et al.: Tensorflow: a system for large-scale machine learning. In: 12th {USENIX} Symposium on Operating Systems Design and Implementation ({OSDI} 2016), pp. 265–283 (2016)

Research on Multidimensional System Security Assessment Based on AHP and Gray Correlation

Xiaolin Zhao[✉], Hao Xu, Ting Wang, Xiaoyi Jiang,
and Jingjing Zhao

Beijing Institute of Technology, Beijing 100081, China
zhaoxl@bit.edu.cn

Abstract. Aiming at the problems of the network security evaluation indexes, which are one-sided and difficult to be strictly quantified, this paper proposes the multidimensional system security evaluation method based on AHP and grey relational analysis. Under the guidance of the construction principle of system security evaluation model, this paper puts the source of factors affecting network security as the criterion of dimension Division, and constructs a multidimensional system security evaluation model for environmental security, network security and vulnerability security. On this basis, this paper combines AHP and grey relational analysis theory, and evaluate system security comprehensively and quantitatively. The multidimensional system security evaluation method based on AHP and grey relational analysis can consider the relationship between qualitative and quantitative factors in system security, and it is highly logical and flexible. This method also can effectively solve the problem that system security is difficult to evaluate objectively and quantitatively, and the system security evaluation can be pushed from a simple rough comparison to a comprehensive quantitative calculation stage.

Keywords: Network security · Security assessment · Analytic Hierarchy Process · Gray correlational analysis

1 Introduction

The number of internet users in China reached 829 million, increasing 3.8 percentage points comparing with 2017 years. It is shown by "43th Statistical Report on Internet Development in China" that the internet penetration rate reached 59.6% at the end of December 2018 [1].

With the implementation of the "internet plus" plan, cyber-system security attacks will intensify and cyberspace security threats have become one of the most serious challenges that affect national security and economic development. For example, Ransomware Wannacry attacked many hospitals, companies, universities and government organization across at least 150 countries, having more than 200 thousand victims in May, 2017. In order to deal with the increasingly serious system security problems, experts believe that we need to fully consider its security during the system design phase and evaluate network system security for controlling the system security

© Springer Nature Singapore Pte Ltd. 2020
W. Han et al. (Eds.): CTCIS 2019, CCIS 1149, pp. 177–192, 2020.
https://doi.org/10.1007/978-981-15-3418-8_13

assessment. At present, the indexes used in quantitative evaluation of network security are relatively unimportant in our country. The lack of consideration of the entire system coupled with the fact that system security is hard to be strictly quantified, which can't meet the current system security needs.

This paper intends to build a multi-dimensional system security assessment model for environment security, network security and vulnerability security based on network theory, Analytic Hierarchy Process (AHP), gray relational analysis theory (GT). AHP is used to determine the weight of each index under the guidance of this model. The gray relational analysis is used to quantitatively evaluate the network security and improve the system security analysis and calculation method. Finally, according to the needs of the experimental task, the simulation system is tested, which shows the effectiveness and feasibility of the method.

2 Related Work

From the published literature, there are some representative methods of network security assessment at home and abroad can be divided into the following three categories [2]:

The security evaluation method based on mathematic model draws on the traditional multi-objective decision theory, and aggregates multiple influencing factors to construct the evaluation function. The advantage of this method is that it can directly reflect the security, such as the traditional weight analysis method, set analysis of the law [3, 4]. But this method also has many deficiencies. For example, the core evaluation function of the structure and the choice of parameters need a unified evaluation criteria and measurement, which often reply on the help of expert knowledge and experience, inevitably with subjective factors.

On the one hand, the system security assessment method based on knowledge reasoning processes uncertainty information by means of fuzzy sets, probability theory and D-S evidence theory [5], on the other hand, by reasoning and aggregating multi-source multi-attribute information [6]. The research focus of system security assessment in knowledge reasoning are: the method based on the fault graph model, the attack tree based method [7], the privilege graph based method, the attack graph model [8], the Bayesian network based method [9], the hierarchical method [5] and so on. Compared with the traditional mathematical model, the method of system security assessment based on knowledge reasoning can simulate the human way of thinking. The evaluation process has a certain degree of intelligence to avoid the influence of human subjective factors on the objectivity of system security assessment. However, the method also have some challenges, such as the inaccessibility of reasoning rules and the combination of explosions, which make them restricted in practical application.

The system security assessment method based on data mining and pattern recognition has strong learning ability by evaluating the security of the system by mining system security modules from training samples or historical data [10]. The process of security assessment based on pattern recognition is mainly divided into two stages: building model and pattern matching. Representative studies include: support vector machine (SVM) method [11], neural network based method [12], gray relational method [13, 14] and Hidden Markov Model based methods [15]. Although the method of system security assessment based on pattern recognition has the advantage of objectivity, it needs a large amount of training data to learn the parameters in the model. It is difficult for the general network system to obtain a large amount of data. At the same time, it is also difficult to use the evaluation method based on pattern recognition to realize the prediction of the network attack event.

The factors which affect security are gray and hierarchical for cyberspace. Analytic Hierarchy Process (AHP) [16] can reflect the evaluation results of the whole system, build multi-level and multi-dimensional evaluation which reflects the hierarchy of the system, and calculate the importance of each factor. However, AHP has defects that its subjectivity is too strong. It is based on the experience of experts, so there are some problems that are difficult to quantify. There is comparison for several traditional methods in Table 1. In order to solve the problem in these methods, this paper establishes a multi-dimensional network assessment model based on AHP and gray correlation. We add a gray-scale quantitative assessment model, which can quantify the collected data more objectively.

Table 1. Comparison for several traditional methods

Method	Data acquisition	Objectivity	Model building	Accuracy of results
Data mining	Difficult	Strong	Easy	Strong
Knowledge reasoning	Easy	Strong	Difficult	Strong
AHP	Easy	Weak	Easy	Weak
What we want?	Easy	Strong	Easy	Strong

Our Contributions

Based on AHP and gray correlation (GC) [17], this paper mainly has the following contributions:

- We established the index system of system security assessment by analyzing the internal relations among the influencing factors;
- The paper uses metasploitable2 as the experimental environment. We established a relatively standard test reference environment. The tools we used are easy to obtain;
- We calculated the overall system security assessment value by combining AHP and GC. It shows the correctness of the algorithm by comparing with other algorithms. It was tested the sensitivity of the factors affecting the algorithm.

The first part of this article is about the introduction of background and the necessity of AHP-GC. The second and third part introduces the theory and calculation method of the algorithm in detail. The fourth part is the experimental design and experimental results of the test part. The last is a conclusion.

3 Multidimensional Network Security Assessment Method Based on AHP-GC

This paper uses AHP-GC multi-dimension security assessment methods. The main process is shown as Fig. 1:

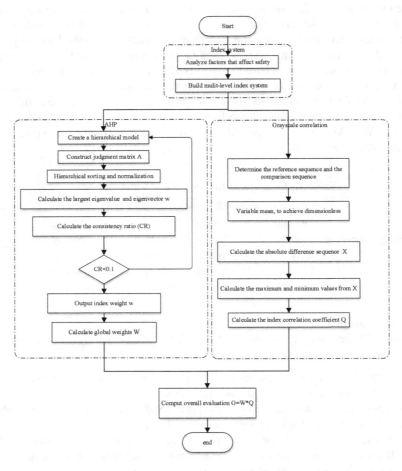

Fig. 1. Overall sequence diagram

Firstly, we need to analyze the factors that affect security, and then establish the comparison matrix between the factors according to the relationship so that AHP can be used to obtain the weight of each index following [16]. Gray correlation analysis is based on the comparison with the reference sequence to get the correlation with the ideal sequence. The correlation can be considered as the score corresponding to each index. In order to solve the security value of the whole system, it is used that the weighted average sum of the scores.

The following describes the establishment of the index model and GC method to obtain indexes of the score.

3.1 Establishment of Multidimensional System Security Assessment Index Model

Based on the classification theory of system security influence factors, this paper divides the system security into three dimensions according to the actual situation, including the host environment security, network security and vulnerability security. The multi-dimensional system security assessment model established in this paper is shown in Fig. 2. The system security includes three sub-metrics, host security, network security and vulnerability security.

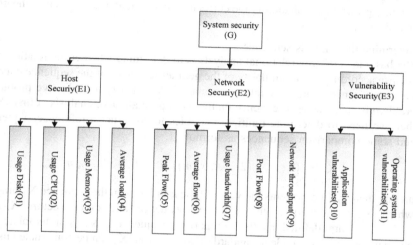

Fig. 2. Muliti-dimensional system security index system

An important factor that really threatens system security is vulnerability. So from a vulnerability perspective, we can divide system security metrics into two parts, known security and unknown security. Known security refers to security issues that have been compromised. The number of vulnerabilities can be found on CNNVD [18] and the extent of the vulnerability can be determined. Another type of security is unknown, vulnerability exists but have not been compromised. When the system is attacked by unknown security, we can only rely on the system anomaly to detect the problem, so we chose the host and network indexes to detect unknown vulnerabilities. Use vulnerability security to evaluate known vulnerabilities.

After the index system is established, the score of each index is collected and the weight of each index is calculated. Finally, the security index of the entire system is obtained through the weighted average calculation method, and the global index is between 0 and 1. The closer the result value is to 1, the safer it is. In order to have a better judgement on the security of the system, we can set the level of security for the system (Table 2).

Criteria for evaluation mainly from the service and vulnerability point of view. If there is a high-risk vulnerability, the system is in an insecure state. If the system is completely out of control, such as crashing, being shut down, etc., it may be receiving a DDOS attack or a great potential for unknown vulnerability. Therefore, it should also be considered as insecure.

The following describes in detail the use of the GC evaluation method of calculating the value.

3.2 Network Security Quantitative Evaluation Method Based on Gray Correlation Analysis

The network security quantitative assessment process based on gray relational analysis can be roughly divided into four steps: determining the analysis sequence, Nondimensionalizing variables, calculating the correlation coefficient and calculating the gray relational degree.

(1) Determine the analysis sequence

The basic idea of gray relational analysis is to determine whether the relationship is close according to the similarity of the geometric shapes of the sequence curves. Therefore, when using gray relational analysis to quantify a qualitative problem, problem is analyzed as a sequence on the basis of qualitative analysis at first. And then we need to determine multiple variables to construct a reference sequence and some comparison sequences as formula 1,

$$\mathbf{X}_i = \{x_i(1), x_i(2), \ldots, x_i(m)\} \ (i = 0, 1, 2, \ldots, n) \tag{1}$$

among then, $x_i(k)$ represents the value of the k-th index in the sequence $\mathbf{X}_i$, among which $\mathbf{X}_0$ is defined as the reference sequence and other vectors $\mathbf{X}_i (i = 1, 2, \ldots, n)$ are defined as the comparison sequences. $\mathbf{X}_0$ is a template for comparison and also an ideal standard of comparison. $\mathbf{X}_0$ can be constructed using the best values of multiple indexes. A comparison sequence is the data sequence consisting of factors that affect the behavior of the system.

(2) Nondimensionalize variables

In the constructed sequence of analyzes, the units of measurement and the orders of magnitude of the various evaluation indexes are not the same in general, but the different dimensions and orders of magnitude are inconvenient for comparison or it is difficult to draw the correct conclusions when comparing. Therefore, there are incompatibilities in the original data. It can't be directly evaluated. In order to reflect the real situation as much as possible and ensure the reliability of the analysis results, the original data of each evaluation index needs to be treated without dimension before the comprehensive evaluation, which is said as dimensionless variables. In this paper, the method of averaging is used to nondimensionalize the analysis sequence. As is shown in formula 2, the basic idea is to use the average of all the data in the analysis sequence as the denominator of the sequence to re-determine the analysis sequence.

$$x_i'(k) = \frac{x_i(k)}{\bar{x}_i} \tag{2}$$

where, $\bar{x}_i$ is the average of the factors of $\mathbf{X}_i$.

(3) Calculate the correlation coefficient

The correlation coefficient is the degree of association between the node pairs in the geometric curves of the reference sequence and the comparison sequence, and the formula is as shown in Formula 3. The correlation coefficient of the kth indexes is,

$$\delta_i(k) = \frac{\Delta\min + \rho\Delta\max}{\Delta x_i(k) + \rho\Delta\max} \tag{3}$$

where, $\Delta x_i(k) = |x(k) - x_i(k)|$ is the value of the k-th data of the absolute difference sequence. Absolute difference sequence is an analytical sequence composed of the absolute value of the difference between the reference sequence and the comparison sequence. As is shown in formula 4, n sets of evaluations constitute n absolute difference sequences, and each set of evaluations is composed of m indexes.

$$\Delta\mathbf{X}_i = \{|x(1) - x_i(1)|, \ldots, |x(m) - x_i(m)|\}(i = 1, 2, \ldots n) \tag{4}$$

$\Delta\max$, $\Delta\min$ respectively represent the maximum and minimum values in the n absolute difference sequences, and their calculation methods are shown in Eqs. 12 and 13.

$$\Delta\max = \max_i(\max(\Delta\mathbf{X}_i)) \tag{5}$$

$$\Delta\min = \min_i(\min(\Delta\mathbf{X}_i)) \tag{6}$$

ρ called the resolution coefficient, the value ρ is generally in the interval $(0, 1)$, the smaller the value, the correlation coefficient between The greater the difference, the stronger the resolution. When the value ρ is less than 0.5463, the resolution is the strongest. Therefore, the usual value ρ is 0.5.

(4) Calculate the gray relational degree

Since the correlation coefficient is the degree of association between the reference sequence and the comparison sequence in each node of the geometric curve, when the correlation degree between the reference sequence and the comparison sequence is compared, the correlation coefficient obtained is more than one. The excessively scattered information makes the overall comparison unusually difficult. Therefore, we need to integrate the reference sequence and the comparative sequence in the geometric curve of each node in the degree of association value. That is the integration of correlation coefficient set as a value. As the reference sequence and comparison of the number of correlation between the sequence of numbers, this value is called gray Correlation.

When calculating the gray relational degree, the index weight can be introduced to combine the correlation coefficient with the hierarchy weight, and the formula for calculating the gray relational degree r is shown in Formula 7. Among them, $\omega(k)$ represents the weight value of the kth evaluation index in the analysis sequence, and the weight of each index satisfies Formulas 8 and 9.

$$r = \sum_{k=1}^{m} \omega(k)\delta(k) \tag{7}$$

$$\omega(k) \in [0, 1] \tag{8}$$

$$\sum_{k=1}^{m} \omega(k) = 1 \tag{9}$$

The gray relational value reflects the size of the correlation between the reference sequence and the comparison sequence. The closer the value is to 1, the greater the correlation between the comparison sequence and the reference sequence is. In this paper, we choose the optimal value of each index in the historical data of the network to build a reference sequence. The closer the value of gray relation is to 1, the better the security of the network to be evaluated.

4 Experimental Design and Analysis

4.1 Experimental Environment Configuration and Index System Interpretation

In order to verify the effectiveness and feasibility of AHP and GC multi-dimensional system security assessment, we set up the experimental environment.

First of all, we need to find a recognized experimental environment, and then conduct comparative experiments.

Experimental Environment to Build. This article chooses metasploitable2 virtual machine. Metasploitable2 virtual machine is a specially Ubuntu operating system. It is designed as a security tool to test and demonstrate common vulnerability attacks. This virtual machine is compatible with VMware, VirtualBox and other virtual platforms. So this is a system which has its own vulnerability. The system can be downloaded from source forge.net [19] After the test environment is set up, we need to scan for system vulnerabilities. We use Nessus [20] for scanning. Nessus is the most widely used system vulnerability scanning and analysis software tool in the world. It can be downloaded from [20]. In addition, the status of the system is monitored to determine potential system intrusion. We use Ganglia [21] to monitor the system. Ganglia is an open source cluster monitoring project sponsored by UC Berkeley and designed to measure thousands of nodes. It can test system performance. There are websites [21] to download.

Experimental Comparison Design. The experimental environment has a lot of exploits that can be exploited, so the final score should tend to be high-risk. At the same time, we set of five experiments by repairing the system vulnerabilities and attacks system. Results of group experiments in five different groups are shown in Table 2.

We can see from the table, S3 level is the dividing line. S1 and S2 can be considered as temporary security. S4 and S5 can be considered dangerous and require warning. S1 is a relatively safe environment, and S5 shows that the worst case, the value of each index close to the maximum value. It may be lost control of computer, unable to measure system attributes such as CPU occupancy, memory usage, etc. The index is observed before The data can be collected. Through the above method to set the experimental environment and experimental control group. By comparing the results of different evaluation methods with the known experimental results to determine the accuracy of the algorithm, and comparing the results of different experimental groups of the same algorithm, the consistency test result of the algorithm is obtained.

Table 2. Experimental comparison design

Number	Level	Assessed value (x)	Assessment method
1	S1	$0.9 \leq x \leq 1$	Patch all vulnerabilities, and no attack
2	S2	$0.8 \leq x < 0.9$	Repair high-risk vulnerabilities, and there are flaws which can't be used, the system is operating normally
3	S3	$0.7 \leq x < 0.8$	Based on the experimental environment, some vulnerabilities are repaired and there are still some exploitable vulnerabilities and low-level DDOS attacks
4	S4	$0.6 \leq x < 0.7$	The default level of the experimental environment, there are high-risk vulnerability. The services are normal
5	S5	$0 < x < 0.6$	In the experimental environment, add DDOS attack to lead to service stopped

Index Interpretation and Collection. This article has 11 indexes, (Q1–Q11). It includes the statistics of the system host status information, network information and vulnerability information. For host status information, it includes hard drive usage (Q1), CPU usage (Q2), memory usage (Q3), and average system load (Q4). Q1 and Q2 have access to get the current resource usage, smaller value is better. Q2 represents the percentage of CPU that is occupied in real time during program execution, the average system load indicates the average load on the CPU. And the information contained is statistical information about the number of the processes that CPU is processing and the processes that wait for CPU for a period of time. The ideal single core load should be around 0.7.

According to the network information, the statistical indexes are Peak Flow (Q5), Average Flow (Q6), Usage bandwidth (Q7), port flow (Q8), and network throughput

(Q9). These indexes monitor traffic from different perspectives variety. Q9 monitors the status of a single port, Q10 monitors the total network operation.

According to vulnerability information, there are two indexes, application level (Q10) and system level indexes (Q11). This index is actually a vulnerability weighted score. The level and rating of the vulnerability comes from CVE.

Experimental data collected are shown in Table 3 based on the host security dimension, network security dimension and vulnerability security dimension respectively. The reference data value is the historical data information of the system to be evaluated for statistics and analysis. The optimal value of each index is extracted; and the comparative data value is the index value collected by the network in real time.

Table 3. Environmental security indexes data information table

Index	Reference	Exp1	Exp2	Exp3	Exp4	Exp5
Q1	6%	0%	8%	63%	23%	99%
Q2	3%	4%	26%	53%	0.4%	99%
Q3	36%	20%	97%	47%	36%	99%
Q4	70%	70%	50%	40%	50%	99%
Q5	2385 KB/sec	1200 KB/sec	128 KB/sec	40 MB/sec	5013 KB/sec	40 MB/sec
Q6	67 KB/sec	67 KB/sec	72 KB/sec	36 MB/sec	129 KB/sec	36 MB/sec
Q7	2%	0%	34%	99%	25%	99%
Q8	396 KB/sec	300 KB/sec	100 KB/sec	36 MB/sec	875 KB/sec	36 MB/sec
Q9	1200 KB/sec	120 KB/sec	150 KB/sec	36 MB/sec	1075 KB/sec	36 MB/sec
Q10	0	0	0	0	1	1
Q11	0	0	0	1	2	2

4.2 Data Preprocessing

In order to avoid the problem of being unable to calculate due to the different units and scales of the collected index data, the collected index data needs to be preprocessed first. Generally, data are normalized to the interval (0, 1) through dimensionless processing, and the index attributes can be monotonously reflected. We hope that the network system is the most secure state when the index value is 1, and the security state decreases with the decrease of the index value until the network system reaches the least secure state when the index value is 0. Considering the characteristics of different indexes, we will adopt different normalization methods.

For indexes Q1, Q2, Q3, Q4 and Q7, their index values vary in the interval (0, 1), and the best reference value is given. Therefore, we calculate the absolute difference between the index value and the reference value to preprocess the index, as shown in Formula 10.

$$x_i' = 1 - |x_i - x_0|, \quad i = 0, 1, 2, \ldots, n \tag{10}$$

Where, x_0 represents the best reference value, and x_i represents the comparison index value. And any of the treated index values is certainly in the interval (0, 1), and the closer it is to 1, the higher the security is. Obviously, $x_0 = 0$.

For indexes Q10 and Q11, we need to normalize the index value to the interval (0, 1) as shown in Formula 11 after calculating the absolute difference according to Formula 10.

$$x_i'' = \frac{x_i' - \min(x_i')}{\max(x_i') - \min(x_i')}, \ i = 0, 1, 2, \ldots, n \tag{11}$$

Where, $\min(x_i')$ is the minimum, and $\max(x_i')$ is the maximum of x_i'. And any of the treated index values is certainly in the interval (0, 1), and the closer it is to 1, the higher the security is.

For indexes Q5, Q6, Q8 and Q9, considering the large data scale span, if calculated according to formulas 7 and 8, the processed index values may be distributed at both ends of 0 and 1, unable to reflect the real security situation, and will affect the subsequent calculation. Therefore, as shown in Formula 19, the index scale is firstly reduced through logarithmic calculation to make its distribution relatively uniform, and the final normalized index value is obtained through the calculation of Formulas 10 and 11.

$$y_i = \ln(x_i), \ i = 0, 1, 2, \ldots, n \tag{12}$$

After the calculation of Formulas 19, 17 and 18, the index value y_i'' can be relatively evenly distributed in the interval (0, 1), and the closer it is to 1, the higher the security is.

4.3 Multidimensional Network Security Evaluation Index Weight Calculation

We use AHP to calculate the weight of each index. First, we give the comparison matrix of the three indexes in the criterion layer, as shown in Table 4.

Table 4. The first level index weight matrix

	E1	E2	E3
E1	1	0.5	1/3
E2	2	1	1/2
E3	3	2	1

Tables 5, 6 and 7 respectively show the pairwise comparison matrix of host security, network security and vulnerability security.

Table 5. Host security (E1) index weight table

	Q1	Q2	Q3	Q4
Q1	1	1/5	1/3	0.25
Q2	5	1	3	1
Q3	3	1/3	1	0.2
Q4	4	1	5	1

Table 6. Network security (E2) index weight table

	Q5	Q6	Q7	Q8	Q9
Q5	1	5	0.5	7	4
Q6	0.2	1	1/7	2	1
Q7	2	7	1	9	7
Q8	1/7	0.5	1/9	1	0.25
Q9	0.25	1	1/7	4	1

Table 7. Vulnerability indexes weight table

	Q10	Q11
Q10	1	1/3
Q11	3	1

After calculation and consistency test, the final weight and consistency test results of each indicator are shown in Table 8.

Table 8. Index weight and consistency validation

Criterions	Weight	Indexes	Weight	Overall weight
E1	0.1638	Q1	0.0734	0.0120
		Q2	0.3772	0.0618
		Q3	0.1378	0.0226
		Q4	0.4116	0.0674
		CR	0.0572	
E2	0.2973	Q5	0.2986	0.0888
		Q6	0.0725	0.0215
		Q7	0.4973	0.1478
		Q8	0.0390	0.0116
		Q9	0.0926	0.0275
		CR	0.0289	
E3	0.5390	Q10	0.25	0.1347
		Q11	0.75	0.4042
		CR	0	
CR	0.0032			

4.4   Result

By using AHP, we obtain the weight vector of every index $\mathbf{W} = (W_1, W_2, \ldots, W_{11})^T$. And the correlation coefficient matrix of indexes $\mathbf{\Delta} = (\delta_1, \delta_2, \delta_3, \delta_4, \delta_5)^T$ could be calculated by using the grey correlation method, where, $\delta_i = (\delta_i(1), \delta_i(2), \ldots, \delta_i(11))^T$ represents the correlation coefficient vector of the j-th experiment. Therefore, Formula 13 can be used to obtain the comprehensive evaluation score of the sequence.

$$\mathbf{G} = \mathbf{W} * \mathbf{\Delta}^T \tag{13}$$

Shown in Fig. 3, we draw 6 correlation curves of the analysis sequence, respectively representing one reference sequence and 5 comparative experiments mentioned in Table 4, where horizontal coordinates represent 11 indicators of multi-dimensional system security index system, and vertical coordinates represent values of pre-processed indicators. On the whole, all curves look close to the reference sequence curve, but the safer the comparison sequence, the closer the curve is to the reference sequence. After calculating, we get the correlation coefficients of every index in 5 experiments, and show them in Table 9.

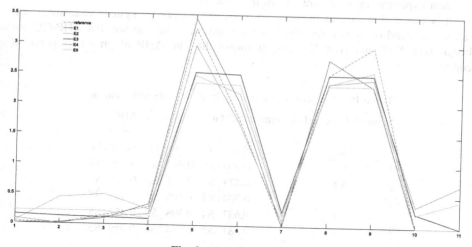

Fig. 3. Correlation curve

Table 9. Comparison of evaluation results

Number	δ_1	δ_2	δ_3	δ_4	δ_5
Q1	0.9474	0.9664	0.7836	0.8914	0.6993
Q2	0.9853	0.5146	0.7992	0.9759	0.6860
Q3	0.8932	0.5675	0.9211	0.9473	0.8678
Q4	0.9093	0.9231	0.6958	0.7922	0.7007
Q5	0.7278	0.3678	0.3820	0.6140	0.3333
Q6	0.6255	0.5162	0.3798	0.8737	0.4436
Q7	0.9818	0.7324	0.6654	0.8516	0.6816
Q8	0.6429	0.7485	0.9886	0.7617	0.7194
Q9	0.4083	0.5251	0.4908	0.4587	0.4139
Q10	1.0000	1.0000	0.6551	0.5647	0.6709
Q11	1.0000	1.0000	1.0000	0.3934	0.5048

We calculate the score of the network system states based on AHP-GC, and compare the method with AHP and AHP-Entropy [22], which are popular method to evaluate network security. The scores and security levels by different methods for different experimental states are shown in Table 10.

It is shown that various methods are basically correct for system assessment and reflect the trend of system security. At the same time, we can see that AHP-GC are better than AHP and AHP-Entropy. It shows that the AHP of gray correlation is correct.

Table 10. The scores and security levels by different methods

Number	Expected outcome	AHP-GC		AHP		AHP-Entropy	
	SL	Score	SL	Score	SL	Score	SL
1	S1	0.950	S1	0.989	S1	0.990	S1
2	S2	0.873	S2	0.861	S2	0.879	S2
3	S3	0.704	S3	0.508	S5	0.461	S5
4	S4	0.653	S4	0.398	S5	0.357	S5
5	S5	0.581	S5	0.064	S5	0.059	S5

Sensitivity Analysis

By looking at the weights of the different indexes in Table 9, you can see that all the indexes have a weight value greater than 0. 01. The smallest is 0. 0116, standing for hard drive usage and port flow. Weight values can't be too small, otherwise the role of the system's indexes will be ignored. The weight requested is within the acceptable range. The maximum weight value is 0.486, which is the system vulnerability index. This fulfil the requirements. Because vulnerabilities are the direct cause of system security. The environmental and cyber security metrics are just the performance of a vulnerability threat.

In addition, the value in host environment is changed and other is the same in Experiment 1 and Experiment 2, and the number of vulnerability is 0, which shows that the algorithm is sensitive to changes of the host environment. The host environment and network environment of Experiment 2 and Experiment 4 are basically similar. It is different from the number of vulnerabilities. It can be seen that the vulnerability assessment is sensitive and the weights are relatively large.

According to the system security assessment results in Table 10, the results of system security evaluation method written in paper are basically similar with the traditional method. The evaluation result is more accurate based on numerical correction.

Based on the analysis of the experimental results, it is verified that the proposed system security assessment method can comprehensively quantify the indexes of system security in the three dimensions of host environment security, network security and vulnerability security. It accurately and objectively evaluates the comprehensive security of the system. Therefore, the validity and feasibility of the multi-dimensional system security assessment method are verified experimentally based on AHP and gray correlation.

5 Conclusion

At present, the existing indexes of system security assessment are difficult to quantify strictly. This paper presents a multi-dimensional system security assessment method based on AHP and gray relation. The source of network security factors is taken as the criterion of dimension division under the guidance of system security assessment model construction principles. The multi-dimensional system security assessment model which includes host environment security, network security and vulnerability security is constructed to evaluate the system security synthetically.

At the same time, the method overcome the shortcomings of the traditional qualitative assessment methods and quantitative assessment methods combining the AHP and gray relational analysis to quantify the system security. It is logical and flexible to solve the problems existing in comprehensive quantitative assessment of system security Multi-level, multi-factor and non-quantitative issues. The security assessment method proposed in this paper can accurately and effectively quantify the comprehensive security of the network and avoid the subjectivity and one-sidedness of the traditional security assessment methods through experimental verification.

Acknowledgement. This work was supported by National Key R&D Program of China (Grant No. 2016YFB0800700).

References

1. China Internet Network Information Center. http://www.cnnic.net.cn/hlwfzyj/hlwxzbg/hlwtjbg/201902/P020190318523029756345.pdf. Accessed 22 Sep 2019
2. Zhao, M.: Survey on technology of network security assessment. Comput. Sci. Appl. **05**(1), 18–24 (2015)

3. Chen, J.: A network security risk assessment model based on unascertained mathematics. J. Air Force Eng. Univ. **15**(2), 91–94 (2014)
4. Huang, X.: Research on network security evaluation system based on fuzzy comprehensive evaluation method. In: International Conference on Economics (2017)
5. Zhang, Y.: DS theory and hierarchical weight based network security risk assessment. Comput. Appl. Soft. **28**(11), 294–297 (2011)
6. Liu, H.: Network security evaluation model based on uncertainty reasoning. J. Acad. Armored Force Eng. **6** (2006)
7. Yao, L., Dong, P., Zheng, T., et al.: Network security analyzing and modeling based on Petri net and Attack tree for SDN. In: International Conference on Computing. IEEE (2016)
8. Yin, X., Fang, Y., Liu, Y.: Real-time risk assessment of network security based on attack graphs, vol. 92, pp. 75–80 (2013)
9. Qi, Z., Zhou, C., Tian, Y.C., et al.: A fuzzy probability Bayesian network approach for dynamic cybersecurity risk assessment in industrial control systems. IEEE Trans. Ind. Inform. **99**, 1 (2018)
10. Swarup, K.S.: Artificial neural network using pattern recognition for security assessment and analysis. Neurocomputing **71**(4–6), 983–998 (2008)
11. Wang, C., Jing, Z., Li, X.: Research on DDoS attacks detection based on RDF-SVM. In: International Conference on Intelligent Computation Technology and Automation (2017)
12. Zhang, Y.B., Yan, Z.Q.: Researches on the network security evaluation method based on BP neural network. Appl. Mech. Mater. **686**, 470–473 (2014)
13. Wang, C.Y.: Assessment of network security situation based on grey relational analysis and support vector machine. Appl. Res. Comput. **30**(6), 1859–1862 (2013)
14. Yang, J., Chen, Q.B.: Network security evaluation based on grey relation projection multi-criteria decision. Comput. Knowl. Technol. **2011**(29), 76 (2011)
15. Xiang, S., Lv, Y., Xia, C., Li, Y., Wang, Z.: A method of network security situation assessment based on hidden Markov model. In: Li, K., Li, J., Liu, Y., Castiglione, A. (eds.) ISICA 2015. CCIS, vol. 575, pp. 631–639. Springer, Singapore (2016). https://doi.org/10.1007/978-981-10-0356-1_65
16. Li, X., Xu, J., Li, D.: Index system of reliability evaluation for distribution network based on analytic hierarchy process. Proc. Chin. Soc. Univ. Electr. Power Syst. Autom. **21**(3), 69–74 (2009)
17. Tian, G., Zhang, H., Zhou, M.C., et al.: AHP, gray correlation, and TOPSIS combined approach to green performance evaluation of design alternatives. IEEE Trans. Syst. Man Cybern. Syst. **99**, 1–13 (2017)
18. CNNVD: Vulnerability information. http://www.cnnvd.org.cn/web/vulnerability/querylist.tag. Accessed 22 Sep 2019
19. rapid7user. https://sourceforge.net/projects/metasploitable/files/Metasploitable2/. Accessed 22 Sep 2019
20. Tenable. https://www.tenable.com/products/nessus-vulnerability-scanner. Accessed 22 Sep 2019
21. Ganglia: Ganglia Monitoring System. http://ganglia.info/?page_id=66. Accessed 22 Sep 2019
22. Ma, R., Ge, H., Gu, S.G., et al.: A method for determining the reference framework of network security metric index system. J. Cyber Secur. **4**(1), 67–78 (2019)

Research on Software Network Key Nodes Mining Methods Based on Complex Network

Chun Shan[✉], Peng Wang, Changzhen Hu, Xianwei Gao,
and Shanshan Mei

Beijing Key Laboratory of Software Security Engineering Technology,
School of Computer Science and Technology, Beijing Institute of Technology,
Beijing 100081, China
sherryshan@bit.edu.cn

Abstract. Complex software system will bring a lot of software security problems, it is very meaningful to know how to more accurately abstract the software network model from the software system and efficiently find the key nodes in the software network. This research takes open source software as the research object, constructs a directed network model of software system, proposes a new weight calculation method, adds weights to the model to form a directed weighted network, and then regards the software network as a complex network. The defect mining and defect propagation cost are two node mining methods related to the weight and degree of the node. At the same time, the PageRank algorithm is improved to mine the key nodes. Finally, the robustness of the software system execution network model is carried out by different attack methods. The evaluation, through experimental verification and comparison, shows that the mining method proposed in this study can more accurately and efficiently mine key nodes in the software system.

Keywords: Software security · Key nodes · Defect probability · Defect propagation cost · Improved PageRank algorithm

1 Introduction

The security, reliability and robustness of software systems are crucial to the development of the software industry. The complexity of software comes from many aspects. The interaction between multiple elements in the system determines the complexity of the software system. The unique characteristics that you have depend on its topology. Throughout the process, according to the needs of the development design, the complex functions are decomposed into a large number of reusable elements (classes, objects, subroutines, components, etc.). If these elements are treated as nodes, then the interaction between these nodes constitutes a complex software network topology model. The software system and the complex network can be combined to study the complexity of the software system by utilizing the relevant characteristics of the complex network, and analyze the structure and function of the software system from a new perspective. First, the structure of the software system can be represented by a software network model. By treating reusable elements on different scales in large

© Springer Nature Singapore Pte Ltd. 2020
W. Han et al. (Eds.): CTCIS 2019, CCIS 1149, pp. 193–205, 2020.
https://doi.org/10.1007/978-981-15-3418-8_14

complex software systems as nodes and treating the interrelationships (messages, data exchanges, program calls, etc.) between these nodes as edges, you can abstract complex software into a network model or diagram. In order to evaluate the influence of nodes, it is common to research and analyze the relationship between all abstract nodes and nodes in the software network, quantify the status or influence degree of nodes in the whole network through certain conditions, and mine the node key in the software network.

2   Related Work

Some attributes of nodes and edges are considered as key metrics for metrics. These metrics include node degrees [1], center affinity [2], feature vectors, K-shell, median [3], cumulative nominations, edges. The weight and so on. Callaway DS et al. [4] studied the seepage problem of a graph with a completely general distribution, and gave the exact solutions in various cases, including the positional seepage, the key seepage, and the occupancy probability depending on the vertex degree. The larger the node, the more critical the node was, but the impact of the overall information of the software network on the criticality of the node was ignored. Freeman LC [5] proposed a median metric, which means that the node has a higher median value. The more interactions a node had, the more important the node was. However, as the size of the network continues to increase, it was unacceptable to calculate the time-consuming and computational complexity of each node; Maharani et al. [6] believed that the structure and weight of the graph have a great influence on the central value itself. And the eigenvectors of the eigenvectors observed the influence of the data center value of the Twitter data to judge the propagation speed of the information in the social network; Kitsak et al. [7] proposed that the importance of the node depends on its relative position in the whole network. The most effective communicators were those who are at the core of the network and were identified by k-shell decomposition analysis. In the process of mining key nodes, PageRank algorithm is one of the most influential classical algorithms. The PageRank algorithm is mainly used to determine the level of a page by the hyperlink relationship of the network, and thus used for page ranking. Google mainly uses it for search engine optimization operations, and different theoretical researchers have made different improvements based on this algorithm [8].

3   Key Node Mining Method Based on Weight and Degree

By calculating the defect probability and defect propagation degree of the software system node, the key nodes of the software system can be obtained from the weight and the degree of the node, in order to more comprehensively measure a node as a key node or further find a more accurate key nodes, followed by the key node mining algorithm based on page rank or PageRank, this algorithm mainly obtains the information of key nodes from the aspect of node in-degree.

3.1   Complex Network Characteristics Metrics for Software Networks

First choose a typical object-oriented software system, the selection principle is based on whether the software features meet the needs, whether there is community support, document integrity. Choose to download the source code for Hystrix open source software from GitHub. To abstract the software from the class level, use the reverse tool to get the UML class diagram. After writing the program to count the number of methods of each class, add it as a weight to the class diagram file, use the complex network analysis tool Pajek to transform the UML into a directed weighted network model, and then use Pajek to obtain its abstract network model. The metric values are then studied for the degree distribution of the corresponding network model of the software system. The statistical results in Table 1 below indicate that the software network model of the experimentally selected system meets the characteristics of a small world network with a shorter average path length and a larger clustering coefficient. We assume that the complexity of all methods in the class is the same, let the weight W = n, which is the number of methods in the class.

Table 1. Statistical characteristics of the software network model corresponding to the system in the experiment

Software system	Number of nodes	Number of sides	Average shortest path length	Average aggregation coefficient	Average aggregation coefficient corresponding to random network	Average degree
Hystrix	375	307	1.366	0.126	0.008	1.637

3.2   Defect Possibility

This study proposes a method for estimating the likelihood of a node defect, and regards the defect possibility as a conditional probability that the node cannot guarantee that the function of the class is normal (or the system is operating normally). Hypothesis defect probability indicator $R(M) = \{R(M_j)|j = 1, 2, \ldots, n\}$, node defect possibility $R(D_i|M_j)$ can be calculated by Bayesian inference:

$$R(D_i|M) = \frac{R(M|D_i)R(D_i)}{R(M)} \qquad (1)$$

The defect probability of the node N1 can be calculated first by the weight, and the degree of use is mainly corrected by the in-degree of entry. Let N1 have the possibility of defects:

$$R(D_{N1}|M) = \frac{R(M|D_{N1})R(D_{N1})}{R(M)} \qquad (2)$$

$R(D_{N1})$ is a priori indicator, that is, the initial evaluation of the probability of a weight-to-node (class) defect. $R(M|D_{N1})$ can be obtained by the out-degree of outgoing, here is the proportion of the degree of out-degree in degrees. $R(M)$ represents the sum of weights and degrees($R(M)$ is not zero), This formula does not consider the case where the out-degree is zero. In the special case, if the degree of exit is zero, the probability of the defect is the ratio of the weight to $R(M)$. The defect possibilities of each node of the open source software system are showed in Table 2:

Table 2. HystrixNode defect possibility evaluation value

Node number	Weight	out-degree	in-degree	Defect possibility value
215	83	2	0	0.976470588
141	34	2	0	0.944444444
174	32	2	0	0.941176471
345	29	2	0	0.935483871
264	28	2	0	0.933333333
184	25	2	0	0.925925926
241	10	2	0	0.833333333
23	9	2	0	0.818181818
85	6	2	0	0.75
265	6	2	0	0.75
38	4	2	0	0.666666667
61	4	2	0	0.666666667
374	4	2	0	0.666666667
124	3	2	0	0.6
135	3	2	0	0.6
273	3	2	0	0.6
16	2	2	0	0.5
278	2	2	0	0.5
369	7	3	2	0.35
92	53	1	2	0.31547619
53	42	1	2	0.311111111
234	5	4	2	0.303030303
159	30	1	2	0.303030303
103	1	3	0	0.25
364	1	3	0	0.25
306	8	1	2	0.242424242
240	32	1	3	0.222222222
35	29	1	3	0.21969697

From the statistics in the table above, we can clearly see the impact of the node's weight on the calculation of the defect probability of this node. In Table 2, we can see that when the degree is the same, the weight of the node is larger, and the probability of the defect is larger. When the weight is the same and the out-degree of the difference is different, the effect of the out-degree of the defect on the probability of the defect is greater than the weight. The impact on the likelihood of defects is greater.

3.3 Defect Propagation Cost

The degree of affinity of a node can reflect the total number of classes or modules that are indirectly and directly dependent on a given class or module, characterizing how much the node affects the entire graph or network. Let node x, y ∈ $V(G)$, $H(x)$ denote the set of all nodes in Figure G that are reachable from x. Assuming that there is a directed path of arbitrary length from x to y, then y is said to be reachable from x. In graph theory, the set $H(v)$ is defined as the reachable set of a given node v. The degree of the degree of the node v is defined as the number of elements in the set $H(v)$.

Starting from any node v_i in the software network, the ratio of the sum of the degrees on the shortest path of all nodes that can be reached along the directed edge and the degree of sweep is the defect propagation cost, which is recorded as:

$$T(v_i) = \frac{\sum_{j \neq i}^{v_j \in H(v_i)} D_{v_i v_j}}{N^2}, D_{v_i v_j} = \min_{v_j \in H(V_i)} D_{v_i v_j} \tag{3}$$

$H(v_i)$ is the set of all nodes that the node v_i can reach through the directed edge, that is, the reachable set of v_i. N is the degree of spread of the node v_i. $D_{v_i v_j}$ is the sum of the out-degrees of a node v_i and v_j in $H(v_i)$, If there are multiple paths between the nodes v_i and v_j, select a shortest path and calculate the sum of all out-degrees. When the out-degree of v_i is zero, $T(v_i) = 0$. Give a simple example to illustrate how to calculate the defect propagation cost of a software network, as shown in Fig. 1.

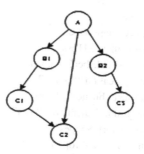

Fig. 1. An example of the cost of software network defect propagation

In the simple network above, there are five nodes associated with node A, and each node corresponds to a class in the object-oriented software. Class A is directly adjacent or directly dependent on B1, B2, and C2. Therefore, if class B1, B2, or C2 changes and is attacked, class A will change accordingly. Similarly, class A is indirectly dependent on classes C1, C2, and C3.

$H(A) = \{B1, B2, C1, C2, C3\}$

$D_{AB_1} = 1; \quad D_{AB_2} = 1;$

$D_{Ac_1} = 2; \quad D_{AC_3} = 2;$

$D_{AC_2} = 1$ (Abandon AB1C1C2 to select the shortest path of AC2 and calculate the out-degree);

$T(A) = \dfrac{D_{AB_1} + D_{AB_2} + D_{Ac_1} + D_{AC_3} + D_{AC_2}}{5^2} = \dfrac{7}{25} = 0.28$

By calculating the defect propagation cost of the open source software system nodes in the experiment, the obtained node defect propagation costs are listed in order from small to large. Due to the large scale of the system, only the calculation of the cost of propagation through the defect is listed in the table. The method sorts some of the obtained nodes, as shown in the following Table 3:

Table 3. Defect propagation cost of nodes in Hystrix

Node number	Class corresponding to the node	Defect propagation cost
234	"com.netflix.hystrix.HystrixCommand"	0.2400
369	"com.netflix.hystrix.HystrixObservableCommand"	0.3125
103	"Factory.HystrixCommandGroupDefault"	0.3125
364	"Factory.HystrixCommandKeyDefault"	0.3125
137	"command.AbstractHystrixCommand"	0.3330
278	"IntegerDynamicProperty"	0.3600
358	"AbstractHystrixCommand.Action"	0.3878
262	"command.BatchHystrixCommand"	0.3878
256	"LongDynamicProperty"	0.4375
331	"BooleanDynamicProperty"	0.4375
184	"HystrixCollapser.Scope"	0.4440
345	"HystrixObservableCollapser.Scope"	0.4444
47	"RequestCollapser.CollapsedTask"	0.444
215	"HystrixServoMetricsPublisherCommand"	0.5000
141	"ExecutionHookDeprecationWrapper"	0.5000
174	"HystrixServoMetricsPublisherCollapser"	0.5000
264	"HystrixServoMetricsPublisherThreadPool"	0.5000
241	"RequestCollapserFactory.Scopes"	0.5000
4	"strategy.properties.BooleanProperty"	0.5000
23	"StringProperty"	0.5000
252	" IntegerProperty"	0.5000
85	"ChainProperty"	0.5000
265	"ExecutionIsolationStrategyHystrixProperty"	0.5000
38	"MethodProvider.SpecificFallback"	0.5000
374	"MethodProvider.DefaultCallback"	0.5000
124	"HystrixCollapserKeyDefault"	0.5000
135	"TryableSemaphoreNoOp"	0.5000

3.4   Improved Algorithm for Key Node Mining Based on PageRank

Basic Principle of PageRank Algorithm

PageRank, the page rank, also known as the Page Ranking, was a web page sorting algorithm proposed by Larry Page and Sergey Brin in 1998. The main method is to use the hyperlink relationship of the network to determine the level of the page, which is used for page ranking. This algorithm is the main basis used by Google to measure the relevance and importance of web pages, and is often used as a performance factor for web page optimization in the evaluation of search engine optimization operations.

On the Internet, in addition to text, animation, pictures, audio, and video, the information in each web page is also transmitted through a large number of links and other web pages. The appearance of these links can help us find some relative information. Important page.

Explain as shown in the left diagram of Fig. 2. At this time, each web page is treated as a node, and the link relationship between web pages is regarded as an edge. Generally speaking, when the webpage A chain is directed to the webpage B, it can be concluded that the webpage A feels that the webpage B has a use value and is a relatively important webpage. The more pages you link to a web page, the more important the linked web page becomes; the more important web pages that are linked to the web become more important.

Suppose only one page is included in a collection: A, B, C, and D. As shown in the right figure of Fig. 2.

- If pages B, C, and D both point to A, then the PageRank (abbreviation) value of A will be the sum of the values of pages B, C, and D, namely: $PR(A) = PR(B) + PR(C) + PR(D)$.

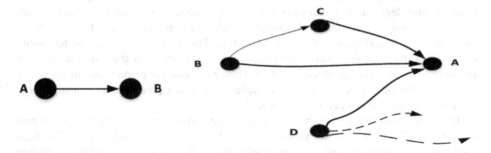

Fig. 2. Web link example diagram

- If page B is linked to C in addition to linking to page A, and page D also has links to the other two pages except page A. Since the PR value of a page cannot be voted twice at the same time. So B gives half the PR value of each page. Similarly, only one-third of the PR value of page D is counted on the PR of A. at this time, $PR(A) = PR(B)/2 + PR(C)/1 + PR(D)/3$. In other words, the PR value of a page is divided equally according to the total number of links, namely: $PR(A) = PR(B)/L(B) + PR(C)/L(C) + PR(D)/L(D)$.

- For any web page i in the network, its PR value can be expressed as follows:

$$PR_i = \sum_{j \in B_i} \frac{PR_j}{L_j} \tag{4}$$

Where B_i is the set of all web pages linked to webpage i, and L_j is the number of other webpages (outgoing) linked by webpage j.

Improved Algorithm Implementation

Since the PageRank algorithm is to find the nodes that are cited more frequently in the webpage, and the idea of measuring the importance of the nodes in terms of the in-degree of accessibility in this section is consistent, we propose an improved PageRank based on the probability of node out and the probability of defects. The algorithm is the KeyNode algorithm. The KeyNode algorithm is defined as follows:

$$KN(i) = \left(\sum_{j=1}^{m} \frac{KN(j)}{D_{out}(j)} \right) \times R(i) \tag{5}$$

KN is the KeyNode algorithm model for calculating the key nodes of the software network in this experiment; $D_{out}(j)$ is the out-degree of the node j pointing to the node i, and the out-degree of the nodes in each system in the network model has been sorted; There are a total of m neighbors that point to node i. $R(i)$ refers to the defect possibility of node i. This algorithm is a recursive algorithm. The recursive exit, i.e. the KN value of the initial node, is the ratio of the probability of the defect of the initial node to its out-degree. In the running process of the software system, the greater the out-degree of a node and the higher the probability of defects, the greater the influence of this node, the easier it becomes to become a key node.

In the previous chapter, we have abstracted the software network model G, referred to as $G_{hystrix}$. The set of nodes in the model is V, and the set of edges is E. The final output of this algorithm is the key node set *KNset*。 The pseudo code of the algorithm execution process is as follows:

```
Input: G_hystrix
Output: KNset
Begin
(1) KNset = Ø ;
(2) for ( i = 1; i ≤ m ; i + +) {
// Calculate the total number of nodes in the software network
diagram separately as m
```
(3) $KN(i) = \frac{R(i)}{D_{out}(i)}$;
```
// Initial node i has only n out-degree nodes, no in-degree
(4)      for ( j = 1; j ≤ n; j + +)
// Traversing node j of node i to calculate KN
```
(5) $KN(j) = \left(\sum_{l=1}^{t} \frac{KN(l)}{D_{out}(l)} \right) \times R(j)$;
```
// KN value of j
(6)                    KNset. Add ("KN(j)") ;
// Put the KN value of the node into the collection     (7) }
(8)    Weight(KNset) ;
// Sort the KN values of the nodes in the collection
(9)    output KNset
End
```

Let the initial value of the set KNset be an empty set. When the algorithm runs, firstly, the total number of nodes of the software system network needs to be traversed. This traversal is only applicable to nodes that are related to other nodes, that is, nodes whose degree is not zero. Starting from the node i whose out-degree is not 0in-degree 0 (after sorting out-degree), calculate the value of KN(i); then calculate the KN value of the adjacent node j of node i, respectively, since node j may also There is more than one adjacent node, so (5) in the algorithm is actually the result of the breadth traversal of the node j; the obtained KN value of j is added into the set KNset, and after the traversal, the KNset is sorted in descending order; the output is obtained. A collection of key nodes.

Executed in the open source software system abstract model, you can get the key nodes of the system. Here only the top ranked nodes are listed, in order: 369, 137, 286, 41, 288, 92, 234, 53, 159, 60, 309, 228, 180, 108, 352, 291, 116, 51, 64, 344, 370, 168, 71, 73, 127. It can be concluded that the key nodes in the improved PageRank algorithm and the defect probability and defect propagation cost are the key nodes with certain repeat nodes [9]. In the software system Hystrix, the key node and the defect probability obtained by the improved algorithm are the same key node ratio of the key node is 5/28, and the ratio of the same key node obtained by the defect propagation cost method is 3/28. The ratio of the same key nodes ranked by the two methods is 2/28.

4 Experimental Analysis and Verification

Research on the robustness or vulnerability of software networks should clarify the target of attack and the way of attack [10]. Properly removing some nodes has been considered an important way to destroy complex networks [11]. This paper uses a combination of random attack and selective attack. This study chooses the relationship between the relative size of the largest connected components f and e in the computing network to measure the anti-aggressiveness of the network. The maximum connected component, the ratio of the number of nodes to the total number of nodes in the network, i.e. the relative size f, is mainly used to measure the overall connection of the network, as a quantitative measure of network robustness. The specific expression of the maximum connected component relative size f is as follows:

$$f = \frac{n}{N} \tag{6}$$

N represents the number of summary points in the network, and n represents the number of nodes owned by the largest connected component. We can get the connection diagram of Hystrix as shown in Fig. 3 below.

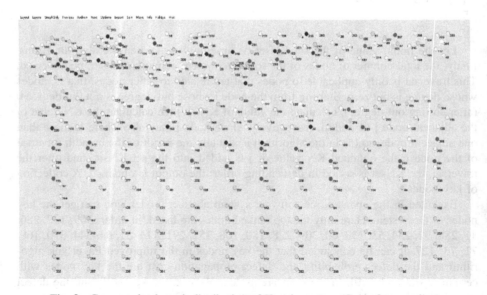

Fig. 3. Connected subgraph distribution of Hystrix system (Color figure online)

The different colors of the nodes in the above figure represent different numbers of methods in each class in the software system, that is, the weights of the nodes in the graph are different, and the colors with large node weights are deeper, which in turn distinguish different nodes. By calculation, we obtain that the largest connected subgraph in Hystrix is composed of 24 nodes. The number of other connected subgraphs and the number of nodes composing the connected subgraph are shown in Table 4.

Table 4. The case of connected components in Hystrix

The number of nodes that make up the connected subgraph	24	23	19	15	9	6	5	4	3	2	1
Number of connected subgraphs	1	1	2	11	1	4	9	3	10	27	32

We use MATLAB to calculate the relationship between the relative size of the maximum connected component and the failure nodes under random attack. In the process of calculation, the proportion of the failure nodes increases in the order of equal difference. In selective attack, we mainly attack the key nodes obtained to verify the correctness of the key nodes. Through simulation experiments, we get the scatter plots between the attacked nodes and the proportion of the maximum connected component in Hystrix under different attack modes, as shown in Fig. 4 below.

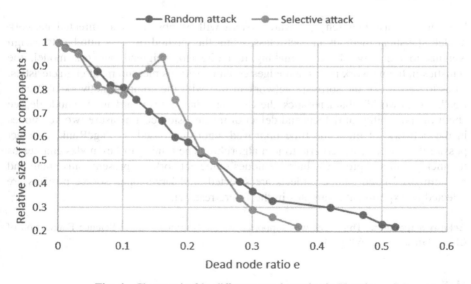

Fig. 4. Changes in f in different attack modes in Hystrix

It can be seen from the figure that the software network: Hystrix shows good attack resistance against random attacks. As the proportion of failed nodes increases, the relative size of the largest connected components also shows a stable and slower downward trend, but it is attacked. When the node reaches about half of the total number of nodes, the relative size of the largest connected component reaches about 0.2. At this time, the software system is in a state of paralysis and cannot continue to work. In the selective attack mode, the ratio of the maximum connected component in the software network to the proportion of the attacked node shows a less consistent change. When the failed node in the network is before 0.1, the relative size of the maximum connected component shows a steady downward trend, but the ratio of f is unexpectedly increased between the ratio of the attacked node between 0.1 and 0.6, which is due to the maximum. When a node in the connected component fails, a connected network may become multiple connected networks. More maximum connected networks may appear in the topology network of the software system, so the curve in the figure will show a short-term rising phase. After that, as the proportion of the failed nodes increases, the relative size of the largest connected component will drop sharply, and then the proportion of nodes that are attacked reaches nearly 0.4, the software system cannot work normally, and the network is in a paralyzed state. The difference between a selective attack and a random attack is that when a selective attack is performed, the key nodes in the network are first attacked, which causes the system to stop working when the attack node is less than the random attack failure node, thereby verifying The key nodes found in this article are correct.

5   Conclusion

First in the class hierarchy software system will be abstracted as directed network model, statistical methods in each class, using the method of class number to assign weights to the network edge, making it a directed weighted network model, the statistics in the network nodes and edges contains various measurement characteristics, so as to verify that the software network in line with the complex network of "scale-free", "small world" characteristics, the value and then put forward and the node degree about the possibility of defects and defect of transmission cost measure two key nodes in the network, at the same time improved algorithm based on PageRank, a defect possibility as one of the criteria to join algorithm, The mining of key nodes enables us to quickly find and protect vulnerable nodes in the network. At present, only small and medium-sized open source projects are selected, and larger open source projects are selected as experimental samples in the future research.

Acknowledgement. This work was supported by the National Natural Science Foundation of China (Grant No. U1636115).

References

1. Li, Y., Zhang, Y., Deng, Y.: Degree centrality based on the weighted network. In: 24th Chinese Control and Decision Conference (CCDC), China, pp. 3976–3979. IEEE (2012)
2. Landherr, A., Friedl, B., Heidemann, J.: A critical review of centrality measures in social networks. Bus. Inf. Syst. Eng. **2**(6), 371–385 (2010)

3. Kitsak, M., Havlin, S., Paul, G., et al.: Betweenness centrality of fractal and non-fractal scale-free model networks and tests on real networks. Phys. Rev. E **75**(5), 056115 (2007)
4. Callaway, D.S., Newman, M.E.J., Strogatz, S.H., et al.: Network robustness and fragility: percolation on random graphs. Phys. Rev. Lett. **85**(25), 5468–5471 (2000)
5. Freeman, L.C.: Centrality in Social Networks' Conceptual Clarification. Soc. Netw. **1**(3), 215–239 (1979)
6. Maharani, W., Gozali, A.A.: Degree centrality and eigenvector centrality in twitter. In: International Conference on Telecommunication Systems Services and Applications, pp. 1–5. IEEE (2015)
7. Kitsak, M., Gallos, L.K., Havlin, S., et al.: Identifying influential spreaders in complex networks. Nat. Phys. **6**(11), 888–893 (2010)
8. Andersen, R., Chung, S.: Local graph partitioning using pagerank vectors. Soc. Netw. **12**(4), 475–486 (2006)
9. Opsahl, T., Agneessens, F., Skvoretz, J.: Node centrality in weighted networks: generalizing degree and shortest paths. Soc. Netw. **32**(3), 245–251 (2010)
10. Malik, H.A.M., Abid, F., et al.: Robustness of dengue complex network under targeted versus random attack. Complexity (2017). https://doi.org/10.1155/2017/2515928
11. Mahesar, A.W., Shah, A., Wahiddin, M.R.: Node status detection and information diffusion in router network using scale-free network. In: Proceedings of the 10th International Network Conference (INC 2014), p. 95, Lulu.com (2014)

Research and Development of TPM Virtualization

Liang Tan[1,2(✉)], Huan Xiao[1], and Juan Wang[3]

[1] College of Computer Science, Sichuan Normal University, Sichuan, China
tanliang2008cn@126.com
[2] Institute of Computing Technology, Chinese Academy of Sciences,
Beijing, China
[3] School of National Cyberspace Security, WHU, Wuhan 430072, China

Abstract. Combination of Cloud Computing and Trusted Computing is an important method to build a trusted cloud environment, and the most critical problem is the virtualization of TPM (Trusted Platform Module, TPM). But in view of the current research, TPM virtualization still not only does not meet the whole TCG specification, but also has a lot of security issues, and it is becoming the bottleneck of building a trusted cloud environment by combination of Cloud Computing and Trusted Computing. This paper introduces the basic concepts, types and basic requirements of TPM virtualization. The classification model of TPM virtualization is put forward by the I/O device virtualization technology. The main research work of the key technologies of TPM virtualization, such as architecture, key management, certification trust extension, migration and so on, are described in detail, moreover taking time as the clue, we can display a panoramic view of the evolution of related key technologies. Combined with the existing research results, the research direction and challenges of TPM virtualization under TCG architecture are discussed.

Keywords: Trusted computing · Cloud computing · Virtual platform module (TPM) · TPM virtualization · vTPM

1 Introduce

The Trusted Platform Module (TPM) is the core of trusted computing [1–9]. It is the root of trust in trusted computer systems and the key technology for trusted computing. TCG (Trusted Computer Group, TCG) [1] defines the core functions of the trusted computing platform: measurement, storage and reporting are all dependent on TPM; trusted roots of trusted computing platform: Root of Trust for Measurement (RTM), Root of Trust for Storage (RTS), and Root of Trust for Report (RTR) are all directly related to TPM. The RTM consists of a set of PCR memories in the CRTM (Core Root of Trust for Measurement, CRTM) and the TPM. The RTS consists of a TPM and a storage root key SRK. The RTR consists of a TPM and an EK. TCG is not only the initiator of trusted computing ideas, but also the organizer and promoter of trusted computing technology. In order to promote the widespread application and further extension of trusted computing, TCG has established a series of working groups, initially including Embedded System, Infrastructure, IoT, Mobile, PC Client, Server, Software Stack, Storage, Trusted Network

Communications and TPM, etc. [1], where the TPM Working Group is the basic and core working group are responsible for the drafting, revising and publishing the TPM specification, which has evolved from TPM1.0 and TPM1.2 to the current TPM2.0 [2–5].

In recent years, cloud computing [10–20], which is an emerging computing service, has rapidly emerged in various industries with its unique advantages of broadband interconnection, resource sharing, flexible configuration, on-demand services, and charging by volume. Users greatly reduce the burden of computing and storage by entrusting computing tasks and data to cloud service providers. It is worth noting that the operating environment provided by the cloud computing to the user (Tenant) is based on the virtual machine [10, 11]. The user's operating environment and data are stored in the cloud, thus users lose direct control of the physical environment. How to provide users with secure cloud computing services is an urgent problem [21]. Scholars in trusted computing at home and abroad are agilely aware of the credibility of that trusted computing can enhance the credibility of cloud computing environments. One of the effective ways to solve this problem is to build a virtual machine trusted running environment through TPM virtualization, such as vTPM (virtual TPM, vTPM) [22]. Trusted Computing Group TCG also quickly followed up on related work. First, in 2008, two new working groups, Cloud and Virtualized Platform, were added [1]. Cloud is mainly responsible for the drafting, revising and publishing the multi-tenant infrastructure, TMI specification, while the Virtualized Platform is mainly responsible for the drafting, revising and publishing the trusted virtual platform specification. One of its core tasks is TPM virtualization; secondly, the TPM 2.0 specification, announced in 2013, explicitly supports TPM virtualization [2–5].

The research on TPM virtualization has a great significance. In a cloud environment, TPM virtualization provides a trusted guarantee for the guest virtual machine running environment. TPM virtualization allows each guest virtual machine to logically have a single "unique" TPM, referred to as vTPM, which just like having a real physical TPM. The guest virtual machine environment can use features such as measure, storage, and reporting provided by vTPM. In particular, the trust chain transfer of the guest virtual machine environment can be implemented through the integrity check function of vTPM, the data protection function of the vTPM is used to implement the sealed storage of the guest virtual machine environment data, and the remote virtual certificate function of the vTPM is used to implement proof of identity of the guest virtual machine environment. In academia, since S Berger proposed the vTPM architecture in 2006 [22], research on TPM virtualization has gradually obtained widespread attention from many scholars and research institutions at home and abroad. In some international conferences, such as: TRUST2008 [23], ESI 2008 [24] (Proceedings of the 2008s International Conference on Emerging Security Information), UCC2015 [25] (IEEE/ACM 8th International Conference on Utility and Cloud Computing), CSS 2015 [27] (2015 IEEE 7th International Symposium on Cyberspace Safety and Security), TrustCom2012 [27] (2012 IEEE 11th International Conference on Trust, Security and Privacy in Computing and Communications), MINES 2012 [28] (2012 IEEE 11th International Conference on Trust, Security and Privacy in Computing and Communications), CIS 2012 [29] (2012 Eighth International Conference on Computing Platform, Computational Intelligence and Security), Proceedings of the 2013 ACM workshop on Cloud computing security workshop [45], etc. There are a number of high-quality articles on vTPM issues, including vTPM system architecture, key management, certificate trust extension, and migration. TPM virtualization issues (or related issues) at academic conferences on "National Trusted Computing and Information Security", "National Computer Network and Information Security", and "China Information and Communication Security" held in recent years in China is also a hot topic. In the industry, major IT giants also pay attention to TPM virtualization. A typical representative is Microsoft. Although Microsoft previously had the Next-Generation Secure Computing Base (NGSCB), in order to further improve the security of the cloud environment, vTPM is supported in Hyper-V [30] in Windows Server 2016 and Windows 10. Orchard's virtualization platform Vbox [31] has supported vTPM in 2009. Most notable is that VMware, one of the virtualization industry giants, announced in 2015 that it supports vTPM in vSphere 6.0 [32]. In addition, well-known open source virtualization platforms such as XEN [33], KVM [34], etc., both support vTPM.

Despite this, the degree of convergence between trusted computing and cloud computing lags far behind market expectations. vTPM has not become the main security solution for major cloud platforms. TPM virtualization is one of the main bottlenecks affecting the application, promotion and popularization of trusted virtualization platform products, which seriously hinders the extension and expansion of trusted computing in the cloud environment. In particular, although China has developed a TCM (Trust Cryptographic Module) (TCM) related standard with independent intellectual property rights [9], similar to the TPM standard, compared with TPM2.0, the TCM standard has not considered the related issues of TCM virtualization. At present, there is no detailed and comprehensive review paper on TPM virtualization. In order to have a general understanding of the progress of this research and to promote domestic research in this direction, it is very meaningful to review the research progress of TPM virtualization.

This paper introduces the basic concepts, types and basic requirements of TPM virtualization, proposes a technical classification model of TPM virtualization, elaborates on the main research progress of key technologies such as system architecture, key management, certificate trust extension and migration of TPM virtualization, and summarize these work. Combined with the existing research results, the research direction and challenges of TPM virtualization under TCG architecture are discussed.

2   Basic Concepts of TPM Virtualization

In order to meet different functional requirements, there have been many different virtualization solutions for the x86 architecture. Combined with the computer system structure and the abstraction level adopted by virtual machines, virtual machine systems can be divided into instruction level virtualization, hardware level virtualization, operating program library virtualization [22–25]. For hardware-level virtualization, there are three main technologies, including full virtualization, para-virtualization, and hardware-assisted virtualization, all of which include CPUs, Memory and I/O virtualization. This article discusses TPM virtualization under the x86 architecture, which is a virtualized I/O device virtualization category.

2.1   Definition of TPM Virtualization

Definition 1: TPM virtualization, which is the application of I/O device virtualization technology to the TPM in the virtual computing platform, so that each virtual machine in the platform can use trusted computing functions to improve securely, independently and autonomously the credibility and security of the operating environment to meet the trusted needs of virtual machine users.

As can be seen from Definition 1, the concept of TPM virtualization has three implications. First, in terms of virtualization technology, TPM virtualization is essentially I/O device virtualization. Second, in terms of functionality, each virtual machine can use the trusted computing capabilities provided by the TPM; Thirdly, in terms of security objectives, each virtual machine can improve the credibility and security of its own operating environment and meet the trusted requirements of virtual machine users through TPM virtualization.

2.2 Basic Types of TPM Virtualization

For hardware-level virtualization, depending on the virtualization implementation of VMM (Virtual Machine Monitor, VMM), the implementation of I/O device virtualization will be different. The core is the storage location of the I/O device's native driver and how the VMM handles the I/O devices. TPM is a slow I/O device attached to the motherboard through the LPC bus. What kind of I/O device virtualization implementation technology is adopted depends on the method implementation of the VMM virtualization. Therefore, according to the different virtualization methods of VMM, we divide the TPM virtualization methods into three categories.

1. TPM virtualization under full virtualization

In full virtualization, the VMM can virtualize the virtual machine to the same physical environment as the physical TPM. All Guest OSs see a unified set of virtual TPM devices, and each I/O operation privileged instruction of the guest OS to the virtual TPM device will be trapped in the VMM, and then directly controlled by the TPM, so there is no need to modify the Guest OS. For x86 architectures, certain privileged instructions do not trap in the VMM, and at this time, binary code translation techniques will be used.

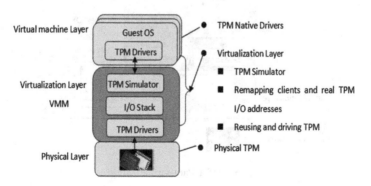

Fig. 1. TPM stand-alone Hypervisor model

According to the difference of the TPM native drive location, we can also classify this type of virtualization into a TPM independent model and a TPM host mode. The virtualization method of putting the TPM native driver directly into the VMM is called the TPM independent model, as shown in Fig. 1. The virtualization method of placing the TPM native driver in the host is called the TPM host model, as shown in Fig. 2.

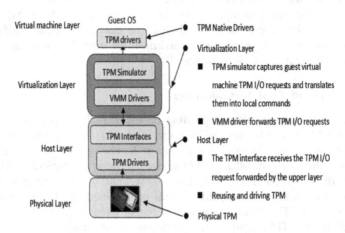

Fig. 2. TPM hosted-based model

2. TPM virtualization under para-virtualization

In the para-virtualization mode, all the privileged instructions accessing the TPM in the Guest OS need to be code-replaced, so the front-end virtual device drivers of different environments need to be developed. When the application makes an access request, the front and back drivers work together to complete the access. As shown in Fig. 3.

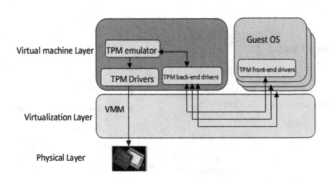

Fig. 3. TPM Para-virtualization

3. TPM virtualization under hardware-assisted virtualization

Under hardware-assisted virtualization, the VMM needs assistance of hardware to complete the virtualization of the TPM. At this time, the kernel of the Guest OS doesn't need to be modified. With the TPM virtual device model in the virtual machine management domain, the impact of the TPM privileged instructions on the host is eliminated by Intel's VT-x technology or AMD's AMD-V technology, which will run at different privilege levels. The VMM is implemented with different privilege levels to implement TPM virtualization, as shown in Fig. 4.

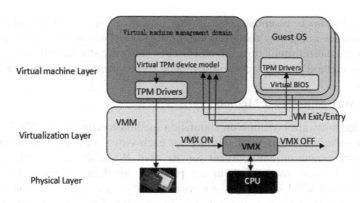

Fig. 4. Hardware-based TPM virtualization

2.3 Basic Requirements of TPM Virtualization

The purpose of TPM virtualization is to provide trusted computing services for virtual machines, to help virtual machines establish a trusted computing environment, and to make users who use virtual machines think that there is no significant difference between using a trusted computer system with a physical TPM. Therefore, when virtualizing TPM, there are four basic requirements [22–25].

1. **Equivalence**
   The so-called equivalence means that, except for the time factor, when the application or user in the virtual machine uses the TPM function, the rest must be the same as the computer system that owns the physical TPM alone, including the measurement, storage, and reporting of trusted computing.
2. **Relevance**
   The so-called relevance includes two aspects. One is that it should be related to the vTPM throughout the life cycle of the virtual machine, including the migration of the virtual machine. The second is that the vTPM maintains a correlation with the hardware TPM.
3. **Safety**
   The so-called security includes two aspects. One is that the physical TPM should be fully managed by the VMM, the guest virtual machine operating system,

applications or users cannot directly access the TPM; the second is that the security of the TPM virtualization software system and architecture. Virtual platforms must meet these two security requirements for TPM virtualization.

4. **Convenience**

   The so-called convenience refers to that after the TPM virtualization was completed, it is convenient to maintain, upgrade and migrate.

3   Technical Classification Model of TPM Virtualization

TPM virtualization is essentially I/O device virtualization. We divide TPM virtualization into three categories according to I/O device virtualization technology. One is software instantiation simulation, the other one is hardware sharing, and the third one is aggregation method. Below we introduce these three categories one by one.

3.1   Software Simulation Method

The so-called software instantiation simulation method means that the VMM creates a software simulation virtual TPM instance for each virtual machine that needs to provide a trusted execution environment for the user. When the user needs the trusted computing functions, most of them are provided by their corresponding software simulation virtual TPM instance. The physical TPM only provides a small number of functions, such as key management, certificate extension, and so on. The basic architecture is shown in Fig. 5.

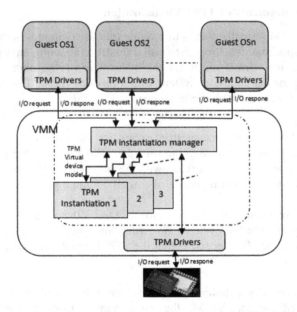

Fig. 5. Software simulation mode of TPM virtualization

This method can be done in either full virtualization, para-virtualization, or hardware-assisted virtualization. The essence of this method is to assign each virtual machine an instance of TPM software that has the same functions as the hardware TPM—vTPM. The vTPM usually runs in the VMM, virtual machine management domain, or isolated device domain, and can implement most functions of the TPM. The advantages of this method are simple implementation, flexibility, high performance and easy migration. The disadvantage is that the security isn't high, but because the vTPM runs in the VMM, virtual machine management domain or isolated device domain, therefore, in addition to privileged security threats and shared security, it can prevent general security threats[1], that is, basic security can be guaranteed. Therefore, this method is currently the mainstream way to implement TPM virtualization on each virtual platform.

3.2 Hardware Sharing Method

The so-called hardware sharing method means that each virtual machine accesses the physical TPM in a time-sharing manner. Generally, the service requests and responses of the TPM are implemented in an asynchronous manner. When multiple client virtual machines issue TPM I/O requests to form a request queue, the VMM performs scheduling through certain policies and processes them in the TPM. After the TPM processed a request, the processing result is placed in the response queue, and the response result is returned to the corresponding virtual machine by the TPM virtual device model. The basic architecture is shown in Fig. 6.

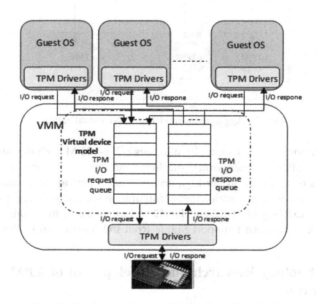

Fig. 6. Hardware share model of TPM virtualization

---

[1] The relevant connotations of general security threats, privileged security threats and shared security threats are described in the literature [61]

This method can be done in either full virtualization, para-virtualization, or hardware-assisted virtualization. The essence of this method is that the hardware TPM provides trusted computing functions for virtual machines. The advantage is high security, and it can prevent general security threats, privileged security threats, and some shared security threats, but the disadvantages are also obvious, it's complicated, the mobility is poor, and since the TPM is a slow peripheral that is attached via the LPC bus, as the number of virtual machines increases, the sharing performance drops dramatically and it cannot be used at all.

3.3   Aggregation Method

The so-called aggregation method is to aggregate multiple TPM virtual functions in one TPM – VF-vTPM, and then directly allocate or schedule the vTPM to the virtual machine for use. The basic architecture is shown in Fig. 7.

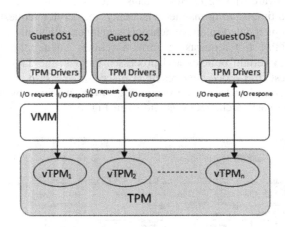

Fig. 7. Aggregation model of TPM virtualization

The aggregation method essentially allocates a VF-vTPM with the same functions as the hardware TPM for each virtual machine, and the vTPM runs inside the TPM. The advantages of this method are high security, good performance, and good scalability. However, the implementation and configuration are complex and the mobility is poor. In fact, the existing TPM 1.2 and TPM2.0 chips cannot achieve this method at all, because the LPC bus doesn't support Single Root I/O Virtualization (SR-IOV) at all.

4   Key Technology Research and Development of TPM Virtualization

TPM virtualization involves key technologies in system architecture, key management, certificate trust extension, and migration, which are detailed in this section. Since the trust chain model and remote proof of trusted virtual machines belong to the category of "trusted computing platform", this section will not discuss and analyze.

4.1 System Architecture of TPM Virtualization

The so-called system architecture refers to the complete composition of the system and its reasonable logical function modules. According to the technical classification model of TPM virtualization in Sect. 3, we summarize the existing research results of TPM virtualization system architecture into three categories, one is the software simulation TPM virtualization system architecture; the other one is the hardware sharing TPM virtualization system architecture; the third one is the aggregated TPM virtualization system architecture. The so-called "software emulation type TPM virtualization system architecture" refers to the complete component architecture and reasonable functional modules for providing a complete composition architecture and reasonable functional modules for the virtual machine to access the software simulation TPM instances. The so-called "hardware sharing TPM virtualization system architecture" refers to the complete component architecture and reasonable functional modules that provide access to the hardware TPM for the virtual machine. The so-called "aggregated TPM virtualization system architecture" refers to the complete component architecture and reasonable functional modules that provide virtual machines with access to the TPM virtual function (VF).

Software Simulation TPM Virtualization System Architecture. For the "software simulation TPM virtualization system architecture", whether domestic or foreign, whether academic or industrial, there are many research results.

In academia, the research results in this area were first proposed by S Berger[2] et al. of IBM TJ Watson Research Center in 2006 [22], as shown in Fig. 8. The system architecture includes vTPM, vTPM manager, and Client-Side TPM, Driver, Server-Side TPM driver, TPM and other entities, where vTPM, vTPM manager and Server-Side TPM driver are in the privileged domain, Client-Side TPM driver is in the virtual machine domain, and TPM is in the underlying hardware layer of the entire virtual system. vTPM is a software-simulated TPM that provides most of the trusted computing functions for the virtual machine. The vTPM manager is responsible for the lifecycle management of all vTPMs, including creating, suspending, restoring, and deleting vTPM instances, and forwarding the vTPM instance request to which the virtual machine is bound and returning the corresponding response. Each vTPM can be associated with the hardware TPM through the vTPM manager, and the associated content mainly includes PCR mapping and certificate chain extension. The Server-Side TPM driver is a privileged domain-side TPM driver. The Client-Side TPM driver is a virtual machine-side TPM driver. The Server-Side TPM driver communicates with the Client-Side TPM driver through the VMM. This literature is the foundation of TPM para-virtualization, and most of the research in this area is based on this idea.

---

[2] Although S Berger is a researcher at the IBM T. J. Watson Research Center, the published results are academic papers, so he is still attributed to academia.

216   L. Tan et al.

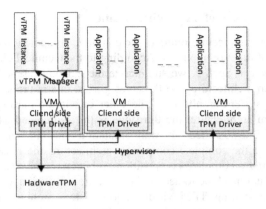

Fig. 8. vTPM architecture

In 2007, the literature [36] also proposed a general system architecture GVTPM for TPM virtualization, as shown in Fig. 9. The system architecture includes entities such as GVTPM, GVTPM manager, GVTPM Factory, GVTPM Protected Storage Service, etc. GVTPM is a software entity that provides trusted computing functions. GVTPM Manager includes Key & Session Manager and TPM Driver, is responsible for GVTPM lifecycle management, GVTPM binding to virtual machines and key and session management. The GVTPM Factory is responsible for providing the GVTPM manager with the ability to create and delete GVTPM services. The GVTPM Protected Storage Service is responsible for providing non-volatile storage for the GVTPM manager. It can be seen from the above analysis that the basic ideas of the literature [22] and literature [36] are consistent, the difference is that the implementation of the vTPM manager function has changed. In the literature [22], the vTPM manager is responsible for the vTPM life cycle management and the protection storage of sensitive information, which is implemented by two other important entities, GVTPM Factory and GVTPM Protected Storage Service in the literature [36]. And the literature [36] doesn't specify that GVTPM manager, GVTPM Factory and GVTPM Protected Storage Service are located in a certain specific area. The advantage of the system architecture proposed in literature [22] and literature [36] is that the vTPM instance is separated from the virtual machine, which is easy to implement, flexible to deploy, has little impact on the VMM, and is light burden for TPM. For example, the vTPM, vTPM manger, GVTPM, and GVTPM Manager instances are placed in the administrative domain, although which is vulnerable to privileged security threats, shared security threats, and heavy privileged domains, it can protect against general security threats.

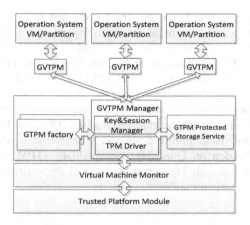

Fig. 9. vTPM general architecture

In order to improve the vTPM anti-privilege security threat capability, in the literature [22], proposing a vTPM architecture variant, as shown in Fig. 10, where the vTPM function is provided by an external security coprocessor plug-in, IBM's PCIXCC, which can provide maximum security for sensitive data such as private keys in a vulnerable environment. The first virtual machine is the owner of the hardware. It obtains a vTPM instance for itself. Other vTPM instances are reserved for other virtual machines. A Proxy process is responsible for passing TPM I/O instruction information between the server driver and the external security coprocessor plug-in. It is worth noting that the vTPM running in PCIXCC is still a software type vTPM, and it's is relatively small. Many security functions, such as cryptographic operations, are provided by hardware in PCIXCC. The advantage of this system architecture is that the vTPM instance and the vTPM manager are located in the security processor and aren't vulnerable to privilege security. But it needs to add additional hardware and cost.

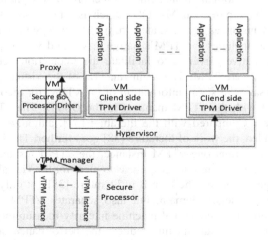

Fig. 10. Security coprocessor-based VTPM architecture

In 2007, the literature [37] based on Xen for the first time to separate the vTPM instance from the privileged domain, as shown in Fig. 11, the vTPM manager and the vTPMD daemon still run in Domain0, and the vTPM instances run in the LibOS-based Trusted VM domain. The applications in the DomU pass the TPM command to the vTPM instances through vTPMmanager and vTPMD. The vTPM instances can also return the running result to the applications in the DomU through vTPMD and vTPM manager. The privileged domain and the isolated domain exchange information through the inter-domain communication mechanism IDC. The biggest advantage of the system architecture is to improve the vTPM's ability to resist shared security threats, reduce the burden on Domain0, and facilitate vTPM migration. However, vTPM has no connection with TPM, and the trust of the underlying virtual platform cannot be extended to virtual machines.

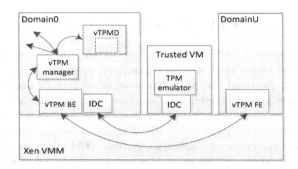

Fig. 11. Single isolated domain vTPM architecture for Xen

In 2008, the literature [38] further separated the vTPM manager, vTPM instances and privilege domain, as shown in Fig. 12. Firstly, an important function in the privileged domain, the domain management function, was separated. The Domain Builder domain is built based on MiniOS, which is called DomB, and the vTPM manager and vTPM instances are separated from the privileged domain to DomB. In addition, DomB also includes the TPM's native driver and virtual platform configuration storage. The native driver is to facilitate the interaction between the vTPM manager and the hardware TPM. The main function of the virtual platform configuration storage is to save the status information of the vTPM for recovery. The DomU can directly interact with the vTPM manager in the DomB. The vTPM front-end in DomU is unchanged. Compared with the literature [37], although only one isolated domain has been added, the work of literature [38] goes further. The isolated domain of the literature [37] only runs one vTPM instance, the vTPM instance lifecycle management, binding to the VM, and integrity measurement for the virtual machine are still done in the privileged domain. The DomB in literature [38] not only separates vTPM instances from the privileged domain, but also separates vTPM instance lifecycle management, VM binding, and virtual machine integrity measurement from the privileged domain. This system architecture reduces the performance burden and shared security threats of privileged domain.

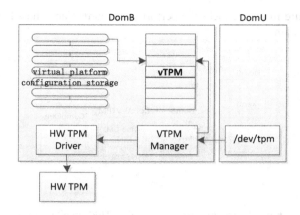

Fig. 12. Single isolated domain vTPM architecture

In 2009, OpenTC, a trusted computing project sponsored by the European Commission, presented a research report on the TPM virtualization architecture [39]. This report not only introduced the background and motivation of TPM virtualization, defined the vTPM status data structure, analyzed the existing vTPM architecture, restrictions, vTPM life cycle, vTPM and VM binding, etc., but also added vTPM attribute-based proof and migration functions [40] to the vTPM architecture, and a dual isolation domain is proposed on the Xen platform. The system architecture further separated the functions of DomB in literature [38]. As shown in Fig. 13. Two domains are included in the system architecture, one of which is DomB, which is similar to DomB in literature [38], but its functions is reduced. There are no vTPM manager and vTPM instances in the DomB. DomB, including VP-Bulider, HIM, CMS, and BMSI, is responsible for securely creating trusted virtual domains. VP-Bulider is responsible for creating virtual domain, HIM is trusted virtual domain integrity measurement management, CMS is virtual domain configuration, and BMSI is the basic management and security interface; second is the other one of which is DomU-vTPM. DomU-vTPM domain, including VTPM-DM, TIS and H-BMSI, runs vTPM instances, where VTPM-DM is the vTPM device model, TIS is trusted Computing interface specifications, H-BMSI is TPM-related basic management and security interfaces. When a vTPM instance is generated, the vTPM generates the EK through the H-BMSI. The private key is protected by the BMSI of the DomB and can only be accessed by the vTPM through the H-BMSI. The hash cipher of the public key, as an external nonce of the vTPM performing reference operations through the H-BMSI interface, implicitly associates with the integrity measurement of Xen, DomB, and vTPM; when starting a new virtual machine, first attached the vTPM domain ID associated with the virtual machine to the configuration table of the virtual machine, the VP-Builder then measures the vCRTM of the virtual machine, and the result of the measurement is stored in the HIM database as the vPCR0 value, and then the VP-Builder verifies the device model of the vTPM to ensure that the virtual machine can correctly access the TIS interface provided by the vTPM device model. Finally, VP-Builder VP-Builder updates the HIM database and establishes the interdependence between vTPM and VM. This system architecture further reduces the performance burden and shared security threats of privileged domain.

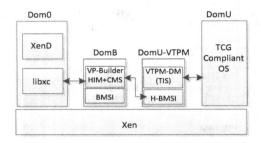

Fig. 13. Double isolated domain vTPM architecture

In China, the similar literatures appeared in 2010. The literature [41] believes that considering the entire privileged domain as TCB will threaten the security of vTPM, because TCB is too large, it is easy to generate loopholes. In order to solve this problem, a new vTPM architecture is proposed in the literature [41], as shown in Fig. 14. The vTPM, vTPM manager, and TPM native drivers originally in the privileged domain are separated into the management domain DomA by creating a new administrative domain, DomA. There are two purposes for creating an administrative domain. One is to protect the vTPM and its related components from unauthorized access and invocation. The other one is to modify the access process of the TPM and protect the DomA through the TPM to improve the security of the vTPM and its related components. The idea of the system architecture is basically the same as that of the literature [37–39].

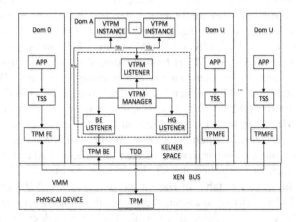

Fig. 14. Dom A -based vTPM architecture

In 2015, in order to prevent attackers in the cloud environment from using the virtual machine's rollback mechanism (an important and common used function) to launch attacks, the domestic literature [42] proposed a trusted virtual platform module (rollback- resilient TPM, rvTPM) system architecture to resist rollback attacks based on Xen, and implemented the rvTPM prototype system in Xen, as shown in Fig. 15. There are four modules: (1) Information Collection Module, which is responsible for collecting information about rollback events. (2) An information registration module that records and shares status information collected by the information collection module. (3) Rollback module, which performs snapshot and rollback operations. (4) Rollback log module, which records the rollback events. As can be seen from Fig. 12, the information collection module, the rollback module, and the rollback log module are in Dom0, and the information registration module is in Xen VMM. The vTPM back-end driver interacts with information collection module, rollback module, and rollback log module, and the rvTPM manager interacts with the information registration module. Compared with the previous literatures, the system architecture follows the earlier TPM para-virtualization method, but it can prevent virtual machine rollback attacks, reduce general security threats, and further improve the security of the management domain and vTPM.

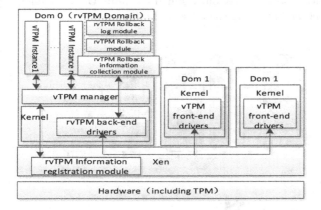

Fig. 15. rvTPM architecture for Xen

In the open source community, virtual platform systems Xen and KVM support TPM virtualization. Xen [34] is the earliest open source virtual platform system that supports TPM virtualization. Many academic researches on TPM virtualization use Xen as an experimental platform. In the beginning, Xen's TPM virtualization system architecture is shown in Fig. 16. The system architecture includes vTPM instances, vTPM manager, vTPM back-end driver and front-end driver, TPM and other entities. The TPM instances, vTPM manager, vTPM back-end driver are in Dom0, vTPM front-end driver is in the virtual machine domain, and TPM is in the underlying hardware layer of the whole virtual system.

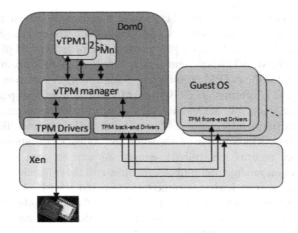

Fig. 16. Early vTPM architecture for Xen

In July, 2013, Xen published the version 3.2, and the TPM virtualization system architecture changed further. As shown in Fig. 17. Xen separates vTPM manager, vTPM and VM bindings, and other functions from Dom0, reducing performance burden of Dom0 and reducing shared security threats.

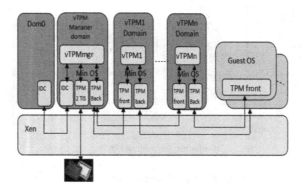

Fig. 17. Current vTPM architecture for Xen

KVM [35] supports TPM virtualization later than Xen, and KVM's TPM virtualization relies heavily on QEMU. In 2007, QEMU supported access to the TPM emulator through patches, enabling virtual machines to use the trusted computing functions provided by the TPM emulator. In April, 2013, QEMU added new patches to enable virtual machines to directly use physical TPM through Pass Through technology, but in this way, only one virtual machine can use the TPM device on one physical machine, and the physical computer and the virtual machine cannot use the TPM chip at the same time, which limits the application of the trusted computing functions on the virtual machines. In December, 2013, QEMU added new patches again, enabling multiple virtual machines to simultaneously use TPM functions simulated by software. The functions and interfaces of virtual TPM are consistent with physical TPM chip. The system architecture is shown in Fig. 18. The system architecture includes libtpms, QEMU with TPM, SeaBIOS, Kernel IMA, and other entities. The libtpms library is used to provide TPM functions to QEMU, including symmetric/asymmetric encryption, secure storage, integrity measurement, and security signatures. QEMU with TPM actually adds a TPM device type and a back-end driver for the TPM device in QEMU. The back-end driver of the TPM device receives the TPM device operation sent by the virtual machine, parses the operation type and calls the corresponding interface of libtpms. The TPM device operates and returns the results of the operation to the virtual machine. SeaBIOS is an open source implementation of a BIOS under the x86 architecture that completes the initialization of the hardware. The system architecture is complex, involving many components and entities, and libtpms has few links with the underlying physical TPM, and there are also privileged security threats and shared security threats.

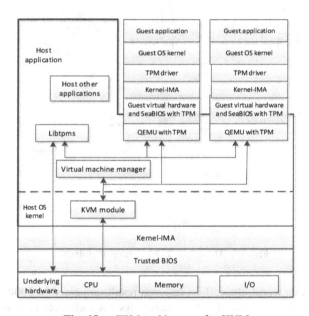

Fig. 18. vTPM architecture for KVM

For the industry, VMware [33] also announced that supporting for vTPM in vSphere 6.0 [33] in 2015; Microsoft [34] supports vTPM in its Windows sever 2016 Hyper-V, Orical [32] VBox supports vTPM through IBM PCIXCC. But neither VMware, Microsoft nor Orical has disclosed its system architecture.

In summary, because software simulation TPM virtualization has the characteristics of simple implementation, good flexibility, high performance and convenient migration, whether it is academic, industrial or open source community, there are many researches on software simulation type TPM virtualization system architecture, and more research results have been obtained. To sum up, the software simulation TPM virtualization system architecture mainly focuses on two aspects. First, how to prevent various security threats, especially privileged security threats and shared security threats, to improve the security of the system architecture; secondly, how to improve the performance of TPM virtualization and reduce the security and performance impact on the virtual platform.

Hardware Sharing TPM Virtualization System Architecture. For the "hardware sharing TPM virtualization system architecture", there are many studies in foreign academic circles, and there are relatively few studies in domestic academic circles. There is no similar design and implementation across the industry and the open source community.

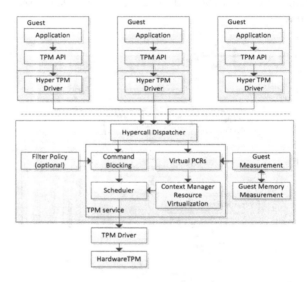

Fig. 19. Hardware TPM sharing architecture

In the academic world, the earliest research results appeared in 2008. The literature [23] first proposed the physical TPM sharing system architecture, which belongs to "hardware sharing TPM virtualization". As shown in Fig. 19, the system architecture includes the HyperTPMDriver in the guest VM, the HyperCallDispatcher in the VMM, the TPM service, the Filter Policy, the Guest Measurement, the Guest Memory Management, and the TPM Driver. The HyperCallDispatcher accepts requests from various guest virtual machines and distributes them. The TPM service, is the core of the entire system architecture, provides TPM function services for each guest virtual machine, including Command Blocking, Virtual PCRs, ContextManage, Resource Virtualization, and Scheduler. Because the physical TPM is an exclusive device with limited resources, when sharing a physical TPM, each guest VM not only needs Resource Virtualization to share limited key resources, such as key pool, authorization session pool, etc., but also needs to manage the context of its runtime and schedule it. Filter Policy is a filtering policy. Guest Measurement and Guest Memory Management are mainly responsible for the integrity measurement and memory management of the guest virtual machine. However, this literature is not specifically implemented. The advantage of this system architecture is that it has high security and can prevent general privileged security threats and shared security threats. However, the management and scheduling of TPM are both in VMM and the VMM becomes larger, which increases the general security threats and the performance is not high.

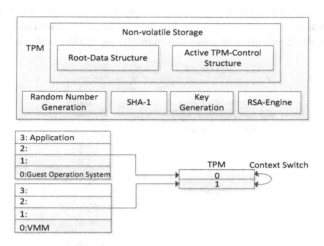

Fig. 20. Supporting shared hardware TPM architecture and CPU protection mechanism

In the same year, the literature [24] redesigned a new TPM to support virtualization, and its structure is shown in Fig. 20. Compared with the existing TPMs, it can support multi-client virtual machine sharing, that is, it is like owning a TPM for each virtual machine. As can be seen from the structure diagram, compared with TCG's TPM, a non-volatile storage is added, which contains two key data structures, one is Active TPM-Control, and the other is Root-Data. The Active TPM-Control data structure includes: SRK, PCRs, AIK, EK, monotonic counters, other non-volatile storage values, delegate authorization tables, TPM context data, DAA parameters f, and associated authorization data. The Root-Data data structure contains specific sensitive data, such as seal keys. When a virtual machine issues a TPM I/O request, the VMM is scheduled to load the virtual machine's TPM-Control data structure into the TPM and decrypt it. The TPM performs the virtual machine's I/O request according to the TPM-Control data structure and The result is returned to the guest virtual machine. Once another client virtual machine issues a TPM I/O request, the VMM will use the key in the Root-Data data structure to encrypt the TPM-Control data structure inside the TPM and load the TPM-Control data structure of the next virtual machine. The CPU hardware protection mechanism is also proposed in this literature. The VM runs on the CPU ring 1, the VMM runs on the CPU ring 0, the VM running on the ring 1 can only operate its own TPM-Control data structure, and the VMM can manage the TPM-Control data structure of all VMs. In addition, an extended command set for managing TPM-Control data structures and sensitive instructions is provided, and algorithms and processes such as sensitive instruction processing, TPM-Control context switching, and TPM scheduling are described in detail. The biggest difference between this literature and the literature [36] is that TPM sharing is implemented by adding new functions and hardware protection mechanisms of the CPU in the TPM, so that the TPM changes from an exclusive device to a shareable device. The advantage of this system architecture is that it is more secure, can prevent general security threats and shared security threats, but it needs to prevent privileged security threats; on the other hand, it has higher performance. Since the system architecture manages and schedules the TPM by means of the CPU hardware protection mechanism, the VMM increases less software code.

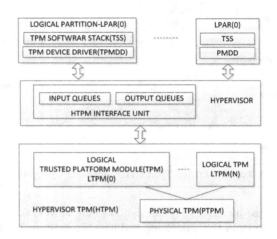

Fig. 21. Sharing hardware TPM architecture for data process system

Literature [43] is a patent granted by the US Patent Office in May, 2008, and it proposes a physical TPM sharing scheme for data processing systems. As shown in Fig. 21, the system architecture includes TPM TSS and TPM DEVICE DRIVER in the logical partition system LPAR, IPUT QUEUES, OUTPUT QUEUES and HTPM ITERFACE UNIT in VMM, multiple LTPMs (Logical TPMs) in HTPM, and a physical TPM. The two entities in the LPAR TPM TSS and TPM DEVICE DRIVER are mainly used to provide interfaces and drivers for applications in the LPAR access to the TPM. In the VMM, IPUT QUEUES indicates all request queues that access the TPM, and OUTPUT QUEUES indicates the response queues. HTPM ITERFACE UNIT indicates the interface to access HTPM in VMM. LTPM is responsible for providing vast majority trusted computing functions for LPAR, and TPM is mainly responsible for sensitive data protection. When the VMM creates a LPAR, it immediately creates an LTPM to bind to it. During data processing, the application in the LPAR sends a TPM request to the VMM to form a request queue IPUT QUEUES. The VMM schedules the request in the request queue to the HTPM, and the LTPM and the TPM jointly process the request and return a response OUTPUT QUEUES. The biggest feature of the system architecture is that the TPM generates multiple LTPMs and binds the LTPMs to the LPARs scheduling through the VMM. Since LTPM is located in HTPM, it is safer.

In 2011, the literature [44] believed that with the development of technology and application updates, such as mobile computing and cloud computing, TPM has not adapted to the needs of new technologies and the diversification of user needs. To this end, the paper proposed a new TPM system architecture Dynamic-Context TPM (dcTPM), as shown in Fig. 22. The system architecture includes a FPGA system-on-chip, various peripheral control interfaces, and multiple physical TPMs. The FPGA on-chip system environment is uCLinux, which has a dctmp daemon, which is not only responsible for linking with host PC, memory, I/O, etc., but also responsible for controlling multiple software emulation vTPMs, and controlling multiple hardware TPMs through the LPC bus. Whether it is a software vTPM or a physical TPM, its context is managed by dcTmp, and dcTmp is scheduled according to the specific requirements of the user. The system architecture is characterized by integrated software TPM and hardware TPM, which is more flexible, can better meet the requirements of users, and has high security.

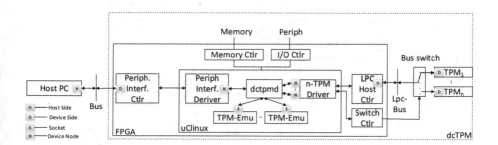

Fig. 22. dcTPM architecture

Literature [45] is a patent granted by the US Patent Office in September 2012, and proposes a system architecture that supports both software-simulated TPM virtualization and hardware-sharing TPM virtualization. As shown in Fig. 23, the system architecture mainly includes the UOS domain, the SOS domain, the vTPM-VM domain, the TPM Conduit, and hardware. UOS is the user virtual machine domain. The SOS domain is the service virtual machine domain. The vTPM-VM domain is a vTPM management domain, which includes vTPM0 to vTPMn Context, vTPM Context Manager and TPM ConduitBE. The vTPM0 to vTPMn Context mainly contains n + 1 vTPMs and their contexts. The vTPM Context Manager is responsible for managing n + 1 vTPMs and their contexts. The TPM Conduit BE is the back-end driver for TPM Conduit and is responsible for interacting with TPM Conduit. The TPM Conduit is located in the VMM and is responsible for distributing TPM requests from UOS or SOS and returning responses from the vTPM-VM domain or Multi-Context iTPM. In the hardware layer, in addition to the traditional CPU, Memory and I/O, it also includes Muti-Context iTPM, ME, VE and ICH, where Muti-Context iTPM is a physical TPM, ME is its management engine, and VE is its virtualization engine, ICH is its input and output controller. The Muti-Context iTPM has two working modes, one is the independent device working mode, which is consistent with the traditional TPM. The second is the sharing mode, which supports TPM Context management. When a UOS or SOS sends a TPM access request, according to the specific requirements of this request, such as TPM version, performance requirements, etc., TPM Conduit forwarded the request to the vTPM-VM domain, which is processed and responded by the software type vTPM, or forwarded to the Muti-Context iTPM, handled and responded by the Muti-Context iTPM. Liking the literature [44], the system architecture also integrates the software TPM and hardware TPM, which is more flexible and can better meet the requirements of users, but the security is not as good as the literature [44]. In the literature [44], management of software and hardware TPM are implemented in FPGA, and this architecture is implemented by the VMM, which obviously makes the VMM larger, increases the general security threats.

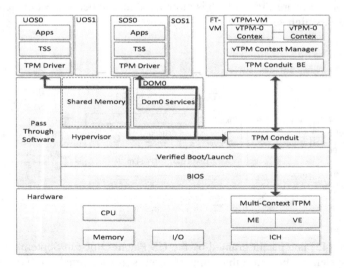

Fig. 23. Architecture for supporting both software simulation vTPM and Hardware sharing vTPM

In 2013, in order to create and manage a concurrent security execution environment for multi-core systems, the literature [46] proposed the HV-TPM system architecture, as shown in Fig. 24. The system architecture includes an I/O INTERFACE, SCHEDULING, and RUN-TIME. STATE, STORAGE Per-VM Persistent State and STANDARD TPM COMPONENTS, where I/O INTERFACE includes two entities, one is DRTM Support, which supports dynamic integrity measurement; the other is Virtualization Support, which supports I/O virtualization. SCHEDULING is responsible for the management and scheduling of the request queue. The RUN-TIME STATE contains the VM status table and the current context of the TPM. The STORAGE Per-VM Persistent State is responsible for storing the status data that each virtual machine needs to maintain continuously. The system architecture is characterized by the creation and management of concurrent security execution environments for multi-core systems based on HV-TPM.

In 2013, the literature [47] proposed the para-virtualization architecture of TPM 2.0, as shown in Fig. 25. It is believed that the core functions of TPM2.0 are easy to support para-virtualized design. Therefore, it is not necessary to use software vTPM to simulate the functions of TPM 2.0 in VMM layer. Each virtual machine uses TPM Service to share TPM. The entire host computing platform includes VMM, privileged virtual machines, para-virtualized TPM service, and hardware. The TPM manager in the privileged virtual machines is responsible for the management of the hardware TPM. Para-virtualized TPM service includes Command Filter, Resource Manager, Log Manager, Sheduler, and Migration Manager. Command Filter is the TPM command parsing and filter, Resource Manager is responsible for TPM service resource management, Log Manager is responsible for TPM service log management, Sheduler is responsible for TPM scheduling, and Migration Manager is responsible for TPM virtualization migration. The advantage of the system architecture is that the security is high, but the management and scheduling of the TPM are both in the VMM and the VMM becomes larger, which affects the performance of the VMM and increases the general security threats of the VMM.

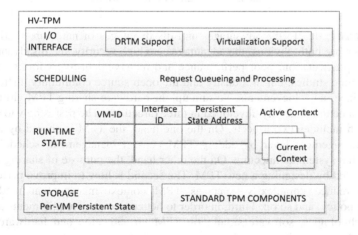

Fig. 24. HV-TPM architecture

In the industry, VMWare's VMWare, Citrix's XenServer, Microsoft's Hyper-V, IBM's PowerVM, etc., have not seen the release and display of relevant results. In the open source community, including Xen, KVM, QEMU, Bochs, etc., this implementation has not been seen.

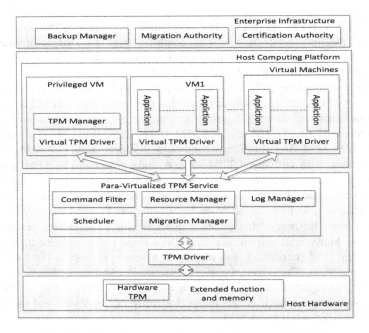

Fig. 25. Virtualization architecture for hardware TPM 2.0

In summary, due to the advantages and disadvantages of hardware-sharing TPM virtualization are both obvious, the advantages are high security, the disadvantages are complex implementation, poor performance and inconvenient migration, so there are many academic studies, but in industry and the open source community, there are few related engineering achievements. To sum up, the hardware-sharing TPM virtualization system architecture is mainly developed in three directions. The first is how to share the TPM, which includes two aspects. On the one hand, the TPM is shared by the virtualization management layer by adding TPM context management, scheduling, and improving the system architecture. On the other hand, the purpose of sharing the TPM is implemented by designing a new TPM. The second is how to improve performance, mainly to reduce complexity, such as TPM context management mode, TPM scheduling policy, and so on. Third, in order to better meet user requirements and adapt to new technologies, software simulation TPM virtualization and hardware sharing TPM virtualization architectures have obvious convergence trends.

Aggregated TPM Virtualization System Architecture. For the "aggregate TPM virtualization system architecture", no matter whether it is academia, industry or open source community at home and abroad, there is very little research work at present, and no results have been published or displayed.

The key technology for "aggregated TPM virtualization" is based on I/O hardware virtualization technology, SR-IOV [48], a hardware-based virtualization standard protocol proposed by the PCI-SIG team, and it's a subset of the PCI-Express protocol. The SR-IOV standard allows for efficient sharing of PCI-Express devices between virtual machines, and embeds a module in the PCI-Express hard core (this module is implemented in hardware). It theoretically can achieve the I/O performance and utilization which is comparable to the performance of the machine. SR-IOV technology is mainly applied to network card devices, which improves the speed and efficiency of virtual machines access to the network. Since the TPM is not a PCI device but a LPC device, the existing PCI device virtualization specification cannot be applied to the virtualization of the TPM device.

At present, part of the work of the TCG VPWG (Virtualized Platform Work Group) also involves how to build multiple vTPMs within the TPM to support virtualization, but it has not disclosed related solutions [1]. The domestic literature [49] studied the I/O hardware virtualization technology – SR-IOV, and proposed a virtual environment security isolation model based on SR-IOV technology for the security isolation of virtual computing environment. The model uses encryption card and Pass Through technology to implement network data isolation and data encryption isolation, where the function implemented by the encryption card is one of the main functions of the TPM.

We believe that although the TCG TPM specification only specifies the functions and architecture of the TPM, there is no limit to the implementation technology. However, it does indicate the interfaces between the TPM and the computing system: LPC. This limitation actually hinders the improvement of communication performance between the TPM and the computing system, and cannot meet the performance requirements of multiple virtual machines, dynamics, and concurrent aspects of the cloud environment. Therefore, it is an urgent task to study the TPM and its system architecture that meet the hardware virtualization technology SR-IOV.

4.2 Key Management of vTPM

The key management of the vTPM, is the same as the key management of the TPM, also includes setting the key type, attributes, storage hierarchy, and key lifecycle management. In order to meet the consistency of user usage and the consistency of the program interfaces, the key management of vTPM and TPM should be nearly the same.

The earliest paper on the vTPM architecture [22] pointed out that the key organization structure of each vTPM is similar to the independent key hierarchy of the TPM, and the key type is the same as the key type of the TPM, that is, in addition to the endorsement key, the other six types of keys, including storage key, identity certificate, signature key, binding key, legacy secret, and symmetric key, form a key tree, and the vSRK is the root of the key tree. The private key of the child node key is protected by the private key of the parent node key. The management of various key lifecycles, including key generation, loading, registration, and destruction, is in the privileged domain and doesn't depend on the physical TPM. The benefits are that it facilitates the rapid generation of keys and facilitates vTPM migration. The key in the key hierarchy is encrypted by the symmetric storage key in the TPM and stored on the peripheral.

However, this literature doesn't discuss vTPM key attributes. In fact, due to the implementation mechanism and software features of vTPM, the key attributes of vTPM present new features.

Literature [36] pointed out that the key attributes should change due to the different vTPM operating environment, which may violate the TCG specification's definition of the TPM key attributes. For example, the vEK key of vTPM, according to the TCG specification, should be a non-migratable key that can only be used to apply for an AIK certificate, but in vTPM, vEK is a migratable key in order to facilitate the migration of vTPM. It is used not only to apply for vAIK certificates, but also to encrypt or sign status data during vTPM migration. Therefore, vEK keys can only be legacy keys. Another example is the vAIK key of vTPM. According to the TCG specification, it should not be migrateable. It can only be used to sign the PCR value inside the TPM, but the vPCR of the guest virtual machine resides in the external memory, therefore, it happens outside the physical TPM that using the vAIK to sign the vPCR, which obviously doesn't conform to the TCG specification of the identity key. So the vAIK key can only be the signature key in the TCG specification. For another example, vTPM's storage root key vSRK. According to the TCG specification, it should be non-migtable. The key tree can only be protected inside the TPM, but in vTPM, the vSRK resides in external memory, and in order to facilitate vTPM migration, vSRK is also a migratable key. So vSRK should also be a legacy key (or encryption key). Therefore, although each vTPM has a separate key hierarchy similar to TPM, and its key attributes are shown in Table 1, this key tree hierarchy should be flatter. However, this literature doesn't discuss the storage structure of vTPM keys and key lifecycle management.

Table 1. Relationship between the key type of vTPM and the key type of hardware TPM

Virtual key type	Hardware TPM_Key_Type
Virtual endorsement key	TPM_LEGACY
Virtual storage key	TPM_LEGACY
Virtual attestation identity key	TPM_SIGNING
Virtual signing key	TPM_SIGNING
Virtual binding key	TPM_BINDING

Literature [50] proposed a key storage structure, which is suitable for VM-vTPM migration. As shown in Fig. 26. The vSRK is the root of the vTPM key tree, vAIK is the identity certificate key of the vTPM, SRK is the root of the TPM key tree, and AIK is the identity verification key of the TPM. gSRK and SK belong to the middle layer key. The vSRK is protected by the intermediate layer key, gSRK, which is protected by SRK and is a non-transportable asymmetric key. The purpose of introducing gSRK is to enable vSRK to migrate. SK is protected by AIK and is also a non-migratory key.

The purpose of SK is to associate vAIK with AIK to sign the migrated data. In addition, the vTPM key is divided into two categories, one is the internal keys, including vSRK, partial encryption, signature, binding and legacy key. Internal keys are not migrated when a virtual machine is migrated. The other type is an external keys, including partial signatures, encryption, and legacy keys, which are keys that sign and encrypt the migrated data when a virtual machine is migrated. In order to prevent link attacks of vTPM migration transactions when a virtual machine is migrated, a vAIK can only be used for one data migration of a VM. Therefore, vAIK is also non-migratorizable. However, this literature doesn't discuss the lifecycle management of vTPM keys.

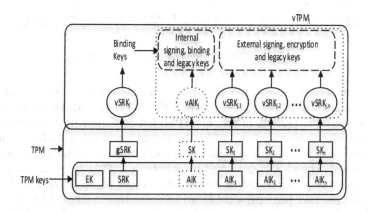

Fig. 26. Key structure suitable for VM-vTPM migration

In October, 2013, TCG published TPM 2.0. The main change in key management is the generation method of master key. The TPM master key, including EK, SRK, etc., is generated by the key seed using the key derivation algorithm KDF. This not only saves TPM storage space, but also establishes a unified key management mechanism and migration mechanism for vTPM. After the TPM 2.0, vTPM has not changed in key type, storage hierarchy, etc. The main changes are reflected in the master key generation and master key attributes. Literature [47] is the first to propose that distributing the key for the vTPM of the virtual machine based on the key seed and generating an endorsement key and key tree, as shown in Fig. 26. As shown in Fig. 27, the vEK of the virtual machine vTPM is directly generated by the EPS, and the vEK cannot be migrated. The vSRK of the virtual machine vTPM is replaced by a general storage key, namely: a duplicateable storage key, and it can be migrated. SPS directly generates SRK instead of vSRK. Each virtual machine vTPM forms a key subtree with vSRK as the root, and the key subtree of all virtual machines is further composed of SRK as a larger key tree. However, this literature doesn't discuss vAIK.

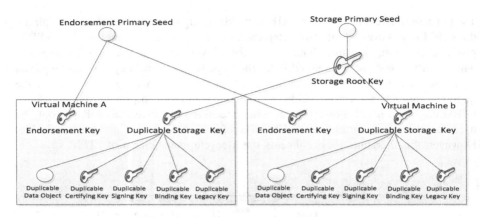

Fig. 27. vTPM key structure based on key seed

In 2015, the domestic literature [57] proposed a new generation of TPM virtualization framework design: Ng-vTPM, in which the vTPM key organization structure is designed, as shown in Fig. 28. In the Ng-vTPM, not only the virtual endorsement key vEK, the virtual storage root key vSRK, the virtual identity key vAIK (virtual attestation identity key), but also the signature key, encryption key, binding key and legacy key are designed. The vEK is generated by the physical TPM EPS and represents the real platform identity. It is used to identify the virtual machine Ng-vTPM and can defend against the fake platform identity. vSRK is the root key of the key hierarchy in Ng-vTPM, which is a migratable asymmetric storage key. The keys located in the vSRK storage hierarchy are identified as migratable keys. vAIK is the identity certificate key of the virtual machine, which is requested by the vEK to be verified by the certificate authority.. When each key is created and the parent key is used to encrypt the secret part of the subkey, different authorization sessions are used to ensure that the keys are not accessible without authorization. Moreover, according to the life cycle of the key, these keys are divided into three groups: vEK, internal migratable group and external non-migratory group. However, storing the SRK in the vTPM management domain violates the TCG specification, and a vTPM has multiple vSRKs, which is also inconsistent with the TCG specification.

From the above analysis, we can see that vTPM key management research mainly focuses on how to set key types and attributes, storage hierarchy and key lifecycle management. Since vTPM must meet the migration requirements, there is always a dilemma between setting the key type and meeting the migration requirements. Either it needs to change the key attributes that originally meets the TCG specification, or it needs to introduce key redundancy, which both can not meet the consistency requirements of vTPM and TPM key management, reducing the convenience of users using vTPM. In addition, the software emulation vTPM provides trusted computing services for virtual machines, especially cryptographic computing services are completed in the virtual platform's memory (not within the TPM), and it are vulnerable to general security threats, privileged security threats, and shared security threats. It will seriously affect the security of virtual machines and vTPM.

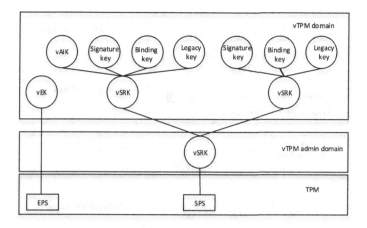

Fig. 28. Key structure of Ng-vTPM

4.3   vTPM Certificate Trust Extension

The credential trust extension of the vTPM refers to how to extend the certificate trust relationship of the physical TPM to the vTPM certificate and construct the certificate trust chain relationship from the TPM to the vTPM.

At present, a lot of research has been done on vTPM certificate trust extension at home and abroad. Literature [22] proposed four design ideas for constructing vTPM certificate chain in the research, but the last one is related to special hardware, so as not to lose generality, this paper does not discuss. We only discuss the first three:

(1)   vTPM vEK to hTPM AIK Binding, as shown in Fig. 29. In this method, both vEK and vAIK are generated by vTPM, vEK is bound by TPM's AIK signature, and vAIK is used by Privacy CA. The private key is signed and the authenticator authenticates with the public key of the Privacy CA. This method not only extends the underlying certificate trust to the virtual machine, but also the vTPM certificate structure is consistent with the TPM, which is easy to understand and porting the existing results, but the disadvantages include two aspects. One is to use the TPM AIK to sign the vEK, which violates the TCG specification. In the TCG specification, AIK can only sign the information generated inside the TPM, but vEK is the external information of the TPM. Second, the validity period of the AIK is usually very short. The failure of the AIK causes the signature of the vEK to be invalid, which causes the vAIK to invalid, which requires frequently re-apply vAIK from Privacy CA, so the performance burden of the Privacy CA is heavy.

(2)   hTPM AIK signs vTPM vAIK, as shown in Fig. 30, signing the vAI of the vTPM directly with the AIK of the TPM does not require a Privacy CA. This approach not only extends the underlying certificate trust to virtual machines, but also reduces the burden on the Privacy CA. However, the scheme relies on the APM of the TPM to sign the vAIK, which violates the TCG specification, and the failure of AIK will also invalidate its signature on vAIK. Therefore, needing to frequently

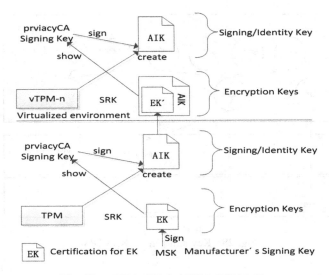

Fig. 29. vTPM vEK to hTPM AIK binding

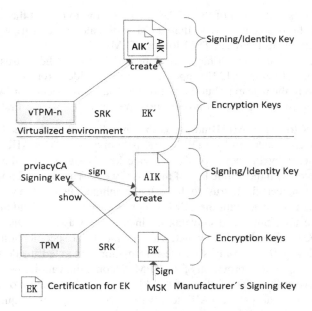

Fig. 30. hTPM AIK signs vTPM vAIK

update the signature of the AIK on the vAIK, which increases the performance burden.

(3) Local CA issue vEK Certificate, that is, the vEK for vTPM is issued by the local certificate authority (Note: not the Privacy CA), as shown in Fig. 31. The advantage of this solution is that the vEK is relatively stable and does not change

with the changes of the underlying virtual platform and the TPM. The disadvantage is that not only the additional certificate authority needs to be added, but also the TPM is not bound, that is, the trusted certificate extension of the TPM is not passed to vTPM.

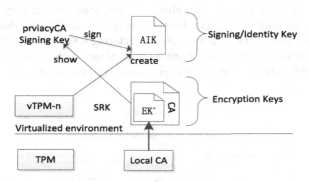

Fig. 31. Local CA issue vEK certificate

The literature [52] proposed the "vTPM vEK to hTPM EK Binding" scheme, that is, the vEK is bound by the TPM EK signature, as shown in Fig. 32. The advantage of this scheme is to avoid invalidation of the vEK signature due to the failure of AIK, the binding relationship with the TPM is clear and simple, and the underlying TPM certificate trust is extended to the virtual machine. But the disadvantage is that it violates the TCG specification, that is, the EK certificate cannot be used for signature.

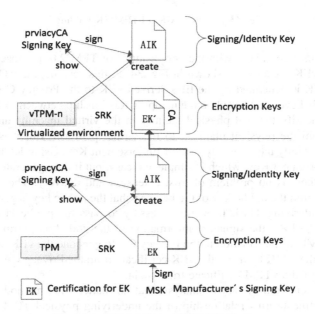

Fig. 32. vTPM vEK to hTPM EK binding

In addition, in order to improve the first four schemes, the literature [53] proposed the "vTPM vAIKto hTPM SK Binding" scheme, which introduces the signature key SK as an intermediary to implement the indirect signature of the AIK on vAIK, so that the AIK no longer sign TPM external data, which can better meet the TCG specification. And generating vAIK doesn't depend on PrivacyCA, which reduces the burden of PrivacyCA, as shown in Fig. 33. However, this solution not only increases the complexity of generating vAIK certificates, but also doesn't solve the problem that AIK failure will cause vAIK to failure. And refactoring vAIK needs to regenerate SK, which brings the new performance burden. In addition, each vAIK certificate corresponds to one SK, which generates a large amount of key redundancy.

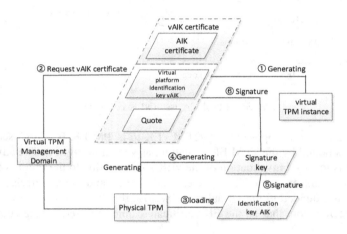

Fig. 33. vTPM vAIKto hTPM SK binding

Literature [57] combined with the new features of TPM 2.0, proposed the "hTPM EPS Product vEK" scheme, as shown in Fig. 34. In this scheme, the vTPM's identity certificate vAIK is generated by the EPS derived vEK to the Privacy CA verification. The literature believes that based on the mapping relationship between vEK and EPS, it can directly identify the real physical identity in the virtual machine and establish a trust chain from the physical platform to the virtual platform. But it is actually not working. EPS is only the basic key seed of Endorsement Key. Using KDF algorithm to generate Endorsement Key, which is simple and easy, but it only generates the key pair of vEK, and there is no problem of trust extension and delivery. The outside world cannot derive from the public key of the key pair that the public key is generated by the EPS of the underlying TPM. It is still necessary to pass the public key of the vEK generated by the EPS, the signature information of the underlying virtualization platform, and the vTPM information to the Privacy CA to generate the vEK certificate, and then generate the vAIK by using the vEK certificate from the Privacy CA to implement the extension of the vTPM certificate trust chain.

It can be seen from the above analysis that no matter what method is adopted to extend the certificate trust relationship of the underlying physical TPM to the vTPM certificate is not perfect, there is a violation of the TCG specification, or increasing the key redundancy, or increasing the performance burden of the Privacy CA. Some schemes can't even extend the certificate trust. These will reduce the convenience and trust of the user.

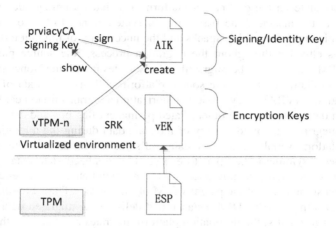

Fig. 34. hTPM EPS product vEK

4.4   vTPM Migration

vTPM migration refers to migrating vTPM from the source virtual platform to the destination virtual platform. The vTPM migration can be classified according to different classification methods. According to whether the source virtual platform and the destination virtual platform are in the same cloud, it can be divided into vTPM intra-cloud migration and vTPM inter-cloud migration; according to whether the source virtual platform and the destination virtual platform are the same, it can be divided into vTPM homogeneous migration and vTPM heterogeneous migration; according to the migration mode, it can be divided into static migration and dynamic migration; at present, the most distinguishing methods used in the study are static migration and dynamic migration. Therefore, this section will be explained in terms of vTPM static migration and dynamic migration.

Static Migration of vTPM. The so-called vTPM static migration is to lock the vTPM, stop the vTPM service, and then migrate the vTPM related status data. The vast majority of current research is mainly to design vTPM static migration protocol, including vTPM single migration protocol, and VM and vTPM bundle migration protocol in the existing research results. Regardless of the vTPM single migration protocol or the VM and vTPM bundle migration protocol, the basic steps of the protocol are nearly the same. The only difference is that the vTPM is locked while the VM is locked, and the vTPM related state data is migrated while the VM related state data is migrated. Therefore, in this section, we all regard as the same type of research for vTPM individual migration and VM-vTPM bundle migration.

In 2006, the literature [22] first designed the static migration protocol of vTPM. In the migration protocol, transmitting the source vTPM instance state data to the destination platform securely by using session key encryption. The destination platform restores the vTPM instance and deletes the source vTPM instance. As shown in Fig. 35. First, the platform migration control process engine creates a vTPM instance with an empty state on the destination platform, generates a unique identifier Nonce associated with the instance, and passes the encrypted Nonce to the source platform. Nonce's goal is to prevent replay attacks and the uncertainty of migration destinations, and Nonce is effective throughout the migration process. The source platform then locks the vTPM that needs to be migrated and associates it with the Nonce passed from the destination platform. Third, the source platform collects state data of the source vTPM, including: NVRAM, key session authorization and transmission callback status, authorization data, counters, and other related permanent flag bits and data. In order to ensure the integrity and confidentiality of the state data during the migration process, the source platform serializes the state data and signs it with an asymmetric key, and then generates a symmetric key pair to encrypt the serialized state data and the signature value to generate the migration data. The symmetric key is encrypted and protected by a storage key of the parent vTPM of the source vTPM. Fourth, the source platform deletes the source vTPM instance and delivers the migrated data to the destination platform. Finally, the destination platform migrates and decrypts the state data of the source vTPM, performs integrity verification and Nonce verification, and finally restores the target vTPM instance. It is worth noting that in order to the destination platform to be able to decrypt the migration data of the source vTPM, the parent vTPM storage key of the source platform must be migrated to the destination platform.

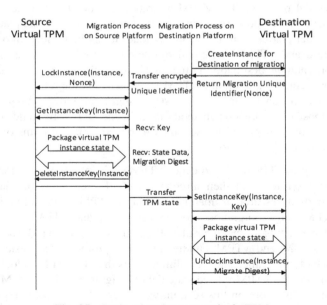

Fig. 35. Static migration protocol of vTPM

In 2007, the literature [52] analyzed the vTPM migration protocol in literature [22], and pointed out three shortcomings in the design of the vTPM migration protocol. First, the literature [22] uses the symmetric key encryption source vTPM state data, and uses the storage key of the source platform parent vTPM to protect the symmetric key. However, the protocol doesn't describe the migration of the storage key; secondly, the protocol is not well designed. For example, what key is used to encrypt the unique identifier Nonce of the destination platform vTPM, which is not stated in the protocol; finally, whether it is vTPM migration or key migration, it belongs to the TCG-IWG (Infrastructure Working Group: IWG) working group. The scope of work of the DMTF (Data Migration Task Force: DMTF) task group, but the design of the protocol is nearly not related to the work of the task group.

In 2008, the literature [40] improved the vTPM migration protocol in literature [22]. The biggest difference from the literature [22] is that the protection of the session key no longer by using the storage key of the parent vTPM. After the source migration control process engine initiated the migration and the destination migration control process engine created a new vTPM instance, the source vTPM requires to establish a trusted channel between the source platform and the destination platform. The session key is negotiated through the trusted channel. The subsequent process is basically the same as the literature [22], as shown in Fig. 36.

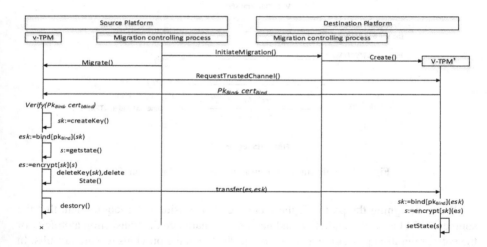

Fig. 36. Static migration protocol of vTPM based on trusted channel

In 2011, the literature [54] again improved the static migration protocol proposed in literature [22], as shown in Fig. 37. This literature proposed a 4-stage VM-vTPM migration process. In the first stage, establishing a TLS session; in the second stage, proving the source platform and the destination platform; in the third stage, migrating VM-vTPM state data, and starting the VM and vTPM of destination platform, deleting the VM and vTPM of source platform; in the fourth stage, ending the TLS session.

Compared with the literature [40], the source and destination credibility certificates have been added.

In 2012, the domestic literature [55] improved the literature [22], [40] and [54]. This literature proposed a two-stage vTPM migration. In the first stage, establishing trusted channel, and in the second stage, migrating the data. In the establishing trusted channel satge, requiring mutual authentication, attribute-based identity verification, parameter negotiation, and session key exchange. In the data migration satge, it is nearly the same as the literature [22] and [40]. As shown in Fig. 38.

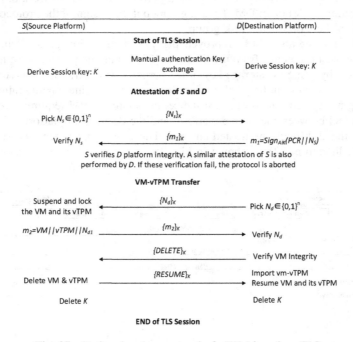

Fig. 37. Static migration protocol of vTPM based on TLS

When designing the protocol, the literature also considers the requirement that the source vTPM has non-repudiation and needing to guarantee the transaction atomicity of the entire migration process, which is more perfect than the previous research results. In the same year, the domestic literature [56] also proposed the design and implementation of a secure VM-v TPM migration protocol, including 4 stages. In the first satge, establishing secure session; in the second satge, remoting proofing of the destination platform; in the third satge, transporting vTPM and VM state data; in the fourth satge, deleting the VM and its vTPM on the source platform and restore it on the destination platform. It is nearly consistent with the previous research results.

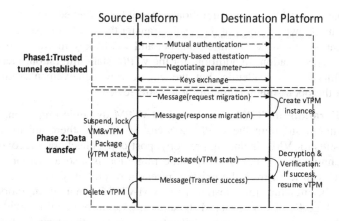

Fig. 38. vTPM static migration protocol for high security requirements

In 2015, the domestic literature [57] redesigned the vTPM migration protocol based on TPM 2.0. In this literature, dividing vTPM into two parts, one is the key migration of vTPM; the other is the state data migration of vTPM. In order to solve the migration timing problem of VM-vTPM, proposing a VM-vTPM instance pair migration protocol, which is divided into four stages: two-party identity authentication stage, two-party remote certification stage, data transmission stage and subsequent processing stage. The protocol process is shown in Fig. 39. And theoretical proof was carried out in this literature. However, this literature is too crude for the description of vTPM key migration.

In addition, the migration of TPM is also studied in literature [24] and [47]. But these two literatures are mainly aimed at the migration of physical TPM, not the migration of vTPM. Therefore, it is not analyzed here.

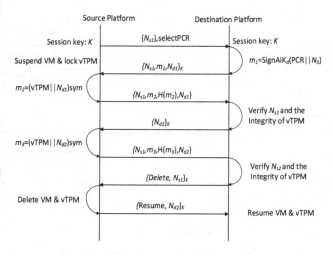

Fig. 39. VM-vTPM static migration protocol

In summary, the vTPM static migration protocol has achieved more research results and is maturing. However, most of the results transfer the vTPM key structure as one of the vTPM status data, which is unreasonable, and vTPM key migration must comply with the TCG specification. In addition, for the vTPM static migration, there are many research results in the academic, but the engineering achievements related to the industry and the open source community are still few.

Dynamic Migration of vTPM. The so-called vTPM dynamic migration, that is, the migration without stopping the vTPM service. At present, there are many dynamic migration results for VMs, including pre-copy, post-copy, checkpoint recovery, and log playback technologies. The vTPM dynamic migration is also a memory copy technology, which can learn from the existing research results of VM.

In 2015, the literature [58] designed the VM-vTPM dynamic migration protocol. As shown in Fig. 40. The VM-vTPM dynamic migration protocol is divided into two satges. The first stage is the integrity verification stage, and the second satge is the data

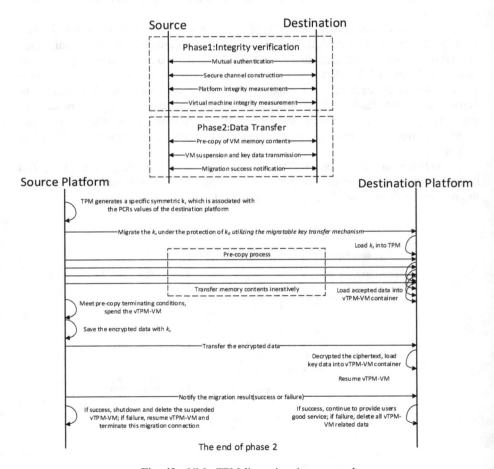

Fig. 40. VM-vTPM live migration protocol

migration satge. In the first satge, the mutual authentication of the source platform and the destination platform, the construction of the secure channel, the integrity measurement of the platform, and the integrity measurement of the virtual machine are included. In the second satge, the migration of the VM-vTPM and the VM-vTPM lock using the pre-copy method, key data migration and migration success notification are included.

In addition, the literature [59] has done similar work on the KVM platform, and the device state of the vTPM is further considered in the migration process. In addition, other research results of vTPM dynamic migration have not been seen yet.

In summary, the existing results in the VM and vTPM memory copy, the discussion is not detailed enough, whether it is to copy the VM first, then copy the vTPM, or copy the vTPM first, then copy the VM, or copy the VM and vTPM at the same time, which is no explanation in the results.

vTPM Migration System. The so-called vTPM migration system refers to the software and hardware systems that manage, control and implement vTPM migration. It usually includes the roles, entities, architectures, and interoperability protocols that implement the migration.

In the academic, there has not been a publicly available, practical vTPM migration system. In the industry, whether it is VMware's vSphere 6, Microsoft's Hyper-V, or Orical's VBox, there is no public display of the commercial vTPM migration system. In the open source community, only Xen gives a good vTPM migration. Since Xen 3.2,

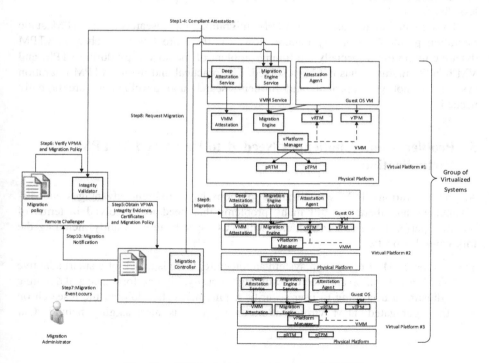

Fig. 41. vTPM migration architecture of VPWG

vTPM can run in a separate domain of Unikernel, the separate domain is essentially a lightweight virtual machine that can be migrated using Xen's virtual machine migration system, but Xen can only migrate vTPM between similar platforms.

In 2011, TCG's VPWG (Virtual Platform Working Group: VPWG) proposed the vTPM migration system architecture and migration protocol under the trusted virtual platform in the Virtualized Trusted Platform Architecture Specification [58]. As shown in Fig. 41. The migration architecture has a total of 12 entities, including Migrate Controller, Integrity Validator, Deep Attestation Service, VMM Attestation, Attestation Service, Migration Engine Service, Migration Engine, Virtual Platform Manager (vPlatform Manager), Virtual Trusted Root (vRTM), Virtual TPM (vTPM), and Physical Trusted Root (PRTM) and Physical TPM (pTPM). The roles involved include remote challengers, migration managers, and more. In the first 4 steps of the migration protocol, the migration challenger proves compatibility between the source platform and the destination platform; in the steps 5 and 6, the Integrity Validator in the migration challenger obtains VPAM integrity evidence, certificates, and migration policies from the Migration Control (Migrate Controller) and verifies them; in the step 7, once the migration manager receives the migration event, a migration command is issued to the migration engine in step 8; in step 9, the migration engine migrates the VM-vTPM that needs to be migrated. After the migration was completed, the Migration Manager notifies remote challenger that migration was successfully. Compared with the existing research results, the specification details the entities involved in the migration, which is closer to the practical system, but the migration protocol itself is less discussed.

To sum up, in the aspect of vTPM migration, the researches on vTPM static migration protocol are nearly mature, however, there are few researches on vTPM dynamic migration, especially the timing problem of memory copy during vTPM and VM bundle migration has not been solved. The practical and mature vTPM migration system has not yet appeared, and further research and development are urgently needed.

5   Problems and Challenges Needed to Be Solved in TPM Virtualization

At present, various TPM virtualization solutions have different advantages and disadvantages, and there are still many problems that need to be solved in terms of security, performance and compliance with TCG specification. Mainly including the following 4 aspects:

(1) On the TPM virtualization system architecture, there is a lack of a smart adaptive TPM virtualization architecture with high security, high performance and dynamic adjustment according to user security requirements. In addition, the research on the aggregated TPM virtualization architecture is also lagging behind. Our

thinking cannot be limited to the details of the TCG specification. We should learn from the basic ideas of trusted computing and boldly innovate in technology.

(2) In the key management of vTPM, the problems and challenges include two aspects. On the one hand, since vTPM must meet the migration requirements, there is always a dilemma between setting the key type and meeting the migration requirements. It is necessary to change the key attributes that originally satisfies the TCG specification, or introduce key redundancy, which cannot meet the consistency requirement of the key management of the vTPM and the TPM, and reduces the convenience of the user to use the vTPM. On the other hand, the trusted computing services provided by the software emulation vTPM for virtual machines, especially the cryptographic computing services, are all completed in the virtual platform's memory (not within the TPM), which is vulnerable to general security threats, privileged security threats and sharing security threats, which will seriously affect the security of user virtual machines and vTPM.

(3) In terms of certificate trust extension, in order to extend the certificate trust relationship of the physical TPM to the vTPM certificate. No matter what way is used, there is a case where the certificate usage violates the TCG specification, or a key redundancy is introduced, and no Satisfactory solution has not been found.

(4) In the vTPM migration solution, the current researches focus on the vTPM static migration protocol between the same virtual platforms in the cloud. However, the vTPM static migration protocol, the vTPM dynamic migration protocol, and the vTPM migration system between heterogeneous virtual platforms in the cloud require further research and development.

6 Conclusion

The combination of trusted computing and cloud computing technology can guarantee the credibility of the cloud computing environment in a certain extent, and promote the expansion and extension of cloud computing in a wider range of application. One of the effective ways to solve this problem is to to build a virtual machine trusted environment through TPM virtualization. How to securely and efficiently virtualize TPM and improve users' trust in cloud environment is the key to the integrated development of trusted computing and cloud computing. At the same time, TPM virtualization is not only a technical issue, it also involves many aspects such as standardization, supervision mode, application mode, etc. Therefore, it is not enough to explore TPM virtualization from a technical perspective, and it requires the joint efforts of the information security academic community, industry and relevant government departments to achieve this.

Acknowledgements. This work was supported by the National Natural Science Foundation of China (Grant No. 61373162), and the Sichuan Provincial Key Laboratory Project (Grant No. KJ201402).

References

1. Trusted Computing Group. https://www.trustedcomputing-group.org. Accessed 08 Sept 2019
2. TPM Specification, Version 2.0/Part 1, Architecture. https://www.Trustedcomputinggroup. org/wp-con-tent/uploads/TPM-Rev-2.0-Part1-Architecture-01.36_public-review.pdf. Accessed 08 Sept 2019
3. TPM Specification, Version 2.0/ Part 2, Structures. https://www.Trustedcomputinggroup. org/wp-con-tent/uploads/TPM-Rev-2.0-Part2-Structures-01.36_public-review.pdf. Accessed 08 Sept 2019
4. Specification, Version 2.0/ Part 3, Commands. https://www.trustedcomputinggroup.org/wp-content/uploads/TPM-Rev-2.0-Part3-Commands-01.36-code_public-review.pdf.   Accessed 08 Sept 2019
5. TPM Specification, Version 2.0/Part 4, Supporting Routines. https://www.trustedcomputi nggroup.org/wp-content/uploads/TPM-Rev-2.0-Part3-Commands-01.36-code_public-revie w.pdf. Accessed 08 Sept 2019
6. Changxiang, S., Huanguo, Z., Dengguo, F., et al.: Information security review. Scientia Sinica Ser. E: Inf. Sci. 37(2), 129–150 (2007)
7. Changxiang, S., Huanguo, Z., Huaiming, W., et al.: Research and development of trusted computing. Scientia Sinica Ser. E: Inf. Sci. 40(2), 139–166 (2010)
8. Dengguo, F., Yu, Q., Dan, W., et al.: Research on trusted computing technology. J. Comput. Res. Dev. 48(8), 1332–1349 (2011)
9. State Cryptography Administration: Trusted Computing Cryptographic Support Platform Function and Interface Specification (2007)
10. Rimal, B.P., Choi, E., Lumb, I.: A taxonomy and survey of cloud computing systems. In: Proceedings of the 2009 Fifth International Joint Conference on INC, IMS and IDC, pp. 44–51. IEEE, Seoul (2009)
11. Yao, S., et al.: An efficient multi-objective scheduling method for data flow in cloud environment. J. Softw. 28(3), 1–19 (2017)
12. Siyao, X., Weiwei, L., Zijun, W.: Virtual machine placement algorithm based on peak load characteristics. J. Softw. 27(7), 1876–1887 (2016)
13. Wei, W., Zeyu, G., Wenbo, Z., et al.: A cloud computing system fault detection method based on adaptive monitoring. Chin. J. Comput. 39(163), 1–15 (2016)
14. Guofeng, W., Chuanyi, L., Hezhong, P., et al.: Overview of internal threats in cloud computing models. Chin. J. Comput. 39(145), 1–21 (2016)
15. Lifang, R., Wenjian, W., Xing, X.: Adaptive cloud computing service portfolio with uncertain perception. J. Comput. Res. Dev. 53(12), 2867–2881 (2016)
16. Junjie, L., Fenghua, L., Qiongni, L., et al.: Optimized high-dimensional index and KNN query under MapReduce framework. Acta Electronica Sinica 44(8), 1873–1880 (2016)
17. Amazon Elastic Compute Cloud (EC2). http://aws.amazon.com/ec2/. Accessed 08 Sept 2019
18. Google App Engine (GAE). https://appengine.google.com/. Accessed 08 Sept 2019
19. Microsoft Azure Services Platform. http://www.microsoft.com/azure/. Accessed 08 Sept 2019
20. Elastic Utility Computing Architecture for Linking Your Programs To Useful Systems (Eucalyptus). http://www.eucalyptus.com/. Accessed 08 Sept 2019
21. Chuang, L., Wenbo, S., Kun, M., et al.: Cloud computing security: architecture, mechanism and model evaluation. Chin. J. Comput. 36(9), 1765–1784 (2013)

22. Berger, S., Cáceres, R., Goldman, K.A., et al.: vTPM: virtualizaing the trusted platform modual. In: Proceedings of the 15th USENIX security Symposium, pp. 305–320. ACM, Vancouver (2006)
23. England, P., Loeser, J.: Para-Virtualized TPM sharing. In: Lipp, P., Sadeghi, A.-R., Koch, K.-M. (eds.) Trust 2008. LNCS, vol. 4968, pp. 119–132. Springer, Heidelberg (2008). https://doi.org/10.1007/978-3-540-68979-9_9
24. Stumpf, F., Eckert, C.: Enhancing trusted platform modules with hardware-based virtualization techniques. In: Proceedings of the 2008 Second International Conference on Emerging Security Information, pp. 1–9. IEEE, Cap Esterel (2008)
25. Lei, S., Deqing, Z., Hai, J.: Xen Virtualization Technology. Huazhong University of Science and Technology Press, Hangzhou (2009)
26. AlBelooshi, B., Salah, K., Martin, T., et al: Securing cryptographic keys in the IaaS cloud model. In: 8th International Conference on Utility and Cloud Computing (UCC), pp. 397–401. IEEE, Limassol (2015)
27. Zhilou, Y., Qiao, W., Weipin, Z., et al.: A cloud certificate authority architecture for virtual machines with trusted platform module. In: IEEE 7th International Symposium on Cyberspace Safety and Security (CSS), pp. 1377–1380. IEEE, New York (2015)
28. Dexian, C., Xiaobo, C., Yu, Q., et al.: TSD: a flexible root of trust for the cloud. In: IEEE 11th International Conference on Trust, Security and Privacy in Computing and Communications, pp. 119–126. IEEE, Liverpool (2012)
29. Xin, W., Zhiting, X., Yi, R.: Building trust into cloud computing using virtualization of TPM. In: Fourth International Conference on Multimedia Information Networking and Security, pp. 59–63. IEEE, Nanjing (2012)
30. Dongliang, X., Xiaolong, W., Yunwei, G., et al.: TrustVP: construction and evolution of trusted chain on virtualization computing platform. In: Eighth International Conference on Computational Intelligence and Security (CIS), pp. 623–630. IEEE, Guangzhou (2012)
31. Microsoft MVP. http://anilerduran.com/vtpm-in-windows-server-2016-hyper-v/. Accessed 08 Sept 2019
32. Oricale. https://www.virtualbox.org/. Accessed 08 Sept 2019
33. VMware. http://www.vmware.com/. Accessed 08 Sept 2019
34. Xen project. http://www.xenproject.org/. Accessed 08 Sept 2019
35. KVM project. http://www.linux-kvm.org/. Accessed 08 Sept 2019
36. Scarlata, V., Rozas, C., Wiseman, M., et al.: TPM virtualization: building a general framework. In: Pohlmann, N., Reimer, H. (eds.) Trusted Computing, pp. 43–56. Springer, Heidelberg (2007). https://doi.org/10.1007/978-3-8348-9452-6_4
37. Anderson, M.J., Moffie, M., Dalton, C.I.: Towards trustworthy virtualization environments: Xen library OS security service infrastructure. Hewlett-Packard Lab. 2007(1), 43–51 (2007)
38. Murray, G., Milos, G., Hand, S.: Improving Xen security through disaggregation. In: VEE 08: Proceedings of the Fourth ACM SIGPLAN/SIGOPS International Conference on Virtual Execution Environments, pp. 151–160. ACM, Seattle (2008)
39. David, P., Serdar, C., Chris, D., et al.: TPM virtualisation architecture document. Open Trusted Computing (2009)
40. Sadeghi, A.-R., Stüble, C., Winandy, M.: Property-based TPM virtualization. In: Wu, T.-C., Lei, C.-L., Rijmen, V., Lee, D.-T. (eds.) ISC 2008. LNCS, vol. 5222, pp. 1–16. Springer, Heidelberg (2008). https://doi.org/10.1007/978-3-540-85886-7_1
41. Xin, J., Lina, W., Rongwei, Y., et al.: Administrative domain: security enhancement for virtual TPM. In: International Conference on Multimedia Information Networking and Security, pp. 767–771. IEEE, Nanjing (2010)
42. Weiqi, D.: Research on key issues of trusted construction of cloud computing execution environment. Huazhong University of Science and Technology (2015)

43. Bade, S.A., Betz, L.N., Kegel, A.G., et al.: Method and system for virtualization of trusted platform modules. US Patent 7 380 119, May, 2008
44. Feller, T., Malipatlolla, S., Kasper, M., et al.: dcTPM: a generic architecture for dynamic context management. In: International Conference on Reconfigurable Computing and FPGAs, pp. 211–216. IEEE, Cancun (2011)
45. Smith, N.M.: Method and apparatus for virtualization of a multi-contexthardware trusted platform module (TPM). US Patent 2009/0 055 641 A1, February 2009
46. Jayaram Masti, R., Marforio, C., Capkun, S.: An architecture for concurrent execution of secure environments in clouds. In: Proceedings of the 2013 ACM workshop on Cloud computing security workshop, pp. 11–22. ACM, Berlin (2013)
47. Yap, J.Y., Tomlinson, A.: Para-virtualizing the trusted platform module: an enterprise framework based on version 2.0 specification. In: Bloem, R., Lipp, P. (eds.) INTRUST 2013. LNCS, vol. 8292, pp. 1–16. Springer, Cham (2013). https://doi.org/10.1007/978-3-319-03491-1_1
48. Pci-sig-single root iov. http://www.pcisig.com/specifica-tions/iov/Single_root/. Accessed 08 Sept 2019
49. Mingda, L., Longyu, M.: A virtual environment security isolation model based on SR-IOV technology. In: Proceedings of the 31st National Computer Security Academic Exchange Conference, pp. 84–89. CNKI, Xiamen (2016)
50. Xinlong, L., Rui, J., Huafeng, K.: Secure and reliable VM-vTPM migration in private cloud. In: 2nd International Symposium on Instrumentation and Measurement, Sensor Network and Automation (IMSNA), pp. 510–514. IEEE, Toronto (2013)
51. Yongjiao, Y., Fei, Y., Junpeng, M., et al.: Ng-vTPM: a new generation of TPM virtualization framework design. J. Wuhan Univ. (Nat. Sci. Ed.) 61(2), 103–111 (2015)
52. Goyette, R.: A review of vTPM: virtualizing the trusted platform module. In: Network Security and Cryptography Symposium, pp. 1–17 (2007)
53. Lina, W., Hanjun, G., Rongwei, Y., et al.: Research on the construction method of trusted virtual execution environment based on trust extension. J. Commun. 32(9), 1–8 (2011)
54. Danev, B.: Enabling secure VM-vTPM migration in private clouds. In: ACSAC 2011 Proceedings of the 27th Annual Computer Security Applications Conference, pp. 187–196. ACM, Orlando (2011)
55. Xin, W., XinFang, Z., Liang, C., et al.: An improved vTPM migration protocol based trusted channel. In: International Conference on Systems and Informatics (ICSAI), pp. 870–875. IEEE, Yantai (2012)
56. Yinchao, Y., Zai, L., Zuoning, C.: Design and implementation of a secure VM-v TPM migration protocol. Appl. Electron. Tech. 38(4), 130–133 (2012)
57. Armbrust, M., Fox, A., Grith, R., et al.: A view of cloud computing. Commun. ACM 53(4), 50–58 (2010)
58. Peiru, F., Bo, Z., Yuan, S., et al.: An improved vTPM-VM live migration protocol. Wuhan University J. Nat. Sci. 20(6), 512–520 (2015)
59. Yuqing, H., Bo, Z., Jue, X., et al.: A KVM-based v TPM virtual machine dynamic migration scheme. J. Shandong Univ. (Nat. Sci. Ed.) 52(6), 69–75 (2017)
60. Virtual platform working group (VPWG) on virtualized trusted platform architecture specification. https://www.trusted-computinggroup.org/wp-content/uploa-ds/TCG_VPWG_Architecture_V1-0_R0-26_FINAL.pdf. Accessed 08 Sept 2019
61. Yan, D., Huaiming, W., Peichang, S., et al.: Trusted cloud service. Chin. J. Comput. 38(5), 133–149 (2015)

A Secure Certificateless Identity Authentication Scheme Based on Blockchain

Weijun Ao[1]($\boxtimes$), Shaojing Fu[1,2], Chao Zhang[1], and Ming Xu[1]

[1] College of Computer, National University of Defense Technology, Changsha, China
[2] Sate Key Laboratory of Cryptology, Beijing, China
554335022@qq.com

Abstract. Centralized systems based on the trusted third-party are widely used in identity authentication. However, there is a single point of failure inherent in the centralized systems. As a natural decentralized architecture, blockchain can bring the advantages of decentralization, trustworthiness and immutability to the identity authentication systems. The existing blockchain-based identity authentication systems can solve the problem of single point of failure, but there are still problems such as certificate management. In this paper, we propose an identity authentication scheme based on blockchain and certificateless public key cryptography. The scheme implements a decentralized database by deploying smart contracts in the Ethereum blockchain, and uses the certificateless public key signature algorithm during the authentication process. Compared with other blockchain-based identity authentication systems, our scheme not only prevents the single point of failure, but also avoids the deficiency of certificate management, and resists impersonation attacks and man-in-the-middle attacks. The security analysis and performance analysis show the security and stability of our scheme.

Keywords: Blockchain · Certificateless public key · Identity Authentication

1 Introduction

With the development of science and technology, the Internet has increasingly changed peoples lives, the following information security problems have become more and more prominent. As a core technology of information security technology, identity authentication, refers to authenticating the user's real identity in the computer or network, plays an important role in protecting information security. Nowadays, many identity authentication systems are based on the trusted third-party authentication server to authenticate the user's identity, and verify the user's identity through the user's knowledge (such as password), owned (such as certificates, tokens) and biological characteristics (such as fingerprints, iris)

© Springer Nature Singapore Pte Ltd. 2020
W. Han et al. (Eds.): CTCIS 2019, CCIS 1149, pp. 251–266, 2020.
https://doi.org/10.1007/978-981-15-3418-8_16

[10]. However, traditional third-party-based identity authentication systems have some inherent problems of centralized systems, such as single point of failure and poor transparency, and face serious security challenges [13].

With the increasing acceptance of digital currencies, blockchain, as the core technology of digital currencies, has attracted extensive attention from industry and academia [16]. In recent years, the research on the application of blockchain in identity authentication has focused on the direction of Public Key Infrastructure (PKI) [11]. For PKI based on blockchain, PKI is established by using blockchain. It solves the problem of PKI Certificate transparency and single point of failure faced by traditional PKI systems, and it also prevents the hackers from implementing the man-in-the-middle attack by attacking the trusted Certificate Authority (CA) to maliciously sign false certificates (Take the Bitcoin blockchain as an example, a hacker needs at least 51% computational power to attack successfully). In 2014, MIT scholar Conner proposed Certcoin, the first distributed PKI based on blockchain [6]. Decentralized PKI is achieved by recording the user's certificates in the public ledger of the blockchain. The issuance process of the certificate can be queried by any user. Subsequent studies have improved the model of Certcoin, such as Privacy-awareness in Blockchain-based PKI (PB-PKI) proposed by Axon in 2015 [2]. In addition to establishing a decentralized CA through the blockchain, PB-PKI divides the nodes of the blockchain into trusted neighbor nodes and untrusted global nodes, and protects the online key through the offline key, reducing the risk of users' privacy information disclosure. Matsumoto researched the problem of CA's insufficient investment in resisting attacks, and proposed an instant karma PKI framework (IKP) [12]. IKP is based on the Ethereum blockchain, introduces a detector mechanism to report illegal certificates in time, encourages CA to issue certificates correctly by economic means, and imposes economic penalties on CA that issue illegal certificates. Although identity authentication based on blockchain and PKI can effectively solve the certificate transparency and single point of failure of PKI, but the management and maintenance of public key certificates will consume huge computing resources [18]. In 2003, Al-Riyami and Paterson proposed a new cryptosystem – Certificateless Public Key Cryptography (CL-PKC) [1]. In CL-PKC, Key Generating Centre (KGC) only knows part of the user's private key. Even if KGC is hacked or KGC's communication information is intercepted, it will not result in the disclosure of users' private keys. Compared with the traditional public key cryptosystem, CL-PKC no longer relies on digital certificates, and has the advantages of efficiency and security [17].

In this paper, we introduce an identity authentication scheme based on blockchain and certificateless public key cryptography. This is the first time that certificateless public key cryptosystem and blockchain are combined to apply to identity authentication. The decentralized feature of blockchain can help to solve the problem of single point of failure. The use of the certificateless public key cryptosystem avoids the real-time online and management pressure of the certificate.

2 Preliminary Knowledge

2.1 Blockchain

Blockchain is a chained-block data structure that combines data blocks sequentially in time order, a kind of distributed ledger which guarantees the consistent storage, non-tampering and non-forgery of data through cryptography. Blockchain provides a new way to solve trust-building problem among entities in distributed environment by using distributed data storage, consensus mechanism and other technologies [15]. The blockchains decentralized feature can help to solve the problem of trust establishment between nodes of decentralized system, so as to achieve decentralized identity authentication [7].

From the perspective of data, blockchain is a distributed database that is virtually impossible to change. Its "distributed" is not only reflected in the distributed data backup storage, but also reflected in the distributed data records, that is, all nodes participate in the data maintenance. Blockchains store data through data blocks and chain structures. All transactions within a certain period of time are processed by cryptographic algorithms to form blocks. Each data block consists of a block header and a block body, with a unique hash corresponding to the block address. The current block is connected to the previous block by storing the hash of the previous block, and the blocks are connected in series to form a chain structure [5]. The block header encapsulates the hash of the previous block, timestamp, Merkle root and other information. The block body stores transaction information, and each transaction is digitally signed by the transaction party to ensure that the data is not forged and cannot be tampered with. Each completed transaction will be permanently recorded in the block for all users to query. The Data structure of blockchain is shown in Fig. 1.

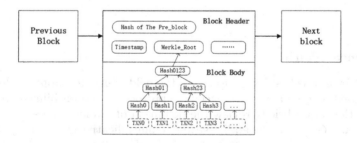

Fig. 1. Data structure of blockchain

Blockchain originated from Bitcoin, but people pay much more attention to blockchain than Bitcoin itself. With the development of technology, blockchain has also moved from the 1.0 stage represented by bitcoin to the 2.0 stage represented by smart contract.

Smart contract [4] is a script stored on the blockchain that can run automatically. Once written, the terms of the contract cannot be changed. In 1994, Szabo first proposed the concept of smart contract, which is defined as "a transaction agreement to implement the terms of the contract through a computer", that is, to automatically execute the contract through a code program [9]. As long as the terms of the contract are met, the transactions will take place automatically without third-party supervision. Although the concept of smart contract has been proposed for a long time, it was not until the release of the Ethereum platform that it provided the basis for the rapid development of smart contracts.

Ethereum, as the representative of Blockchain 2.0, is based on Turing-complete Ethereum Virtual Machine (EVM), which can perform the coding of arbitrary complex algorithms. It can provide the necessary foundation for Smart contract development by relying on EVM, and allow anyone to develop Decentralized Application (Dapp) running through blockchain in the platform. In Ethereum, the smart contract is programmable, and can be regarded as an automatic agent. It has its own account and address, can send and receive messages and values, and can execute the corresponding code according to the contract content. The model of the Ethereum smart contract is shown in Fig. 2.

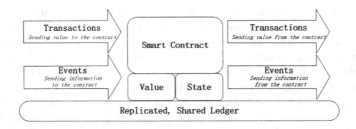

Fig. 2. Model of Ethereum smart contract

2.2   Bilinear Pairing

Bilinear Pairing was first introduced into the field of cryptography by Joux, who first proposed a three-party key exchange protocol based on bilinear pairing in 2000 [14]. Hence, we briefly review the definition of bilinear maps.

Let G_1 and G_2 denote an addictive and a multiplicative cyclic groups of prime order q, let p and g denote a generator of G_1. We call a map $\hat{e} : G_1 \times G_1 \to G_2$ is a bilinear pairing if it satisfies:

(1) The map $\hat{e}$ is bilinear: for all $a, b \in Z$, $\hat{e}(ap, bq) = \hat{e}(p, q)^{ab}$.
(2) The map $\hat{e}$ is non-degenerate: there is $p, q \in G_1$, such that $\hat{e}(p, q) \neq 1$ is established.
(3) The map $\hat{e}$ is efficiently computable: for all $p, q \in G_1$ there is an efficient algorithm to calculate $\hat{e}(p, q)$.

2.3   Security Assumption

The identity authentication scheme design based on blockchain and certificateless public key proposed in this paper mainly refers to the idea of certificateless public key cryptosystem proposed in literature [1]. According to the security attack model defined by it, two types of attacker should be considered in the security analysis of the scheme:

(1) Type I Attacker F_1: Simulate an external attacker, F_1 does not have access to *master-key*, but may request *public key* and replace it.
(2) Type II Attacker F_2: Simulate an honest but curious KGC, F_2 does have access to *master-key*, but may not replace *public key* of entities.

3   Framework Design

3.1   System Structure

As shown in Fig. 3, the identity authentication scheme design proposed in this paper includes four participating entities:

(1) Key Generating Center (KGC): Responsible for generating and distributing *partial private key*.
(2) Authentication server: Responsible for user registration, identity authentication and other functions.
(3) User client: Responsible for generating *private key* and completing the identity authentication process with the authentication server.
(4) Blockchain: Responsible for implementing decentralized database by deploying *Smart Contract* 1 and *Smart Contract* 2 on the Ethereum blockchain. The main function of *smart contract* 1 is to store the hash value of the system *master-key s* and the system parameters *params*. It can prevent hackers from maliciously modifying the *master-key* after KGC attacked. The main function of *smart contract* 2 is to store the *ID* and other informations of registered users.

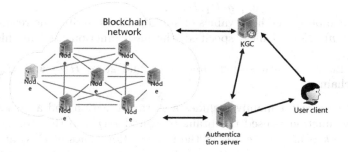

Fig. 3. Model of system structure

Table 1. Notations

$s, H(s)$	*master-key* and its hash value
PK_i, PK_0, PK_{KGC}	*Public key* of User Client u_i, Authentication Server and KGC
params	System parameters
x_i, ID_i	Secret value, *ID* Of User Client u_i
D_i, S_i	*partial private key, private key* Of User Client u_i
x_0, ID_0	Secret value, *ID* Of Authentication Server
D_0, S_0	*partial private key, private key* Of Authentication Server
pw_i	Password of User
e_i, e_j	Random number generated during the registration phase
f_i, f_j	Random number generated during the authentication phase
Req_1, Req_2	Request information
Res_1, Res_2	Response message
$T_i, W, Y, T_0, O_1, O_2, O_3$	Variables used during protocol interaction

3.2 Algorithm Description

Notations. The notations used in this paper are shown in Table 1.

Setup. The setup phase is mainly completed by KGC.

(1) Given the security parameter sp. KGC selects the prime q, and selects $s \in z_q^*$ as the *master-key*, then calculates and publishes the *public key* $PK_{KGC} = g^s$.

(2) G_1 and G_2 denote the multiplicative groups of prime order q, g denote a generator of G_1, $\hat{e} : G_1 \times G_1 \to G_2$ is a Bilinear pairing. KGC chooses hash functions $H_1 : \{0,1\}^* \to G_1^*$ and $H_2 : \{0,1\}^* \to G_1^*$. The system parameters $params = <G_1, G_2, \hat{e}, q, g, H_1, H_2>$.

(3) KGC computes the hash values of s and $params$, writes the results as $H(s)$ and $H(p)$ (Note: Unless specified, the hash function used in this paper is $SM3$).

(4) KGC interacts with *smart contract* 1 and store $H(s)$ and $H(p)$ on the blockchain.

Smart Contract 1 mainly includes a storage function and a query function. The query function is used to obtain $H(s)$ and $H(p)$. In the storage function, the variable k is used to represent the modification times of $H(s)$ and $H(p)$. A modifier is implemented with the "if" function, ensures that only the contract-owner (KGC) can store $H(s)$ and $H(p)$ on the blockchain and $H(s)$ and $H(p)$

cannot be changed by attacker after storage. The pseudocode of the storage function is as follows.

Algorithm 1. (*smart contract* 1)Store $H(s)$ and $H(p)$

Input: $H(s)$ and $H(p)$
Output: bool
1 **if** *(msg.sender $\neq$ KGCAddress $\|$ $k \geq 1$)* **then**
2 $\quad$ | $\quad$ revert();
3 **else**
4 $\quad$ | $\quad$ $hash_s = H(s)$;
5 $\quad$ | $\quad$ $hash_p = H(p)$;
6 $\quad$ | $\quad$ $k++$;
7 $\quad$ | $\quad$ return *true*;
8 **end**

Set Private Key and Public Key. Flow chart of setting public-key and private-key is shown in Fig. 4.

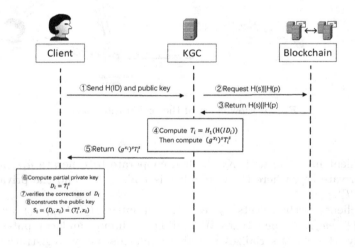

Fig. 4. Flow chart of setting public-key and private-key

(1) User client u_i randomly selects $x_i \in z_q^*$ as the *secret value*, calculates and publishes the *public key* $PK_i = g^{x_i}$.

(2) User client u_i sends $H(ID_i)$ (the hash value of identifier ID_i) and *public key* PK_i to KGC.

(3) KGC interacts with the *smart contract* 1 to obtain $H(s)$ and $H(p)$, computes the hash value of the s and *params* stored by itself (record the result as $H'(s)$ and $H'(p)$). Compare $H'(s)\|H'(p)$ with $H(s)\|H(p)$("$\|$" represents

string concatenation). If they are different, issue a warning message (It means that KGC has been attacked and is no longer trusted). If same, compute $T_i = H_1(H(ID_i))$ and $(g^{x_i})^s T_i^s$, then send $(g^{x_i})^s T_i^s$ to u_i;

(4) User client u_i get *partial private key* D_i by computing $D_i = \frac{(g^{x_i})^s T_i^s}{(g^s)^{x_i}} = T_i^s$, and verifies the correctness of D_i by checking $\hat{e}(T_i^s, g) \stackrel{?}{=} \hat{e}(H_1(H(ID_i), PK_{KGC})$. If the equation is true, constructs the *publickey* as $S_i = (D_i, x_i) = (T_i^s, x_i)$.

For authentication server, *secret value* is x_0, *public key* is $PK_0 = g^{x_0}$, *private key* is $S_0 = (T_0^s, x_i)$, where $T_0 = H_1(H(ID_0))$.

Registration Phase. Flow chart of the registration phase is shown in Fig. 5.

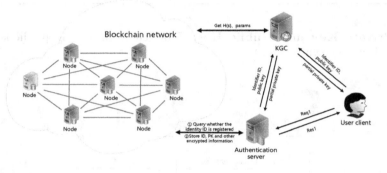

Fig. 5. Flow chart of the registration phase

(1) The client interacts with KGC, then cooperate to generate u_is public key and private key, where the public key is $PK_i = g^{x_i}$, and the private key is $S_i = (T_i^s, x_i)$.
(2) The client firstly selects $e_i \in z_q^*$, computes $H_2(ID_i||pw_i)$ and $W = H_2(ID_i||pw_i)g^{e_i}$, then takes W and D_i as inputs and computes $W^{x_i} T_i^s$. Finally, the client serializes the above information as registration-request message $Req_1 = (ID_i, PK_i, g^{e_i}, W^{x_i} T_i^s, H_2(ID_i||pw_i))$and sends it to the server.
(3) The authentication server interacts with the *smart contract* 2 to check whether the identity ID_i is registered. If registered, returns the registration-rejected message to the client. If unregistered, computes $T_i' = H_1(H(ID_i))$, and verifies the correctness of $W^{x_i} T_i^s$ by checking

$$\hat{e}(W^{x_i} T_i^s, g) \stackrel{?}{=} \hat{e}(H_2(ID_i||pw_i)g^{e_i}, g^{x_i})\hat{e}(T_i', PK_{KGC}).$$

If equal, server selects $e_j \in z_q^*$ and computes g^{e_j}, $Y = H_2(ID_0||PK_0)g^{e_j}$. Then the authentication server sends the registration-response message

$Res_1 = (ID_0, PK_0, g^{e_j}, Y^{x_0}T_0^s)$ to the client. If not, sends registration-failure message to the client.

(4) The authentication server serializes e_j, g^{e_i}, $H_2(ID_i||pw_i)$. Then encrypt it to get ciphertext $C(ID_i)$(Note: Unless specified, the encryption function used in this paper is $AES - 256 - CBC$). Finally, the authentication server uses ID_i as index to store PK_i and $C(ID_i)$ in the blockchain.

(5) The client computes $T_0' = H_1(H(ID_0))$, then verifies the correctness of $Y^{x_0}T_0^s$ by checking

$$\hat{e}(Y^{x_0}T_0^s, g) \overset{?}{=} \hat{e}(H_2(ID_0||PK_0)g^{e_j}, PK_0)\hat{e}(T_0', PK_{KGC}).$$

If equal, the user is successfully registered, and the client writes ID_0, PK_0, g^{e_j}, e_i to the storage. If not, registration fails.

Algorithm 2. (*smart contract* 2)Store PK_i and $C(ID_i)$

Input: ID_i, $PK_i||C(ID_i)$
Output: bool
1 mapping(uint => bytes) public ClientData;
2 **if** *(msg.sender $\neq$ KGCAddress)* **then**
3 | revert();
4 **else**
5 | uint16 $i = 0$;
6 | **for** *(; i < ClientData.length; i++)* **do**
7 | | ClientData[ClientId].push(ClientData[i]);
8 | **end**
9 | return *true*;
10 **end**

Smart Contract 2 also includes a storage function and a query function. But because *Smart Contract* 2 supports modifications to the stored data, and the data structure is more complex, so the code is more complicated. In the query function, we use ID_i as index to obtain PK_i and $C(ID_i)$. In the storage function, We use the mapping of uint and bytes to store the $PK_i||C(ID_i)$. A modifier is implemented with the "if" function too, ensures that only the contract-owner (The authentication server) can store data on the blockchain. The pseudocode of the storage function is shown above.

Certification Phase. Flow chart of the Certification phase is shown in Fig. 6.

(1) User inputs the identifier ID_i and password pw_i on the client login interface.
(2) The client computes $H_2(ID_i||pw_i)$, then selects $f_i \in z_q^*$ and computes g^{f_i}. Finally, the client sends an authentication request $Req_1 = (ID_i, g^{f_i}, H_2(ID_i||pw_i))$ to the authentication server.
(3) The authentication server interacts with the *smart contract* 2 to check whether the identity ID_i is registered. If unregistered, returns the

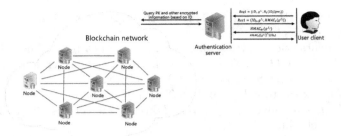

Fig. 6. Flow chart of the Certification phase

authentication-failure message to the client. If registered, gets the user's public key PK_i and $C(ID_i)$ with identity ID_i as the index, decrypts $C(ID_i)$ to get e_j, g^{e_i} and $H_2(ID_i||pw_i)$. The authentication server compares $H_2(ID_i||pw_i)$ with it in Req_1. If they are unequal, the authentication fails. If equal, computes $k = (g^{e_i})^{e_j}$ and $O_1 = HMAC_k(g^{f_i})$. Then selects $f_j \in z_q^*$ and computes g^{f_j}. Finally, the authentication server sends the authentication-response message $Res_1 = (ID_0, g^{f_j}, O_1)$ to the client.

(4) The client obtains the corresponding g^{e_j}, e_i in the storage by using the ID_0 as an index, then computes $k' = (g^{e_j})^{e_i}$ and $O_1' = HMAC_{k'}(g^{f_i})$. The client verifies whether O_1 and O_1' are equal. If they are not equal, the authentication fails and the client terminates the authentication process. If equal, the client completes the authentication of the server, then computes $O_2 = HMAC_{k'}(g^{f_j})$. Finally, the client sends O_2 as Req_2 to the authentication server.

(5) The authentication server computes $O_2' = HMAC_k(g^{f_j})$, then compares O_2 and O_2'. If O_2' is equal to O_2, the server completes the authentication of the client, then computes $O_3 = HMAC_k((g^{f_j})^{f_i}||ID_0)$. And the authentication server sends O_3 as Res_2 to the client. If not, the authentication fails and the server terminates the authentication process.

(6) The client computes $O_3' = HMAC_k'((g^{f_i})^{f_j}||ID_0)$, then compares O_3 and O_3'. If O_3 is equal to O_3', the client outputs authentication-success information. If not, The client outputs authentication-failure information.

Password Update

(1) In order to update password from pw_i to pw_i' when u_i is successfully authenticated, The client computes $U = g^{e_i e_j} g^{f_j f_i} \times H_2(ID_i||pw_i')$ ($\times$ denotes the multiplication operation of G_1) firstly, then sends the password-update-request message $Req0 = (ID_i, U, (g^{f_j})^{e_i})$ to the authentication server.

(2) The authentication server gets g^{e_i} with identity ID_i as the index, then computes $(g^{e_i})^{f_j}$. The server compares $(g^{e_i})^{f_j}$ and $(g^{f_j})^{e_i}$. If they are not equal, the server terminates the password update process. If they are equal, get the value of $H_2(ID_i||pw_i')$ by computing $\dfrac{U}{g^{e_i e_j} g^{f_j f_i}}$. Finally, the server

encrypts $H_2(ID_i||pw_i')$ and stores it in the blockchain instead of the original $H_2(ID_i||pw_i)$.

4 Security Analysis

This section analyzes the security of the identity authentication scheme based on blockchain and certificateless public key cryptography proposed in this paper.

Firstly, consider the two adversaries mentioned in literature [1]. For type I attacker F_1, it can replace u_i's public key with its chosen public key. In the paper, u_i's *public key*, ID and other information are stored in the blockchain (*Smart contract* 2). Due to the decentralized and transparent of the blockchain, the u_i's public key cannot be changed after successful registration. Moreover, any change of the information on the blockchain will be recorded in the block, which is easy to be backtracked. Therefore, F_1 cannot replace the u_i's original public key, only other attacks can be carried out. For type II attacker F_2, although KGC has mastered all of partial private keys, it does not have the ability to replace the public key because it cannot interact with *Smart Contract* 2. Moreover, because $H(s)||H(p)$ is stored in the blockchain (*Smart Contract* 1), and the client will verify correctness of *master-key* s and *params* after receiving the *partial private key* D_i, the *private key* will be generated after the verification is passed. Therefore, the malicious KGC cannot replace the u_i's *public key* or change the system's *master-key*, and only can try other attack methods.

In addition to using blockchain to defend against two types of adversaries, In the field of public key cryptography, the scheme design proposed in this paper also has the following security features:

4.1 Defending Impersonation Attack

For identity authentication, the main attack methods is impersonation attack. There are three attack modes of impersonation attack: passive attack, active attack and parallel attack [8]. Passive attack means that an attacker can steal the session script between the claimant (user client) and the verifier (authentication server) before impersonating the claimant. Active attack refers to that the attacker first disguises himself as the verifier and interacts with the claimant for many times to obtain some useful information, then proves to the verifier that he is the owner of the identity ID of a claimant with the obtained information. Parallel attack mean that an attacker can interact with multiple different verifier in parallel. For active attack and Parallel attack, it is assumed that the attacker can interact with the verifier to obtain the *public key* PK_i of the u_i, and interact with KGC to obtain the partial private key D_i of the u_i.

According to the introduction of the algorithm in Sect. 2, the security of the authentication phase depends on the key $k = g^{e_i e_j}$ of the HMAC algorithm. Since the security of HMAC algorithm has been proved in literature [3], as long as the attacker can obtain k in the previous user registration phase, it can be considered that the identity authentication scheme proposed in this paper can be breached.

And the security of k value depends on the registration process between the client and the authentication server by using the certificateless public key signature algorithm.

According to the evidence in literature [1], for two types of attackers, the following conclusions are made:

(1) Suppose CDH is established on group G_1, for attacker F_1, the scheme presented in this paper based on the Random Oracle model is unforgeable under adaptive selection message attack (EUF-CMA). That is to say, if any attacker F_1 can forge the signature within time T_1 by performing queries on the hash function H_1, H_2, secret value generation, public key generation, KGC generation partial private key and signature generation at most p_1 times, p_2 times, p_3 times, p_4 times, p_5 times, p_6 times with advantages of ε_I. Then there exists an algorithm A_1, which can overcome the CDH problem on group G_1 with advantage ε_1 during the time t_1. Where,

$$\varepsilon_1 \geq \frac{(p_5 + p_6)^{p_5 + p_6} \varepsilon_I}{p_1 (p_5 + p_6 + 1)^{p_5 + p_6 + 1}}$$

$$t_1 \leq T_1 + (q_1 + q_5 + q_6) t_{G_1} + q_2 + q_3 + q_4$$

(t_{G_1} represents the time of 1 exponential operation on group G_1).

(2) Suppose CDH is established on group G_1, for attacker F_2, the scheme presented in this paper based on the Random Oracle model is unforgeable under adaptive selection message attack (EUF-CMA). That is to say, if any attacker F_2 can forge the signature within time T_2 by performing queries on the hash function H_1, H_2, secret value generation, public key generation, KGC generation partial private key and signature generation at most p_1 times, p_2 times, p_3 times, p_4 times, p_5 times, p_6 times with advantages of ε_2. Then there exists an algorithm A_2, which can overcome the CDH problem on group G_1 with advantage ε_{II} during the time t_2. Where,

$$\varepsilon_2 \geq \frac{(p_3 + p_6)^{p_3 + p_6} \varepsilon_{II}}{p_2 (p_3 + p_6 + 1)^{p_3 + p_6 + 1}}$$

$$t_2 \leq T_2 + (q_2 + q_6) t_{G_1} + q_1 + q_3 + q_4$$

4.2 Defending Man-in-the-middle Attack

In a man-in-the-middle attack, an attacker can intercept communication information between the user client and the authentication server, and even tamper with the data before transmitting. When an attacker simply eavesdrops on the interaction between the user and the server, this is equivalent to a passive attack, as discussed above. It is assumed that the attacker is not only satisfied with eavesdropping, but also maliciously tampers reply information before transmitting. In this case, no matter which party, the authentication server or the client, receives the modified information, and it will directly end the authentication process, the authentication fails. Through the above discussion of the active attack in the impersonation attack, the attacker cannot successfully obtain useful information in the process of tampering with the information, which can only lead to user authentication failure. Therefore, the scheme design can prevent man-in-the-middle attacks to a certain extent.

5 Efficiency Analysis

This section presents the performance analysis of the proposed scheme in terms of computation and communication overhead.

5.1 Computational Overhead

Firstly, give a definition. EXP_1 denotes one exponent calculation on Group G_1. $Pairing$ denotes one bilinear pairing operation. H_1 denotes one hash on group G_1. H denotes one hash that is not on group G_1. M_1 denotes one multiplication (division) on the group G_1. M_2 denotes one multiplication on the group G_2. $Hmac$ denotes one HMAC operation. $Code$ denotes one encryption (decryption) operation.

In the key-generation phase. The client and server first need to perform the $1EXP_1$ operation for generating the public key, and perform $EXP_1 + M_1$ operation to obtain a *partial private key* sent by the KGC. When KGC interacts with the blockchain, it also performs $2H$ operations to verify whether the *master-key* and the parameter are modified. Finally, the correctness of the *partial private key* is verified by $H_1 + 2Pairing$ operation. Therefore, a total of $2EXP_1 + M_1 + 2H + H_1 + 2Pairing$ operation is required to generate public key and private key.

In the registration phase. The client first performs $H_1 + 2(M_1 + EXP_1)$ operation times to generate registration information. Then the server performs $3Pairing + M_1 + M_2 + H_1$ operations to verify the registration information, and performs $H_1 + 2(M_1 + EXP_1)$ operations to generate return information. The server also needs $1Code$ operation to encrypt the information of ID_i. Finally, the client performs $3Pairing + M_1 + M_2 + 2H_1$ operations to verify the return information of the server. Therefore, a total of $5H_1 + 6M_1 + 2M_2 + 4EXP_1 + 6Pairing + Code$ operations is required to complete a registration.

In the certification phase. The client first performs $EXP_1 + H_1$ operation to generate authentication request information. Then the server performs $1Code$ operation decryption to obtain the information of ID_i, and $2EXP_1 + Hmac$ operations to generate the authentication information. Then the server performs the $EXP_1 + 2Hmac$ operations to verify the identity of the client. Finally, the client performs $EXP_1 + Hmac$ operations to determine if the server has successfully authenticated the client. Therefore, a total of $6EXP_1 + 6Hmac + H_1 + Code$ operations is required to complete a certification.

When the client updates the password, it only needs to perform $EXP_1 + M_1 + H_1$ operations to send password-update information to the server. The server can also complete the password-update process by simply performing $EXP_1 + M_1 + Code$ operations. Therefore, a total of $2EXP_1 + 2M_1 + H_1 + Code$ operations is required to complete a password-update.

5.2 Communication Overhead

Firstly, give a definition. $|p|$ denotes the length of the element in z_q^*. $|id|$ denotes the length of the Identity ID. $|hmac|$ denotes the length of the result in the HMAC algorithm.

In the registration phase. The length of the registration information $Req_1 = (ID_i, PK_i, g^{e_i}, W^{x_i}T_i^s, H_2(ID_i||pw_i))$ sent by the client is $4|p| + |id|$. The length of the server return information $Res_1 = (ID_0, PK_0, g^{e_j}, Y^{x_0}T_0^s)$ is $3|p| + |id|$. Therefore, to complete a registration, the required communication overhead is $7|p| + 2|id|$.

In addition to the communication overhead between the client and the server, the server needs to interact with the blockchain twice during the registration process. One is to query whether ID_i has been registered to the blockchain, and the other is to store PK_i and $C(ID_i)$ into the blockchain. Because the plaintext of $C(ID_i)$ is $(e_j, g^{e_i}, H_2(ID_i||pw_i))$, so the length of the $C(ID_i)$ is $3|p|$, and the length of the data sent to blockchain is $4|p|$.

In the certification phase. The length of the authentication-request information sent by the client $Req1 = (ID_i, g^{f_i}, H_2(ID_i||pw_i))$ is $2|p| + |id|$. The length of the server return information $Res1 = (ID_0, g^{f_j}, O_1)$ is $|p| + |id| + |hmac|$. Then the client sends the information of the $|hmac|$ length to the server. Finally, the server sends the $|hmac|$ length information to the client to determine whether the authentication user identity is successful. Therefore, to complete a authentication, the required communication overhead is $3|p| + 2|id| + 3|hmac|$.

In addition, the server needs to interact with the blockchain in order to obtain the information(PK_i and $C(ID_i)$) about ID_i in an authentication process. As in the registration phase, the length of data obtained from the blockchain is $4|p|$.

When the password needs to be updated, the length of the password-update request information $Req_{up} = (ID_i, U, (g^{f_j})^{e_i})$ sent by the client is $2|p| + |id|$. The server also needs to interact with the blockchain through web3.js to store $H_2(ID_i||pw_i')$ in the blockchain.

In the test, we use testrpc to generate a private chain simulation blockchain environment, and simulate the authentication server deploying smart contracts on this blockchain. We tested the time cost on querying and storing operations between the authentication server and the blockchain 1000 times, and take the mean every 50 times. The result is shown in Fig. 7. As the interaction between the authentication server and the blockchain increases, the time cost of storing data each time is approximately 0.81 s, and the time cost of querying data is approximately 0.75 s.

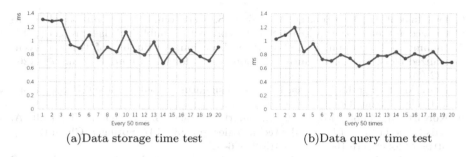

(a)Data storage time test   (b)Data query time test

Fig. 7. The average time cost between the authentication server and the blockchain.

6 Conclusion

In order to solve the shortcomings of the centralized identity authentication system, this paper proposes an identity authentication scheme based on blockchain and certificateless public key cryptography. Compared with the traditional identity authentication, this scheme combines the certificateless public key cryptosystem and blockchain to apply to identity authentication for the first time, utilizes the decentralized feature of the blockchain to effectively solve the single point failure problem, avoids the certificate management problem of the traditional public key cryptosystem by using the certificateless public key cryptosystem. But the scheme still has some shortcomings. For example, the protocol interaction in this scheme is based on the bilinear pairing cryptosystem. Due to the high computational cost of bilinear pairings and the communication overhead between the server and the blockchain, the system overhead is large. So, our future work will focus on cross-domain identity authentication and system efficiency.

Acknowledgments. This work is supported by the National Nature Science Foundation of China (NSFC) under grant 61572026, 61672195, Open Foundation of State Key Laboratory of Cryptology (No: MMKFKT201617).

References

1. Al-Riyami, S.S., Paterson, K.G.: Certificateless public key cryptography. In: Laih, C.-S. (ed.) ASIACRYPT 2003. LNCS, vol. 2894, pp. 452–473. Springer, Heidelberg (2003). https://doi.org/10.1007/978-3-540-40061-5_29
2. Axon, L.: Privacy-awareness in blockchain-based PKI. Technical Report (2015)
3. Bellare, M.: New proofs for NMAC and HMAC: security without collision-resistance. In: Dwork, C. (ed.) CRYPTO 2006. LNCS, vol. 4117, pp. 602–619. Springer, Heidelberg (2006). https://doi.org/10.1007/11818175_36
4. Christidis, K., Devetsikiotis, M.: Blockchains and smart contracts for the Internet of Things. IEEE Access **4**, 2292–2303 (2016)
5. Dunphy, P., Petitcolas, F.A.: A first look at identity management schemes on the blockchain. IEEE Secur. Privacy **16**(4), 20–29 (2018)

6. Fromknecht, C., Velicanu, D., Yakoubov, S.: CertCoin: a NameCoin based decentralized authentication system 6.857 class project. Unpublished class project (2014)

7. Hammi, M.T., Hammi, B., Bellot, P., Serhrouchni, A.: Bubbles of Trust: a decentralized blockchain-based authentication system for IoT. Comput. Secur. **78**, 126–142 (2018)

8. Hota, M., Panigrahi, L., Jena, D.: Digital signature based on EC-DLP. Siddhant - J. Decis. Making **10**(1), 6–13 (2010)

9. Kõlvart, M., Poola, M., Rull, A.: Smart contracts. In: Kerikmäe, T., Rull, A. (eds.) The Future of Law and eTechnologies, pp. 133–147. Springer, Cham (2016). https://doi.org/10.1007/978-3-319-26896-5_7

10. Liu, A., Du, X., Wang, N., Li, S.: Research progress of blockchain technology and its application in information security. J. Softw. **29**(7), 2092–2115 (2018)

11. Lu, J., Cao, X., Yang, P.: Two-factor identity authentication model based on blockchain and face recognition. J. Appl. Sci. **37**(2), 164–178 (2019)

12. Matsumoto, S., Reischuk, R.M.: IKP: Turning a PKI around with decentralized automated incentives. In: 2017 IEEE Symposium on Security and Privacy (SP), pp. 410–426. IEEE (2017)

13. Muftic, S.: Blockchain identity management system based on public identities ledger, 25 April 2017. (US Patent 9,635,000)

14. Nowak, M.A., May, R.M.: Evolutionary games and spatial chaos. Nature **359**(6398), 826 (1992)

15. Raju, S., Boddepalli, S., Gampa, S., Yan, Q., Deogun, J.S.: Identity management using blockchain for cognitive cellular networks. In: 2017 IEEE International Conference on Communications (ICC), pp. 1–6. IEEE (2017)

16. Sullivan, C., Burger, E.: E-residency and blockchain. Comput. Law Secur. Rev. **33**(4), 470–481 (2017)

17. Wang, Z., Han, Z., Liu, J., Zhang, D.W., Chang, L.: ID authentication scheme based on PTPM and certificateless public key cryptography in cloud environment. J. Softw. **27**(6), 1523–1537 (2016)

18. Zhang, F.T., Sun, Y.X., Zhang, L., Geng, M., Li, S.: Research on certificateless public key cryptography. J. Softw. **22**(6), 1316–1332 (2011)

A Trust-Based Security Research Method for Internet of Things Terminal

Zhe Liu[1,2(✉)], Bo Zhao[1,2], and Jiyang Li[1,2]

[1] School of Cyber Science and Engineering, Wuhan University, Wuhan, China
liangjishijie@sina.com
[2] Key Laboratory of Aerospace Information Security and Trusted Computing,
Ministry of Education, Beijing, China

Abstract. The Internet of things has a broad application prospect, but under the environment of the Internet of things, terminals are facing extremely serious security threats. The existing security research focuses on authentication and encryption and other technologies, and the lightweight embedded equipment provides the possibility for the hardware security enhancement of the Internet of things terminal. Therefore, this paper introduces the basic concepts of trust and trustworthiness into the Internet of things terminal security improvement. By adding the trusted module to the Internet of things terminal equipment, it enhances the security of the Internet of things terminal from the perspective of active defense and trustworthiness, and obtains good results in practical application.

Keywords: Internet of Things · Trust concept · Security · Authentication mechanism

1 Introduction

The concept of Internet of things was first appeared at the end of the 20th century. The Internet of things can "digitize" the real world, so real world can be presented in the virtual world through the Internet of things, and then "reduce" the space distance between the real world, and the cost of data transmission; so the Internet of things has been widely used.

Because of the broad application prospect of the Internet of things, scholars from domestic and overseas have done plenty of research on the Internet of things and its terminals. Xu et al. [1] proposed a network method considered Byzantine fault tolerance and two resource allocation algorithms for Internet of things fog computation. This method can resist the influence of Byzantine error and improve the efficiency of transmitting and processing big data of Internet of things. Tao et al. [2] proposed a terminal cache management mechanism driven by node location information; this method reduced the time delay of Internet of things transmission and the network load of Internet of things; besides this method could improve the transmission efficiency. Liu et al. [3] applied the Internet of things to the crab breeding monitoring system as a whole, and realized the local and remote comprehensive intelligent monitoring of crab breeding base, so as to realize the intelligent control of bait casting machine, oxygen

© Springer Nature Singapore Pte Ltd. 2020
W. Han et al. (Eds.): CTCIS 2019, CCIS 1149, pp. 267–280, 2020.
https://doi.org/10.1007/978-981-15-3418-8_17

booster and other Internet of things terminals. Zanella et al. [4] conducted a comprehensive survey of supporting technologies, protocols and architectures of urban Internet of things. It covered a complete urban information system and makes transformation and upgrading of existing urban information terminals. Jin et al. [5] implemented the framework of intelligent city through the Internet of things (IoT), covering the complete urban information system and transforming and upgrading the existing urban information terminals. Tao et al. [6] built industrial Internet of things center (IIHub) to deal with heterogeneous devices in intelligent manufacturing of Internet of things, rapidly configure and realize, and realized intelligent interconnection when online services were generated, and completed the rapid configuration and realization of intelligent interconnection, and made intelligent analysis and accurate management.

The Internet of things is widely used, but we are also facing various security problems. Zhang et al. [7] believes that under the Internet of things environment, there are still security problems such as unsafe system construction, limited equipment resources, inaccessible physical equipment, systems with loopholes, privacy data leakage, peripheral equipment security threats, key program intrusion and various system attacks. Conti et al. [8] believes that with the wide application of the Internet of things system, the data collection and analysis of the Internet of things will face great challenges. Especially in the absence of a proper authentication system, it is difficult to detect malicious operators in the Internet of things environment. Sadeghi et al. [9] argued that it is difficult for industrial Internet of things systems to meet the required functional requirements and assume security and privacy risks. However, existing security solutions cannot be extended to large networks with heterogeneous devices and network physical systems with limited resources and real-time requirements, so they do not meet the security requirements of the Internet of things.

The main motive of this paper studied the Internet of things terminal security, introducing the concept of trust into the Internet of things secure terminal certification, and realized the measurement of terminal trust through the authentication mechanism of trust and the supervision mechanism after trust. First, the Internet of things (IoT) terminals are implanted with devices that have been certified as trustworthy. Secondly, encryption algorithm is introduced to authenticate the device when the hardware is started. Only certified devices can access the Internet of things, and conduct Internet of things data interaction, so as to ensure the credibility of Internet of things terminal access; Finally, trust measures are performed on devices that are trusted to reduce the occurrence of untrusted behaviors. Through trust authentication, the possibility of unreliable devices accessing to the Internet of things can be reduced from the perspective of trust. Compared with other security protection methods facing more Internet of things terminals, this method reduces the number of protected Internet of things terminals and improves the security of the Internet of things in the field of terminal security.

2 Related Work

In the Internet of things environment, the device terminal of the Internet of things is the data collector and a basis of data security. If Internet of things data collection cannot guarantee data security, the subsequent data transmission and quantification and other aspects are out of the question. Scholars at home and abroad have done plenty of research on the Internet of things terminal security, and also made some achievements.

Ma et al. [10] transformed trust into a quantitative investigation of expected credit and risk, and proposed a method suitable for distributed Internet of things terminal trust management. This move realizes the security management of the Internet of things terminal devices without increasing the terminals of the Internet of things. However, this paper does not improve the review mechanism of the multiple factors involved in blockchain, which may easily lead to the phenomenon of false trust of multiple parties involved in blockchain records.

Fang et al. [11] analyzed the working principle of the control system under the condition of the Internet of things, and proposed the security model s-iotc of the general control system under the environment of the Internet of things. By adding the security authentication module at the disturbance place, the security of the system could be guaranteed. However, the scheme proposed in this paper is relatively early, and there is little relevant support in practical application, so the usability of Internet of things devices is slightly deficient.

Tan et al. [12] proposed a remote certification scheme for the terminal trusted environment of the Internet of things terminal, which set the trusted attribute or the trusted behavior proof for the static and dynamic environment respectively, and verified the credibility of the terminal of the Internet of things through the dual factors of attribute and behavior. However, the summary of verification process is prone to leak device state information, and the implementation of credible proof occupies too much system resources, which is not suitable for lightweight Internet of things device system. At the same time, there is also a lack of consideration of the problem of data credibility reduction caused by unreliable failure of the device itself.

Davidson et al. [13] proposed a new symbol execution technology FIE in the context of the Internet of things, which was built on the KLEE symbol execution engine and is mainly used to verify some simple firmware image security attributes often found in practice and to find vulnerabilities of Internet of things terminals. This move improved the Internet of things terminal security by means of detection mode; but since KLEE execution engine requires manufacturer code support, its scalability and compatibility may not be applicable to all Internet of things devices.

Lin et al. [14] made a summative analysis of security risks in nb-iot networks by using the physical non-cloning function (PUF). PUF was then integrated into the chips of nb-iot user devices for security enhancements such as chip binding and anti-counterfeiting. In this paper, PUF function was introduced into the Internet of things terminal security authentication, but it lacks the authentication process technology in the whole Internet of things environment, so the security coverage is still relatively limited.

Kotenko et al. [15] developed a device monitoring system for monitoring Internet of things terminals based on the architecture of big data and machine learning framework, and assessed that the provided framework provided improved information processing productivity and higher accuracy of attack detection. However, due to the excessive reliance on machine learning and big data, it is easy to misjudge the device state under the existing machine learning technology, and it is easy to have a relatively large resource load on the server device, so the application level is relatively weak.

At present, the light weight of embedded devices provides the possibility for the hardware security enhancement of Internet of things terminals. The current chip technology is sufficient to increase the corresponding security chip in the Internet of things terminal with limited space. Meanwhile, the power consumption of the Internet of things terminal has a relatively good control to some extent, which provides feasible technical support for the addition of trusted module in the Internet of things terminal [16].

Based on the above factors, this paper introduced the basic concept of trust into the security improvement of Internet of things terminals. By adding a trust measurement module to Internet of things terminal devices, it enhanced the security of Internet of things terminals from the perspective of active defense and trust, allowing Internet of things devices to take the security advantage from the perspective of initiative.

3   The Design of Internet of Things Terminal Authentication Based on Trust

Our design process for the security authentication of Internet of things terminals is shown in the following Fig. 1, respectively setting the trust root module and authentication module in the terminal and remote server.

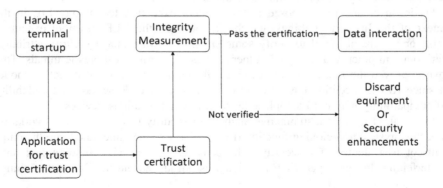

Fig. 1. Trust start design scheme

This design scheme introduces the basic idea of trust [17, 18]. Starting from terminal security and based on the trust root set autonomously, the trust chain transmission is constructed to extend the trust to the whole system and ensure the overall trust level of the system [19].

3.1 Trust Chain Architecture and Process

The trust chain architecture built is shown in Fig. 2. The trust chain includes the trust platform, measurement and security functions provided by the sub-module of the trust, and builds the terminal security software module as the trust root.

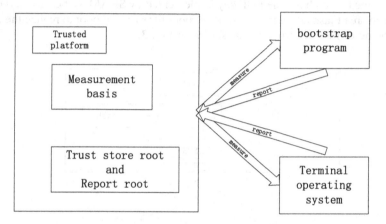

Fig. 2. Trust chain architecture diagram

The overall design process is as follows:

(1) Powering on the terminal, then the code with measurement function is imported through the bootstrap program, and the measurement value is stored as the starting point of the trust chain.
(2) Starting from this trust starting point, we measure the trust value of the Internet of things terminal kernel.
(3) Judge the measurement results, then give kernel control under the condition of trust; The middle layer and application layer are measured by kernel trust state.
(4) A complete trust chain is formed after trust measurement, and the final result is uploaded to the server, indicating that it is trusted at startup.

Internet of things terminal through the complete trust chain and through the trust verification, the real start of the Internet of things terminal. Compared with the way to add hardware modules to realize terminal startup, the trust chain designed and implemented in this project does not need to change the hardware architecture, and the overall architecture is more complete. The start-up process has good trust, and no additional hardware overhead is required, so the device security can be effectively guaranteed. For the Internet of things terminal system, its system structure is relatively simple, and the software and hardware components are seldom changed or changed. It is more suitable to use the star trust structure, and can reduce the trust loss compared with the chain structure.

3.2 Trust to Start the Design Scheme

According to the basic idea mentioned in the previous order, on the premise of not affecting the hardware architecture of mobile terminals, this project takes bootloader (uboot) as the trusted base, the PUF key implemented by SRAM as the trusted root, and the storage area Flash as the trusted storage root of the trusted boot to realize the trusted boot scheme of mobile terminals, as shown in Fig. 3.

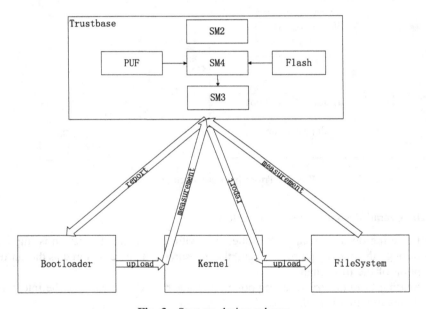

Fig. 3. Start-up design scheme

The overall design steps are as follows:

(1) PUF key serves as the trust root, and all initial PCR values are encrypted by SM4 algorithm and stored in Flash. BootLoader verifies kernel integrity through TPM before loading kernel.
(2) Use SM3 algorithm to calculate the kernel PCR value, then extract the standard value from Flash and use PUF key to decrypt and compare with the measured value.

(3) Trustroot reports the results to bootLoader. If the verification passes, bootLoader loads kernel.

It should be noted that before loading the file system, kernel calculates the PCR value of key files in the file system by calling the trust root, extracts the standard value from Flash, decrypts it and compares it.

(4) The trustroot will report the result to kernel. If the verification passes, the kernel will load the file system, thus forming the security trust environment started.

According to the above design ideas and schemes, the following trusted startup process can be formed (Fig. 4):

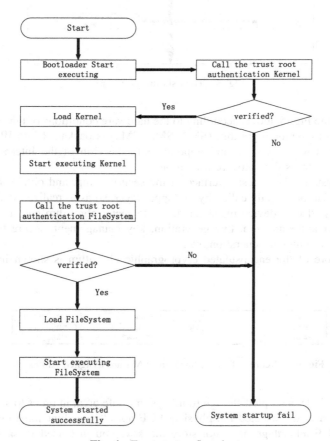

Fig. 4. Trust startup flowchart

3.3 Trustroot Design

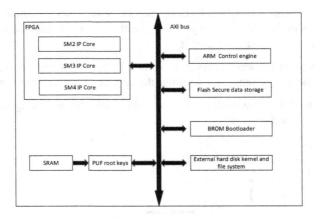

Fig. 5. Trust startup flowchart

As shown in the Fig. 5 above, according to the hardware conditions of the terminal, the design of cryptographic algorithm (SM2, SM3, SM4) is packaged into IP core form, which is added to the system and imported into the chip of the Internet of things terminal, and used as the software trust root.

We encapsulate the access interface of the security chip, and obtain the interface package that can be directly called by the upper layer, so as to realize the functions of simulated trusted root device management, state secret algorithm call, remote proof, including user authentication, key generation, key management, secure hash, secure storage, random number generation, etc.

The IP core of the encapsulated cryptographic algorithm is shown in the Fig. 6 below:

sm3_ip_0	S00_AXI	S00_AXI_reg 0x43C4_0000	64K	0x43C4_FFFF
sm4_ip_0	S00_AXI	S00_AXI_reg 0x43C5_0000	64K	0x43C5_FFFF
sm2_ip_0	S00_AXI	S00_AXI_reg 0x43C3_0000	64K	0x43C3_FFFF

Fig. 6. IP cores of SM2, SM3 and SM4 are assigned addresses

Due to include encrypted storage root keys in a safe area, in order to save cost and improve security, we selected the physical PUF not cloning function to generate the root keys, PUF advantage need not store the key, you just need to save help data associated with a key, start the next time use refactoring functions can restore the root keys, and help data even if lost or stolen, the attacker can use the restore the root keys, security has been greatly improved.

4 Results and Validation

4.1 National Secret Algorithm Implementation

Here, SM2, SM3 and SM4 are packaged into the IP core in the form of Verilog and imported into the chip independently designed. Write the system. Bit with SM2, SM3 and SM4 algorithms into the chip, and run the test function, and the results are displayed in the serial port, as shown in Figs. 7 and 8:

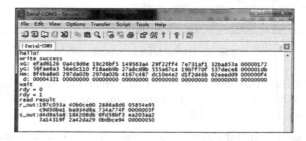

Fig. 7. The results of operation SM2 algorithm in serial port

```
Hello world
61 62 63 80 00 00 00 00 00 00 00 00 00 00 00 00 00 00 00 00 00 00 00 00 00 00
  00 00 00 00 00 00 00 00 00 00 00 00 00 00 00 00 00 00 00 00 00 00 00 00 00 0
0 00 00 00 00 00 00 00 00 18
count = 1
61626380 00000000 00000000 00000000 00000000 00000000 00000000 00000000 00000000
  00000000 00000000 00000000 00000000 00000000 00000000 00000018
text_i 61626380
text_A 7380166f
cmd_o      2
cmd_o      2
output_temp  66c7f0f4
baseaddr_SM3 + 36 14
begin
66c7f0f4 62eeedd9 d1f2d46b dc10e4e2 4167c487 5cf2f7a2 297da02b 8f4ba8e0
end
01 23 45 67 89 ab cd ef fe dc ba 98 76 54 32 10
Hello from xilinx!
 1234567 89abcdef fedcba98 76543210
dataout:681edf34 d206965e 86b3e94f 536e4246
sm4 272
68 1e
enc:
68 1e df 34 d2 06 96 5e 86 b3 e9 4f 53 6e 42 46
dec:
Hello from xilinx!
 1234567 89abcdef fedcba98 76543210
dataout:1234567 89abcdef fedcba98 76543210
sm4 272
 1 23
01 23 45 67 89 ab cd ef fe dc ba 98 76 54 32 10
```

Fig. 8. Serial port shows the results of SM3 and SM4 algorithms

4.2 Specific Implementation of Trusted Start

(1) By setting the prompt code in the uboot source code, we can observe the execution of the code when the system starts from the serial port, and extract the information shown in the following Fig. 9:

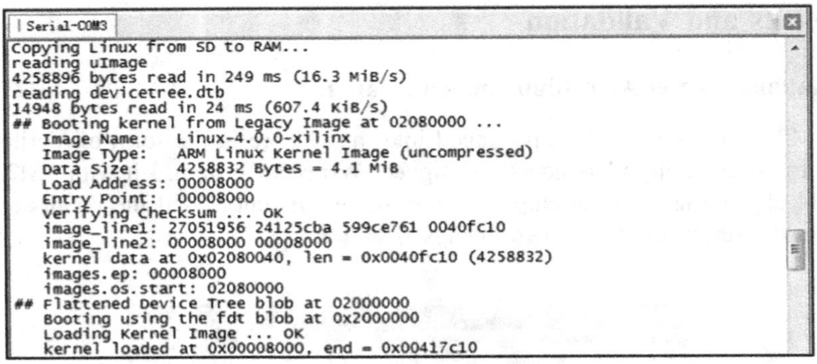

Fig. 9. Uboot boot information

Thus, it is known that the total length of kernel file uImage is 4258896 bit, including 64 bit of header information for parsing, the actual length is 4258832 bit, and the loading address in memory (DDR3) is 0x00008000-0x00417c10.

(2) Insert the test code into the uboot source code, directly read the data of the kernel loading address after the completion of kernel loading, and obtain part of the kernel data (64 bit), which is compared with the information in the uImage file, and the results are consistent (Figs. 10 and 11):

Fig. 10. Read 64 bit data

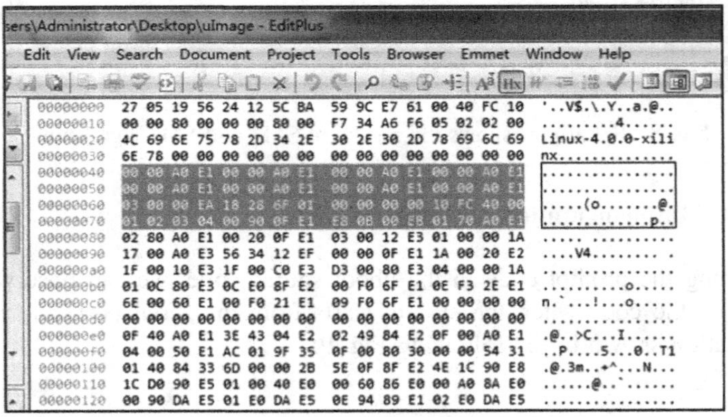

Fig. 11. Actual uImage data

(3) Add the call interface of IP core of SM3 algorithm in the uboot source code, hash the 64 bit data obtained (Fig. 12):

```
## Flattened Device Tree blob at 02000000
   Booting using the fdt blob at 0x2000000
   Loading Kernel Image ... OK
   kernel loaded at 0x00008000, end = 0x00417c10
00 00 a0 e1 00 00 a0 e1 00 00 a0 e1 00 00 a0 e1
00 00 a0 e1 00 00 a0 e1 00 00 a0 e1 00 00 a0 e1
03 00 00 ea 18 28 6f 01 00 00 00 00 10 fc 40 00
01 02 03 04 00 90 0f e1 e8 0b 00 eb 01 70 a0 e1

64byte_hash:
23206364 58a4404b 7dcffb33 b5944cb8 20428e61 df0a91ec 3ad9fc89 47d19aa0
```

Fig. 12. Partial kernel data hash results

(4) On this basis, the integrity measurement is verified, and the general process is as follows: expand the read address length to the length of kernel data, extract and hash the whole kernel data, and get the following results. The results obtained by multiple starts are consistent (Fig. 13):

```
## Booting kernel from Legacy Image at 02080000 ...
   Image Name:    Linux-4.0.0-xilinx
   Image Type:    ARM Linux Kernel Image (uncompressed)
   Data Size:     4258832 Bytes = 4.1 MiB
   Load Address:  00008000
   Entry Point:   00008000
   Verifying Checksum ... OK
   image_line1: 27051956 24125cba 599ce761 0040fc10
   image_line2: 00008000 00008000
   kernel data at 0x02080040, len = 0x0040fc10 (4258832)
   images.ep: 00008000
   images.os.start: 02080000
## Flattened Device Tree blob at 02000000
   Booting using the fdt blob at 0x2000000
   Loading Kernel Image ... OK
   kernel loaded at 0x00008000, end = 0x00417c10
Hash:
   070155b8 734bdc4e 1f0dd9a5 fa9335a3 eb84fd93 b8b0f250 63eefa8e 2f2a522f
```

Fig. 13. Complete kernel data hash results

Based on these experimental results, the realization of the kernel and the integrity of the device tree measures, in order to ensure the security of the data and do not disappear after using, hash value with PUF key encrypted stored in a Flash, every time system start refactoring PUF key, then the new access to the integrity of the data encryption and decryption and compare the measurements, that can only be successful start-up system at the same time.

When kernel is not attacked or modified, the measurement value matches the standard value, the verification is successful, and the control right is transferred, as shown in the Fig. 14 below:

```
Copying Linux from SD to RAM...
reading uImage
4258888 bytes read in 219 ms (18.5 MiB/s)
reading devicetree.dtb
14948 bytes read in 20 ms (729.5 KiB/s)
## Booting kernel from Legacy Image at 02080000 ...
   Image Name:   Linux-4.0.0-xilinx
   Image Type:   ARM Linux Kernel Image (uncompressed)
   Data Size:    4258824 Bytes = 4.1 MiB
   Load Address: 00008000
   Entry Point:  00008000
   Verifying Checksum ... OK
## Flattened Device Tree blob at 02000000
   Booting using the fdt blob at 0x2000000
   Loading Kernel Image ... OK
   Kernel HashCheck Start ... Success!
   Loading Device Tree to 1fff9000, end 1ffffa63 ... OK
   FDT HashCheck Start ... Success!

Starting kernel ...
```

Fig. 14. Integrity verified

When the content of kernel file is tampered with by malicious virus, the measurement value changes and does not match the standard value. The system cannot be started and the system enters the reset state, as shown in the Fig. 15 below:

```
Copying Linux from SD to RAM...
reading uImage
4258896 bytes read in 218 ms (18.6 MiB/s)
reading devicetree.dtb
14948 bytes read in 20 ms (729.5 KiB/s)
## Booting kernel from Legacy Image at 02080000 ...
   Image Name:   Linux-4.0.0-xilinx
   Image Type:   ARM Linux Kernel Image (uncompressed)
   Data Size:    4258832 Bytes = 4.1 MiB
   Load Address: 00008000
   Entry Point:  00008000
   Verifying Checksum ... OK
## Flattened Device Tree blob at 02000000
   Booting using the fdt blob at 0x2000000
   Loading Kernel Image ... OK
   Kernel HashCheck Start ... Fail!
resetting ...
```

Fig. 15. Failed integrity check

After the above process, we can consider that the terminal has completed the trusted start and trusted certification process, and from the perspective of terminal certification, the Internet of things terminal security improvement work has been completed.

5 Conclusion

Based on the idea of trust, this paper aims at the current security defects faced by the terminals of the Internet of things, and starts with the existing structure of the terminals of the Internet of things. Under the premise of changing the internal structure of Internet of things terminals as little as possible, security chips and modules are added to complete the authentication of Internet of things terminals through trusted start and trusted authentication and verification, which is realized in simulation and practical applications.

However, it should be noted that the security of the Internet of things is not only the security of terminal authentication, but also includes the interaction security between the whole network of the Internet of things and the terminal. Therefore, in this paper, according to the actual needs, the solution of terminal security is proposed and achieved. However, other aspects of security should also be considered in the subsequent research, so as to have more excellent room for improvement in the overall environment security under the Internet of things environment.

References

1. Xu, J., Ota, K., Dong, M., Liu, A., Li, Q.: SIoTFog: byzantine-resilient IoT fog networking. Front. Inf. Technol. Electron. Eng. **19**(12), 1546–1558 (2018)
2. Tao, J., Shi, S.J., Feng, F., Gao, Y.: Research on location-driven buffer management of end nodes in Internet of Things. Chin. J. Comput. **42**(02), 22–35 (2019)
3. Liu, Y., Li, J., Cao, S., Xing, B.: Design and application of monitoring system for crab breeding base based on Internet of Things. Trans. Chin. Soc. Agric. Eng. **34**(16), 205–213 (2018)
4. Zanella, A., Bui, N., Castellani, A., Vangelista, L., Zorzi, M.: Internet of Things for smart cities. IEEE IoT J. **1**(1), 22–32 (2014)
5. Jin, J., Gubbi, J., Marusic, S., Palaniswami, M.: An information framework for creating a smart city through Internet of Things. IEEE IoT J. **1**(2), 112–121 (2014)
6. Tao, F., Cheng, J., Qi, Q.: IIHub: an industrial Internet-of-Things hub toward smart manufacturing based on cyber-physical system. IEEE Trans. Ind. Inf. **14**(5), 2271–2280 (2018)
7. Peng, A., Zhou, W., Jia, Y., Zhang, Y.: Survey of the Internet of things operating system security. J. Commun. **39**(03), 22–34 (2018)
8. Contia, M., Dehghantanhab, A., Frankec, K., Watsond, S.: Internet of Things security and forensics: challenges and opportunities. Future Gener. Comput. Syst. **78**(2), 544–546 (2018). Jin, H.G., Hong, H., Sui, J., et al.: Fundamental study of novel mid-and
9. Sadeghi, A.-R., Wachsmann, C., Waidner, M.: Security and privacy challenges in industrial Internet of Things. In: 2015 52nd ACM/EDAC/IEEE Design Automation Conference (DAC), 8–12 June 2015, pp. 1–6 (2015)
10. Ren, Y., Li, X., Liu, H., Cheng, Q., Ma, J.: Blockchain-based trust management framework for distributed Internet of Things. J. Comput. Res. Dev. **55**(07), 1462–1478 (2018)
11. Yang, J., Fang, B., Zhai, L., Zhang, F.: Research towards IoT-oriented universal control system security model. J. Commun. **33**(11), 49–56 (2012)
12. Tan, L., Chen, J.: Remote attestation project of the running environment of the trusted terminal. J. Softw. **25**(06), 1273–1290 (2014)
13. Davidson, D., Moench, B., Ristenpart, T., et al.: FIE on firmware: finding vulnerabilities in embedded systems using symbolic execution. In: USENIX Conference on Security. USENIX Association, pp. 463–478 (2013)
14. Lin, Y., Jiang, F., Wang, Z., Wang, Z.: Research on PUF-based security enhancement of narrow-band Internet of Things. In: 2018 IEEE 32nd International Conference on Advanced Information Networking and Applications (AINA), 13 August 2018, pp. 1–8 (2018)

15. Saenko, I., Branitskiy, A.: Framework for mobile Internet of Things security monitoring based on big data processing and machine learning. IEEE Access **6**, 72714–72723 (2018)
16. Duan, B., Li, L., Lai, J., Zhan, J.: Research on hardware vulnerabilities mining method for industrial control device based on dynamic taint analysis. Netinfo Secur. (04), 47–54 (2019)
17. McKnight, D.H., Chervany, N.L.: What trust means in ecommerce customer relationships: an interdisciplinary conceptual typology. Int. J. Electron. Commer. **6**(2), 35–59 (2001)
18. Mui, L.: Computational models of trust and reputation: agents, evolutionary games, and social networks. Massachusetts Institute of Technology, Cambridge (2002)
19. McKnight, D.H., Chervany, N.L.: The meanings of trust. Technical Report MISRC Working Paper Series 96-04, University of Minnesota, Management Information Systems Research Certer (1996)

A QoS&SLA-Driven Multifaceted Trust Model for Cloud Computing

Runlian Zhang[1,4(✉)], Qingzhi Wang[2], Jinhua Cui[3], and Xiaonian Wu[1]

[1] Guangxi Key Laboratory of Cryptography and Information Security, Guilin University of Electronic Technology, Guilin 541004, China
zhangrl@guet.edu.cn
[2] Qingdao Technological University, Qindao College, Qindao 266106, China
[3] College of Computer, National University of Defense Technology, Changsha 410073, China
[4] Guangxi Colleges and Universities Key Laboratory of Cloud Computing and Complex Systems, Guilin 541004, China

Abstract. Quality of Service (QoS) plays a vital role in cloud computing while Service Level Agreements (SLA) to a service contract is indispensable as well. Selecting a trusted cloud service based on service performance, thus, is raising fundamental concern. This work presents a QoS&SLA-driven multifaceted trust model for efficiently evaluating the trustworthiness of a cloud service in the light of its multiple differential service attributes. Owing to the uncertainty of QoS, the interval number theory is naturally introduced into our trust model. In the trust evaluation, moreover, an adaptive weight adjustment method that depends on connection number is exploited to dynamically accommodate their respective factors. The proposed trust model is the composition of two types of trust metrics, which are QoS trust and user satisfaction trust. QoS trust, specifically, that indicates the level of actual performance of the cloud service. User satisfaction trust virtually reflects to what extent actual service performance is in accord with SLA. Finally, we assess the proposed trust model based on real datasets derived from CloudHarmony, which makes the approach more objective and effective for cloud computing.

Keywords: Trust model · Quality of Service · Service Level Agreements · Interval number theory

1 Introduction

The cloud paradigm gains increasing acceptance because of its cost-efficient computing manner. Cloud services have been enclosed into standard computer programs in the form of services for cloud users. Still, there exist several challenges such as the related issues of security, privacy and trust [1]. One major difficulty is to determine which cloud service provider is trustworthy and reliable as per the requirement and application for cloud users. Meanwhile, cloud service providers should monitor the status of cloud services whenever and wherever possible so as to provide the better cloud services and resist various attacks.

© Springer Nature Singapore Pte Ltd. 2020
W. Han et al. (Eds.): CTCIS 2019, CCIS 1149, pp. 281–295, 2020.
https://doi.org/10.1007/978-981-15-3418-8_18

Trust is an integral component in the cloud paradigm as a result of the indispensable interactions between the cloud user and the service provider. Bridging the trust among them, however, is a sophisticated procedure. Nowadays, many researchers have developed several trust frameworks from different perspectives to achieve it. Policy-based trust model [2–4] can establish and authenticate trust relationship through the certificate policies which mainly realize the privilege management to protect sensitive resources and services. Behavior-based trust framework [5–8] intends to make trust decision with the assistance of past experiences wherein the positive experience generally increases the estimate of the trustworthiness while the negative reduces it. Reputation-based trust framework [9–11] can aggregate a large number of user's ratings. Consequently, it covers more situations and has a broader view on the service provider than a single user does.

However, most existing trust models utilize subjective assessment of the cloud users, which enables them depend heavily on recommendation mechanisms to quantify trustworthiness of cloud services. Trustworthiness evaluation is a complex process closely related to many factors which usually are determined via the subjective weight assignment model. With the complicated and various service attributes, prior works basically lack adaptability when assigning weights to trust attributes. To address the above problem, this paper proposed a Multifaceted Trust Framework based on Quality of Services (QoS) and Service Level Agreements (SLA) for cloud computing environments. The main contributions of this work are illustrated as follows:

- We propose an objective QoS-based scheme instead of involving user's subjective ratings. In virtue of advantages of the interval number theory, trust evaluation with considerations of multi-dimensional trust factors is implemented. This can exhibit a better view of objectivity and uncertainty of trust evidence unlike that in the traditional trust model.
- We present how to regulate the trust factor weights adaptively according to changes of trust factors. Exploiting multivariate connection number theory, we eliminate limitations of traditional weighting methods for multiple trust factors, in which the weights are assigned subjectively.
- We resolve the issue of user satisfaction on the basis of the nearness degree of trust factors between monitored values and that in SLA. That genuinely indicates the objective achievement scale on SLA index system.
- We conduct comprehensive experiments to compare the effectiveness of the proposed model and existing trust models. The results show the proposed is more objective and effective.

The remainder of the paper is organized as follows. Some existing works are first reviewed in Sect. 2. In Sect. 3, we then describe our proposed trust model followed by presenting our simulation results in Sect. 4. Finally, we conclude our work in Sect. 5.

2 Related Works

Trust in our daily life often serves as a foundation for making decisions in various complex situations [12]. Naturally, the cloud paradigm involves in it as well, in which trust is as a subjective mutual measurable relationship between the service and the user in certain specific context. Especially, It not only has the guarantee of service quality on the cloud computing, but also help users select the most trustworthy cloud services [13]. For instance, QoS-based and SLA-based trust mechanisms are an effective measurement solution to the trustworthiness of cloud services.

Manuel [14] introduced a trust model based on previous credentials and present capabilities of a cloud resource provider wherein trust was measured in terms of four attributes such as availability, reliability, turnaround efficiency and data integrity. In addition, it presented how a service level agreement is prepared while combining users' QoS requirements and capabilities of cloud resource provider.

Li et al. [15] proposed an adaptive and attribute-based trust model in which rough set theory is employed to trust analysis with considerations of multi-dimensional trust attributes, and utilizing the IOWA operator aggregates the global trust degree according to time series.

Fan et al. [16] developed a trust management framework for the calculation of both the objective and the subjective trust of a CSP. This framework with two-layer trust evaluation model depends on a set of TSPs distributed over the clouds.

Tan et al. [17] proposed a SLA trust model based on behavior evaluation. Time and successful transaction are integrated to calculate the trust value, especially in an iterative way. Providers are chosen according to the fulfillment of SLA parameters monitored in the serving process and the users' demands.

Chakraborty et al. [18] identified and formalized several parameters that can be extracted from SLA or retrieved during the sessions. It designed a trust evaluation engine to estimate trustworthiness of a CSP. The framework can cater to different requirements of different consumers as it calculates trust based on individual consumer's policies.

Ding et al. [19] designed a CSTrust framework for conducting cloud service trust worthiness evaluation by combining QoS prediction and customer satisfaction estimation. It defined the usage structure factor to reduce the influence of negative neighbors in similarity computation. Moreover, it presented the similarity parameter to determine how many neighbors' records have been adopted to predict missing QoS value.

Sidhu and Singh [20] presented the design of a trust evaluation framework that uses the compliance monitoring mechanism to determine the trustworthiness of service providers. The framework generates trust on CSPs by evaluating the compliance of QoS parameters and then by utilizing the improved TOPSIS method.

Alhanahnah et al. [21] proposed a context-aware multifaceted trust framework (CAMFT) to help evaluate trust in cloud service providers. It considers two kinds of trust factors: SLA trust factors and non-SLA trust factors, both of which are measured in virtue of AHP method and fuzzy simple additive weighting, respectively.

Tang et al. [22] proposed a trustworthy selection framework for cloud service, named TRUSS. The integrated trust evaluation method is comprised of both objective and subjective trust assessment. The objective one is based on QoS monitoring while the subjective is with the dependence of user feedback ratings.

3 QoS&SLA-Driven Trust Model

This section first discusses the trust preliminaries to the model. In the following, we present the architecture of QoS&SLA-driven multifaceted trust model in the cloud computing environment.

3.1 Trust Preliminaries

Trustor. A trustor is an agent that trusts another entity. In our model, the trustor is the cloud user (CU). Let CU be a collection of the cloud user, $CU = \{cu_1, cu_2, \cdots\cdots, cu_n\}$.

Trustee. A trustee is an entity that the trustor trusts. In our model, the trustee is the cloud service (CS). Let CS be a collection of the cloud service, $CS = \{cs_1, cs_2, \cdots\cdots, cs_m\}$.

Trust. Trust is a trait having congruence between the desired and perceived participation and it is characterized by hope, faith, confidence, assurance and initiative [12]. Here, trust is defined as a belief level that a cloud user puts on a cloud service for a specific action according to previous observation of QoS performance and user satisfaction. In this paper, the trustworthiness of the cloud service ranges from 0 to 1. A value of 1 means completely trustworthy and 0 means the opposite.

QoS Trust. QoS parameters represent the first hand information or evidence after the CU interacts with the CS. QoS trust is a kind of trust calculated by QoS parameters, which reflects how much extent the cloud user trusts the cloud provider from the point of view of QoS.

User Satisfaction Trust. SLA is an important document that gives a clear definition of the formal agreements about service terms like performance, availability and billing. User satisfaction trust is a kind of trust calculated by user satisfaction degree, which reflects how much extent the cloud service can actualize the SLA.

Global Trust. Global trust, which reflects the trust degree of the cloud service from the cloud user's point of view, is an integration of QoS trust and user satisfaction trust.

Reputation. Reputation is the sum of impressions held by all cloud users. Here the cloud service's reputation is assumed as the aggregate generated through the global trust from different cloud users.

3.2   Trust Model

Figure 1 shows the system architecture of our proposed trust model, which is mainly composed of five components: cloud service provider, cloud user, performance monitor, SLA agent and trust management module. A cloud service provider deploys its services and provides services to cloud users. A cloud user is the consumer of cloud services. The performance monitor is used to monitor the actual service performance at runtime. The SLA agent is responsible for the negotiation between the cloud service provider and the cloud user about the SLA details, which will finally publish a SLA document to the cloud service provider and the cloud user. With the SLAs, a cloud user can identify whether a service satisfies his/her service requirements. The trust management module is charge of evaluating the trustworthiness of cloud services through the monitored evidence.

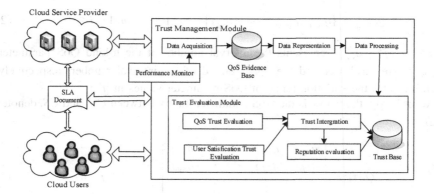

Fig. 1. QoS&SLA-driven trust model

4   Trusts and Reputation Evaluation for the Cloud Services

In this section, we describe trusts and reputation evaluation for the cloud services. First of all, we discuss QoS trust evaluation and the calculation of trust factor weights. The second part presents user satisfaction trust evaluation. The next part discusses how to integrate QoS trust and user satisfaction trust, which is followed by discussion of reputation evaluation.

4.1   QoS Trust

QoS is a measure of service quality that the service provider offers to the service user. In cloud paradigm, QoS data involves many parameters such as up-time, down-time, delay, bandwidth etc. Performance monitor component is responsible for obtaining QoS data continuously. Suppose we can obtain QoS parameters of the interaction between the CS and the CU by the performance monitor component, these parameters are denoted as follows.

$$QoS_{s,j} = \{Q_{s,j,1}, Q_{s,j,2}, \cdots\cdots, Q_{s,j,k}\} \qquad (1 \le s \le m, 1 \le j \le n) \qquad (1)$$

$Q_{s,j,u}$ represents u-kind QoS parameter value of the interaction between CSs and CUj. $QoS_{s,j}$ represents QoS parameter set of the interaction which indicates abilities of the CS to provide appropriate service according to the requirements of the CU. We hence evaluate the trustworthiness of the CS based on QoS parameters which refers to QoS trust.

The QoS data is dynamically obtained several times during a pre-defined time, and randomly varies with the time of transmission. Such an operation will form a sequence of QoS data. Comparing to the fixed value, the uncertain one is more appropriate for the QoS data representation while the interval number is indeterminate. So the QoS data is expressed in the interval number, denoted by $QoS_{s,j}^t$. Based on the sliding window, we pull the QoS data between CSs and CUj at $[t', t]$. It is denoted as follows.

$$QoS_{s,j}^t = \{\tilde{q}_{s,j,1}, \tilde{q}_{s,j,2}, \cdots\cdots, \tilde{q}_{s,j,k}\} \qquad (1 \le s \le m, 1 \le j \le n) \qquad (2)$$

$\tilde{q}_{s,j,u} = [q_{s,j,u}^-, q_{s,j,u}^+]$ represents the interval number of the u-kind QoS parameter. $q_{s,j,u}^-, q_{s,j,u}^+$ are the lower and the upper bound of the interval number, respectively, which indicates the variation range of QoS parameter values in $[t', t]$.

Accordingly, the below is the QoS parameter matrix between CU_j and CS, denoted by $Q_j(t)$.

$$Q_j(t) = \begin{bmatrix} \tilde{q}_{1,j,1} & \tilde{q}_{1,j,2} & \cdots\cdots & \tilde{q}_{1,j,k} \\ \tilde{q}_{2,j,1} & \tilde{q}_{2,j,2} & \cdots\cdots & \tilde{q}_{2,j,k} \\ \vdots & \vdots & \vdots & \vdots \\ \tilde{q}_{m,j,1} & \tilde{q}_{m,j,2} & \cdots\cdots & \tilde{q}_{m,j,k} \end{bmatrix} \qquad (1 \le j \le n) \qquad (3)$$

Each QoS parameter has different ranges, and the according values are significant distinct. Furthermore, some are beneficial parameters and others are cost parameters. For the beneficial parameter, the bigger value is the better. For the cost parameter, the smaller value is the better. Accordingly, we normalize these values to the no-dimensional form. So, each QoS parameter is transformed into the beneficial parameter within the range of [0, 1]. The concrete computational methods are as follow.

For the beneficial parameter:

$$[r_{s,j,u}^-, r_{s,j,u}^+] = \left[\frac{q_{s,j,u}^-}{\max\limits_{1 \le s \le m} q_{s,j,u}^-}, \frac{q_{s,j,u}^+}{\max\limits_{1 \le s \le m} q_{s,j,u}^+} \right] \qquad (s = 1, 2, \cdots\cdots, m) \qquad (4)$$

For the cost parameter:

$$[r_{s,j,u}^-, r_{s,j,u}^+] = \left[\frac{\min\limits_{1 \le s \le m} q_{s,j,u}^-}{q_{s,j,u}^-}, \frac{\min\limits_{1 \le s \le m} q_{s,j,u}^+}{q_{s,j,u}^+} \right] \qquad (s = 1, 2, \cdots\cdots, m) \qquad (5)$$

So the normalization value of each QoS parameter is written $\tilde{r}_{s,j,u}$, $\tilde{r}_{s,j,u} = [r_{s,j,u}^-, r_{s,j,u}^+]$. The standardized matrix of values of the QoS parameter is shown below.

$$
RQ_j(t) = \begin{bmatrix} \tilde{r}_{1,j,1} & \tilde{r}_{1,j,2} & \cdots\cdots & \tilde{r}_{1,j,k} \\ \tilde{r}_{2,j,1} & \tilde{r}_{2,j,2} & \cdots\cdots & \tilde{r}_{2,j,k} \\ \vdots & \vdots & \vdots & \vdots \\ \tilde{r}_{m,j,1} & \tilde{r}_{m,j,2} & \cdots\cdots & \tilde{r}_{m,j,k} \end{bmatrix} \qquad (1 \le j \le n) \qquad (6)
$$

Connection number is a structural function used to describe the certainty and uncertainty of objects and the relationships among them. To better express the certainty and uncertainty of QoS parameters, these values are denoted with "mean value + max deviation" binary connection number (a kind of connection number) instead of the interval number. Let $r_{s,j,u}$ be the binary connection number of $\tilde{r}_{s,j,u}$.

$$
\begin{cases} r_{s,j,u} = A_{sju} + B_{sju}i \\ A_{sju} = \dfrac{r_{s,j,u}^+ + r_{s,j,u}^-}{2} & (1 \le s \le m, 1 \le j \le n, 1 \le u \le k, -1 \le i \le 1) \\ B_{sju} = \dfrac{r_{s,j,u}^+ - r_{s,j,u}^-}{2} \end{cases} \qquad (7)
$$

Then $q_{s,j,u}$ is transformed into trigonometric function as follows.

$$
\begin{cases} q_{s,j,u} = r_{sju}(\cos\theta_{sju} + i\sin\theta_{sju}) \\ r_{sju} = \sqrt{A^2 + B^2} & (-1 \le i \le 1, A \ne 0) \\ \theta_{sju} = \arctan\frac{A}{B} \end{cases} \qquad (8)
$$

Each QoS parameter affects the trust evaluation to varying degrees. Note that we cannot determine the parameter weights in advance. At most time, while the CSP can maintain stable QoS performance, the trust degree of the CSP will change with fluctuations in QoS parameter values. In current settings, we don't take the CU's preferences into account, and instead suppose each QoS parameter has the same importance in interactions. The CSPs always provide the stable and reliable services at most cases, so there exists the basic principle that the smaller the fluctuation of certain QoS attribute is, the less the effect of this QoS parameter on trust evaluation is, conversely, and that the bigger fluctuation will incur the severely effect. Therefore, the bigger the QoS parameter value fluctuates, the greater the weight should be given. Let w_u be the weight of the u-kind QoS attribute.

$$
\begin{cases} w_u = \dfrac{D_u}{\sum D_u} \\ D_u = \dfrac{\sum(r_{sju} - \bar{r}_{sju})^2}{m-1} \end{cases} \qquad (1 \le u \le k) \qquad (9)
$$

Here, $\bar{r}_{sju}$ is the average value of the norm of each QoS attribute. The QoS trust degree of the service provider is computed by principle model, denoted by $QT_{s,j}^t$.

$$QT_{s,j}^t = \sum r_{sju} w_u \qquad (1 \le s \le m, 1 \le u \le k) \tag{10}$$

4.2   User Satisfaction Trust

A service level agreement is legal contract between a cloud user and a cloud service provider, which is usually promised by the service provider to the user. That contains many QoS parameters like main memory, response time, bandwidth, and so on. However, actual monitored QoS parameter is normally different from the one promised by the service provider in the SLA. As a general rule, if monitored QoS parameter value is greatly close to it in the SLA, the user satisfactory is much higher accordingly. We hence compute user satisfactory trust by using interval number nearness degree.

Suppose the QoS parameter value in SLA is denoted as $SQoS_{s,j}$.

$$SQoS_{s,j} = \{\tilde{a}_{s,j,1}, \tilde{a}_{s,j,2}, \cdots\cdots, \tilde{a}_{s,j,k}\} \qquad (1 \le s \le m, 1 \le j \le n) \tag{11}$$

Here $\tilde{a}_{s,j,u} = [a_{s,j,u}^-, a_{s,j,u}^+]$ is the interval number representation of the u-th$(1 \le u \le k)$ QoS parameter value. The deviation degree $L(\tilde{a}_{s,j,u}, \tilde{q}_{s,j,u})$ between the u-th QoS parameter value $SQoS_{s,j}$ and $QoS_{s,j}^t$ is as follows.

$$L(\tilde{a}_{s,j,u}, \tilde{q}_{s,j,u}) = \frac{\left|a_{s,j,u}^+ - q_{s,j,u}^+\right| + \left|a_{s,j,u}^- - q_{s,j,u}^-\right|}{a_{s,j,u}^+ - a_{s,j,u}^- + q_{s,j,u}^+ - q_{s,j,u}^-} \tag{12}$$

The nearness degree $T(\tilde{a}_{s,j,u}, \tilde{q}_{s,j,u})$ between the u-th QoS parameter value $SQoS_{s,j}$ and $QoS_{s,j}^t$ is described below.

$$T(\tilde{a}_{s,j,u}, \tilde{b}_{s,j,u}) = \begin{cases} \frac{1 - L(\tilde{a}_{s,j,u}, \tilde{b}_{s,j,u})}{1 + L(\tilde{a}_{s,j,u}, \tilde{b}_{s,j,u})} & 0 \le L(\tilde{a}_{s,j,u}, \tilde{b}_{s,j,u}) < 1 \\ 0, & L(\tilde{a}_{s,j,u}, \tilde{b}_{s,j,u}) \ge 1 \end{cases} \tag{13}$$

So the user satisfactory trust $ST_{s,j}^t$ is shown as the following. The lower the deviation degree is, the higher the nearness degree is. Consequently, the user satisfactory trust gets higher.

$$ST_{s,j}^t = \frac{1}{k} \sum_{u=1}^{k} T(\tilde{a}_{s,j,u}, \tilde{b}_{s,j,u}) \tag{14}$$

4.3   Trust Integration

To obtain the global trust, we enable the integration of the QoS trust and the user satisfaction trust. Importantly, we think the historical trust value is one of influence factors, so the global trust degree of the service provider is computed by principle model, denoted by $GT_{s,j}^t$.

$$GT_{s,j}^t = \alpha GT_{s,j}^{t-1} + \beta QT_{s,j}^t + \gamma ST_{s,j}^t \qquad (\alpha + \beta + \gamma = 1) \qquad (15)$$

Here, α, β, and γ are positive weights of the trust parameters.

4.4   Reputation

Trust and reputation are related, but different. Basically, trust is between two entities, but the reputation of an entity is the aggregated opinions of a community towards that entity. Usually, an entity that has high reputation is trusted by many other entities in that community. In this model, the global trust is the trustworthiness of a cloud service from the perspective of a cloud user. Reputation is the trustworthiness of a cloud service from the perspective of all cloud users. We collect the global trust of the cloud service provider from different cloud users to generate their reputation. Let RT_s^t be the reputation of the cloud service provider s.

$$RT_s^t = \frac{1}{n} \sum_{j=1}^{n} GT_{s,j}^t \qquad (16)$$

5   Evaluation

In this section, we mainly conducts trusts evaluation on sample dataset extracted from Cloud Harmony Project in the fashion of emulation on Matlab [23]. The values for security parameters are α, β, and γ, which are empirical values obtained from multiple experiments. As the weight factors in Eq. (15), which is used to determine how much the final integrated global trustworthiness is affected by the last global, QoS's and user satisfaction's trustworthiness, respectively. Weights of QoS parameters are evaluated by Eq. (9).

Cloud service models covered in our experiments include IaaS, SaaS and PaaS. The sample dataset consists of 3 kinds of cloud service instances as shown in Table 1. The sample dataset involves 6 QoS parameters, specifically, which are Network Latency, downlink data speed (256 KB–10 MB/2 threads), downlink data speed (1–128 KB/4 threads), uplink data speed (256 KB–10 MB/2 threads), uplink data speed (1–128 KB/4 threads) and service success rate. These QoS values were fetched from Cloud Harmony website.

Table 1. Cloud service instance specifications

Cloud service model	Cloud service type	Cloud service
IaaS (I)	Compute	Google Compute Engine-europe-west4 (I1)
		Microsoft Azure Virtual Machines - australia-east (I2)
		Alibaba Elastic Compute Service - ap-southeast-1 (I3)
		Amazon EC2-ap-southeast-2 (I4)
PaaS (P)	Storage	IBM Bluemix-us-south (P1)
		Alibaba Cloud Object Storage-cn-shenzhen (P2)
		Google Cloud Storage-asia (P3)
		Microsoft Azure Cloud Storage-us-west (P4)
SaaS (S)	CDN	Azure CDN from Verizon (S1)
		Tata Communications CDN (S2)
		MaxCDN (S3)
		Rackspace Cloud CDN (S4)

5.1 Trusts Evaluation of Cloud Services

In virtue of Cloud Harmony, QoS data of 12 cloud services is first collected. QoS parameters involved are Network Latency (ms), downlink data speed (256 KB–10 MB/2 threads) (Mb/s), downlink data speed (1–128 KB/4 threads) (Mb/s), uplink data speed (256 KB–10 MB/2 threads) (Mb/s), uplink data speed (1–128 KB/4 threads) (Mb/s), service success rate. This is 12×6 matrix representing 12 cloud services and 6 attributes. The initial trust degree is set to 0.5. Positive weights of the trust parameters are $\alpha = 0.2$, $\beta = 0.4$, and $\gamma = 0.4$.

Figure 2 illustrates the trustworthiness of cloud services. It is clear that the trustworthiness changes with interactions. There are three kinds of trustworthiness that focus on different aspects. One is QoS, another is user satisfaction. Particularly, we put the two together into the global trust assessment. The values are different but the trend of the change is similar intuitively, which shows the relationship that QoS trustworthiness goes higher as user satisfaction gets higher. Thus, it is conformed to the general regularity, and indicates that our framework is more quantitative and objective.

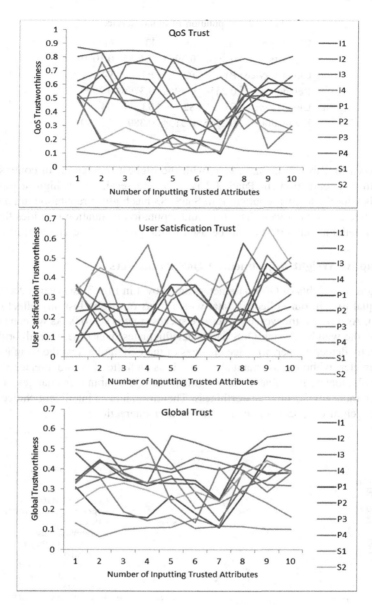

Fig. 2. Trustworthiness of cloud service

5.2   Reputation Evaluation of Cloud Services

We acquire QoS values of 12 cloud services from 10 cloud users. The reputations of 12 cloud services are evaluated based on the methods above. The results are shown in Table 2.

Table 2. Reputation of cloud Service

Cloud service	I1	I2	I3	I4
Reputation	0.3608	0.3975	0.4255	0.1099
Cloud service	P1	P2	P3	P4
Reputation	0.2558	0.4958	0.3796	0.2509
Cloud service	S1	S2	S3	S4
Reputation	0.2965	0.3134	0.389	0.3799

As shown in Table 2, in IaaS, I3 is with the highest reputation. In contrast, I4 is with the lowest reputation. In PaaS, P2 is a storage service with highest reputation while P4 is with the lowest reputation. In SaaS, S3 has highest reputation among CDN services while S1 is the lowest. The trust and reputation evaluation provides the cloud user with a reliable support that can be used in the process of service selection.

5.3   Adaptive Weight Adjustment of QoS Parameters

The changes of weights of QoS parameters are shown in Fig. 3. Service success rate is always equal to 1 in our collected data, which turns out to be lost any effect on trust evaluation. As a result, the weight of service success rate is set to 0. As we can see from the results, the weight of each QoS parameter fluctuates over time. Our algorithm can automatically detect the performance changes of the CSP and adjust the weight of each QoS parameter without any manual work. It is definite that the greater the QoS parameter fluctuates, the greater the weight of the QoS parameter changes. That can incur much more impact on trustworthiness. Therefore, it is an intelligent choice to self-adjust the weight of QoS parameters without user interaction.

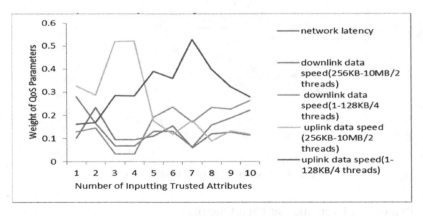

Fig. 3. The change of weight of QoS parameters

5.4   Comparisons with Other Methods

Figure 4 shows the comparing result of our model with TOPSIS, AHP and Liner Weighted methods. Due to limited space, we only give the comparing result of 3 cloud services.

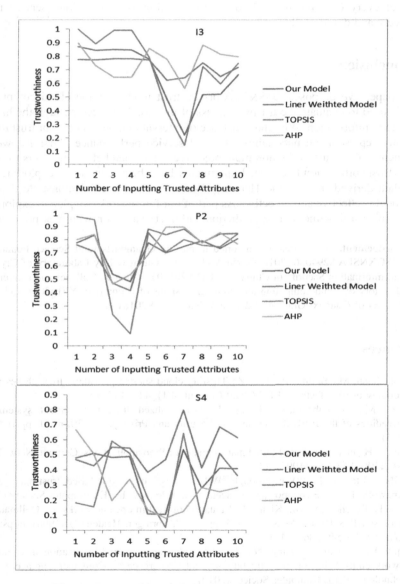

Fig. 4.   Trustworthiness of cloud service in different models

It is evident that all the trust models are effective in evaluating the trustworthiness of the CS. Under the different trust model, the trend of the change of the trustworthiness is also similar. Our model has shown advantage over other models in the sense that it is objective. QoS data in interval number representation can better indicate the uncertainty of QoS data. Adaptive weight adjustment of QoS parameters can avoid the impact of subjective factor on the trust evaluation. Our model can reflect the contribution of every QoS parameter into the trustworthiness of the cloud service more objectively and dynamically.

6   Conclusion

In this paper, we proposed QoS&SLA-driven trust model for the cloud computing, which is used to evaluate the trustworthiness of the cloud services through the history service QoS information. With the assistance of interval number theory, our trust model can better represent the uncertainty of cloud service performance. Adaptive weight adjustment makes trust evaluation more objective, which can help cloud users to select a more trustworthy cloud service. Experiments have been conducted exploiting real cloud data derived from Cloud Harmony Website. The results demonstrate that our trust model is effective and objective. As part of our future work, we plan to explore the solution of trust timeliness, trust prediction and trust evaluation with user preferences.

Acknowledgement. This article is supported in part by Guangxi Natural Science Foundation (No. 2018GXNSFAA294036, 2018GXNSFAA138116), Guangxi Key Laboratory of Cryptography and Information Security of China (No. GCIS201705), Guangxi Colleges and Universities Key Laboratory of cloud computing and complex systems of China (No. YF16205), and Innovation Project of Guangxi Graduate Education (No. YCSW2018138).

References

1. Alhanahnah, M., Bertok, P., Tari, Z.: Trusting cloud service providers: trust phases and a taxonomy of trust factors. IEEE Cloud Comput. **4**(1), 44–54 (2017)
2. Blaze, M., Feigenbaum, J., Lacey, J.: Decentralized trust management system. In: Proceedings of the IEEE Symposium on Security and Privacy, vol. 30, no. 1, pp.164–173 (1996)
3. Chu, Y.-H., et al.: REFEREE: trust management for Web applications. Comput. Netw. ISDN Syst. **29**(8), 953–964 (1997)
4. Li, N., Mitchell, J.C., Winsborough, W.H.: Design of a Role-based trust-management framework. In: IEEE Symposium on Security and Privacy. IEEE Computer Society (2002)
5. Beth, T., Borcherding, M., Klein, B.: Valuation of trust in open networks. In: Gollmann, D. (ed.) ESORICS 1994. LNCS, vol. 875, pp. 1–18. Springer, Heidelberg (1994). https://doi.org/10.1007/3-540-58618-0_53
6. Liqin, T., Chuang, L., Yang, N.: Behavior value analysis and application in evaluating network entity behavior trust. In: International Conference on Computer Engineering and Technology. IEEE Computer Society (2010)
7. Pandey, S., Daniel, A.K.: Fuzzy logic based cloud service trustworthiness model. In: IEEE International Conference on Engineering and Technology (2016)

8. Yang, Z., Luo, J.: A behavior trust model based on fuzzy logic in cloud environment. Int. J. Perform. Eng. **14**, 665–672 (2018)
9. Comi, A., et al.: A reputation-based approach to improve QoS in cloud service composition. In: 24th IEEE International Conference on Enabling Technologies: Infrastructures for Collaborative Enterprises. Institute of Electrical and Electronics Engineers Inc., Larnaca (2015)
10. Singh, A., Chatterjee, K.: A multi-dimensional trust and reputation calculation model for cloud computing environments. In: 2017 ISEA Asia Security and Privacy Conference. Institute of Electrical and Electronics Engineers Inc., Surat (2017)
11. Bilecki, L.F., Fiorese, A.: A trust reputation architecture for cloud computing environment. In: IEEE/ACS International Conference on Computer Systems and Applications (2017)
12. Rathore, H., Badarla, V., George, K.J.: Sociopsychological trust model for wireless sensor networks. J. Netw. Comput. Appl. **62**, 75–87 (2016)
13. Chiregi, M., Navimipour, N.J.: A comprehensive study of the trust evaluation mechanisms in the cloud computing. J. Serv. Sci. Res. **9**(1), 1–30 (2017)
14. Manuel, P.: A trust model of cloud computing based on quality of service. Ann. Oper. Res. **233**(1), 281–292 (2015)
15. Li, X., Du, J.: Adaptive and attribute-based trust model for service-level agreement guarantee in cloud computing. IET Inf. Secur. **7**(1), 39–50 (2013)
16. Fan, W., Perros, H.: A novel trust management framework for multi-cloud environments based on trust service providers. Knowl.-Based Syst. **70**, 392–406 (2014)
17. Tan, Z., et al.: A novel trust model based on SLA and behavior evaluation for clouds. In: 14th Annual Conference on Privacy, Security and Trust, pp. 581–587(2017)
18. Chakraborty, S., Roy, K.: An SLA-based framework for estimating trustworthiness of a cloud. In: IEEE 11th International Conference on Trust, Security and Privacy in Computing and Communications, pp. 937–942 (2012)
19. Ding, S., et al.: Combining QoS prediction and customer satisfaction estimation to solve cloud service trustworthiness evaluation problems. Knowl.-Based Syst. **56**, 216–225 (2014)
20. Sidhu, J., Singh, S.: Improved TOPSIS method based trust evaluation framework for determining trustworthiness of cloud service providers. J. Grid Comput. **15**(1), 81–105 (2017)
21. Alhanahnah, M., et al.: Context-aware multifaceted trust framework for evaluating trustworthiness of cloud providers. Future Gener. Comput. Syst. **79**, 488–499 (2018)
22. Tang, M., et al.: Towards a trust evaluation middleware for cloud service selection. Future Gener. Comput. Syst. **74**, 302–312 (2017)
23. CloudHarmony Homepage. http://www.cloudharmony.com/

A Lossless Data Hiding Scheme in Public Key Encrypted Domain Based on Homomorphic Key-Switching

Yan Ke[✉], Minqing Zhang, Tingting Su, and Jia Liu

Key Laboratory of Network and Information Security under the Chinese People
Armed Police Force (PAP), College of Cryptography Engineering in Engineering
University of PAP, Xi'an 710086, China
15114873390@163.com

Abstract. This paper proposes a lossless data hiding in encrypted domain
(RDH-ED) scheme. To realize the data extraction directly from the encrypted
domain without the private key, a key-switching based least-significant-bit
(KS-LSB) data hiding method has been designed. In application, the user first
encrypts the plaintext and uploads ciphertext to the server. Then the server
performs KS-LSB to obtain the marked ciphertext. Additional data can be
extracted directly from the marked ciphertext by the server without the private
key, which enables the (trusted or untrusted) third party to manage ciphertext
flexibly under the premise of keeping the plaintext secret. The Experimental
results demonstrate that the embedding capacity is 1bit per bit of plaintext. Data
hiding would not affect the accuracy and the security of encryption.

Keywords: Information security · Reversible data hiding in encrypted
domain · LWE · Key switching

1 Introduction

REVERSIBLE data hiding in encrypted domain (RDH-ED) is an information hiding
technique that aims to not only accurately embed and extract the additional messages in
the ciphertext, but also restore the original plaintext losslessly [1, 2]. RDH-ED is useful
in some distortion intolerable applications, such as ciphertext management or retrieval
in the cloud, ciphertext annotation for medical or military use. With the increasing
demand for information security and the development of the encrypted signal processing techniques, RDH-ED has been an issue of great attention in the field of privacy
protection and ciphertext processing.

From the viewpoint of the cryptosystem that RDH-ED methods are based on,
existing RDH-ED methods could be classified into two categories: Symmetric encryption based RDH-ED [1, 3–14], and public key encryption based RDH-ED. Symmetric
cryptography that has been introduced into RDH-ED includes stream encryption [1, 3–6,
13], advanced encryption standard (AES) [7, 8], and RC4 encryption [9].

According to the methods of utilizing the redundancy in the cover for data hiding,
symmetric encryption based RDH-ED methods were classified into two categories

© Springer Nature Singapore Pte Ltd. 2020
W. Han et al. (Eds.): CTCIS 2019, CCIS 1149, pp. 296–309, 2020.
https://doi.org/10.1007/978-981-15-3418-8_19

[1, 2]: "vacating room before encryption (VRBE)" [1, 7, 8, 10, 13] and "vacating room after encryption (VRAE)" [3–6]. The room, namely the redundancy in the cover, is vacated for reversible data hiding. The first RDH-ED method was proposed by Zhang for encrypted images [3], and then [4, 5] enhanced its capacity. Qian *et al.* proposed a similar method to embed data in an encrypted JPEG bit stream [6]. AES was introduced in [7] to encrypt the cover image. Each block containing n pixels could carry one bit data. The embedding rate (ER) is $1/n$ bits per pixel (bpp). Then difference prediction was introduced before encryption in [8], and AES was used to encrypt pixels except the embedding ones, thus resulting in a better embedding capacity (EC) and reversibility. However, it needed decryption first before data extraction in the above RDH-ED methods, which restricted the practicability in practical applications. The separable RDH-ED was proposed in [11, 12]. Separability has been so far an important attribute of practicality for current RDH-ED.

The redundancy introduced by VABE or VARE is independent from the encryption, resulting in the mutual restriction between decryption distortion and the embedding capacity, which is a major obstacle to the realization of separability and a high EC. There existed two main solutions proposed: one is to improve the quality of redundancy introduced before encryption. For example in [13], a separable high embedding algorithm was proposed by making full use of prediction error introduced before encryption. Second, the correlation of the plaintext is preserved in the ciphertext, so that RDH in spatial domain, such as difference expansion technique (DE) [15], histogram shifting technique (HS) [16–18], could be implemented in the encrypted domain. For example in [14], a new framework of RDH-ED was proposed, in which a specific stream cipher was used to preserve the correlation between the neighboring pixels. The above mentioned symmetric encryption based algorithms are fast and efficient in practice, which has significant research value and technological potential in the future.

However, there are also technical defects in symmetric encryption based RDH-ED. The correlation of plaintext would be destroyed because of the *confusion* and *diffusion* principles of symmetric encryption. To achieve reversible data hiding, it usually needs to introduce embedding redundancy. While it is difficult to vacate room after encryption, the current attention focuses more on the VEBE method [13], by which more computational expense is introduced into the client end for data hiding. The preprocessing in the plaintext is similar to data compression, and the compression capability determines the performance of RDH-ED. As for the methods of preserving plaintext correlation by a specific encryption [14], it currently mainly relies on reusing the same random sequence to encrypt a specific pixel block. It could provide certain security guarantees, but key reusing would weaken the encryption intensity of the symmetric encryption in theory. The more correlation among ciphertext is remained, the more the encryption intensity is reduced. The RC4 encryption was declared breached in 2013 [19], RDH-ED based on early RC4 has certain limitations in future security applications. In addition, symmetric encryption requires a geometrically increasing amount of encryption keys with the number of communication participants. The local key storage cost is high for each user.

Compared with symmetric encryption, public key encryption has some advantages for RDH-ED, which is worthy of our attention: first, public key encryption requires a linear increasing amount of key usage in the communication network. The local key storage cost is only the private key of the user's own, while all the public keys are publicly released. It has been widely used in electronic finance and network communication protocols, which provides application prospects for RDH-ED. Second, public key encryption introduces ciphertext extension, namely, the redundancy from the ciphertext itself. Through a certain embedding strategy [28], we could select embedding positions and improve EC effectively. Third, flexible cryptosystems of the public key encryption, especially the homomorphic encryption, provide reliable technical supports for RDH-ED. However, there are still technical limitations and application dilemmas in public key based RDH-ED. We shall discuss those in Sect. 2. This paper focuses on the current state of public key based RDH-ED, aiming at making full use of LWE-based fully homomorphic encryption (FHE) technique to implement DE encapsulation. A novel RDH-ED method is proposed, which is superior to the current public key based RDH-ED in practicality, security and reversibility.

The rest of this paper is organized as follows. The following section introduces the art of state about public encryption based RDH-ED and analyzes the potential of DE for RDH-ED. Section 3 introduces the techniques of FHE, key-switching, and bootstrapping. Section 4 describes the detailed processes of the proposed full homomorphic encryption encapsulated difference expansion. In Sect. 5, the three judging standards of RDH-ED, including *correctness*, *security* and *efficiency*, are discussed theoretically and verified with experimental results. Finally, Sect. 6 summarizes the paper and discusses future investigations.

2   Public Encryption Based RDH-ED

Currently, researches of public key encryption based RDH-ED are mainly based on Paillier encryption [20–26]. and learning with Error (LWE) encryption [27–29]. Probabilistic and homomorphic properties of the above cryptography allow the third party, *i.e.*, the cloud servers, to conduct operations directly on ciphertext without knowing the private key, which shows potential for more flexible realizations of RDH-ED.

The first Paillier encryption based RDH-ED was proposed by Chen *et al.* [20]. Shiu *et al.* [21] and Wu *et al.* [22] improved the EC of [20] by solving the pixel overflow problem. Those algorithms were VRBE methods. Li *et al.* in [25] proposed a VRAE method with a considerable EC by utilizing the homomorphic addition property of Paillier encryption and HS technique. The above algorithms were all inseparable. Data extraction was implemented only in the plaintext domain. It was a crucial bottleneck of public key encryption based RDH-ED to realize data extraction directly from the encrypted domain. Wu *et al.* proposed two RDH-ED algorithms for the encrypted images in [24]: a high-capacity algorithm based on Paillier cryptosystem was presented for data extraction after image decryption. The other one could operate data extraction in the encryption domain. Zhang *et al.* [23] proposed a combined scheme consisting of a lossless scheme and a reversible scheme to realize separability. Data was extracted from the encrypted domain in the lossless scheme and from the plaintext domain in the reversible scheme. In [26], Xiang embedded the ciphertext of additional data into the LSBs of the encrypted pixels by employing homomorphic multiplication. Only the ciphertext of additional data could be obtained during extraction directly from ciphertext. To distinguish the corresponding plaintext of the ciphertext of additional data without the private key, a one-to-one mapping table from ciphertext to plaintext was introduced while the ciphertext of additional data for embedding was not from encryption but from the mapping table. However, the exposure and accumulation of a large number of the mapping tables to an untrusted third party might increase the risk of cryptanalysis in theory, while the Paillier algorithms cannot resist *adaptive chosen ciphertext attack* (ACCA or CCA2) [30].

LWE based RDH-ED was first proposed in [26] by quantifying the LWE encrypted domain and recoding the redundancy from ciphertext. Ke *et al.* fixed the parameters for LWE encryption and proposed a multilevel RDH-ED with a flexible applicability and high EC in [27]. However, the data-hiding key used for extraction overlapped partly with the private key for decryption, thus resulting in limitation for embedding by a third party. In [29], separability could be achieved by preserving correlation from the plaintext in the ciphertext through a modified somewhat LWE encryption. However, the correlation among ciphertext was strong, and it was theoretically vulnerable to cryptanalysis attacks. This paper proposes a lossless data hiding in encrypted domain (RDH-ED) scheme. To realize the data extraction directly from the encrypted domain without the private key, a key-switching based least-significant-bit (KS-LSB) data hiding method has been designed. In application, the user first encrypts the plaintext and uploads ciphertext to the server. Then the server performs KS-LSB to obtain the marked ciphertext. Additional data can be extracted directly from the marked ciphertext by the server without the private key, which enables the (trusted or untrusted) third party to manage ciphertext flexibly under the premise of keeping the plaintext secret. The Experimental results demonstrate that the embedding capacity is 1bit per bit of plaintext. Data hiding would not affect the accuracy and the security of encryption.

3 Preliminaries

3.1 LWE Encryption

The private key is denoted as s, and the public key A is generated by s and e satisfying Eq. (1), where e is sampled randomly:

$$A \cdot s = 2e \tag{1}$$

Encryption:
The plaintext is $m \in \{0, 1\}$ Set $m = (0, 0, \ldots 0)$ Generate a 0–1 sequence a_r uniformly and output the ciphertext:

$$c = m + A^T a_r \tag{2}$$

Decryption:

$$\left[[\langle c, s \rangle]_q \right]_2 = \left[[\langle m + A^T a_r, s \rangle]_q \right]_2 = \left[\left[m^T s + (A^T a_r)^T s \right]_q \right]_2$$

$$= \left[[m + a_r^T A s]_q \right]_2 = \left[[m + a_r^T 2e]_q \right]_2 = m \tag{3}$$

where $[.]_q$ means to perform modulo q. The correctness lies in that the total introduced noise could be restrained to meet:

$$a_r^T e < q/4 \tag{4}$$

3.2 Key–Switching [32]

There is data expansion in LWE encrypted ciphertext [28], but in FHE, a secondary expansion would occur when ciphertext got multiplied. The homomorphic multiplication between the ciphertext matrices returns the ciphertext tensor product, and the private key is also subjected to the tensor product operation before being used to decrypt the new ciphertext. Therefore, the amount of data will again expand geometrically.

In our scheme, the ciphertext of the pixel bits will get expanded after each multiplication. It also occurs after addition or subtraction between encrypted pixels due to the cases of bit carry or bit borrow, resulting in a large number of multiplication and exclusive or operations among ciphertext of pixel bit. If the secondary expansion cannot be eliminated or controlled, the amount of ciphertext data can produce an excessively extension that is unacceptable in practice. Key-switching can effectively eliminate the extension by replacing the extended ciphertext with new ciphertext of any shorter length without decrypting it, and ensure the new ciphertext corresponds to the same decryption as the extended ciphertext.

We use the key-switching technique to eliminate the ciphertext secondary expansion in FHEE-DE, that is, key-switching is implemented following each homomorphic operation. What is more, a key-switching based LSB data hiding method is proposed in this paper.

4 The Proposed Scheme

4.1 (a) Parameters Setting and Function Definition

The cryptosystem is parameterized by the integers: n (the length of the private key), $q \in (n^2, 2n^2)$ (the modulus), $d \geq (1 + \varepsilon)(1 + n)\log_2 q$ (the dimension of the public key space), $\varepsilon > 0$. If q is a prime, all the operations in the cryptosystem are performed modulo q in $\mathbb{Z}_q$, $\beta = \lceil \log_2 q \rceil$. We denote the noise probability distribution on $\mathbb{Z}_q$ as χ, $\chi = \overline{\psi}_{\alpha q}$, where the discrete Gaussian distribution $\overline{\psi}_{\alpha q} = \lceil qx \rfloor \bmod q | x \sim N(0, \alpha^2)$, and $\lceil qx \rfloor$ denotes rounding qx to the nearest integer [28].

Definition 1: The private key generating function:

$$s = SKGen_{n,q}(\cdot) \tag{5}$$

which returns the private key $S = \in Z_q^n : s = (1, t)$ where $t = Z_q^{n-1}$ is sampled from the distribution χ.

Definition 2: The public key generating function:

$$A = PKGen_{(d,n),q}(s) \tag{6}$$

in which a matrix $W \in Z_q^{d \times (n-1)}$ is first generated uniformly and a vector $e \in Z_q^d$ is sampled from the distribution χ, then the vector $b \in Z_q^d$ is obtained:

$$b = Wt + 2e \tag{7}$$

the n-column matrix $A \in Z^{d \times n}$ is consisting of b followed by $-W$, $A = (b, -W)$. A is returned as the public key.

Remark: Observe that $A \cdot s = 2e$ for Eq. (8).

Definition 3: The encrypting function:

$$c = Enc_A(m) \tag{8}$$

which returns a vector c as the ciphertext of one bit plaintext $m \in \{0, 1\}$ with the public key A: Set $m = (m, 0, 0, \ldots, 0) \in Z_2^n$ Generate a random vector $a_r \in Z_2^d$ uniformly and output c:

$$c = m + A^T a_r \tag{9}$$

Definition 4 [32]: The function $BitDe(x)$, x, $\in Z_q^n$, decomposes x into its bit representation. Namely, it outputs $(u_1, u_2, u_3, \ldots, u_\beta,) \in Z_q^{n\beta}$, $x = \sum_{j=0}^{\beta-1} 2^j \cdot u_j$, $u_i \in Z_2^n$.

Definition 5: The decrypting function:

$$m = Dec_s(c) = \left[[\langle c, s \rangle]_q \right]_2 \tag{10}$$

which returns the plaintext bit $m \in \{0, 1\}$ with the private key s. If the inputs of the decryption function are in binary form, we could regard such a function as a decryption circuit, denoted as $Dec *_S (C)$, $C = BitDe(c)$, $S = BitDe(s)$.

Definition 6 [32]: The function $Powerso$ $f(x)$, $x \in Z_q^n$, outputs the vector $(x, 2x, 2^2x, \ldots, 2^{\beta-1}x,) \in Z_q^{n \cdot \beta}$.

Next, we will give the procedure of key-switching, which takes a ciphertext c_1 under s_1 and outputs new ciphertext c_2 that encrypts the same plaintext under the private key s_2.

Definition 7 [32]: The switching key generating function:

$$B = SwitchKGen(s_1, s_2) \tag{11}$$

where $s_1 \in Z_q^{n1}$, $s_2 \in Z_q^{n2}$. $A_{temp} = PKGen_{(n1 \bullet \beta, n2)}$, $q(s_2)$. The matrix $B \in Z_q^{(n1 \cdot \beta) \times n2}$ can be obtained by adding $Powersof(s_1)$ to A_{temp}'s first column.

Ciphertext c_2 can be obtained by using the switching key:

$$c_2 = BitDe(c_1)^T \cdot B \tag{12}$$

In our scheme, there is a *key-switching based LSB data hiding* method proposed to ensure that the servers could directly extract additional data from ciphertext without using the private key. We generate a pseudo-random binary sequence k for the servers to randomly scramble the additional data before KS-LSB data hiding. The switching key for KS-LSB data hiding is:

$$B_{LSB} = SwitchKGen(s, s) \tag{13}$$

where $s \in Z_q^n$. All different keys are distributed as shown in Table 1:

4.2 Encryption

For the pixel pair (X, Y), whose iLSBs are denoted by b_X^i, b_Y^i, $(i = 1, 2, \ldots, 8)$.

Each bit is encrypted by LWE encryption with a new public key. We omit the symbol "$_A$" in Eq. (8) for short in this paper: $c_X^i = Enc(b_X^i)$, $c_Y^i = Enc(b_Y^i)$, $i = 1, 2, \ldots, 8$.

4.3 Key-Switching Based LSB Data Hiding

Step 1: Randomly scramble the additional data sequence b_s by using data hiding key k to obtain the to-be-embedded data b_r:

$$b_r = k \oplus b_s \tag{14}$$

where $b_r \in b_r$.

Denote the last element of $c_{X'}^1$ as c_{LX1}, whose LSB would be replaced by b_r (X is the "1" signed pixel by M_{ava}).

Step 2: If $b_r = LSB(c_{LX1})$, $c_{X'}^1$ maintains the same, or if $b_r \neq LSB(c_{LX1})$, $c_{X'}^1$ is refreshed by:

$$c_{X'}^1 = BitDe(c_{X'}^1)^T \cdot B_{LSB}.$$

Step 3: Repeat Step 2 until $LSB(c_{LX1}) = b_r$.
The marked ciphertext is obtained: $c_{X'}^1$ and $c_{Y'}^i (i = 1, 2, \ldots, 8)$.

According to the framework in Fig. 1(a), after receiving the marked ciphertext, the client user could implement the decryption on the marked ciphertext to obtain X and Y by using s: $b_{X'}^i = Dec_s(c_{X'}^i)$, $= Dec_s(c_{Y'}^i)$, $(i = 1, 2, \ldots, 8)$.

4.4   LSB Extraction from the Marked Ciphertext

Additional data could be directly extracted from ciphertext without the private key s (X is the "1" signed pixel by M_{ava}):

$$b_r = LSB(c_{LX1}) \tag{15}$$

$$b_s = k \oplus b_r \tag{16}$$

5   Theoretical Analysis and Experimental Results

5.1   Correctness

The correctness of the proposed scheme includes the lossless restoration of plaintext and the accurate extraction of the embedded data. The test images, 512×512 8-bit grayscale images, are from image libraries, USC-SIPI (http://sipi.usc.edu/database/database.php?volume=misc) and Kodak (http://r0k.us/graphics/kodak/index.html).

The experimental results of six test images were selected in this section to demonstrate the correctness. The six test images are as shown in Fig. 2. The preprocessing LWE encryption & decryption, key switching, and KS-LSB were all implemented on MATLAB2010b with a 64-bit single core (i7-6800 K) @ 3.40 GHz.

Parameters setting: Solving the LWE problem with given parameters is equivalent to solving Shortest Vector Problem (SVP) in a lattice with a dimension $\sqrt{n \log_2(q)} / \log_2(\delta)$.

Considering the efficiencies of the best known lattice reduction algorithms, the secure dimension of the lattice must reach 500 ($\delta = 1.01$) [33, 34]. An increase in n will result in a high encryption blowup. To balance security and the efficiency of practical use, we set $n = 240$, $q = 57601$, $d = 4573$. To ensure the fidelity of the marked plaintext, we set $h_{fid} = 10$.

Fig. 1. The test images. (a) Lena; (b) Baboon; (c) Crowd; (d) Tank; (e) Peppers; (f) Plane.

5.1.1   Accuracy of Plaintext Recovery

In the proposed scheme, the user directly decrypts the marked ciphertext to get the plaintext. We calculated the PSNR of the plaintext.

The values of PSNR with the maximum EC are listed in Table 1. From the results of PSNR, it could be seen that there is no embedding distortion in the plaintext.

Table 1. The PSNR (*dB*) with the maximum EC (*bits*).

Image	EC	PSNR
Lena	110195	∞
Baboon	69286	∞
Crowd	104882	∞
Tank	108963	∞
Peppers	110558	∞
Plane	114834	∞
Average	103120	∞

5.1.2   Accuracy of Data Extraction

There are three cases of data extraction in this paper. The realization of the three cases is the embodiment of the separability of the proposed scheme:

(a) The third-party server directly extracts the embedded data from the marked ciphertext by using KS-LSB extraction. Figure 2(a) shows the comparison result bit by bit between the extracted data and the additional data with an EC of 100000 bits in the

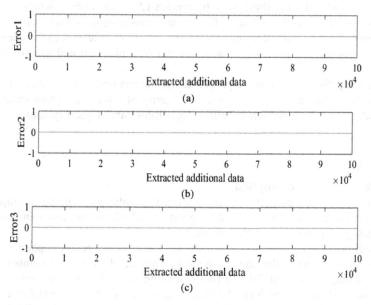

Fig. 2. Errors of the extracted data: (a) Error1 from KS-LSB extraction on the marked ciphertext; (b) Error2 from DE extraction on the marked plaintext; (c) Error3 from LWE decryption on the encrypted additional data.

experiment. It demonstrates that the extraction accuracy was 100%. (b) The user decrypts the marked ciphertext to obtain the marked plaintext, and then uses DE extraction to extract data. As shown in Fig. 2(b), the extraction accuracy is 100%. (c) The third-party server first performs FHEE-DE extraction on the marked ciphertext to obtain the encrypted embedded data. The user decrypts it to obtain the embedded data. The accuracy is as shown in Fig. 2(c).

5.2 Security

Security of RDH-ED mainly includes two aspects: (a) Data hiding should not weaken the security of the original encryption or leave any hidden danger of security cracking. (b) The embedded information cannot be obtained by an attacker without the extraction key or the private key.

In [27, 28], through the derivation of the probability distribution function (PDF) on the marked ciphertext and the experimental analysis of the statistical features, it was proved that the ciphertext distribution before and after data hiding did not change, so that the security of the RDH-ED method was proved by certain reasoning. In this paper, we do not have to make relevant derivation on PDF or the statistical features, because all the operations of the proposed scheme are equivalent to the operations of re-encryption [31], and the encryption security can be directly guaranteed by the re-encryption principles.

The processes of implementing KS-LSB on the ciphertext are equivalent to the processes of re-encrypting the ciphertext, which would not reveal anything about the private key or reduce the encryption security. The additional data is scrambled using sequence encryption by the third party before KS-LSB data hiding, which ensure the confidentiality of the additional data. During the transmission or processing by third-party servers, the third party does not obtain any information related to the client user's private key, nor did it expose any relationship between plaintext and its corresponding ciphertext.

In summary, the security of the proposed scheme can realize the security that LWE encryption has achieved. What is more, the security of LWE encryption reaches anti-quantum algorithm analysis, while Paillier algorithms cannot resist quantum algorithm analysis.

5.3 Efficiency

5.3.1 Public Key Consumption

A new ciphertext can be obtained by performing only once matrix multiplication between a switching key and the old ciphertext, which is fast and can ensure the confidentiality of plaintext and the private key.

KS-LSB data hiding is to randomly change the LSB of specific ciphertext by key switching until the LSB is the same as the to-be-embedded bit. Let the number of times of key switching performed for one bit embedding be λ, that is, the public key consumption of KS-LSB for one bit embedding is λ. Since the LSB of the ciphertext is 0 or 1 randomly appeared with a probability of 0.5, $\lambda+1$ obeys the geometric distribution as shown in Table 2. It demonstrates that it would be a small probability event with a probability less than 3% to operate more than 4 times key switching to realize one bit embedding. The theoretical value of λ is 0.8906. In the experiment, we performed 1000 KS-LSB data hiding tests. The actual λ was 0.995 on average, indicating a high embedding accuracy and efficiency.

Table 2. The probability distribution of β

λ	0	1	2	3	4	5
P	0.5	0.25	0.125	0.0625	0.0313	0.0156

5.3.2 Elapsed Time

The public key encryption algorithms, including the Paillier algorithm and the LWE algorithm, have ciphertext extension. In [28], the ciphertext extension of Paillier and LWE encryption was discussed in detail. Due to the application of the separability of RDH-ED, ciphertext is usually stored in the server or the cloud, the local storage cost of users is not too much. However, the elapsed time of encryption, decryption, data hiding, and data extraction is related to the efficiency in practice. In this section, we mainly demonstrate the elapsed time of each operation. Table 3 lists the elapsed time of the four main operations.

The elapsed time is specifically the time (milliseconds) when one bit plaintext gets decrypted, or one public key is generated and consumed by the operation, e.g., one bit of plaintext gets encrypted after each elapsed time of encryption.

Table 3. Elapsed time (*ms*) of once operation in FHEE-DE

Operation	Encryption	Decryption	Key switching
Elapsed time	20.5971	0.0067	0.1054

The brief structure and linear operations of LWE provide low time consumption, which are significant in practice. The results in Table 3 indicate that the elapsed time of the proposed method is acceptable for practical use.

6 Conclusion

This paper proposes a lossless data hiding in encrypted domain (RDH-ED) scheme. To realize the data extraction directly from the encrypted domain without the private key, a key-switching based least-significant-bit (KS-LSB) data hiding method has been designed. The Experimental results demonstrate that the embedding capacity is 1bit per bit of plaintext. Data hiding would not affect the accuracy and the security of encryption.

References

1. Ma, K., Zhang, W., Zhao, X., Yu, N., Li, F.: Reversible data hiding in encrypted images by reserving room before encryption. IEEE Trans. Inf. Forensics Secur. **8**(3), 553–562 (2013)
2. Shi, Y.-Q., Li, X., Zhang, X., Wu, H.: Reversible data hiding: advances in the past two decades. IEEE Access **4**(5), 3210–3237 (2016)
3. Zhang, X.: Reversible data hiding in encrypted image. IEEE Signal Process. Lett. **18**(4), 255–258 (2011)
4. Zhou, J., Sun, W., Dong, L., Liu, X., Au, O.C., Tang, Y.Y.: Secure reversible image data hiding over encrypted domain via key modulation. IEEE Trans. Circuits Syst. Video Technol. **26**(3), 441–452 (2016)
5. Wu, X., Sun, W.: High-capacity reversible data hiding in encrypted images by prediction error. Signal Process. **104**(11), 387–400 (2014)
6. Qian, Z., Zhang, X., Wang, S.: Reversible data hiding in encrypted JPEG bitstream. IEEE Trans. Multimedia **16**(5), 1486–1491 (2014)
7. Puech, W., Chaumont, M., Strauss, O.: A reversible data hiding method for encrypted images. In: Proceedings of the SPIE 6819, Security, Forensics, Steganography, and Watermarking of Multimedia Contents X, 2008, p. 68191E (2008)
8. Zhang, W., Ma, K., Yu, N.: Reversibility improved data hiding in encrypted images. Signal Process. **94**(1), 118–127 (2014)
9. Li, M., Xiao, D., Zhang, Y., Nan, H.: Reversible data hiding in encrypted images using cross division and additive homomorphism. Signal Process.: Image Commun. **39**(11), 234–248 (2015)
10. Cao, X., Du, L., Wei, X., Meng, D., Guo, X.: High capacity reversible data hiding in encrypted images by patch-level sparse representation. IEEE Trans. Cybern. **46**(5), 1132–1143 (2016)
11. Zhang, X.: Separable reversible data hiding in encrypted image. IEEE Trans. Inf. Forensics Secur. **7**(2), 826–832 (2012)
12. Wu, H.-Z., Shi, Y.-Q., Wang, H.-X., et al.: Separable reversible data hiding for encrypted palette images with color partitioning and flipping verification. IEEE Trans. Circuits Syst. Video Technol. **27**(8), 1620–1631 (2016). to be published
13. Puteaux, P., Puech, W.: An efficient MSB prediction-based method for high-capacity reversible data hiding in encrypted images. IEEE Trans. Inf. Forensics Secur. **13**(7), 1670–1681 (2018)
14. Huang, F.J., Huang, J.W., Shi, Y.Q.: New framework for reversible data hiding in encrypted domain. IEEE Trans. Inf. Forensics Secur. **11**(12), 2777–2789 (2016)
15. Tian, J.: Reversible data embedding using a difference expansion. IEEE Trans. Circuits Syst. Video Technol. **13**(8), 890–896 (2003)
16. Ni, Z., Shi, Y.-Q., Ansari, N., Su, W.: Reversible data hiding. IEEE Trans. Circuits Syst. Video Technol. **16**(3), 354–362 (2006)
17. Ou, B., Li, X., Zhao, Y., Ni, R., Shi, Y.-Q.: Pairwise prediction-error expansion for efficient reversible data hiding. IEEE Trans. Image Process. **22**(12), 5010–5021 (2013)
18. Li, X., Yang, B., Zeng, T.: Efficient reversible watermarking based on adaptive prediction-error expansion and pixel selection. IEEE Trans. Image Process. **20**(12), 3524–3533 (2011)
19. AlFardan, N.J., Bernstein, D.J., Paterson, K.G., et. al.: On the security of RC4 in TLS and WPA (2013). http://cr.yp.to/streamciphers/rc4biases-20130708.pdf
20. Chen, Y.-C., Shiu, C.-W., Horng, G.: Encrypted signal-based reversible data hiding with public key cryptosystem. J. Vis. Commun. Image Represent. **25**(5), 1164–1170 (2014)

21. Shiu, C.-W., Chen, Y.-C., Hong, W.: Encrypted image-based reversible data hiding with public key cryptography from difference expansion. Signal Process.: Image Commun. **39**, 226–233 (2015)

22. Wu, X., Chen, B., Weng, J.: Reversible data hiding for encrypted signals by homomorphic encryption and signal energy transfer. J. Vis. Commun. Image Represent. **41**(11), 58–64 (2016)

23. Zhang, X.-P., Loong, J., Wang, Z., et al.: Lossless and reversible data hiding in encrypted images with public key cryptography. IEEE Trans. Circuits Syst. Video Technol. **26**(9), 1622–1631 (2016)

24. Wu, H.-T., Cheung, Y.-M., Huang, J.-W.: Reversible data hiding in paillier cryptosystem. J. Vis. Commun. Image Represent. **40**(10), 765–771 (2016)

25. Li, M., Li, Y.: Histogram shifting in encrypted images with public key cryptosystem for reversible data hiding. Signal Process. **130**(1), 190–196 (2017)

26. Xiang, S.-J., Luo, X.: Reversible data hiding in homomorphic encrypted domain by mirroring ciphertext group. IEEE Trans. Circuits Syst. Video Technol. **28**(11), 3099–3110 (2018)

27. Ke, Y., Zhang, M., Liu, J.: Separable multiple bits reversible data hiding in encrypted domain. In: Shi, Y.Q., Kim, H.J., Perez-Gonzalez, F., Liu, F. (eds.) IWDW 2016. LNCS, vol. 10082. Springer, Cham (2017). https://doi.org/10.1007/978-3-319-53465-7_35

28. Ke, Y., Zhang, M., Liu, J., Su, T., Yang, X.: A multilevel reversible data hiding scheme in encrypted domain based on LWE. J. Vis. Commun. Image Represent. **54**(7), 133–144 (2018)

29. Li, Z.X., Dong, D.P., Xia, Z.H., et al.: High-capacity reversible data hiding for encrypted multimedia data with somewhat homomorphic encryption. IEEE Access **6**(10), 60635–60644 (2018)

30. Paillier, P., Pointcheval, D.: Efficient public-key cryptosystems provably secure against active adversaries. In: Lam, K.-Y., Okamoto, E., Xing, C. (eds.) ASIACRYPT 1999. LNCS, vol. 1716. Springer, Heidelberg (1999). https://doi.org/10.1007/978-3-540-48000-6_14

31. Gentry, C.: Fully homomorphic encryption using ideal lattices. In: Proceedings of the 41st ACM Symposium on Theory of Computing, STOC 2009, pp. 169–178 (2009)

32. Brakerski, Z., Gentry, C., Vaikuntanathan, V.: (Leveled) fully homomorphic encryption without bootstrapping. ACM Trans. Comput. Theory **6**(3), 1–36 (2014)

33. Gama, N., Nguyen, P.Q.: Predicting lattice reduction. In: 27th Annual International Conference on the Theory and Applications of Cryptographic Techniques, Advances in Cryptology-Eurocrypt 2010, Istanbul, Turkey, pp. 31–51 (2008)

34. Ruckert, M., Schneider, M.: Estimating the security of latticed-based cryptosystems (2010). http://eprint.icur.org/2010/137.pdf

A Detection Approach for Buffer Overflow Vulnerability Based on Data Control Flow Graph

Jinfu Chen$^{(\boxtimes)}$, Qihao Bao, Qingchen Zhang, Jinchang Hu,
and Patrick Kwaku Kudjo

School of Computer Science and Communication Engineering,
Jiangsu University, Zhenjiang 212013, China
jinfuchen@ujs.edu.cn

Abstract. Buffer overflow vulnerability is currently one of the major security problems for programming languages written in C/C ++. To address this issue, existing studies have proposed varied detection techniques to eliminate buffer overflow vulnerability. However, these approaches are still far from finding an ideal solution to completely reduce buffer overflow vulnerability. This paper presents a detection approach for buffer overflow vulnerability based on Data Control Flow Graph (DCFG). The proposed approach first uses the dangerous function identification method to determine the dangerous points and the type of dangerous functions. We then construct the constraint rules of the dangerous function at the dangerous point to establish the constraint system. Finally, the constraint system is solved to obtain the result of the vulnerability determination. To explore this approach, we performed an extensive experiment and compared empirically with existing vulnerability detection tools. The result shows that the proposed method has a good effect on buffer overflow vulnerability detection, and can effectively improve detection efficiency.

Keywords: Buffer overflow · Security vulnerability · Data Control Flow Graph · Dangerous function · Vulnerability detection

1 Introduction

With the development of computer technology, more and more people are increasingly enjoying the convenience brought by information systems. The inevitable problem in the continuous development of information technology is the increasing number of software bugs that constitute security vulnerabilities. The National Institute of Standard and Technology (NIST) define software vulnerability as a weakness or error in an information system, security procedure and implementation that could be exploited. Among the reported cases of security vulnerabilities, buffer overflow vulnerability is the most common and major security problems for programming languages written in C/C++. Buffer overflow vulnerabilities occur as a result of errors that allow an attacker to cause the program to write beyond the bounds of an allocated memory allocation, which leads to data overflow [1, 2]. The attacker uses the vulnerability to create fake data and eventually obtains control of the computer system [3]. In the 1980s, the first

© Springer Nature Singapore Pte Ltd. 2020
W. Han et al. (Eds.): CTCIS 2019, CCIS 1149, pp. 310–324, 2020.
https://doi.org/10.1007/978-981-15-3418-8_20

worm successfully attacked hundreds of computers within a very short period of time and had a huge impact. Currently, the Public Vulnerability Library (CVE) has formed a number of internationally influential vulnerability standards to improve vulnerability analysis [4]. Furthermore, the National Vulnerability Database (NVD) uniquely identifies, classifies, and describes vulnerabilities, which is strictly compatible with CVE and builds a comprehensive, multichannel vulnerability release mechanism [5–7].

At present, the main technologies of buffer overflow detection include dynamic detection, static detection and constraint analysis detection. Static detection performs vulnerability detection before the program, without running the program. Dynamic detection determines the performance of the test program during the execution of the program, and checks the difference between the operation result and the expected result [8, 9]. Strictly speaking, the static detection approaches are effective and can detect vulnerabilities in the early stages of software development [10]. Hence, researchers and software developers prefer the static approach to buffer overflow vulnerability detection. Constraint analysis is a static analysis method that establishes a program's constraint system and solves this system. The purpose of establishing a constraint system is to use the constraint rules to generate the constraints of the program, and the solution of the system in order to check the constraints to determine the properties of the program. In addition, the constraint system is composed of inequality relations between multiple constraint variables, and the nature of the program is found by analyzing the constraint relationship between program states. The aforementioned approaches have significantly improved buffer overflow vulnerability detection. However, these methods alone are insufficient for building and deploying secure systems to mitigate security vulnerabilities. To this aim, this paper presents a detection approach for buffer overflow vulnerability based on Data Control Flow Graph (DCFG).

Data Control Flow Graph (DCFG) is a new code graphical representation that combines Data Flow Graph (DFG) and Control Flow Graph (CFG). A DCFG corresponding to a program can generally be represented by DCFG = (V, E, λ, μ), where V represents a set of nodes, E represents a set of directed edges, λ represents the label function of the directed edges, and μ represents assignment function of the node attributes. Data Control Flow Graph (DCFG) has the advantages of both Data Flow Graph (DFG) and Control Flow Graph (CFG). It can fully reflect data dependencies between each operation of the program, but also be able to accurately describe the data flow changes from the creation to use of each variable in the program. Moreover, Data Control Flow Graph (DCFG) can also show the control information of the program code.

Our approach first uses the dangerous function identification method to determine the various dangerous points and the type of dangerous functions and then constructs the constraint rules of the dangerous function at the dangerous point to establish the constraint system. Finally, the constraint system is solved to obtain the result of the vulnerability determination.

We make the following contributions in this work:

(1) We propose a detection approach for buffer overflow vulnerability based on Data Control Flow Graph (DCFG).

(2) We used a comparative experiment to evaluate the effectiveness of the proposed model and the benchmark vulnerability detection tools.

The remainder of this paper is organized as follows: Related work is discussed in Sect. 2. The detective method of stack buffer overflow vulnerabilities is described in Sect. 3. The analysis of the method is detailed in Sect. 4, and the conclusion is presented in Sect. 5.

2 Related Work

Software vulnerability can be defined as the logical defects, or errors that occur during the software life cycle. We usually classify vulnerabilities into functional vulnerabilities and security vulnerabilities [11, 12]. Functional vulnerabilities can affect the normal operation of the program. Security vulnerabilities generally do not affect the daily use of the program. The Common Vulnerabilities and Exposure (CVE) defined vulnerabilities as deficiencies found in computer systems that, when exploited, can adversely affect the confidentiality, integrity, or availability of information [13, 14]. In summary, the characteristics of software vulnerabilities can be summarized as follows: First, software vulnerabilities are defects in the internal logic of software systems; secondly, software vulnerabilities exist in certain environments; third, software vulnerabilities can cause computers to be remotely controlled and threaten Information security [15].

The number of software vulnerabilities has increased in recent years, hence, methods and techniques for analyzing software vulnerabilities are becoming more and more important. Static analysis is an effective software vulnerability analysis technique. Static analysis can determine whether a vulnerability exists by analyzing the syntax and structure of the source code without executing the program, and therefore does not increase the overhead of program execution. In the following, we present the three widely used static detection techniques: symbolic execution, model checking, and constraint analysis.

(1) Symbolic execution determines the corresponding symbol expression for each path of the program, then analyzes the specific path, and judges whether the program behavior is correct according to the input and output, thereby analyzing whether the program has defects. To the best of our knowledge, symbolic execution is the most widely used vulnerability detection technique.

(2) The model test uses the state machine or the directed graph to establish the corresponding model for the program behavior, and describes the security properties of the target software. It further analyzes whether the target software meets the corresponding properties by determining whether a certain state of the software system is reachable. Due to the high software complexity, the current model test can only construct an abstract model for vulnerability detection in terms of software vulnerability detection.

(3) Constraint analysis is a static analysis method that establishes a program's constraint system and solves this system. The purpose of establishing a constraint system is to use the constraint rules to generate the constraints of the program, and the solution of the system is a static check of the constraints, and then determine the properties of the program. The constraint system is composed of inequality relations between multiple constraint variables, and the nature of the program is found by analyzing the constraint relationship between program states [16].

3 Proposed Method: A Novel Vulnerability Detection Approach Based on Data Control Flow Graph

As is shown in Fig. 1, the detection framework of DCVDM includes the following parts: DCFG generation module, a dangerous function identification module, constraint analysis module, and vulnerability determination module. In the following, we briefly describe these major components:

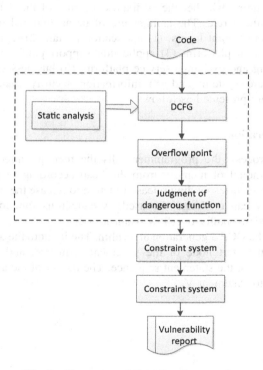

Fig. 1. The proposed detection framework.

(1) DCFG generation: the main purpose of the module is to generate its corresponding DCFG based on the source code. The main process is as follows: enter the start and end nodes of the sequence of statements, and then process the initial and used nodes of the program's variables. Determine whether the current node already exists. If the current node already exists, add the current node to the DCFG. Otherwise, discard the current node and analyze the next node of the current node. When all nodes have finished accessing, output DCFG.

(2) dangerous function identification: the main flow of the module is to traverse the DCFG according to the DCFG that has been generated, and record the vulnerability-related dangerous points on the executable path during the traversal process. Finally, determining the relevant information of the dangerous function existing in the target code.

(3) constraint analysis module: associates the integer containing the buffer allocation space length and the coverage space length at the dangerous function overflow point, and abstracts the buffer correlation function into the operation of the buffer attribute. Finally, establish an attribute constraint rules.

(4) vulnerability determination: the result of the vulnerability determination is obtained by judging whether the attribute constraint of the dangerous point satisfies the constraint rule. The architecture of urban regional health information system consists of eight layers: (1) application portal; (2) regional health information application platform; (3) application support platform; (4) data center; (5) data sharing and exchange service platform; (6) business systems; (7) specification standard system; and (8) information security system. The detailed explanations are presented as follows.

3.1   DCFG Generation

In the encoding process, the programmer calls the memory allocation function to request a certain amount of memory from the heap according to the need, and the program must call the corresponding release function to release the memory, otherwise the current memory can no longer be used. A dangerous function is a dangerous function that is prone to buffer overflow when in use.

Algorithm 1 is the DCFG generation algorithm. The input to the algorithm is V_i and V_j, V_i represents the start node of the statement sequence, and V_j represents the termination sequence of the statement sequence. The output of the algorithm is DCFG from statement V_i to statement V_j.

ALGORITHM 1.   Algorithm for the DCFG generation

INPUT: V_i, V_j
OUTPUT: DCFG
1. DCFG = new DCFG();
2. DV = new DV();
3. vector<string> en;
4. int num = 0;
5. **for** (int n = i; n <= j; n++) **do**
6.   pn = S_n;
7.   **if** (pn.name == init_decl) **then**
8.   DCFGNode = new DCFGNode (pn.id, en);
9.   addDCFGNode (DCFGNode, DCFG);
10.   addDCFGNode (DCFGNode, DV);
11.   num = num+1;
12.   **else if** (pn.name == use_decl) **then**
13.   DCFGNode = new DCFGNode (pn.id, en);
14.   addDCFGNode (DCFGNode, DCFG);
15.   addDCFGNode (DCFGNode, DV);
16.   num = num+1;
17.   **else if** (pn.name == goto_expr) **then**
18.   whileSubDCFG = new DCFG();
19.   int wLastId = getWhileLastId(pn);
20.   whileSubDCFG = constructwhilestmt (num, wLastId);
21.   addDCFGNode (whileSubDCFG.head, DCFG);
22.   num = wLastId +1;
23.   **else if** (pn.name == cond_expr) **then**
24.   condSubDCFG = new DCFG();
25.   condSubDCFG = constructcondstmt(pn);
26.   addDCFGNode (condSubDCFG.head, DCFG);
27.   num = num+1;
28.   **else if** (en belong to DV) **then**
29.   DCFGNode = new DCFGNode(en.id, en);
30.   addDCFGNode (DCFGNode, DCFG);
31.   num = num+1;
32.   **end if**
33. **end for**
34. return DCFG;

In the process of generating DCFG, it is necessary to separately analyze the structure of the sequence, selection and loop in the program statement. Lines 1–4 of the algorithm declare the relevant variables, lines 7–11 deal with the initial nodes of the program variables, and lines 12–16 processes the variables of the program using nodes. Lines 17–27 deal with the selection, loop, and other structures. Lines 28–33 determine whether the current node already exists in the DV. If so, you need to add the current node to the DCFG. Otherwise, discard the current node and analyze the current node.

A node that terminates the current algorithm when all nodes have access. Line 34 outputs the DCFG from statement V_i to statement V_j.

3.2 Dangerous Function Identification

After the DCFG has been obtained from the source code, we can now determine the dangerous functions based on the DCFG. The DCFG-based dangerous function identification (DCFG-DFI) algorithm is shown in Algorithm 2. The main idea is to traverse the DCFG, record the vulnerability-related dangerous points on the executable path during the traversal process, and compare the dangerous function set to determine the existence of the target code.

ALGORITHM 2.   Algorithm for the DCFG-based dangerous function identification **(DCFG-DFI)**

INPUT: DCFG
OUTPUT: dans
1. root = DCFG.head;
2. vector<unsigned int> users;
3. vector<stack<unsigned int>> dans;
4. Traverse (root.id);
5. Traverse (id)
6. **begin**
7.   **if** (id == 0) **then**
8.   return;
9.   **end if**
10. node = DCFG.getNodeById(id)
11. flag = has(users, node);
12. **if** (flag) **then**
13.   pos = index (users, node);
14.   **if** (MMF(node) || MCF(node) || UV(node)) **then**
15.   dans[pos].push(id);
16.   **end if**
17.   **end if**
18. return dans;
19. end

The input to the DCFG-DFI algorithm is the DCFG of the target program, and the output is **_dans_**, which records the information about all the vulnerabilities related to the vulnerability that caused the current vulnerability. Lines 1–3 of the algorithm declare the relevant variables, and line 4 calls the Traverse() function to traverse the DCFG. Lines 6–19 obtain and record information about the dangerous points related to the vulnerability. The execution time of the algorithm is mainly spent on the node traversal. Since the total number of nodes analyzed does not exceed the total number of nodes of the DCFG, the time complexity of the DCFG-DFI algorithm is O(n).

3.3   Constraint Analysis

For the constraint analysis, the following basic concepts are defined.

Definition 1: For variable **v**, define **type(v)** as the type of variable **v**, which can be an integer type or other type. **Type(v) = int** indicates that **v** is an integer variable. **ope(v)** and **cov(v)** represent two attribute operations on the buffer: get the allocated space length and the length of the cover space, and **type(ope(v)) = int**, **type(cov(v)) = int**.

Definition 2: For the function **fun**, if the *i*th parameter is an integer variable, **ope_i** represents the length of the allocation space corresponding to the *i*th parameter, and **cov_i** is the length of the coverage space corresponding to the *i*th parameter.

The establishment of the constraint system is to use the constraint rule to generate the constraints of the program. The construction of the constraint rule is mainly divided into two steps: the initialization of the attribute and the transfer of the attribute. At the point of an overflow of the dangerous function, the constraint attribute system of the buffer attribute to be accessed is constructed, and the constraint rule that needs to be verified is generated. This article mainly describes the construction of constraint rules for the three dangerous functions, namely "Strncpy()", "Memcpy()" and "Gets()".

When the dangerous function is Strncpy, the constraint rules for the buffer attribute can be expressed using in Eq. 1:

$$\frac{type(v) = int,\, type(w) = int}{Strncpy(v, w)} \Rightarrow$$
$$ope(v, w) < cov(v, w),\, ope(v, w) - cov(v, w) < 0. \tag{1}$$

Type(v) = int indicates that the type of the variable **v** is an integer. **w** is also an integer variable. **v** and **w** are the used variables of the function Strncpy. The generated constraint is that the allocation space length of the variable **v** points to the buffer is smaller than the length of the coverage space, and the length of the allocation space of the variable **w** to the buffer is smaller than the length of the coverage space.

When the dangerous function is Memcpy, the constraint rules for the buffer attribute are as shown in Eq. 2:

$$\frac{type(v) = int,\, type(w) = int}{Memcpy(v, w)} \Rightarrow$$
$$ope(v, w) < cov(v, w),\, ope(v, w) - cov(v, w) < 0. \tag{2}$$

Type(v) = int indicates that the type of the variable **v** is an integer. **w** is also an integer variable, and **v** and **w** are the used variables of the function Memcpy. The generated constraint is that the allocation space length of the variable **v** points to the buffer is smaller than the length of the coverage space, and the length of the allocation space of the variable **w** to the buffer is less than the length of the coverage space.

In a similar fashion, when the dangerous function is Gets, the constraint rules for the buffer attribute are as shown in Eq. 3:

$$\frac{type(v) = int}{Gets(v)} \Rightarrow$$
$$ope(v) < 0. \tag{3}$$

Type(v) = int indicates that the type of the variable **v** is an integer, and the variable of the **v** function Gets is used. The generated constraint is that the variable **v** points to the buffer's allocated space length is less than zero.

The constraint system can be established by analyzing the program according to the generation rules of the above buffer attribute constraints. The solution of the system is a static check of the constraints, and then determine the properties of the program. At this point, the security vulnerability detection problem has been transformed into a dangerous point if the attribute constraint to satisfy the constraint rule.

3.4 Judgment of Vulnerability

The input to the DCVJ algorithm is the set of ***dans*** related to the vulnerability-related hazard, and the output is the ***stin*** that records all the dangerous information of the current vulnerability. As shown in Algorithm 3, the type of dangerous function is first determined. If the vulnerability related constraint of the type is satisfied, the relevant constraint rules of the current vulnerability are returned. Then its verify the constraint rules and return all hazard information for the current vulnerability. After this, it then checks for the next dangerous point [17].

ALGORITHM 3.   Algorithm for the DCFG-based vulnerability judging (**DCVJ**)

INPUT: dans
OUTPUT: stin
1. int O;
2. int C;
3. **for** (int i = 0; i < dans.size()-1; i++) **do**
4.   stin = dans[i];
5.   **if** (strncpy) **then**
6.   return strncpyconstraint(stin);
7.   **if** (O<C)
8.   return StrncpyError(stin);
9.   **else if** (Memcpy) **then**
10.   return strncpyconstraint(stin);
11.   **if** (O<C)
12.   return MemcpyError(stin); /
13.   **else if** (Gets) **then**
14.   return strncpyconstraint(stin);
15.   **if** (O>0)
16.   return GetsError(stin);
17.   **end if**
18. **end for**

Line 1–2 of the algorithm define the buffer space and the coverage space. Similarly, line 5–8 judge whether it is the Strncpy type, line 9–12 also judges whether it is the Memcpy type, and line 13–16 determine whether it is the Gets type. The execution time of the algorithm is mainly spent on the judgment of the dangerous function type. Since all the dangerous functions of the analysis are in the dangerous point set *dans*, the time complexity of the DCVJ algorithm is $O(n)$, where **n** is the total number of dangerous points.

4   The Experiment Analysis and Results

This section of the paper presents the experimental procedure design to assess the performance of the proposed method, namely DCVDM. In addition, DCVDM is compared with other vulnerability detection tools such as cppcheck, flawfinder, and splint in terms of their false-negative rate and false-positive rate. Table 1 gives a brief summary of the experimental procedure.

In presenting the result of this study, we used the following terms to describe our findings. The total number of vulnerabilities in the test case set is recorded as TVN, the total number of vulnerabilities reported by the tool is recorded as TRN, the total number of real vulnerabilities reported by the tool is recorded as TTP, and the number of false-positive vulnerabilities reported by the tool is recorded as TFN. Thus, TRN = TTP + TFN. According to the definitions of the false-negative rate and the false-positive rate, there is a false-negative rate when FNR = (TVN-TTP)/TVN, and a false-positive rate when FPR = TFN/TRN. A lower false-negative rate FNR and false-positive rate FPR of a tool indicate better detection effectiveness.

Table 1. Experimental program

Type	Tool	Data	Purpose
Stack-Overflow	cppcheck	CWE121_Stack_based_ Buffer_Overflow	FNR
	flawfinder		
	splint		FPR
	DCVDM		
Heap-Overflow	cppcheck	CWE122_Heap_based_ Buffer_Overflow	FNR
	flawfinder		
	splint		FPR
	DCVDM		
Over-read	cppcheck	CWE126_Buffer_Over_Read	FNR
	flawfinder		
	splint		FPR
	DCVDM		

(1) Stack-Overflow [18]

Table 2 shows the results of the flawfinder, cppcheck, and splint tools and the DCVDM for the CWE121_Stack_based_Buffer_Overflow. Figure 2 also shows the false-negative rate and false-positive rate. The following is an analysis of the false-negative rate and false-positive rate of different tools.

Table 2. The result of CWE121_Stack_based_Buffer_Overflow

Type	TVN	Tool	TRN	TTP	TFN	FNR	FPR
CWE121_Stack_based_ Buffer_Overflow	1032	cppcheck	311	121	190	88.28%	61.09%
		flawfinder	2304	259	2045	74.90%	88.76%
		splint	340	133	207	87.11%	60.88%
		DCVDM	926	439	487	57.46%	52.59%

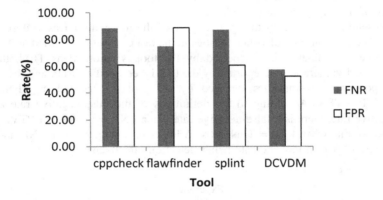

Fig. 2. The FNR and FPR of CWE121_Stack_based_Buffer_Overflow.

FNR: from the comparison of the three tools, namely flawfinder, cppcheck and splint, FNR of flawfinder is the lowest, which is 74.90%, and FNR of cppcheck is the highest, reaching 88.28%. Again, it can be seen from the analysis as presented in Table 2 that DCVDM has the lowest FNR of 57.46%, which is lower than the other three tools. It can be seen that the stack buffer overflows, and DCVDM performs better on FNR.

FPR: with regards to the FPR detection rate, our finding shows that the FPR of flawfinder is the highest, reaching 88.76%; the FPR of cppcheck and splint were quite low, however they were all above 60%, which indicate a certain level of validity. Again, in comparing the performance of the tools, we observed that the DCVDM has the lowest FPR of 52.59%, which is lower than the other three tools such as flawfinder, cppcheck, and splint. It can be seen that the stack buffer overflows, and DCVDM performs better with regards to FPR.

(2) Heap-Overflow

Table 3 shows the results of the flawfinder, cppcheck, and splint tools and DCVDM for the CWE122_Heap_based_Buffer_Overflow. Figure 3 shows the false-negative rate and false-positive rate. The following is an analysis of the false-negative rate and false-positive rate of different tools.

Table 3. The result of CWE122_Heap_based_Buffer_Overflow

Type	TVN	Tool	TRN	TTP	TFN	FNR	FPR
CWE122_Heap_based_ Buffer_Overflow	398	cppcheck	500	227	273	42.96%	54.60%
		flawfinder	560	111	449	72.11%	80.18%
		splint	228	114	114	71.36%	50.00%
		DCVDM	218	132	86	66.83%	39.45%

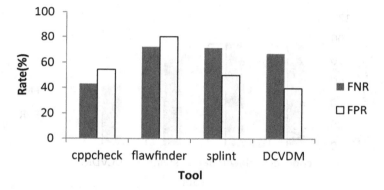

Fig. 3. The FNR and FPR of CWE122_Heap_based_Buffer_Overflow.

FNR: from the comparison of the three tools of flawfinder, cppcheck and splint, the FNR of cppcheck is 42.96%, which is the lowest of the three tools and the best in FNR. FNR of flawfinder is 72.11%, which is the highest. From the comparison of the four tools of flawfinder, cppcheck, splint and DCVDM, the FNR of DCVDM is 66.83%. It can be seen that DCVDM's FNR needs to be further reduced.

FPR: from the comparison of the three tools of flawfinder, cppcheck and splint, the FPR of splint is 50%, which is the lowest of the three tools and the best in the false-positive rate indicator. The false-positive rate of flawfinder is 80.18%. From the four tools of flawfinder, cppcheck, splint and DCVDM, DCVDM has the lowest false-positive rate of 39.45%. It can be seen that the DCVDM performs better on the false alarm rate index.

(3) Over-read

Table 4 shows the results of the flawfinder, cppcheck, and splint tools and the DCVDM for the CWE126_Buffer_Over_Read. Figure 4 shows the false-negative rate and false-positive rate. The following is an analysis of the false-negative rate and false-positive rate of different tools.

Table 4. The result of CWE126_Buffer_Over_Read

Type	TVN	Tool	TRN	TTP	TFN	FNR	FPR
CWE126_Buffer_Over_Read	560	cppcheck	293	16	277	97.14%	94.54%
		flawfinder	434	22	412	96.07%	94.93%
		splint	197	109	88	80.54%	44.67%
		DCVDM	386	245	141	56.25%	36.53%

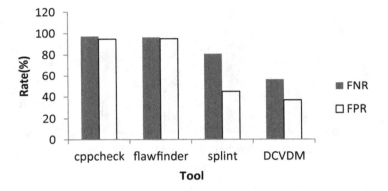

Fig. 4. The FNR and FPR of CWE126_Buffer_Over_Read.

FNR: from the comparison of the three tools of flawfinder, cppcheck and splint, the FNR of splint is 80.54%, which is the lowest among the three tools and the best in the false-negative rate index. The false-negative rates of both flawfinder and cppcheck are above 96%. They only use text matching in the vulnerability detection process, resulting in a high false-negative rate. From the four tools of flawfinder, cppcheck, splint and DCVDM, DCVDM has the lowest false-negative rate of 56.25%, which is much lower than the other three tools. It can be seen that the DCVDM performs better on the buffer rate.

FPR: from the comparison of the three tools of flawfinder, cppcheck and splint, the FPR of splint is 44.67%, which is the lowest of the three tools and the best in the false-positive rate indicator. The false-positive rate of both flawfinder and cppcheck is close to 95%, which is determined by human error. From the comparison of the four tools of flawfinder, cppcheck, splint and DCVDM, DCVDM has the lowest false-positive rate of 36.53%. It can be seen that DCVDM performs better in the false alarm rate.

5 Conclusions

In this paper, we propose a detection approach for buffer overflow vulnerability based on DCFG (Data Control Flow Graph) to detect three common vulnerabilities: "Strncpy ()", "Memcpy()" and "Gets()". To start with, introduce the process of converting source code into corresponding data control flow graph. Additionally, traverse DCFG to find the dangerous function and get the overflow point position. Finally, Comparing the buffer space of the function operation with the size of the space to be covered at the overflow point position to get the results of the vulnerability test.

In addition, we designed three vulnerability detection methods, which can detect specific type of vulnerability in the program segment to be tested. The results of the cases studied in this paper showed that the proposed method is feasible and effective in analyzing and detecting the three mentioned types of vulnerability existing in the tested program segments. Finally, the experiment prove that this method can be better applied to vulnerability detection of software and improve detection efficiency. It can detect the vulnerability in the software system more accurately and improve the security of the system.

Acknowledgements. This study was funded by the National Natural Science Foundation of China (NSFC grant numbers: U1836116 and 61872167), the Project of Jiangsu Provincial Six Talent Peaks (Grant numbers: XYDXXJS-016), and the Graduate Research Innovation Project of Jiangsu Province (Grant numbers: KYCX171807).

References

1. Liao, X., Wang, Y., Fan, X., et al.: National security vulnerability database classification based on an LDA topic model. J. Tsinghua Univ. **52**(10), 1351–1355 (2012)
2. Xu, J., Kalbarczyk, Z., Patel, S., et al.: Architecture support for defending against buffer overflow attacks. In: Proceedings of the 2nd Workshop on Evaluating and Architecting System dependability (EASY) (2002)
3. Liu, W., Yang, L., Zhang, W.: Modelling binary oriented software buffer-overflow vulnerability in process algebra. In: Seventh International Symposium on Parallel Architectures, Algorithms and Programming, pp. 20–25. IEEE (2015)
4. Zhang, Y., Wu, S., Liu, Q., et al.: Design and implementation of national security vulnerability database. J. Commun. **32**(06), 93–100 (2011)
5. Jimenez, M., Papadakis, M., Bissyandé, T.F., et al.: Profiling android vulnerabilities. In: IEEE International Conference on Software Quality, Reliability and Security, pp. 222–229. IEEE (2016)
6. Chen, Z., Zhang, Y., Chen, Z.: A categorization framework for common computer vulnerabilities and exposures. Comput. J. **53**(5), 551–580 (2010)
7. Baker, Y.S., Agrawal, R., Bhattacharya, S.: Analyzing security threats as reported by the United States Computer Emergency Readiness Team (US-CERT). In: 2013 IEEE International Conference on Intelligence and Security Informatics, pp. 10–12. IEEE (2013)
8. Feist, J., Mounier, L., Potet, M.L.: Statically detecting use after free on binary code. J. Comput. Virol. Hacking Tech. **10**(3), 211–217 (2014)
9. Han, X., Shuang, W., Jiayi, Y.E., et al.: Detect use-after-free vulnerabilities in binaries. J. Tsinghua Univ. **57**(10), 1022–1029 (2017)

10. Pan, Q., Cui, Z., Wang, L.: Static detection approach for SQL injection vulnerability in android applications. J. Front. Comput. Sci. Technol. **12**(08), 1225–1237 (2018)
11. Bisbeyii, R., Hollingworth, D.: Protection analysis: final report. Prot. Anal. Final Rep. **44**(Supplement s6), 59–63 (1978)
12. Liang, J., Sankar, L., Kosut, O.: Vulnerability analysis and consequences of false data injection attack on power system state estimation. IEEE Trans. Power Syst.: Publ. Power Eng. Soc. **31**(5), 3864–3872 (2015)
13. Yamaguchi, F., Golde, N., Arp, D., et al.: Modeling and discovering vulnerabilities with code property graphs. In: Security and Privacy, pp. 590–604. IEEE (2014)
14. Sharma, R., Singh, R.K.: Vulnerability discovery in open- and closed-source software: a new paradigm. In: Hoda, M.N., Chauhan, N., Quadri, S.M.K., Srivastava, P.R. (eds.) Software Engineering. AISC, vol. 731, pp. 533–539. Springer, Singapore (2019). https://doi.org/10.1007/978-981-10-8848-3_51
15. Bishop, M., Engle, S., Howard, D., et al.: A taxonomy of buffer overflow characteristics. IEEE Trans. Dependable Secure Comput. **9**(3), 305–317 (2012)
16. Thome, J.: A scalable and accurate hybrid vulnerability analysis framework. In: IEEE International Symposium on Software Reliability Engineering Workshops, pp. 61–62. IEEE Computer Society (2015)
17. Li, X., Chen, J., Lin, Z., et al.: A mining approach to obtain the software vulnerability characteristics. In: Fifth International Conference on Advanced Cloud and Big Data, pp. 296–301. IEEE Computer Society (2017)
18. Shahriari, H.R., Jalili, R.: Using CSP to model and analyze transmission control protocol vulnerabilities within the broadcast network. In: International Networking and Communication Conference, 2004. INCC 2004, pp. 42–47. IEEE (2004)

Outsourced Data Integrity Auditing for Efficient Batch Dynamic Updates

Kunyao Deng[1(✉)], Ming Xu[1], and Shaojing Fu[1,2]

[1] School of Computer, National University of Defense Technology,
Changsha 410073, China
1878307013@163.com
[2] Sate Key Laboratory of Cryptology, Beijing, China

Abstract. Cloud storage is becoming more and more popular as it provides a good solution for people with insufficient storage space. Provable Data Possession (PDP) is a model that allows to verify the outsourced data's integrity without downloading it. However, existing dynamic data possession verification schemes not only suffer from low efficiency of batch auditing for multi-block Data, but also lack effective mechanism to update multiple blocks at the same time. In this paper, we propose a new dynamic provable data possession scheme for secure cloud data auditing. The scheme leverages BLS signatures and RMHT to support batch auditing and then optimizes batch auditing scenarios with four algorithms to support efficient batch updates. The theoretical analysis show the security of our scheme, and the experimental results show that the scheme has advantages over the existing dynamic integrity audit scheme in terms of computing time and communication cost.

Keywords: Cloud storage · Integrity auditing · Dynamic updates · Merkel Hash Tree

1 Introduction

With the development and popularization of network technology, today's society has stepped into the era of big data. The amount of data exploding conflicts with the limited storage space of users. For this reason, cloud storage has to be used to solve the storage space problem. Cloud storage service providers cluster large amounts of storage resources to provide inexpensive storage services and huge storage space. Users can pass data to the cloud storage service provider without having to focus on where the data is stored and retrieve it from the cloud storage service provider when they need to use the data. However, storing data on the cloud can cause users to lose real control over the data and pose some security threats such as data leakage, tampering and loss. Therefore, it is necessary to verify the integrity of the outsourced data.

PDP [1] provides a solution for remote data integrity verification. In a PDP scheme, client generates data blocks' corresponding homomorphic tags and uses

© Springer Nature Singapore Pte Ltd. 2020
W. Han et al. (Eds.): CTCIS 2019, CCIS 1149, pp. 325–339, 2020.
https://doi.org/10.1007/978-981-15-3418-8_21

these tags as part of the integrity verification evidence. Juel et al. [2] first proposed the POR mechanism, which uses the inserted "sentinel" to verify the integrity of the data and to recover the damaged data. The subsequent solutions [3–7] extends the integrity verification model from the aspects of privacy protection, verification efficiency, supporting for public auditing and so on. In all of the above work, there is no support for data dynamic update or data insertion is not supported.

Later studies have solved this problem by introducing an authentication structure. Erway et al. [8] proposed a new PDP scheme, which uses the rank-based authenticated skip list to mark the sequence of blocks. Wang et al. [9] introduce the Merkel Hash Tree (MHT) to support for fully dynamic data operations. In order to reduce the depth of the authentication structure, Yao et al. [10] used Large Branching Tree instead of MHT. Due to the simple structure of MHT, many scholars [11–13] have optimized the scheme on the basis of MHT in order to support more situations.

There are still some research challenges in cloud data integrity auditing. First of all, the TPA may not complete the verification correctly without knowing the specific structure of the authentication structure. For example, the calculation of the parent node hash value needs to determine the left and right child nodes. Secondly, the current schemes still have the drawbacks of requiring a number of auxiliary information. Third, in actual use, users may update multiple files at the same time. However, most schemes do not support updating multiple blocks at the same time, especially inserting multiple data blocks after one block.

Our contribution can be summarized as follows:

(1) We propose a protocol supporting batch auditing based on the RMHT, which is able to audit multiple blocks at once and alleviate both computational and communication overhead. In addition, a verifier can perform the verification without knowing the structure of the RMHT.
(2) We extend the batch auditing scheme to support efficient batch updating. In our scheme, multiple update operations can be performed simultaneously and the verification of updates only need to be executed once. In particular, our scheme is supported for inserting more than one block after a specified position.

The rest of the paper is organized as follows. In Sect. 2, we define the system model and system components. Then, in Sect. 3, we propose our schemes about batch auditing and batch updating, followed by security and performance analysis in Sect. 4. Furthermore, we analyze the experiment results and show the practicality of our schemes in Sect. 5. Finally, we conclude our work in Sect. 6.

2 Problem Statement

2.1 System Model

Figure 1 shows the basic architecture of cloud storage model. Three entities are involved as follows:

- Client: an entity, who has a lot of data need to be stored and need to outsorce data to cloud because of limited storage capacity.
- Cloud Service Provider (CSP): an entity, has significant storage capacity and computation resource to maintain the clients' data.
- Third Party Auditor (TPA): an entity, who provides users with integrity audit services.

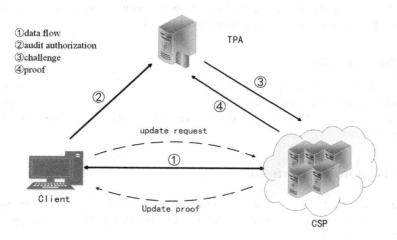

Fig. 1. System model

2.2 System Components

The data integrity auditing mechanism is mainly composed of five algorithms, namely Key generation algorithm (KeyGen), data block's tag generation algorithm (SigGen), Challenge generation algorithm (GenChal), evidence generation algorithm (GenProof), and evidence detection algorithm (VerifyProof). In addition, in order to realize the dynamic operation of data integrity proof, three dynamic operation algorithms are introduced: update execution algorithm (ExecUpdate) and update verification algorithm (VerifyUpdate).

(1) KeyGen: this algorithm is executed by the client. Its purpose is to generate public and private keys and to formulate hash algorithms.
(2) SigGen: this algorithm is run by the client. It uses the private key and file blocks to generate the tags for each block.
(3) GenChal: the TPA performs this algorithm to specify some data blocks to accept integrity challenges and generate a challenge factor for each challenged block.
(4) GenProof: this algorithm is executed by the CSP. Based on the challenge information, the CSP generates evidence based on local storage to prove the integrity of the blocks it stores, including the tag set and hash values of the challenged block.

(5) VerifyProof: the TPA executes this algorithm to verifie the integrity of the challenged blocks based on the public key and the evidence provided by CSP.

(6) ExecUpdate: this algorithm is run by the CSP. After receiving the update request, the CSP updates the data and generates evidence that the data was updated correctly.

(7) VerifyUpdate: this algorithm is executed by the client. Similar to VerifyProof, the client verifies the update was executed correctly based on the public key and the evidence provided by CSP.

2.3   Security Model

In this paper, we believe that csp is untrustworthy, the data it stores may be compromised, and he falsifies evidence for reputation or economic benefit through integrity auditing. Possible threats include replay attacks, delete attacks and forgery attacks.

3   Problem Statement

In this section, to achieve batch auditing and batch updating, we propose a scheme that can authenticate multiple blocks and perform multiple blocks updates.

3.1   Rank-Based Merkel Hash Tree

The structure of a Rank-based Merkel Hash Tree (RMHT) is a binary tree, as shown in Fig. 2, which is intended to efficiently authenticate the nodes which are corresponding to the hashes of authentic data values. Each leaf node of the tree represents a corresponding data block which are sequenced from left to right. For an arbitrary node, a rank value is assigned to it to denote the number of leaves which can be reached from it.

Every node of a RMHT is corresponding to a value, which plays a key part in the process of authentication. The value of the leaf node is related to the safe hash value of its corresponding data block which can be denoted as $h(1\|h(m))$, while the value of a non-leaf node is computed from the hash values of its child nodes and rank value which can be denoted as $h(r\|h_{left}\|h_{right})$.

A RMHT is an excellent authentication structure. With the help of the auxiliary authentication information (AAI), we can authenticate both the values and the positions of data blocks. The authentication path (AP) is the path from the root node to the leaf node and the sibling nodes of the nodes in the authentication path constitutes the AAI. For example, the TPA wan to authenticate the block m_2. The AP is (Root, A, C, m_2) are the AAI is (h_B, h_D, h_{m_1}). The value of the root node h_{Root} can be computed by the hash of the block m_2 and the AAI. By comparing h_{Root} with the old root node value we can verify the integrity of the block m_2.

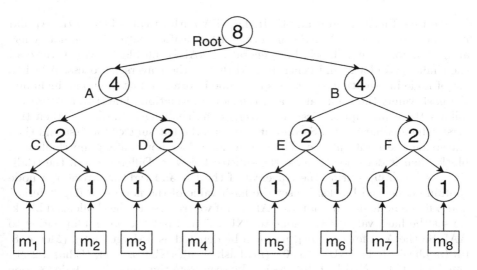

Fig. 2. The Rank-based Merkel Hash Tree

In our scheme, a node contains a tuple consisting of three elements, including the hash value, the rank value, and the side information which indicates that the node is left (0) or right (1) to its parent node respectively.

3.2　Batch Auditing for Multi-block Data

When a client wants to outsource a file $F = (m_1, m_2, \ldots, m_n)$ to CSP, he needs to invoke KeyGen at first. We chose the BLS signature scheme to save communication overhead because of its short signature results. Client generates a secure hash function H, a hash function h, a random signing key (spk, ssk), a random $\alpha \in Z_p$ and $v \leftarrow g^\alpha$. Then he uses (α, ssk) as the private key and (v, spk) as the public key. After that, he invokes KeyGen to generate a signature Ti for each data block m_i: $\sigma_i \leftarrow [H(m_i) \bullet u^{m_i}]^\alpha$ (u is a random element). Later, he constructs a RMHT through $H(m_i)$ and signs the Root R under the private key: $sig_{sk}H(Root) \leftarrow H(R)^\alpha$. The client finally sends $(F, \sigma, sigsk(H(R)))$ to CSP.

The process of batch auditing can be shown in as follows. TPA first generates $chal = i, v_{i s_1 \leq i \leq s_c}$ including the serial number of the challenged block (i) and the corresponding challenge factor. After receiving the challenge, the CSP computes $\mu = \sum_{i=s_i}^{s_c} v_i m_i$ and $\sigma = \prod_{i=s_i}^{s_c} \sigma_i^{v_i}$. Then the CSP generate AAI. The CSP sends $[\mu, \sigma, H(m_i), AAI, sig_{sk}H(Root)]$ as proof to the TPA. In existing schemes, CSP generate a AAI for each block. For multi-block data, there are some shared nodes in their authentication paths. When we authenticate more than one block, it is obviously not efficient to construct the RMHT's root by each leaf node and their AAIs. We plan to use shared nodes to reduce auxiliary authentication information and hash calculations.

We take Fig. 2 as an example. If the TPA authenticates block m_1, m_4 and m_7, node A and node D are both in the authentication path. We are not generating AAI for a single block, but generating AAI for all blocks. We traverse all the challenged blocks and generate AAI during the traversal process. AAI is a list of node information, which has the same information as the node, including the hash value, the rank value, and the side information. The traversal process follows three principles. First, it traverses the challenged block and then traverses the auxiliary node. Second, it traverses the left subtree for first and then traversing the right subtree. Third, if a node does not contain the challenged block, then it does not traverse the subtree below it. Different from the traditional scheme [9], during the traversal, if the left and right subtrees of a node contain challenged blocks, we set the hash value of the node to a flag "Merge" and put the node information to AAI, and if we traverse to the challenged block, we set the hash value of the node to "NULL" and put the node information to AAI. So the AAI for (m_1, m_4, m_7) can be denoted as [(Merge, 8, 0), (Merge, 8, 0), $(m_2.hash, 1, 1)$, (NULL, 1, 0), $(m_3.hash, 1, 0)$, (NULL, 1, 1), (E.hash, 2, 0), $(m_8.hash, 1, 1)$, (NULL, 1, 0)]. As can be seen from the stack, it includes 8 node information, but 4 of them have the flag bit, so the main storage overhead in AAI comes from 4 hash values. If a set of AAI is generated for each challenged data block, the main storage overhead comes from 9 hash values, which shows the superiority of our algorithm. The specific method can be seen in Algorithm 1.

Algorithm 1. AAIGen of multi-block auditing (AAIGen(node,chal))

Require: RMHT, $chal = i_{s_1 \leq i \leq s_c}$
Ensure: AAI
1: $AAI \leftarrow NULL$, node = Root
2: **if** $node.rank = 1$ **then**
3:      AAI.PUSH(¡NULL,1,node.p¿)
4: **else if** $s_c \leq left.rank$ **then**
5:      AAI.PUSH((right.hash,right.rank,1))
6:      AAIGen(left,chal)
7: **else if** $s_1 > left.rank$ **then**
8:      AAI.PUSH((left.hash,left.rank,0))
9:      update chal:chal.i - left.rank
10:      AAIGen(right,chal)
11: **else**
12:      AAI.PUSH((Merge,node.rank,node.p))
13:      split chal to $chal_1$ and $chal_2$ by left.rank
14:      AAIGen(left,$chal_1$)
15:      AAIGen(right,$chal_2$)
16: **end if**

When the TPA receives the integrity proof, he first checks

$$e(\sigma, g) = e(\prod_{i=s_i}^{s_c} H(m_i)^{v_i} \bullet u^\mu, v) \tag{1}$$

If not, then output FALSE; otherwise, the TPA generates root R using $[H(m_i)_{s_1 \le i \le s_c},$ AAI]. We design the Algorithm 2, which is used to calculate the hash of the root. Then TPA authenticates H(Root) by checking

$$e(sig_{sk}H(Root), g) = e(H(Root), v) \tag{2}$$

If the verification is passed, the data is complete, otherwise, the data is damaged.

Algorithm 2. Calculate the H(Root) with AAI(RootGen(AAI,Hash))

Require: AAI, $StackHash \leftarrow H(m_i)_{s_1 \le i \le s_c}$
Ensure: $H(Root) \leftarrow checknode.hash$
 1: $Stacktemp \leftarrow NULL, Nodechecknode \leftarrow NULL$
 2: **while** $AAI \neq NULL$ **do**
 3:   aai = AAI.pop()
 4:   **if** $aai.hash = NULL$ **then**
 5:     temp.push(checknode)
 6:     $checknode \leftarrow< Hash.pop(), 1, aai.p >$
 7:   **else if** $aai.hash = Merge$ **then**
 8:     tempnode = temp.pop()
 9:     checknode.rank = aai.rank
10:     checknode.p = aai.p
11:     checknode.hash = h(checknode.rank || checknode.hash || tempnode.hash)
12:   **else**
13:     tempnode = temp.pop()
14:     checknode.rank += aai.rank
15:     **if** aai.p = 1 **then**
16:       checknode.hash = h(checknode.rank || checknode.hash || tempnode.hash)
17:     **else**
18:       checknode.hash = h(checknode.rank || tempnode.hash || checknode.hash)
19:     **end if**
20:   **end if**
21: **end while**

Figure 3 shows an example process for generating H(Root). The entire participation process is only done by the AAI and Hash stacks. Because each node has a p-value, it can construct a RMHT structure containing the relevant nodes, so H(Root) can be computed correctly. Calculate the hash value of the root node. The order of the generated nodes is identified by a numerical number in the figure.

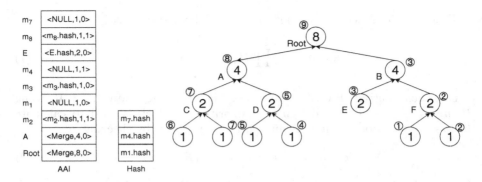

Fig. 3. Example of using AAI to generate H(Root)

3.3   Batch Updating for Multi-block Data

For the update of a single data block, the solution of [9] is fully explained, and we adopt his approach to the updated strategy for each block. So we will omit some details about the update operation and focus on batch processing.

When the client wants to update m blocks at one time, it firstly generates a series of single update requests. Each update request is expressed as "update = (Operation, index, [m], [σ])". For modifying operations, only the first two parameters are useful. For inserting multiple blocks, the last two parameters include all the blocks and tags that will be inserted. For example, (modify, i, [m], [σ]) means replacing the i-th block with m and (insert, i, [m_1, m_2], [σ_1,σ_2]) means insert two blocks m_1 and m_2 after the i-th block.

Upon receiving the update request, the CSP runs ExecUpdate. In addition to updates to actual data, the CSP also need to update the RMHT. All nodes on the authentication path need to be updated except the node being updated. We noticed that the insert and delete operations will cause a change in the node rank information, and the delete operation will also cause changes in the node side information. So, we must not only pay attention to the update of node hash. For inserting multiple data blocks after one block, we generate a subtree for the block and the insert block, and replace the inserted block with the root of the subtree. For other update operations, the scheme is same as [9]. We used the method of updating the subtree first and then updating the parent node to recursively update the entire tree. The specific implementation of the update RMHT can be seen in Algorithm 3.

In the update process of RMHT, since the start node of the update starts from the root, but the update of the root node is related to the update of its child nodes, so we use the recursive way to update, for any non-leaf node, its update order is the first child nodes and then the root node. Since the update of the parent node of the deleted node is cumbersome after the search pointer points to the deleted node, when we search for a non-leaf node, we first judge that whether all the leaves of the left subtree or all the leaves of its right subtree need to be deleted. If all nodes of one side need to be deleted, directly use the

---

Algorithm 3. update RMHT(UpdateTree(node,updateList))

Require: RMHT, UpdateList
Ensure: $H(Root) \leftarrow checknode$
 1: $node \leftarrow Root$
 2: **if** node.rank = 1 **then**
 3:     Update = UpdateList.pop(0)
 4:     **if** $Update.Operatin = Modify$ **then**
 5:         $node.hash \leftarrow Hash(Update.m)$
 6:     **else**
 7:         contrust newSubRMHT by node and Update.m;
 8:         $node \leftarrow newSubRMHT$
 9:     **end if**
10: **else if** node.left.rank ¡ UpdateList.get(0).index **then**
11:     update UpdateList: UpdateList.index - node.left.rank
12:     **if** isAllDelete(node.right) **then**
13:         node = node.left;
14:     **else**
15:         right = UpdateTree(node.right, UpdateList)
16:         update node by new right child
17:     **end if**
18: **else if** $UpdateList.get(last).index \leq node.left.rank$ **then**
19:     **if** isAllDelete(node.left) **then**
20:         node = node.right
21:     **else**
22:         left UpdateTree(node.left, UpdateList)
23:         update node by new left child
24:     **end if**
25: **else**
26:     split UpdateList to $UpdateList_1$ and $UpdateList_2$ by left.rank
27:     left = UpdateTree(node.left, $UpdateList_1$)
28:     right = UpdateTree(node.right, $UpdateList_2$)
29:     update node by new left child and new right child
30: **end if**

---

subtree of the other side to replace the parent node. If not all deleted, consider updating the left and right subtrees respectively, and update the parent node after its left and right subtrees are updated. When the leaf node is searched, since the node we are going to be deleted is considered in its parent node, the search for the leaf node must be a modification update or an insert update. For the modification update, only the hash value of the leaf node needs to be modified. For the insertion update, it will rebuild a RMHT subtree, and replace the leaf node with the newly generated subtree. Figure 4 shows an example of a concurrent update. The sequence number represents the order in which the nodes complete the update.

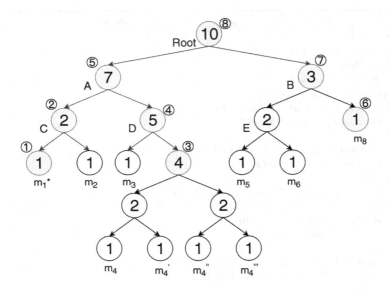

Fig. 4. Example of using AAI to generate H(Root)

After updating the data and the RMHT, the CSP need to generate evidence that the data has been updated correctly. The evidence includes the AAI and hashes of the updated blocks H(m_i), old H(Root)'s signature $sig_{sk}(H(Root))$ and new root H($Root_{new}$). The AAI can be generated by Algorithm 1 when treating the updated blocks as challenged blocks. After receiving the proof of batch updating, the client first generates pre-update value using $\{[H(m_i)], AAI\}$ by Algorithm 2. The client authenticates it by checking

$$e(sig_{sk}H(Root), g) = e(H(Root), v) \tag{3}$$

If the verification is passed, the client first generates new root R using $[[H(m_i)],$ $[H(m_i^*)],AAI]$. Different from the integrity verification, in the process of generating the new root node, we need to process each operated node according to different update operations. The specific implementation of generating new root can be seen in Algorithm 4. In Algorithm 4, we use the rank 0 to represent the deleted node. The result of the operation of the deleted node and any node is another node. Then the client checks the new root node calculated by Algorithm 4 and the new root node in the evidence. If the two roots are the same, the update is executed correctly and the client send new root's signature to the CSP in order to perform subsequent integrity verification.

Algorithm 4. Calculate the updated H(R)(NewRootGen(AAI,UpdateList,Hash))

Require: AAI,UpdateList,Stack Hash
Ensure: $H(Root) \leftarrow checknode.hash$
 1: $Stacktemp \leftarrow NULL, Nodechecknode \leftarrow NULL$
 2: **while** $AAI \neq NULL$ **do**
 3:   aai = AAI.pop()
 4:   **if** $aai.hash = NULL$ **then**
 5:     temp.push(checknode)
 6:     Update = UpdateList.pop(0)
 7:     **if** Update.Operatin = Modify **then**
 8:       checknode $\leftarrow$ [h(Update.m),1,aai.p]
 9:     **else if** Update.Operatin = Insert **then**
10:       contrust newSubRMHT with insert block and inserted block
11:       checkpoint = newSubRMHT.Root
12:     **else**
13:       checknode $\leftarrow$ [NULL,0,aai.p]
14:     **end if**
15:   **else if** $aai.hash \neq Merge$ **then**
16:     **if** checknode.rank = 0 **then**
17:       checknode $\leftarrow$ aai
18:     **else**
19:       checknode.rank += aai.rank
20:       update checknode.hash by aai and checknode
21:     **end if**
22:   **else**
23:     tempnode = temp.pop()
24:     **if** checknode.rank = 0 **then**
25:       **if** tempnode.rank = 0 **then**
26:         checknode $\leftarrow$ [NULL,0,aai.p]
27:       **else**
28:         checknode $\leftarrow$ tempnode
29:       **end if**
30:     **else**
31:       update checknode.hash by tempnode and checknode
32:     **end if**
33:   **end if**
34: **end while**

---

4   Security Analysis

4.1   Correctness Analysis

In the integrity verification process, the correctness of the scheme is to say if the data is not damaged, then the evidence generated by the CSP in response to the challenge must be able to successfully pass the data integrity verification. Therefore, to prove the correctness of the mechanism, just prove that the proof returned by the CSP can be successfully passed.

First, we proof $e(\sigma, g) = e(\prod_{i=s_i}^{s_c} H(m_i)^{v_i}) \bullet u^\mu, v)$:

$$
\begin{aligned}
e(\sigma, g) &= e(\prod_{i=s_i}^{s_c} \sigma_i^{v_i}) \bullet u^\mu, g) \\
&= e(\prod_{i=s_i}^{s_c} ((H(m_i) \bullet u^{m_i})^\alpha)^{v_i}, g) \\
&= e(\prod_{i=s_i}^{s_c} H(m_i)^{v_i}) \bullet (\prod_{i=s_i}^{s_c} u^{m_i})^{v_i}, g)^\alpha \\
&= e(\prod_{i=s_i}^{s_c} H(m_i)^{v_i}) \bullet u^\mu, v)
\end{aligned}
\tag{4}
$$

Second, we proof $e(sig_{sk}H(Root), g) = e(H(Root), v)$:

$$
\begin{aligned}
e(sig_{sk}H(Root), g) &= e(H(Root)^\alpha, g) \\
&= e(H(Root), v)
\end{aligned}
\tag{5}
$$

Therefore, the above two proofs show that our scheme is correct.

In addition, the security of RMHT can be determined by the unidirectionality of the hash function and we introduced location information to ensure that the hashes of the two child nodes are correctly connected in order. Therefore, we can believe that the authentication structure is reliable.

4.2   Resistance to Attack

In the cloud storage environment, we mainly consider replay attacks, delete attacks and forgery attacks.

Resistance to replay attacks: During the verification process, if the data stored by the user on the cloud server changes, the tag information of the data block will also change, so expired labels cannot pass the authentication. In addition, the challenge block number and the challenge factor are randomly generated, and it is impossible to complete the verification by the previous evidence.

Resistance to delete attacks: The CSP may delete data files that the user does not frequently access and use pre-computed data block tags to trick the verifier into passing the integrity certificate. However, the verification process requires an aggregated label, and the CSP cannot make all the aggregates.

Resistance to forgery attacks: According to the characteristics of the BLS system and the unidirectionality of the hash function, the forged data labels cannot pass the data integrity verification.

5   Performance Analysis

We implemented our proposed solution using Java. Our experiment os conducted on a machine possessing Intel(R) Core(TM) i7-8700 CPU @ 3.20 GHz, 24 GB of

RAM, running Windows 10. The test file is 1 GB and is divided into 4096 16 KB-blocks. Then we use jPBC to provide bls signature and the hash algorithm h was instantiated by using SHA256.

In order to demonstrate the performance of the proposed scheme, we compare it with the solution proposed in [11]. The red line is the result of the implementation of [11], while the blue line is the result of our proposed scheme. [11] is a dynamic data auditing scheme based on improved MHT and no batch auditing and updating schemes for multiple blocks are proposed.

We conduct experiments for multi-block batch auditing and demonstrate its efficiency in Fig. 5, where the number of blocks is increased from 1 to 400. As shown in the figure, the communication cost of our scheme is less and the gap is increasing with the increase of the number of blocks. In fact, the more nodes that are challenged on the block authentication path, the fewer the auxiliary information and the smaller the communication overhead. The comparison result of the calculation overhead and the communication overhead are not much different, and the influencing factors are also the same, and will not be described here.

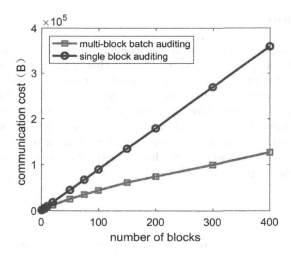

Fig. 5. Communication cost during batch auditing and single auditing

From Fig. 6, it can be observed that multi-block batch updating shows good performance. The update operations are randomly generated. As the number of update blocks increases, the number of update nodes we propose increases significantly. In our scenario, each node is updated at most once. The computational overhead and communication overhead of the update verification process are similar to the multi-block batch audit, and will not be described here.

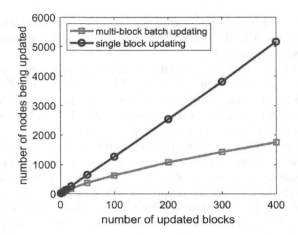

Fig. 6. Number of nodes being updated during batch updating and single auditing

6   Conclusion

Integrity verification is very important in cloud storage situations. In this paper, we proposed an integrity verification scheme that supports multi-block batch updates. In addition to supporting full dynamics, it also supports inserting multiple blocks after one block, which is lacking in other schemes. In our scenario, we verify multiple challenge blocks at once with as little auxiliary information as possible and avoid duplicate node updates when multiple blocks are updated simultaneously. We designed four algorithms to implement our scheme. We compare our scheme with previous work through experiments and the result shows the proposed scheme performs better.

References

1. Ateniese, G., Burns, R., Curtmola, R., et al.: Provable data possession at untrusted stores. In: ACM Conference on Computer and Communications Security, USA, pp. 598–609 (2007)
2. Juels, A., Kaliski Jr., B.S.: PORs: proofs of retrievability for large files. In: ACM Conference on Computer and Communications Security (2007)
3. Ateniese, G., Pietro, R.D., Mancini, L.V., et al.: Scalable and efficient provable data possession. In: Proceedings of the 4th International Conference on Security and Privacy in Communication Networks, NewYork, pp. 1–10 (2008)
4. Ateniese, G., Kamara, S., Katz, J.: Proofs of storage from homomorphic identification protocols. In: Matsui, M. (ed.) ASIACRYPT 2009. LNCS, vol. 5912, pp. 319–333. Springer, Heidelberg (2009). https://doi.org/10.1007/978-3-642-10366-7_19
5. Wang, C., Ren, K., Lou, W., et al.: Toward publicly auditable secure cloud data storage services. IEEE Netw. **24**(4), 19–24 (2010)

6. Shen, W., Qin, J., Jia, Y., et al.: Enabling identity-based integrity auditing and data sharing with sensitive information hiding for secure cloud storage. IEEE Trans. Inf. Forensics Secur. **14**, 331–346 (2018)

7. Wang, C., Wang, Q., Ren, K., et al.: Privacy-preserving public auditing for data storage security in cloud computing. In: Infocom 2010 Proceedings IEEE, pp. 1-9 (2010)

8. Erway, C., Papamanthou, C., Tamassia, R.: Dynamic provable data possession. In: ACM Conference on Computer and Communications Security, pp. 213–222, USA (2009)

9. Wang, Q., Wang, C., Li, J., Ren, K., Lou, W.: Enabling public verifiability and data dynamics for storage security in cloud computing. In: Backes, M., Ning, P. (eds.) ESORICS 2009. LNCS, vol. 5789, pp. 355–370. Springer, Heidelberg (2009). https://doi.org/10.1007/978-3-642-04444-1_22

10. Yao, G., Lei, N.: Large branching tree based dynamic provable data possession scheme. J. Inf. Sci. Eng. **33**(3), 653–673 (2017)

11. Zou, J., Sun, Y., Li, S.: Dynamic provable data possesion based on ranked Merkle hash tree. In: 2016 International Conference on Identification, Information and Knowledge in the Internet of Things (IIKI). IEEE, pp. 4–9 (2016)

12. Zhang, Y., Ni, J., Tao, X., et al.: Provable multiple replication data possession with full dynamics for secure cloud storage. Concurr. Comput.: Pract. Exper. **28**, 1161–1173 (2016)

13. Qi, Y., Tang, X., Huang, Y.: Enabling efficient batch up-dating verification for multi-versioned data in cloud storage. Chin. J. Electron. **28**, 377–385 (2019)

Secure Personal Health Records Sharing Based on Blockchain and IPFS

Xuguang Wu, Yiliang Han$^{(\boxtimes)}$, Minqing Zhang, and Shuaishuai Zhu

Engineering University of China Armed Police Force, Xi'an, China
yilianghan@163.com

Abstract. Personal Health Records (PHR) system has attracted intensive attention due to its universal accessibility and low cost in economics. Because of high cost of storing data and access control, most PHR systems adopt centralized management, where an authoritative management center controls the entire system and PHR data is stored in a trusted third-party service provider. However, there are some disadvantages, such as fully trusting to a control center, suffering from a single point of failure, and data deleting. In this paper, we propose a novel distributed framework based on blockchain and IPFS (Inter Planetary File System), and a suite of mechanisms for data access control to PHR data. Smart Contracts are designed on the blockchain, and all data operations are treated as transactions. The symmetric cryptographic algorithm is used to encrypt the PHR data, and then all encrypted data is stored on IPFS nodes securely in distributed environment. The ciphertext-policy attribute-based encryption (CP-ABE) is used to encrypt the symmetric secret keys, and the corresponding ciphertext is stored and published in IPNS (Inter Planetary Name Space), so as to achieve fine-grained access control. Analytical and experimental results are presented, which show that our framework has ability to provide authenticity, confidentiality, fine-grained access control, forward secrecy, and traceability simultaneously.

Keywords: Personal Health Records · Blockchain · IPFS · IPNS · CP-ABE

1 Introduction

Personal health records (PHR) system has become a research hotspot [1–3]. Information recorded in the PHR includes medical history, use of medicines and so on. The PHR service allows patients to create, manage, control and share their personal health data across the network. With the development of PHR system, patients can save much money and time without the repeated routine medical test or complicated document administration, and doctors can know more medical information and health history about patients.

Recently, architectures and schemes of PHR system have been proposed. As a result of high cost of storing data and access control, most PHR systems adopt

© Springer Nature Singapore Pte Ltd. 2020
W. Han et al. (Eds.): CTCIS 2019, CCIS 1149, pp. 340–354, 2020.
https://doi.org/10.1007/978-981-15-3418-8_22

centralized management, where an authoritative management center controls the entire system and the PHR data is stored in a trusted third-party service provider. Yu et al. [4] in 2010 combined techniques of attribute-based encryption (ABE), proxy re-encryption and lazy re-encryption to solve key distribution and data management in cloud computing, which defines access policies based on data attributes, and allows the data owner to delegate most of the computation tasks. Li et al. [5] in 2013 proposed a novel patient-centric framework and a suite of mechanisms for data access control to PHR stored in semi-trusted servers, which leverages ABE techniques to encrypt each patient's medical health file, to achieve fine-grained and scalable data access control. Liu et al. [6] in 2015 proposed a new primitive Ciphertext-Policy Attribute-Based Signcryption (CP-ABSC) scheme, which was applied for fine-grained access control and secure sharing of signcrypted data in cloud computing. Chen et al. [7] in 2016 proposed an ID-based t out of n oblivious transfer protocol based on the bilinear pairing over eliptic curves and a structure of cloud-based patient-centered PHR scheme, which helps patients to manage their health information. Rao [8] in 2017 proposed a provable secure CP-ABSC scheme in the standard model for cloud-based PHR sharing system, which has ability to provide fine-grained access control, confidentiality, authenticity, signcryptor privacy and public verifiability. Manogaran et al. [9] proposed an secure framework integrating Fog Computing for healthcare system in cloud environment.

However, centralized PHR service has several disadvantages. First, the centralized center is truly trusted by all users. The current model of PHR data service is controlled by a centralized authority, so that private information of users is known by the controller. Information leakage, selling, stealing and other events occur. Second, the centralized service center is suffering from a single point of failure and many attacks. The provider system must be perfectly designed and protected to ensure safe and stable operation. Once the centralized server has gone wrong, the entire system will be vulnerable. The potential attack vectors criminals may attempt include denial of service (DoS) attacks, side channel attacks, authentication attacks and man-in-the-middle attacks, which will result in a single point failure. Third, PHR data can be deleted and modified easily. Ideally, PHR should be kept in a secure place and should not be deleted and altered, even data owners cannot change their data. PHR data truly reflects the patient's physical condition, if the data is modified, it will make difficult for doctors to judgeine the true condition of patients, sometimes leading to unpredictable accidents.

With these issues in mind, decentralized PHR system should be developed to replace the existing centralized schemes. Blockchain technology [10] is an emerging technology that enables data sharing in a decentralized and transnational fashion. Some blockchain based PHR data sharing system are proposed. Unfortunately, most of them still store entire patient records in a trusted third-party center, that is unable to achieve full decentralization. Xia et al. [11] in 2017 proposed a blockchain-based data sharing framework that sufficiently addresses access control challenges associated with sensitive data stored in the cloud using immutability and built-in autonomy properties of the blockchain. Ekblaw et al. [12] suggests implementing a permissioned blockchain structure and encrypting data off the blockchain. Culver implements a permissioned blockchain in which only providers, health plans, and governmental parties participate. Dagher et al. [13] proposed a blockchain-based framework, named Ancile, for secure, interoperable, and efficient access to medical records, while a provider is needed to store the patients data. Zyskind et al. [14] are aware of the trusted third-party storage problem. It is suggested that the patients data can be stored in a off-blockchain key-value store, where data is sufficiently randomized across the nodes and replicated to ensure high availability. But it lacks implementation details and has no effective access control mechanism.

In the paper, we propose a novel distributed framework based on blockchain and IPFS (Inter Planetary File System) [15], and a set of mechanism to ensure secure access to PHR data. Blockchain allows for decentralization, and is the ideal alternative platform for centralized system. IPFS is a peer-to-peer distributed system that provides storage space and makes data synchronized among all nodes. In our proposed framework, Smart Contracts are designed on the blockchain, executing data requests from users and writing down all data operations. All PHR data is stored on IPFS nodes securely in distributed environment. The ciphertext-policy attribute-based encryption (CP-ABE) is used to encrypt PHR data. Our framework has ability to provide authenticity, confidentiality, fine-grained access control, forward secrecy, and traceability simultaneously.

Rest of the paper is organized as follows: In Sect. 2, the IPFS, blockchain and CP-ABE are described. Models and assumptions of our proposed framework is given in Sect. 3. Our framework is given in detail in Sect. 4. Section 5 is dedicated to discuss the security analysis and performance. Finally, the paper is concluded in Sect. 6.

2 Preliminaries

2.1 IPFS

Inter Planetary File System (IPFS) [15] was initially designed by Juan Benet. It is a protocol designed to create a permanent, decentralized way of storing and sharing files. All nodes are in a P2P distributed network, and thus forming a distributed file system with the help of content-addressable and peer-to-peer hypermedia distribution protocols.

IPFS constructs a directed acyclic graph called Merkle DAG [16], where the link between objects is an encrypted hash. This hash allows the hash of the validation content to be the same as the hash used to access it. So that IPFS has no single point of failure and delete data. But it is difficult to access variable data. A mechanism is needed to construct self-certified names, which is called IPNS (Inter Planetary Name Space), where each user has a mutable namespace "ipns/<NodeId>" and a unique id NodeId= hash(node.PubKey). Each user can publish a file to its unique address signed by its private key. When other users access the data, it is able to authenticate the signature to ensure legitimacy.

We select IPFS as storage database using its characteristics. It can be perfectly aligned with the blockchain and provide a decentralization service.

2.2 Blockchain and Ethereum

Blockchain. A blockchain [10] is a distributed database system, which ensures consistency of data between nodes with a consensus algorithm, and gains security and privacy of data through encryption algorithms, and creates an open, transparent and verifiable ledger through the data chain with timestamp.

Smart contracts [17] represent blockchain's next evolution. They are pieces of code created by the users and stored on the blockchain. Smart contracts are defined according to certain rules set by the user. These rules are what govern the behavior of all the transactions and data. Smart contracts are executed by blockchain nodes and its correct execution is guaranteed by a consensus protocol. Once appended to blockchain, the smart contract is accessible by all nodes.

Ethereum. Ethereum [18] is called the blockchain 2.0, whose biggest symbol is the application of smart contracts. Bitcoins are known as "ledger." Accordingly, Ethereum can be seen as a "global computer": the first Turing-complete blockchain system. Through it, programmer can upload applications to the blockchain, and the effective implementation of the program can be guaranteed, so that the function of smart contracts can be realized. Ethereum can apply a variety of industries and areas, such as asset trading, digital notarization, P2P lending, mutual insurance and so on.

We use the platform in this paper to prototype our secure PHR sharing protocol.

2.3 CP-ABE

Attribute-Based Encryption (ABE) [19] uses a set of attributes to describe the characteristics of user identity information. The access structure is introduced into the ciphertext and key, which are generated according to the attribute set. If the private key is associated with attribute set, and the ciphertext is associated with access structure, then this type of ABE scheme is called Ciphertext-policy attribute-based encryption (CP-ABE). The data owner does not need to distribute the attribute key for each user, only needs to manage the rights through the access structure, reducing greatly the complexity of key management and providing more flexible access control.

In this paper, we apply an efficient and provable secure CP-ABE scheme to achieve access control in distributed environment. This scheme is proposed by Ibraimi et al. [20] and is CPA secure under Decision Bilinear DiffieHellman assumption (DBDH). It is composed of four algorithms, namely, Setup, KeyGen, Encrypt, and Decrypt.

3   Models and Assumptions

3.1   System Models

The secure scheme's purpose is to provide a user with a way to store its PHR securely on decentralized IPFS, and to control the data access authority fully. As is shown in Fig. 1, the secure PHR sharing system has three parties: Data users, blockchain, and IPFS/IPNS. The PHR can be accessed from any user with authorized license verified with its own Blockchain account information.

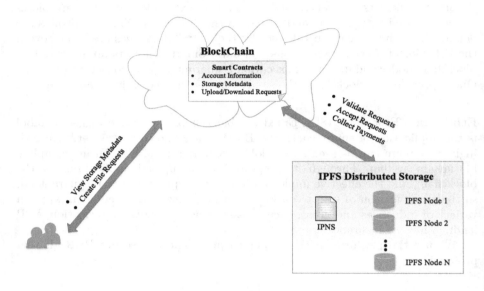

Fig. 1. System mode

Throughout this paper, there are two types "data user": "Data owner" and "Data requester". The "Data owner" is used to describe one or more users of PHR data in this system. "Data requester" is used to describe users who are asking for access to PHR in the existing storage space, such as doctors, friends and family.

Due to limited storage space of blockchain, the stored data are limited to the basic information of users and PHR data, including data owner Id, PHR created time, PHR sizes, and file hashes. The contents of PHR are stored in IPFS/IPNS system with enough storage space and real-time online capacity. There are special smart contracts deployed on the blockchain, which are triggered by users' data access requests. According to these requests, it then uploads or downloads PHR, and records all the operation information and metadata into the blockchain. The data inserted into the blockchain can be protected using public key encryption, and non-authorized users can not read it.

3.2 Design Goals

Our main design goal is to help the data owner achieve fine-grained access control on PHR stored by the decentralized IPFS nodes. At the same time, the stored data cannot be tampered by anyone even the data owner. Data owner should has the ability to specify who can decrypt the PHR data. Any unauthorized users could not get any other user's information by any means. The security and performance requirements are summarized as follows:

- **Authenticity**. The system should establish a mechanism to verify the user's identity information. Only legitimate users are allowed to access the system and gain permission to store and read PHR data.
- **Confidentiality**. The PHR data should be well encrypted by secure encryption schemes. Even if an unauthorized user gets the encrypted data, it has no way to decrypt the data.
- **Fine-grained access control**. Fine-grained access control should be enforced, meaning that PHR data can only be granted to the specified user.
- **Forward secrecy**. Whenever a user's attribute is no longer valid, the PHR data that have been conducted in the past are still secure and will not be affected, even if the system is actively attacked.
- **Traceability**. All users' access records to PHR data should be recorded for subsequent audit. If there is an illegal access incident, the relevant illegal visitors should be recorded, audited and punished.

4 Our Proposed Scheme

4.1 Main Idea

This proposed scheme aims to help the data owner securely store and distribute its PHR to specific users. The IPFS system adopts a decentralized way to store data. Smart contracts are used on the Blockchain as a middle man between users, it can keep track what data is stored and where it is. So that the PHR data can be accessed anywhere, and there are no central authority needed to be trusted.

The scheme adopts the encryption method of KEM-DEM, which is (1) using CP-ABE to encrypt the key DEK of symmetric cryptosystem, called Key Encapsulation Mechanism (KEM); (2) using a symmetric cryptographic algorithm to encrypt the PHRs, called Data Encapsulation Mechanism (DEM). The ciphertext of encrypted DEK using CP-ABE is expressed as C_{key} and stored in IPNS. As is described in Preliminaries section, every user has a mutable namespace "ipns/<NodeId>", and publishes the C_{key} to its own path. The PHR encrypted by DEK is expressed as C_{file}, and stored in IPFS nodes. The KEM ensures that only specific set of users can get DEK to achieve data access control. The DEM solves the problem of efficiency with fast operation speed of the symmetric encryption algorithm.

Each user has a subset of attributes in common, for example, a doctor may have hospital A, professor, and 45 years old etc. If these attributes satisfy a

User Access Structure $\mathbb{T}$, the corresponding user can decrypt the cipher text. Otherwise, the user cannot get any information. Each Data Owner is in charge of the sharing of PHRs and distributes private keys corresponding to users with special attributes.

Table 1 gives the description of notation to be used in our scheme.

Table 1. Notation used in our scheme description

Notation	Description
PK, MPK	System public key and master key
SK	User secret key
PKA	Attribute public key
SKA	Attribute secret key
DEK	Symmetric data encryption key of a data file
$\mathbb{T}$	User access structure
C_{key}	Ciphertext of encrypted DEK using CP-ABE
C_{file}	Ciphertext of encrypted the data file using DEK
$Enc_k(M)$	Use symmetry encryption algorithm to encrypt the plaintext M with key k
$Dec_k(C)$	Use symmetry encryption algorithm to decrypt the ciphertext C with key k

4.2 Ethereum Smart Contract Design

As is shown in Fig. 2, the smart contracts written for our scheme are the heart part. The blockchain can not store any of the bulk PHRs, but the smart contracts on it tie all participants of the system together. They define the system logic and set out transactions rules, so that the system combing blockchain and IPFS can work in a peer-to-peer manner, without a central controller.

The PHRUserInterface is located between users and other smart contracts. Its main work is to establish a secure communication connection with users, receive various requests and pass them to the PHRSecureSharing contract.

The PHRUser contract stores and manages users' information and storage metadata. It contains the IPNS namespace such as "ipns/<NodeId>", where NodeId is the hash value of its public key. This namespace points to a IPFS object, which stores the PHR data ID, $C_{key_i} = \{DEK_i\}_{CP-ABE}$ that is ciphertext of encrypted DEK, and maintains a list of all hash values of ciphertext data stored in the IPFS nodes. The IPNS object contains important access control information, and is managed by PHRDataStorage contract.

The key contract is PHRSecureSharing contract, created only once and referenced by other contracts. It is the link of the whole system, and controls user operations and data operations through the PHRUser contract and the PHRDataStoragedata contract. Its main functions are as follows:

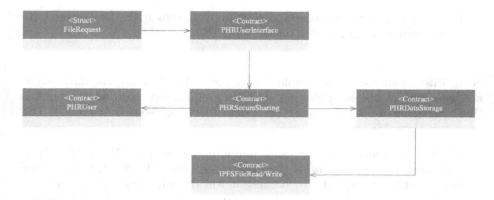

Fig. 2. Smart contract design

- User registration. After receiving a JOIN request from a new user, the PHRSecureSharing contract verifies its Ethereum account, and then maps the valid Ethereum account address to a PHRUser contract.
- User revocation. When a user leaves the system, the PHRSecureSharing contract removes the user information through the PHRUser contract.
- IPNS namespace management. When a user wants to add, delete or modify a PHR, the PHRSecureSharing contract modifies the IPNS namespace, and changes the content of the corresponding IPNS object.
- Transaction record. The system treats each PHR operation as a blockchain transaction. After the consensus mechanism and the workload proved, the selected node recorded it on IPFS nodes, thus forming a permanent record to prevent the information to be tampered.

The PHRDataStoragedata contract records every IPFS nodes' information, for example NodeId, storage space size, communication bandwidth etc.

The IPFSFileRead/Write contract handles reading and writing data directly with IPFS system. After a file is uploaded to IPFS system, it will get a file address, which is the hash value of file content. By contraries, it will get the whole file, when downloading a file.

4.3   Scheme Description

System Setup

- Each user's client application generates its own public/private keys. With the key pairs, each user creates an account, which is used to access blockchain and IPNS/IPFS. In the blockchain system, the application generating and managing key pairs is called Wallet. In the IPNS system, there is a mutable namespace "/ipns/<NodeId>", where NodeId=hash (node.PubKey). Other users can verify this account and then access the corresponding data including all IPFS address of PHR data.

– The data owner can manage and distribute its own PHR, then creates its corresponding public/master keys of CP-ABE.

New File Creation. Before uploading a file to IPFS nodes, the data owner needs to encrypt the data file and generate a ciphertext data, which contains three parts: an unique ID, encrypted data file C_{file}, session key C_{key}. The process is shown as follow.

– Select a random number r, and compute the unique $ID = Hash(r + nowtime)$, where $nowtime$ is the file created time. The file ID of each file should not grow sequentially, because it will risk exposing user' privacy. At the same time, the ID is generated randomly. In this way, it not only avoids the disclosure of private data, but also enhances the user's anonymity.
– Choose a random symmetric data encryption key $DEK \in \mathbf{K}$, where $\mathbf{K}$ is the key space, and encrypt the data file using DEK. We call the encrypted data file as C_{file}.
– Define a tree access structure $\mathbb{T}$, and encrypt DEK using CP-ABE as C_{key}.

Upload New File. When the data owner uploads a new PHR, the Smart Contract on the blockchain is triggered automatically. It carries out the process as follow:

– The data owner uploads a file request to the blockchain through the PHRUser-Interface contract.
– The PHRUserInterface contract contract authenticates the user's legitimacy.
– After that, the data owner sends $\{ID, C_{key}, C_{file}\}$ to the blockchain. Then the three contracts, including PHRSecureSharing contract, PHRDataSorage contract and IPFSFileRead/Write contract, carry out procedural operations, which upload the encrypted data file C_{file} to IPFS, and get a hash address.
– The PHRUser contract adds the hash address, the ID and ciphertext C_{key} to IPNS, which is shown in Fig. 3. Then it storages the Metadata about C_{file} and C_{key} on the blockchain, such as its location, name, size and hash. After that, the data owner receives the IPNS address

ID_1	$\{DEK_1\}_{\text{CP-ABE}}$	File Address of IPFS
ID_2	$\{DEK_2\}_{\text{CP-ABE}}$	File Address of IPFS
...	...	...
ID_n	$\{DEK_n\}_{\text{CP-ABE}}$	File Address of IPFS

Fig. 3. The content of IPNS

Access File. When a data requester accesses a PHR, the Smart Contractes on the blockchain are also triggered automatically. The process are as follow:

- The data requester sends the file request, which includes the PHR's unique ID.
- After validation, the blockchain contractes downloads C_{key} and address of C_{file} from IPNS with the ID.
- After integrity verification, the data requester decrypts C_{key} with its own secret key. If the secret key is not satisfied to access policy $\mathbb{T}$, it outputs null ($\bot$). Or else, the algorithm decrypts the ciphertext, and outputs the correct DEK. According the address, the data requester downloads the encrypted file C_{file} and verifies its integrity through hash functions.

New User Grant. When a new user A wants to join the system, the data owner assigns the corresponding secret key to this user as follows.

- The new user A sends a request.
- The Data Owner varies the authenticity of the user. If not, output $\bot$.
- Judge that whether the attribute of the user belongs to the access control structure.
- If and only if user's attribute set satisfies access control structure, the data owner runs the **KeyGen** algorithm of CP-ABE to generate the secret key SK_A for ciphertext stored on the IPFS nodes.

User Revoke. When a user needs to be revoked, the data owner starts with the intuition of the user revocation operation as follows.

- Find the affected PHR, and determine a minimal set of attributes $\mathbb{T}_{new}$ without which the leaving user's access structure will never be satisfied.
- DEKs of affected data files are encrypted with the new access structure $\mathbb{T}_{new}$ and PK.
- According to the KeyGen algorithm, the attribute secret key components are redefined accordingly, and sent to the users securely.

5   Security Analysis and Performance

5.1   Security Analysis

We analyze the security properties of our proposed scheme, starting with the following immediately available properties.

- **Authenticity.** All users have blockchain accounts, which are used to be verified by Smart Contracts. Only the verified user can read and store its PHR data in this system. The data owner is responsible to control access authority, and could distribute the specific secret key to the user with attributes meeting the access control structure.

– **Confidentiality.** The PHR data is encrypted using symmetric $DEKs$ of the symmetric key algorithm, and $DEKs$ are directly encrypted using standard CP-ABE. The symmetric algorithm is secure, and the security of this intuitive scheme merely relied on the security of CP-ABE. The CP-ABE used in this paper is provably CPA secure under the Decisional Bilinear Diffie-Hellman (DBDH) problem. Therefore, the intuitive scheme is secure under the same model.

– **Fine-grained access control.** The access control mechanism is mainly based on the CP-ABE scheme in paper [12], which is very effective to resist in ciphertext crack and collusion attack. In our proposed scheme, the encrypted PHR is bound to the access control structure, and the decryption key is bound to the user attribute. When the user attribute meets the access control structures, the decryption key can be used to decrypt ciphertexts. The access control structure supports the "AND", "OR" and "Threshold" operations, which satisfies the settings of most access control rules and supports better fine granularity.

– **Forward secrecy.** We have the mechanism of user revocation. If a user is not allowed to access PHR data, the system will find the affected PHR, and run the corroding programs to update new keys. So that the forward secrecy is achieved.

– **Traceability.** The special smart contracts on blockchain are executing automatically, which will write down all the operation information on the Blockchain block. The operation information includes users' requests, PHR created time, access time, file size and so on. Moreover, once the operation information is recorded, it will never be deleted.

– **Anonymity.** On the Blockchain, the public key is an identity from some viewpoint. In practice, you may use the hash of public key as your identity since public keys are large. A consequence of treating public keys as identities is that you can make a new identity whenever you want. We can simply create a new fresh key pair via the KeyGeneration operation. Moreover, each PHR's ID is unique, so that it has no direct relationship with the user's identity.

We also compare the security and function with several existing works, in terms of confidentiality, anonymity, avoiding a single of failure, traceability, and revocation. The six representative are: (1) the BBDS Scheme [11] which is a Blockchain-based electronic medical records sharing scheme in cloud environments; (2) the Ancile scheme [13] which is a blockchain-based framework utilizing smart contracts in an Ethereum-based blockchain for access control and obfuscation of data. (3) the GOA scheme that turns a blockchain into an automated access-control manager, which does not require trust in a third party; (4) the Rao scheme [8] based on a provable secure CP-ABSC scheme; (5) the LYZRL scheme [5] which exploits multi-authority ABE for scalable and secure sharing of PHR on the multiple data owner scenario in cloud computing; (6) the HWLZL [23] scheme based on an identity-based conditional proxy re-encryption scheme.

The results are shown in Table 2. It can be seen that, our scheme is CPA security and achieves confidentiality as others schemes. BBDS, Ancile, GOA and our scheme are based on blockchain, anonymity is achieved. The system only recognizes the ID of the user, but can not know the exact identity. Instead of storaging PHRs on the cloud server, our scheme uses the IPFS as distributed storage platform, so as to avoid a single of failure compared with other schemes. All PHR data operations are treated as transactions recorded on the block chain, and then traceability is obtained. In the aspect of user revocation, our scheme is provided with attribute level as a result of using CP-ABE.

Table 2. Comparison of security

Scheme	Confidentiality	Anonymity	Avoiding a single of failure	Traceability	Revocation
BBDS	Yes	Yes	No	Yes	ACL level
Ancile	Yes	Yes	No	Yes	No
GOA	No	Yes	Yes	Yes	No
Rao	Yes	No	No	No	No
LYZRL	Yes	No	No	No	Attribute level
HWLZL	Yes	No	No	No	No
Our scheme	Yes	Yes	Yes	Yes	Attribute level

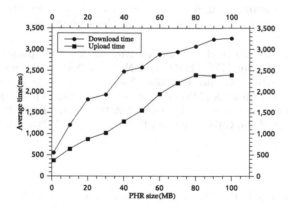

Fig. 4. Consuming time when uploading or downloading PHRs

5.2   Performance

To test the performance of the scheme, we have carried on the simulation. Four HP laptops PC OMEN pro 2 are connected to a Tenda router forming a small distributed network. The configuration parameters of laptop PC are Inter Core i5-7300HQ, 4.00 GB RAM and 120G solid hard disk. Each computer has installed Windows 10 operating system, and runs as Ethereum and IPFS node at the same time.

In this experiment, we test the time of PHR uploading and downloading. The PHR size from 1 MB to 100 MB is uploaded to our system, and then downloaded to the local computer. The results are shown in Fig. 4.

As can be seen from the figure, the file download time is more than the upload time. As file sizes increase, uploading and downloading consuming time are increasing, and their speed is slowly increasing.

6   Conclusion

This paper aims to share PHRs data securely in distributed environment, which is different from existing scheme in centralized cloud computing. A secure PHRs sharing scheme based Blockchain and IPFS is proposed. The data of PHRs is stored in IPFS/IPNS nodes. All the operations of uploading and downloading PHR are recorded on the Blockchain, which is a global database trusted by all parties. The encryption method KEM-DEM is adopt, which ensures data confidentiality and access control. Analysis and experimental results are presented. However, our scheme only achieves CPA security, which is a certain gap between CCA security. In the future, we will improve the security of our scheme.

Acknowledgments. This work is supported by National Cryptology Development Foundation of China (No: MMJJ20170112), National Nature Science Foundation of China under grant 61572521 and 61572550, Natural Science Basic Research Plan in Shaanxi Province of China (2015JM6353), Scientific foundation for innovation team of armed police engineering university (KYTD201805), and Basic Research Plan of Engineering College of the Chinese Armed Police Force (WJY201523, WJY201613).

References

1. Price, M., Bellwood, P., Kitson, N., Davies, I., Weber, J., Lau, F.: Conditions potentially sensitive to a personal health record (PHR) intervention, a systematic review. BMC Med. Inform. Decis. Making **15**(1), 32 (2015)
2. Manogaran, G., Vijayakumar, V., Varatharajan, R., et al.: Machine learning based big data processing framework for cancer diagnosis using hidden Markov model and GM clustering. Wirel. Pers. Commun. **2**, 1–18 (2017)
3. Manogaran, G., Varatharajan, R., Priyan, M.K.: Hybrid recommendation system for heart disease diagnosis based on multiple kernel learning with adaptive neuro-fuzzy inference system. Multimedia Tools Appl. **77**(4), 4379–4399 (2018)

4. Yu, S., Wang, C., Ren, K., Lou, W.: Achieving secure, scalable, and fine-grained data access control in cloud computing. In: 2010 proceedings IEEE INFOCOM, pp. 1–9. IEEE (2010)
5. Li, M., Yu, S., Zheng, Y., Ren, K., Lou, W.: Scalable and secure sharing of personal health records in cloud computing using attribute-based encryption. IEEE Trans. Parallel Distrib. Syst. **24**(1), 131–143 (2013)
6. Liu, J., Huang, X., Liu, J.K.: Secure sharing of personal health records in cloud computing: ciphertext-policy attribute-based signcryption. Future Gener. Comput. Syst. **52**, 67–76 (2015)
7. Chen, S.-W., et al.: Confidentiality protection of digital health records in cloud computing. J. Med. Syst. **40**(5), 124 (2016)
8. Rao, Y.S.: A secure and efficient ciphertext-policy attribute-based signcryption for personal health records sharing in cloud computing. Future Gener. Comput. Syst. **67**, 133–151 (2017)
9. Thota, C., Manogaran, G., Priyan, M.: Centralized fog computing security platform for IoT and cloud in healthcare system. In: Exploring the Convergence of Big Data and the Internet of Things, p. 141 (2017)
10. Nakamoto, S.: Bitcoin: a peer-to-peer electronic cash system (2019)
11. Xia, Q., Sifah, E.B., Smahi, A., Amofa, S., Zhang, X.: BBDS: blockchain-based data sharing for electronic medical records in cloud environments. Information **8**(2), 44 (2017)
12. Ekblaw, A., Azaria, A., Halamka, J.D., Lippman, A.: A case study for blockchain in healthcare: "MedRec" prototype for electronic health records and medical research data. In: Proceedings of IEEE Open Big Data Conference, vol. 13, p. 13 (2016)
13. Dagher, G.G., Mohler, J., Milojkovic, M., Marella, P.B.: Ancile: privacy-preserving framework for access control and interoperability of electronic health records using blockchain technology. Sustain. Cities and Soc. **39**, 283–297 (2018)
14. Zyskind, G., Nathan, O., Pentland, A.S.: Decentralizing privacy: using blockchain to protect personal data. In: IEEE Security and Privacy Workshops, pp. 180–184 (2015)
15. Benet, J.: IPFS-content addressed, versioned, P2P file system, arXiv preprint arXiv:1407.3561
16. Chacon, S., Straub, B.: Pro Git. Apress, New York (2014)
17. Kosba, A., Miller, A., Shi, E., Wen, Z., Papamanthou, C.: Hawk: the blockchain model of cryptography and privacy-preserving smart contracts. In: 2016 IEEE Symposium on Security and Privacy (SP), pp. 839–858. IEEE (2016)
18. Wood, G.: Ethereum: a secure decentralised generalised transaction ledger. Ethereum Proj. Yellow Pap. **151**, 1–32 (2014)
19. Bethencourt, J., Sahai, A., Waters, B.: Ciphertext-policy attribute-based encryption. In: 2007 IEEE Symposium on Security and Privacy. SP 2007, pp. 321–334. IEEE (2007)
20. Ibraimi, L., Tang, Q., Hartel, P., Jonker, W.: Efficient and provable secure ciphertext-policy attribute-based encryption schemes. In: Bao, F., Li, H., Wang, G. (eds.) ISPEC 2009. LNCS, vol. 5451, pp. 1–12. Springer, Heidelberg (2009). https://doi.org/10.1007/978-3-642-00843-6_1
21. Hur, J., Noh, D.K.: Attribute-based access control with efficient revocation in data outsourcing systems. IEEE Trans. Parallel Distrib. Syst. **22**(7), 1214–1221 (2011)
22. Narayan, S., Safavi-Naini, R.: Privacy preserving EHR system using attribute-based infrastructure. In: ACM Cloud Computing Security Workshop. CCSW 2010, Chicago, IL, USA, pp. 47–52, October 2010

23. He, K., Weng, J., Liu, J.K., Zhou, W., Liu, J.-N.: Efficient fine-grained access control for secure personal health records in cloud computing. In: Chen, J., Piuri, V., Su, C., Yung, M. (eds.) NSS 2016. LNCS, vol. 9955, pp. 65–79. Springer, Cham (2016). https://doi.org/10.1007/978-3-319-46298-1_5
24. Caro, A.D., Iovino, V.: jPBC: Java pairing based cryptography. In: Computers and Communications, pp. 850–855 (2011)
25. Mavroyanopoulos, N., Schumann, S.: Mhash library. http://mhash.sourceforge. net/

Author Index

Printed in the United States
By Bookmasters